The White House Vice Presidency

The White House Vice Presidency

The Path to Significance, Mondale to Biden

Joel K. Goldstein

UNIVERSITY PRESS OF KANSAS

Published by the University Press of Kansas (Lawrence, Kansas 66045), which was organized by the Kansas Board of Regents and is operated and funded by Emporia State University, Fort Hays State University, Kansas State University, Pittsburg State University, the University of Kansas, and Wichita State University

Library of Congress Cataloging-in-Publication Data
Goldstein, Joel K. (Joel Kramer), 1953– author.
The White House vice presidency : the path to significance, Mondale to Biden / Joel K. Goldstein.
    pages cm
Includes bibliographical references and index.
ISBN 978-0-7006-2202-3 (cloth : alk. paper) — ISBN 978-0-7006-2203-0 (ebook)
    1. Vice-Presidents—United States—History—20th century. 2. Vice-Presidents—United States—History—21st century. 3. United States—Politics and government—1977–1981. 4. United States—Politics and government—1981–1989. 5. United States—Politics and government—1989– 6. Vice-Presidents—United States—Biography. I. Title.
E176.49.G65 2016
352.23'90973—dc23
2015035632

British Library Cataloguing-in-Publication Data is available.

Printed in the United States of America

10 9 8 7 6 5 4 3 2 1

The paper used in this publication is recycled and contains 30 percent postconsumer waste. It is acid free and meets the minimum requirements of the American National Standard for Permanence of Paper for Printed Library Materials Z39.48-1992.

For Maxine, and for Rachel, Josh, and Jenna

CONTENTS

ACKNOWLEDGMENTS

With distractions and diversions, this book has been in the works for more than a dozen years. Hundreds of people—loved ones, strangers, and many in between—have helped me along the way, and I am grateful to them for their time, kindness, and wisdom. I hope I have thanked them each personally because the limited space here constrains me to mention a few individually but most generically.

I have taught at Saint Louis University School of Law during the life of this project and appreciate its support and the encouragement from my deans and colleagues on the faculty and staff over the years. Stephanie Haley assisted with administrative matters and patiently helped type and retype much of the manuscript. I used materials at various archives listed in the bibliography and found that the archivists who assisted me to be among the most helpful people I have encountered. An O'Donnell Grant from the Scowcroft Institute at the Bush School of Government and Public Service at Texas A & M University helped fund research at the George H. W. Bush Library.

More recently, the University Press of Kansas helped me get to the finish line. Kelly Chrisman Jacques, Jane Raese, and Connie Oehring improved the book through their project management and copyediting. My acquiring editor, Charles Myers, expressed early and enduring interest in the project; helped me define its shape and content; and patiently, skillfully, and thoughtfully worked through a range of issues with me.

Many have generously spoken to me about the vice presidency over the years and shared insights or information with me. Nigel Bowles, Roy Brownell II, Jeff Cohen, Josh Goldstein, Charles Myers, Michael Nelson, and Richard Pious read, and commented very helpfully, on all or part of the manuscript in earlier versions to my great benefit. Many others contributed by generously inviting me to speak or write about the topic or aspects of it in a range of settings, by raising questions for me, and by reacting to my thoughts and work. I am grateful for the education they provided and stimulated.

Some language in chapter 2 previously appeared in Joel K. Goldstein, "Constitutional Change, Originalism, and the Vice Presidency," *Uni-*

versity of Pennsylvania Journal of Constitutional Law 16, no. 2 (November 2013), 369–411; I have drawn some ideas for this book from that article and from some of my other writings on the vice presidency and related topics, which are identified at pages 401–402 of the selected bibliography.

I am fortunate in having friends and family members who, over meals, calls, and on vacations, generously indulged me with questions about vice presidents and vice-presidential wannabes when other topics might have had more appeal to them. My wife, Maxine, and our children, Rachel, Josh, and Jenna, were most patient, even visiting the Natick home of Henry Wilson (U. S. Grant's second vice president) with me. They drew the line only once, to reject my suggestion that, since one of our rescue dogs came with the name "Levi," we call the other "Morton" to honor Benjamin Harrison's vice president. "Primo" was a better name for him, they rightfully insisted.

I came away from the experience convinced of the potential for good in the vice presidency that Jimmy Carter and Walter Mondale created, and that many of their successors refined, and impressed by the capacity of our constitutional system to adapt to changing circumstances, especially when guided by enlightened leaders. I also came away deeply touched by the generosity of many people who selflessly helped me so much on a project important to me. I am grateful to many, but I alone am responsible for the book's judgments and shortcomings.

The White House Vice Presidency

Introduction

"I am nothing but I may be everything," John Adams, the first vice president, wrote of his office.[1] For most of American history, the "nothing" part of Adams's formulation captured the second office, at least so long as the president's heartbeat maintained a normal rhythm. The Constitution prescribed only one ongoing duty for the vice president, presiding over the Senate, a role that conferred little power even when the Senate met, which it did infrequently. Most vice presidents found themselves unwelcome in both the legislative and executive branches. The vice president might become "everything" if called upon to discharge presidential duties upon the death or resignation of the chief executive, an event that occurred nine times from 1789 to 1974. Otherwise, he had status but not power.

The huge disparity between the vice president's humble existence and contingent significance helped make the office a target of derision. The vice presidency was lampooned as unnecessary and ill-conceived. One senator referred to Adams as "his superfluous Excellency."[2] Daniel Webster declined the second spot on the Whig ticket in 1848, explaining, "I do not propose to be buried until I am dead,"[3] a decision he probably regretted when Millard Fillmore, not he, became president when Zachary Taylor died two years later. Thomas R. Marshall, Woodrow Wilson's vice president, wrote that "the only business of the Vice President is to ring the White House bell every morning and ask what is the state of the health of the president."[4] Vice President Nelson A. Rockefeller frequently disparaged his last public office as simply "standby equipment."[5]

Things have changed dramatically. The perception and reality of the vice presidency is quite different now. Seeing Vice President Dick Cheney as the power during the George W. Bush administration, some joked that Bush was a heartbeat from the presidency. One scholar wrote of "the Co-Presidency of Bush and Cheney."[6] This characterization exaggerated Cheney's role, but he was much closer to "everything" than to "nothing."

The phenomenon of "vice-presidential power" did not begin with Cheney's inauguration nor end when he left office. Paul C. Light coined that phrase in 1984 to describe the tenure of Walter F. Mondale (1977–1981),[7] and the concept, to varying degrees, also applies to Mondale's five successors. Adams, Webster, Marshall, and Rockefeller, among many others, could not have imagined Cheney's vice presidency, but they also would have found shocking the roles of Cheney's predecessor, Al Gore, and his successor, Joe Biden, both consequential number twos. Vice-presidential power varies from administration to administration, yet the change is largely institutional, not simply personal. The vice presidency is no longer a sinecure. It matters now. A lot. An office that was "nothing" has become a robust political institution.

In part, this development happened over time. In the early twentieth century, the office began to attract more accomplished men and to take tentative steps toward the executive branch. Recognizing this trend, Irving G. Williams's *The Rise of the Vice Presidency* appeared in 1956[8] as Richard M. Nixon finished his first term as Dwight Eisenhower's vice president. Williams's title accurately described the trajectory of the office but made no claim regarding its level of significance.

In 1982, I wrote *The Modern American Vice Presidency: The Transformation of a Political Institution*,[9] which argued that the modern vice presidency, the office from Nixon to Mondale, had grown due to dramatic changes in American politics and government since Franklin D. Roosevelt became president in 1933. With the depression and World War II, Americans increasingly looked to Washington to address national and international issues. The power of the presidency grew relative to the other branches of government, to political parties, and to local political bosses. Presidential nominees gained the right to choose their running mates, a decision that was previously the province of party leaders. The president's new responsibility for the decision changed the dynamic between the two members of the ticket. The vice president became indebted to his benefactor (even if he was not embraced by the president once in office), more loyal, and more closely identified with the administration. The advent and increased feasibility of air travel and the ubiquity of radio, then television, created new possibilities and challenges for the chief executive. He was expected to respond, or appear to respond, to more problems and to be more places, demands that created a need for high-level help. The Cold War and nuclear age made the first successor more significant and his preparation more essential. The vice president became more visible and his qualifications more important.

These factors drew the vice presidency away from the Senate and toward the executive branch and provided incentive to fill the office with able figures and to give them work other than presiding over the Senate. Especially beginning with Nixon's time in the office, vice presidents increasingly performed executive-branch chores instead of the constitutional Senate role. They chaired commissions, traveled abroad, lobbied for and defended administration programs, and discharged partisan responsibilities. The office began to attract more accomplished people, which enhanced it as a source of presidential candidates. My 1982 book praised the Mondale vice-presidential model but suggested future vice-presidential influence would turn largely on the relations between the president and vice president, the needs of each administration, and the resources contributed by the vice president.

The Modern American Vice Presidency accordingly gave a systemic or contextual explanation for the institutional growth to that time. It saw the vice presidency as evolving in response to developments in other institutions and related its rise to opportunities and incentives presented by these changes. I continue to believe that that account largely explains the rise of the vice presidency during most of that time.

Yet a lot changed with Mondale's vice presidency. It did not simply tinker with the office Nixon and the next five vice presidents had held; it introduced a very different model. Mondale conceived of and, with President Jimmy Carter, implemented a new vision of the office as providing a close presidential adviser and senior troubleshooter. They brought the vice presidency into the White House and converted a developing, but limited, office into one of great significance. Their vision enabled the institution to rise to an elevated plane far above the level where its prior forty-one occupants had operated. It made "vice-presidential power" plausible, not oxymoronic.

The innovations Carter and Mondale introduced outlasted their term. More than three decades later, the essential features of the Mondale model have largely redefined the office. Rather than belonging to an earlier period, Mondale's vice presidency inaugurated a new era. It more closely resembled those of his five successors (George H. W. Bush, Dan Quayle, Gore, Cheney, and Biden) than those of its six immediate predecessors (Nixon, Lyndon B. Johnson, Hubert H. Humphrey, Spiro T. Agnew, Gerald R. Ford, and Rockefeller).

The institution that exists today, the "White House vice presidency," reflects the Mondale design and its further development. The modern institution follows the Mondale model closely though not precisely. Put differently, the Mondale model was the original, the source of, and a version of the "White House vice presidency," but the two terms are not synonymous. The "White House vice presidency" also does not signify that the vice president spends all of his time in the White House—far from it; much necessary work is performed elsewhere. Rather, it means that the vice president has become part of the president's inner circle and works closely with him to achieve administration objectives. It signifies a set of roles, relationships, and resources now associated with the office that allow vice presidents to contribute importantly at the central and highest level of the executive branch.

The White House vice presidency represents a very positive development for the vice presidency, the presidency, and the American constitutional system more generally. It has increased the likelihood that the vice presidency will better serve its contingent constitutional function to provide an able, well-prepared successor. Yet the greatest benefits from the White House vice presidency come from the vice president's enhanced role in the ongoing work of government. An involved vice president can advise the president regularly on the problems that reach the Oval Office from a unique and helpful perspective. Unburdened by attachment to any departmental perspective and as an elected official, the vice president is positioned to take a holistic approach, to see the range of choices much as a president does, and as one who largely shares the president's interests, and to advise accordingly. And because the vice president's political future depends on the administration's accomplishments, a vice president has incentive to help the president succeed. The White House vice presidency also provides a high-level official to handle important duties. Of course, vice presidents still perform ceremonial work. So do presidents. Yet most vice-presidential work now is significant. Vice presidents regularly discharge important assignments that otherwise would require presidential attention or be neglected. The stature of the office, coupled with presidential access, allows the vice president to shoulder significant responsibilities that virtually no other presidential subordinate can handle. A vice president perceived as influential can extend government's capacity and ease the president's burdens.

This recognition, that the White House vice presidency has greatly enhanced American government, far from ending the inquiry, suggests further questions. How did this change happen? Why did the office become much more robust on Mondale's watch than ever before? Why have the essential features of the Mondale model survived more than thirty-five years beyond his term even without constitutional or statutory enactments? And what does the development of the vice presidency teach about institutional change in the American constitutional system?

This book addresses those questions. It describes the changes in the vice presidency beginning with, and brought on by, the Mondale term and argues that they are fundamental and enduring. The book discusses the development of the office since 1976, not to provide a history of those years but to portray the contemporary vice presidency as a governmental institution and to explain why it changed when it did and how that institutional revision has been sustained. The account also provides a study of political leadership. As such, this book uses the vice presidency to explore political behavior of presidents and vice presidents since 1976. Finally, it studies the dynamics of institutional reform, showing how fundamental constitutional change can occur through informal means. The following paragraphs elaborate on these themes.

Mondale's vice presidency built on foundations constructed during the prior quarter century. These included (1) the increased association of vice presidents with the executive branch, (2) the ability of the office to attract more able occupants, and (3) the increased value of the office as a springboard to the presidency. Yet far from continuing a familiar pattern, Mondale's vice presidency represented a bold departure in institutional design in which the old, and some new, threads were woven into a sturdier fabric. Mondale assumed a far more prominent and influential role in the executive branch. Whereas prior vice presidents had operated at the administration's periphery with episodic access and influence, Mondale became one of Carter's closest advisers. Whereas conflict with the president, his inner circle, or both diminished most prior vice presidents, Mondale developed a harmonious relationship with Carter and his closest associates that largely continued throughout their term. Far from being "standby equipment," Mondale was an integral figure in the presidency's ongoing important work. Mondale's success also depended on resources he obtained to support his advising and troubleshooting roles.

The Carter-Mondale period also witnessed significant changes in the process by which vice presidents were chosen and in their campaign and transition roles. Carter and Mondale were not solely responsible for these changes but contributed importantly. For instance, Carter's vice-presidential selection process differed from prior models. It was more deliberative and protracted than its predecessors. Carter did not ignore conventional criteria, but he understood that political and governmental considerations had converged so that choosing a well-qualified running mate had strategic value. The 1976 campaign included the first vice-presidential debate, an innovation that gave running mates greater visibility and impacted subsequent vice-presidential selection and campaign roles.

Some of Mondale's successors were more influential than he; others had less clout. But each retained the resources Mondale obtained, each saw the president regularly, and each found significant ways to contribute. Vice presidents, beginning with Mondale, had far greater opportunities to participate in high-level executive decision-making and assumed more significant assignments as troubleshooters. Although different vice presidents have emphasized distinct activities, they have undertaken more substantive roles on a more consistent basis than did their pre-Mondale predecessors. Their foreign travel and other diplomatic work have been more consequential, their legislative interventions more significant, their domestic troubleshooting more regular and central. Whereas Mondale avoided responsibility for ongoing governmental programs, many of his successors accepted, and at times embraced, such roles. Mondale's successors, and the presidents they served, each contributed to the evolution of the office and anchored a more robust version in firmer foundations.

The selection process for vice-presidential candidates also changed as subsequent nominees developed Carter's innovations. It began and ended sooner. The earlier start can be traced to changes in presidential nominating practices that advanced the resolution of that decision. The earlier conclusion occurred as presidential candidates took advantage of the opportunity to remove the selection from the convention. Vice-presidential selection now includes a formalized vetting process over an extended period during which public discussion of possible nominees occurs. The longer review focuses greater attention on the vice presidency and allows more intensive scrutiny of political running mates. The protracted consideration raises the stakes for the presidential candidate as the perceived quality of the process and of the running mate chosen ultimately reflect on the selector. The preconvention vice-presidential rollout developed as a new standard campaign event.

The vice-presidential debate also became a standard feature of presidential campaigns as, beginning in 1976, the major party vice-presidential candidates engaged in a televised debate in nine of the ten elections (all but 1980). These events gave the vice-presidential candidates national visibility. Although most people choose between the competing presidential candidates, some vice-presidential selections have impacted significant numbers of votes.

The vice president–elect traditionally played only a small role in forming the new administration. Beginning in 1976, they participated in choosing high-level personnel and shaping administration policy, a trend that culminated in 2000, when Cheney actually ran Bush's transition.

Although no vice president has recently succeeded to the White House on the death, resignation, or removal of the chief executive, several succession crises occurred. Presidents transferred power to their vice presidents under the Twenty-Fifth Amendment on the first three occasions in our history. The period raised other issues regarding government continuity that implicated the vice presidency.

The vice presidency also served as a valuable springboard. Bush became the first sitting vice president elected president since 1836. Gore won the popular vote but narrowly lost the election. Mondale won his party's nomination. Vice presidents were largely successful in retaining office. Four of the six (Bush, Gore, Cheney, and Biden) were elected to two full terms with the same president, a feat achieved only six times during the first 188 years.[10] All six were renominated for a second term.

Finally, the period introduced a new type of modern vice president: the eminent vice president without presidential ambitions, with Cheney as the first example. The office has become sufficiently significant that talented people with attractive career options view being vice president as an end in itself, not primarily as a route to the presidency.

It is often useful to categorize discrete vice-presidential activities such as adviser, troubleshooter, and portfolio handler and the distinct facets of the institution such as selection, campaign roles, transition, and duties. Yet such classification can distort as well as edify. Ultimately, the components and activities of the White House vice presidency are interrelated and mutually dependent. The new pattern and criteria of the vice-presidential selection process and vice-presidential campaign performance impact vice-presidential duties, and the expansion of the vice-presidential role imposes new expectations and constraints on selection. Similarly, synergies connect various vice-presidential activities. The vice president's advising role enhances his troubleshooting and vice versa. Far from being separate, the various institutions and activities of the modern vice presidency are linked.

Although the vice presidency has changed and grown in ways that reveal new continuities, the performance of the office varies depending on its occupant, the president, and the context in which they serve. Vice presidents from Bush to Biden have added gloss to the Mondale model. Those variations reflected factors peculiar to each vice president, such as their background, skill, political relationships, strengths, preferences, and circumstances. Each vice president encountered different conditions, from the political context, preferences, and style of the president they served and from the needs of each administration. The Biden vice presidency differs from that of Cheney just as Cheney's differed from Gore's, and so on. The White House vice presidency presents recurring patterns but allows novelty. Similarly, the selection process fluctuates as different individuals act in unique political environments.

The impact of individuals on the White House vice presidency suggests a second theme of this book. The White House vice presidency provides a lens to explore political leadership. The development of that institution was neither fortuitous nor routine. Carter and Mondale made something substantial of an office that, for most of its history, was superfluous or worse, an extraordinary achievement that their predecessors had either not attempted or not accomplished. That required effective political leadership. Carter and Mondale succeeded because of their mutual commitment to the task, their astute analysis of the problems and possibilities of the office, the institutional arrangements they designed, and their personal qualities and skill in implementing their new vision.

The actions of Carter's and Mondale's successors provide additional lessons in political behavior. Each pair faced unique challenges. The responses reflected strategic choices and executions. Some vice presidents strengthened the institution and enhanced its ability to contribute. Others made significant mistakes. Their conduct provides instructive models of political behavior.

Finally, the development of the White House vice presidency provides a case study of the dynamics of institutional growth. Without formal change in the Constitution or statutory law during the period studied, the vice presidency has become highly significant. It has changed from an office without consequential ongoing duties to one that contributes meaningfully and regularly to the executive branch. This development has rested on the repetition of informal practices and patterns of conduct, most of which Carter and Mondale initiated, that subsequent administrations have adopted and sometimes improved or extended. These informal practices include the intense vetting of prospective running mates; the preconvention vice-presidential selection; a vice-presidential debate; the vice president–elect's role in the transition from one administration to the next; the emergence of the vice president as an engaged senior adviser with a West Wing office, a weekly private meeting with the president, and the right to attend presidential meetings and receive presidential information; and the use of the vice president as a primary presidential troubleshooter. None of these practices are legally mandated, yet all are now entrenched features of the White House vice presidency. They could be abandoned, but that seems highly unlikely. These perpetuated practices, and others, help account for the development of the vice presidency into its robust form.

The development of the White House vice presidency illustrates the capacity of informal practice to reshape political institutions. That achievement is even more impressive given two contextual features. It converted a long-marginalized office into a significant political institution, and this change occurred when other governmental institutions were experiencing a quite different trajectory and becoming increasingly dysfunctional.

The dynamic that remade the vice presidency since 1976 accordingly has larger significance. If understanding that phenomenon would allow its replication elsewhere, the story of vice-presidential change is not simply a great success story regarding one institution but instructive about institutional advance and regeneration.

Appreciating the development Carter and Mondale initiated requires understanding the institution they inherited. Accordingly, the next chapter sketches the history of the vice presidency from its creation until 1976.

2

The Vice Presidency
through History

By 1976, the vice presidency was quite different both from the office the founders created and from the one previously known in American history. Whereas the office was initially conceived as an expedient to promote the election of a national president, the growth of national political parties and the Twelfth Amendment to the Constitution in 1804 rendered that function obsolete. Whereas the vice president originally was associated primarily with the legislative branch, with the main responsibility of presiding over the Senate, vice presidents functioned in the executive branch and rarely presided over the Senate long before 1976. Whereas for much of American history, party leaders had selected vice-presidential running mates, the presidential nominee had claimed that prerogative long before 1976. Whereas for much of American history, vice presidents (and candidates for the position) often had modest credentials, by 1976, they were generally of presidential caliber. And yet the office in 1976 remained limited and problematic. Its history, from 1789 to 1976, provides context to assess the subsequent creation of the White House vice presidency.

The Original Constitutional Vice Presidency

The original Constitution gave the vice presidency the following features. The office went to the presidential runner-up, but election as vice president, unlike election as president, did not require a majority electoral vote. Implicitly, the vice president was subject to the same qualifications as the president and shared a common term. Like the president and other civil officers, the vice president was subject to impeachment and removal for treason, bribery, and other high crimes and misdemeanors. The Constitution made the vice president the president of the Senate[1] and the first successor should the president of the United States die, resign, be removed, or be unable to discharge the powers and duties of his office.[2]

Yet neither the ongoing Senate nor contingent presidential succession role explained the creation of the vice presidency.[3] Indeed, Roger Sherman, who served on the committee that proposed the office, justified the Senate presiding role because otherwise the vice president would be "without employment," a claim George Mason and George Clinton echoed at ratifying conventions.[4] Instead, the office was probably created to help the initial presidential election system function. The founders assumed George Washington would be the first president but feared electors would thereafter support their states' favorite sons. In response, they created a system in which each elector cast two votes but required that at least one name someone not from the elector's state. The restricted second votes would help produce a national president; the second office would encourage conscientious balloting. As Hugh Williamson said at the Constitutional Convention, the vice presidency "was introduced only for the sake of a valuable mode of election which required two to be chosen at the same time,"[5] an explanation that would later be repeated.[6]

The words of a few framers cannot conclusively establish collective intent, but circumstantial evidence supports this understanding. The vice presidency and the Electoral College appeared simultaneously at the Constitutional Convention. The only mention of the office in *The Federalist Papers* was in an essay celebrating the presidential electoral system,[7] an association that suggests a relationship even though the author, Alexander Hamilton, offered other justifications.

The founders thought little of the vice presidency relative to the ongoing business of governing. Williamson said the office "was not wanted," and others joined in the disparagement.[8] Recorded comments from the Philadelphia or ratifying conventions did not extoll the office. And perhaps most significantly, the original Constitution did not provide for filling a vice-presidential vacancy. It simply authorized transferring the vice president's functions elsewhere. The Senate would elect a president pro tempore to preside when the vice president was absent or exercising the presidency. Congress could designate an "officer" to follow the vice president in the line of succession. Once the presidential voting ended, a vice president was extraneous.[9]

The Constitution conceived of the vice presidency as a legislative position.[10] Presiding over the Senate, the only ongoing function it conferred, protected the presiding senator's state from losing its equal representation.[11] The vice president could break tie votes.

The Constitution did not separate the vice presidency entirely from the executive branch, because Article II, relating to the presidency, conveyed the vice president's term, selection, qualifications (implicitly), presidential succession role, and susceptibility to impeachment and removal. Yet Article II vested executive powers and duties in the president and gave the vice president an executive role only if the president died, resigned, or was removed or disabled. John Adams described this entirely contingent executive role in recognizing that as vice president, "I am nothing, but I may be everything."[12]

The Constitution disqualified the vice president from presiding over the Senate when "he shall exercise the office of President of the United States"[13] but did not say whether he could handle executive functions while serving as Senate president. This silence might suggest some latitude to assume such roles, or it might yield to the policy underlying the prohibition against presiding over the Senate when acting as U.S. president, reflecting the idea that the vice president could not simultaneously act in both branches.

The Constitution did, however, envision the vice president as the Senate's regular presiding officer, a requirement it underscored by using the mandatory "shall" in assigning that role. Senator Oliver Ellsworth, an active participant at Philadelphia and a constitutional authority of the founding generation, later instructed Vice President Adams, "I find, Sir, it is evident & Clear, Sir, that wherever . . . the Senate are to be, then Sir, you must be at the head of them."[14] The obligatory nature of the Senate presiding duty suggested that, short of exercising the presidency, a vice president's permitted executive assignments, if any, could not interfere with that responsibility.

The original Constitution did not value philosophical or personal compatibility between president and vice president. Although at Philadelphia Elbridge Gerry referred to the "close intimacy" between the two as a reason the vice president should not preside over the Senate, Gouverneur Morris forcefully rebutted that prediction.[15] No one is recorded as echoing Gerry's view, and the ultimate decision to make the vice president the Senate president rejected his concerns. In any event, Morris had the better argument. As originally conceived, the presidency and vice presidency were electorally independent. There was no reason to believe the holders of those offices would be politically or personally allied. Since election of the vice president did not require majority support, the president's political opponents might win the second office. The original system seemed likely to produce an able vice president, although not necessarily of the president's caliber because a majority electoral vote was not required for the second office.

Finally, the founders apparently envisioned the vice president as playing a modest presidential succession role. The Constitution provided that in case of a vacancy due to death, resignation, or removal or of the president's "inability to discharge the powers and duties of the said office [the presidency], the same shall devolve on the Vice President."[16] Textually, "the same" thing "devolve[d]" in all four contingencies. The Philadelphia Convention seemed to intend that the vice president should assume presidential powers and duties, not the office. The penultimate draft provided that in the case of any of the four contingencies (or presidential absence), the vice president "shall exercise those powers and duties until another President be chosen, or until the inability of the President be removed."[17] The Committee of Style, which was empowered to perfect style but not substance, generated the ambiguous language in the Constitution.[18] The Twelfth Amendment supported that view in providing that if the electoral system did not produce a president, "then the Vice-President shall act as President, as in the case of the death or other constitutional disability of the President."

The Original Vice Presidency in Practice

The original constitutional vice presidency lasted only fifteen years, through the presidencies of Washington and Adams and Thomas Jefferson's first term. No succession events occurred during this time, and the office's operation was consistent with its design.

Not surprisingly, an office created to facilitate the presidential election system had little importance in governance. Adams lamented that "my country has in its wisdom contrived for me the most insignificant office that ever the invention of man contrived or his imagination conceived. . . . I can do neither good nor evil."[19] Jefferson thought the vice presidency "the only office in the world about which I am unable to decide in my own mind whether I had rather have it or not have it."[20] He could not imagine "a more tranquil & unoffending station" which would provide "philosophical evenings in the winter & rural days in summer."[21]

Early leaders regarded the vice president as a legislative figure. Washington did not include Adams in his Cabinet.[22] Adams envisioned his office as "the Head of the Legislative" and wrote that the vice presidency "is totally detached from the executive authority and confined to the legislative."[23] His formulation that as vice president he was "nothing," but "I am president also of the Senate," suggested where his professional time was to be spent. Jefferson reached the same conclusion.[24] "As to duty, the constitution will know me only as the member of a legislative body," he wrote to James Madison. Its "spirit" required that the legislative and executive power be separated except where otherwise specified.[25]

Consistent with Ellsworth's instruction, early vice presidents considered themselves bound to preside over the Senate. Abigail Adams complained that her husband never left the presiding officer's chair.[26] Jefferson told the Senate during his vice-presidential inauguration that he was "entering into an office whose primary business is merely to preside over the forms of this House."[27] With few exceptions, he presided each day.[28]

The first vice presidents, Adams and Jefferson, were extraordinary. Aaron Burr, who followed, was able but controversial. But the unanticipated development of national political parties undermined the design of the presidential election system as strategic considerations replaced merit as the voting criteria. By 1796, the first post-Washington election, parties were slating candidates for president and vice president, invariably with regional balancing. The Federalists paired Adams of Massachusetts with Thomas Pinckney (1796) and Charles Cotesworth Pinckney (1800), both of South Carolina. The Democrat-Republican ticket each time joined Jefferson (Virginia) and Burr (New York).

The partisan maneuvering produced different, but anomalous, results in the first post-Washington elections. In 1796, Adams was elected president with seventy-one electoral votes, whereas Jefferson, the rival standard-bearer, became vice president with sixty-eight votes. Four years later, ticketmates Jefferson and Burr each received seventy-three votes. Political leaders understood that a tie could be avoided if one elector voted for the party's presidential but not its vice-presidential candidate, but the Jeffersonians failed to execute that strategy. Some thirty-six ballots in the House of Representatives contingent election were held before enough Federalists abstained to allow Jefferson to prevail.

Although a cross-party result like the one in 1796 was inconvenient, the greater defect was that someone not intended for the presidency could be elected, as almost happened in 1801. The possibility of inversion allowed the minority party to promise electoral votes to the rival vice-presidential candidate in exchange for concessions.[29] To eliminate that specter, Jefferson's supporters pushed through the Twelfth Amendment before the 1804 election. It separated electoral voting for president and vice president, revising the Constitution to address political practice. Some thought the change obviated the need for a vice president and proposed abolishing the office,[30] but these arguments did not prevail, perhaps because they were viewed as a distraction from the basic task at hand.[31] In addition to separating the electoral vote for vice president, the Twelfth Amendment required that a winning candidate receive a majority of that vote and provided that if no vice-presidential candidate received a majority, the Senate would choose a vice president from the two candidates with the most vice-presidential electoral votes. It also made explicit what had been implicit, that "no person constitutionally ineligible to the office of President shall be eligible to that of Vice-President of the United States."[32]

The Nineteenth-Century Vice Presidency

The amendment did not, however, modify the office's duties. Vice presidents continued as the first presidential successor and as the Senate's president, where they regularly presided unless poor health intervened.[33]

Conventional wisdom associates the Twelfth Amendment with the decline of the vice presidency. Some opposed the amendment, anticipating that separate selection would diminish the vice presidency because it would not be the station for the presidential alternative.[34] Although the standard view seems logical, the role of the Twelfth Amendment in the decline of the office has been overstated.

To begin with, the original system was not functioning as designed. The vice presidency was already being used for geographic balance and to entice critical states. The pattern of Virginians running with candidates from Massachusetts and New York began with Washington and Jefferson, not in and after 1804. The vice presidency had already become a prize to be bartered for electoral support, not the station for the number-two man. It was also not likely to remain the presidential breeding ground. Jefferson preferred that succession run through his close ally, Secretary of State Madison, not Burr, and encouraged that result.[35] Those holding consequential offices were better positioned to demonstrate leadership than a vice president.

Nor is it clear that the Twelfth Amendment precipitated a decline in vice-presidential candidates. If that were the case, one would expect vice-presidential quality to plummet consistently after 1804. That did not occur. Clinton, the first vice president under the new system, had been the runner-up for vice president in 1792 and was the governor of New York when elected vice president, although some thought his abilities were declining. Daniel Tompkins, James Monroe's vice president (1817–1825), served ten years as an able governor of New York and had recently declined Madison's offer to be secretary of state in 1814, although his health and financial problems ultimately distracted him during his vice presidency. John C. Calhoun, a leading nineteenth-century political figure, served as vice president under John Quincy Adams and Andrew Jackson. Martin Van Buren, Jackson's second vice president, was elected the eighth president. John Tyler (1841) served in the House of Representatives for four years and was governor of Virginia, U.S. senator for nine years, and president pro tempore of the Senate before becoming vice president. George Dallas (1845–1849) had been a U.S. senator and ambassador to Russia and turned down opportunities to be attorney general; he later served as minister to Great Britain. In other words, most vice presidents for decades after 1804 were pretty able, accomplished public officials.[36]

Though the Twelfth Amendment was not the sole culprit, the office did decline. From 1804 to 1899, only two men who received much support for the presidential nomination emerged as the running mate, Thomas Hendricks and John Logan in 1884. Some vice presidents had modest credentials. Chester Arthur (1881) was a patronage politician whose highest prior office had been collector of customs in the Port of New York. Garret Hobart (1897–1899) had served no higher than the New Jersey legislature. He was more experienced than his Democratic opponent, Arthur Sewall, a Maine industrialist who had never held elective office. William Rufus King (1853) had served in the Senate for nearly thirty years, in the House for five years, as ambassador to France, and as president pro tempore of the Senate, but his health was so poor that he resigned from the Senate about two and one-half months before his term as vice president began and died six weeks into that service.[37]

Nineteenth-century vice-presidential candidates were chosen by party leaders, not by the presidential candidate. Political, not governance, considerations dictated the selections. The second spot was generally used to achieve geographic and/or ideological balance, to heal party wounds, or to enhance the ticket's appeal in a competitive state. Vice presidents accordingly had little reason to feel indebted to the president. Often they disagreed on fundamental issues, a circumstance viewed positively as a way to broaden a ticket's appeal and foster party unity. Vice presidents did not consider themselves part of the presidential administration and sometimes acted contrary to it.[38] Clinton opposed aspects of Jefferson's foreign policy and voted against rechartering the Bank of the United States, which Madison favored.[39] Calhoun split with President Jackson over the Nullification Crisis and cast the deciding vote against the nomination of Van Buren as minister to Great Britain.[40] Arthur opposed some nominations that President James Garfield submitted to the Senate, Hendricks battled with President Grover Cleveland, and Levi Morton's laissez-faire manner of presiding over the Senate contributed to the defeat of one of President Benjamin Harrison's legislative priorities.[41] Vice Presidents Van Buren and Hobart had some influence in the administration due to their relationship with Presidents Jackson and

William McKinley, respectively. They were exceptions. Nineteenth-century vice presidents generally had little to do other than preside over the Senate. Political distance and constitutional separation made the office a sinecure.

Four nineteenth-century vice presidents succeeded to the presidency following a president's death. After William Henry Harrison died in 1841, Tyler insisted that he was president, not simply acting president. Tyler's view was probably wrong and met initial resistance,[42] but his persistence secured his interpretation. Millard Fillmore, Andrew Johnson, and Arthur later followed Tyler's example, thereby embedding the Tyler Precedent in constitutional practice. That interpretation presented a difficulty, however, when a president was disabled, as became evident when Garfield was shot and incapacitated for eighty days before dying. Since the Constitution seemed to envision the same thing devolving in case of disability as in case of death, if Tyler was right, a presidential disability elevated the vice president, thereby supplanting the president. The Cabinet refused to acknowledge Garfield's disability, apparently in part for fear of ousting him.

In the nineteenth century, the vice presidency was not perceived as a good career move for an able and ambitious politician. After 1801, no sitting nineteenth-century vice president other than Van Buren (1836) was elected president, and only one other (John Breckenridge) was nominated. Only three—Clinton, Tompkins, and Calhoun—received second terms. From 1828 to 1900, five presidents were elected to a second term, but none with their first-term vice president, three of whom (Calhoun, Hannibal Hamlin, and Schuyler Colfax) were dumped.[43] The four vice presidents who succeeded to the presidency lacked a strong political base, and none secured his own term.

Finally, the nineteenth century demonstrated that the vice president was expendable. Owing to four presidential deaths and successions, six vice-presidential deaths, and one vice-presidential resignation, from 1812 to 1900, the vice presidency was vacant eleven times for a total of twenty-six years and nine months. Only ten of the twenty-one vice presidents during that period completed their terms. Yet the country survived without any discernable cry for a means to fill vice-presidential vacancies.

At the approach of the twentieth century, the vice presidency had little appeal. "There is very little to be said about the Vice President of the United States," Woodrow Wilson wrote in 1885. "His position is one of anomalous insignificance and curious uncertainty." Wilson concluded the little to be said by observing that the "chief embarrassment" in discussing the office was that "in explaining how little there is to be said about it one has evidently said all there is to say."[44] In 1899, Theodore Roosevelt thought the vice presidency an "honorable position," but he preferred one with "more work in it" such as being a U.S. senator, secretary of war, or governor general of the Philippines.[45] Roosevelt thought the chance for "a Vice President to do much of anything is infinitesimal."[46] (After agreeing to be McKinley's running mate in 1900, Roosevelt became the twenty-sixth president when McKinley was assassinated the next year.) In 1908, Wilson viewed the vice president simply as an officer of the Senate whose powers were "practically negligible."[47] Eight years later, he dismissed the suggestion that he replace Vice President Thomas Marshall with Secretary of War Newton Baker because Baker was too good to be wasted in the vice presidency.[48] "The Vice-President's office is ill-conceived," wrote James Bryce in 1928, and the officer had become "even more insignificant than the Constitution seemed to make him."[49]

The Twentieth-Century Vice Presidency before Nixon

The vice presidency began to assume some small association with the executive branch in the twentieth century. Marshall presided over the Cabinet while Wilson was overseas before discontinuing the practice on the grounds that he should not operate simultaneously in both branches. During the 1920 presidential campaign, Warren G. Harding promised that if elected, he would use his vice president, Calvin Coolidge, as a liaison between the executive and legislative branches. Upon their election, Harding asked Coolidge to attend Cabinet meetings, which Coolidge did, although with misgivings.[50] Coolidge's experience persuaded him that Harding's initiative would help prepare a vice president to assume the presidency.[51] Yet his vice president, Charles G. Dawes, declined such an invitation in order to avoid a precedent that might embarrass a future president.[52] Charles Curtis, Herbert Hoover's vice president, resumed Cabinet attendance,[53] and it has continued ever since.

This innovation did not make the office overly taxing. Marshall praised the vice presidency as a job that lacked responsibilities.[54] In retirement, he added, "I don't want to work but I wouldn't mind being Vice President again."[55] "'A Vice President. . . . has no work,'" Dawes declared in 1927.[56] The 1932 Pulitzer Prize–winning musical comedy, "Of Thee I Sing," parodied fictitious Vice President Alexander Throttlebottom, who sneaked into the White House with a tour group and was unaware of his duty to preside over the Senate.

Franklin D. Roosevelt used his first vice president, John Nance Garner, as an occasional legislative adviser and liaison.[57] Garner helped advance early New Deal legislation, even some that went further than he thought prudent. He also traveled to the Philippines and Japan in 1936 with a Senate delegation and later attended the Mexican opening of the Inter-American Highway. FDR named his second vice president, Henry A. Wallace, chair of the Board of Economic Warfare within the executive branch in 1941 and sent him on goodwill trips to Latin America and China.[58] In 1949, Congress made the vice president a member of the new National Security Council (NSC).[59]

These steps did not link the vice president closely with the executive branch. Wilson and his inner circle refused to confide in Marshall regarding the president's health after a stroke essentially incapacitated him in October 1919. Marshall did not see Wilson for more than seventeen months, until Harding's inauguration.[60] Garner broke with FDR regarding labor union strikes and the court-packing plan and opposed Roosevelt's third-term candidacy. Wallace lost his position as head of the Board of Economic Warfare after a public feud with Secretary of Commerce Jesse Jones.[61] During his vice presidency Harry S. Truman rarely saw FDR. No one told him of the Manhattan Project to build the atomic bomb until after FDR's death.[62]

Presiding over the Senate remained the vice president's central occupation for the first half of the twentieth century. Marshall regarded Cabinet attendance as unconstitutional and unwise since it would interfere with the vice president's constitutional duty and undermine Senate confidence in him.[63] Coolidge regularly presided over the Senate and found the work "fascinating" and the debate "informing."[64] Dawes devoted his vice presidency to trying, unsuccessfully, to change Senate rules in order to limit debate. Curtis thought administering those rules was the vice president's entire job.[65] Truman presided part of virtually each day the Senate was in session during his eighty-two-day vice presidency.[66] Alben W. Barkley, Truman's vice president, recognized that the Constitution imposed on him the "duty" to be the Senate's presiding officer but offered to assume other services.[67] Barkley was the last vice president to devote much professional time to presiding over the Senate.[68]

During the first half of the twentieth century, vice-presidential selection still typically occurred at the end of the convention only after the presidential nomination was resolved and often after prolonged balloting. From 1900 to 1948, only five unsuccessful presidential aspirants received the second spot (Marshall in 1912, Curtis in 1928, Garner in 1932, Frank Knox in 1936, and Earl Warren in 1948). Presidential nominees did not control the choice until 1940 or so and generally refrained from stating a preference. Blatantly political considerations often dictated vice-presidential choice. From 1900 to 1956, 43 percent of the vice-presidential candidates came from states with at least twenty electoral votes, and 40 percent came from those with ten to nineteen electoral votes.[69] Some twenty-four of the twenty-six tickets included geographical balance. Candidates often were chosen to help carry an important swing state, such as Indiana, which provided five of the eight major-party vice-presidential candidates from 1904 to 1916. Conventions often sought ideological balance and joined candidates from different poles of the party. The vice-presidential selection was occasionally determined by a deal, sometimes without the knowledge of the presidential candidate, who traditionally did not attend the convention. In 1912, Wilson's managers promised the vice presidency would go to Marshall in exchange for Indiana's support on the twenty-eighth ballot. Twenty years later, Garner supported FDR in exchange for the second spot.[70] The requirement that a Democratic nominee receive a two-thirds vote had encouraged ideological ticket balancing and deals. Its elimination in 1936 lessened those tactics.

Nonetheless, during the first half of the twentieth century, the vice presidency began to attract more prominent political figures. The eleven vice presidents during this period included governors of New York (Theodore Roosevelt), Indiana (Marshall), and Massachusetts (Coolidge); two Senate majority leaders (Curtis and Barkley); a speaker of the House of Representatives (Garner), three prominent national legislators (Charles Fairbanks, James Sherman, and Truman); a past and future Cabinet member (Wallace); and Dawes, a Nobel Prize winner and holder of leading executive positions. Those who sought the job unsuccessfully were also generally distinguished, including a future president (FDR), two sitting vice presidents (Sherman and Curtis), two past vice presidents (Adlai Stevenson I and Fairbanks), a Senate majority leader (Joseph Robinson), a Senate minority leader (Charles McNary), a future Senate majority leader (John Kern), a future secretary of war (Frank Knox), a prominent governor and future senator from Ohio (John Bricker), and the governor of California and future chief justice of the United States (Warren). Whereas seven vice presidents died in office from 1812 to 1912, none did during the next 50 (or for that matter 100) years,[71] suggesting that greater attention was being paid to health in selecting nominees. Four of the five vice presidents serving with a president who sought reelection (all except Wallace in 1944) were renominated for a second term.

The first half of the twentieth century called attention to the importance of the vice president as the first presidential successor. Succession events affected four of the nine presidencies during this period. McKinley (1901), Harding (1923), and Roosevelt (1945) died in office, and Wilson had a lengthy disability beginning in October 1919 following a major stroke, although no steps were taken to transfer presidential powers. Franklin Roosevelt narrowly escaped assassination on February 15, 1933, a few weeks before his term began. Whereas nineteenth-century presidents by succession were not later elected to the office, Theodore Roosevelt, Coolidge, and Truman all won their own terms.

Yet the office's advance did not silence its critics. In 1948, the great political scientist Clinton Rossiter disparaged the vice presidency as "a hollow shell of an office, an impotent and uncomfortable heir apparency sought by practically no one we should like to see as President."[72] Five years later, Lucius Wilmerding, Jr., a leading student of political institutions, said that the vice presidency had "no duties," and "an office without duties, no matter how great its reversionary prospects, is not an office to inspire or satisfy the expectations of an ambitious mind." He proposed abolishing it.[73]

The Modern American Vice Presidency: Nixon to Rockefeller

These criticisms were overstated, but in any event, the vice presidency was about to be transformed. Major changes in American society and government during the 1930s and 1940s fundamentally altered America's political system, and these developments affected the vice presidency. The New Deal, World War II, and the Cold War changed American government in ways that drew the vice presidency closer to the executive branch. The growth of national government and America's expanded international role strengthened the executive branch and weakened local political machines. The president's domestic and international role increased, and new technology created new possibilities for, and expectations regarding, presidential activity and travel.[74]

The president's enhanced governmental role allowed presidential candidates to claim the leading role in selecting their running mates beginning in 1940, a change that encouraged more compatible and interdependent pairings. That year, Franklin Roosevelt refused to run unless Wallace was his running mate. The convention accepted Wallace, but opposition was so intense that he did not deliver an acceptance speech at that gathering.[75] Four years later, Roosevelt's decision to endorse, but not dictate, Wallace's renomination signaled that he preferred that the convention choose someone else, a course he encouraged by identifying Truman or Justice William O. Douglas as acceptable options. Contemporary Republican nominees acted on the assumption that the choice was theirs to make, and party leaders, though consulted, shared that understanding.[76] The practice was sufficiently secure that all were surprised when Adlai Stevenson II threw the selection to the convention in 1956. This change gave presidents some incentive to involve vice presidents in their administrations and vice presidents reason to see the executive branch as salvation from the insignificant duty the Constitution prescribed.[77]

The tenure of Richard M. Nixon (1953–1961) accelerated the movement of the vice presidency to the executive branch and the rise of the office. President Dwight Eisenhower and Nixon built on the earlier precedents and exploited technological advances to expand Nixon's executive roles. In addition to attending Cabinet and NSC meetings, Nixon handled various assignments for Eisenhower. Nixon undertook diplomatic missions to fifty-four countries, beginning in October 1953, when he left on a seventy-day trip to Asia and the Far East. He took six other official foreign trips as vice president, including a high-profile May 1958 visit to South America, where demonstrators attacked his car, and a 1959 trip to the Soviet Union, where he engaged in a "kitchen debate" with Nikita Khrushchev on the merits of the rival systems.

Nixon worked to combat Senator Joseph McCarthy's anticommunist witch hunts once they turned on Eisenhower's administration[78] and to advance legislation for an interstate highway system and for school construction. He was a frequent administration spokesman and a leading Republican political surrogate, especially during the midterm campaigns in 1954 and 1958. Eisenhower's aversion to partisan activity created an opening for the ambitious Nixon, who carried the burden in the 1956 reelection campaign.

Eisenhower named Nixon to chair the President's Committee on Government Contracts to address racial discrimination in government conduct. Eisenhower claimed that Nixon discharged these duties "voluntarily" because the vice president, "with the constitutional duty of presiding over the Senate, is not legally a part of the Executive branch and is not subject to direction by the President."[79] Formally, Eisenhower may have been right, but politically, Nixon had reason to accede to the president's "requests." The executive branch work offered greater opportunity to advance Nixon's political ambitions.

The vice president's role as presidential successor also gained greater prominence as Eisenhower experienced three serious illnesses — a heart attack in September 1955, an ileitis attack and operation in 1956, and a stroke in 1957. These first presidential disabilities in the nuclear age drew attention to the competence and preparation of the person a heartbeat away and to arrangements to handle presidential inability. At Eisenhower's direction, Nixon chaired Cabinet and NSC meetings on these occasions, a deliberate departure from Wilson's ostracism of Marshall during his disability. The Department of Justice supported a proposed constitutional amendment to allow a temporary transfer of presidential power to the vice president if the president were disabled, and Eisenhower and Nixon entered into an agreement empowering Eisenhower or Nixon to effect a temporary transfer of presidential powers should Eisenhower be incapacitated.[80] Eisenhower was the first president whom the Twenty-Second Amendment to the Constitution precluded from seeking another term, which allowed Nixon to plan his presidential race in 1960. Nixon became the first sitting vice president in 100 years to be nominated for the presidency but narrowly lost to John Kennedy.

Other administrations followed the Eisenhower-Nixon precedents. Kennedy named Johnson to chair the President's Committee on Equal Employment Opportunity, the successor to Nixon's government contracts committee, and the Space Council. When Johnson, fearing controversy, resisted the first assignment, Kennedy insisted that his participation was mandatory because Nixon had fulfilled that role.[81] Kennedy sent Johnson on eleven trips to thirty-three nations.[82] Although many were ceremonial, Johnson handled consequential missions to Asia, including Vietnam in May 1961; to Germany in August 1961 after the Soviet Union erected the Berlin Wall; and to Greece, Turkey, Iran, and Cyprus in August 1962 to advise of aid reductions.[83]

These executive branch assignments pulled the vice president further from Capitol Hill to the other end of Pennsylvania Avenue, constitutionally and physically. In 1961, Johnson became the first vice president given an office in what is now the Eisenhower Executive Office Building near the White House,[84] space provided so that he could meet his executive "responsibilities most effectively."[85] The Kennedy Department of Justice found that especially since 1933, the vice presidency had moved "closer and closer" to the executive[86] and that tasks Wallace, Nixon, and Johnson had performed as well as the statutorily created NSC membership had "tended to increase the identification of the Vice President with the executive branch and the general acceptability of a delegation of executive functions to him."[87] When it was proposed, at Johnson's urging, that the new vice president preside over the Senate Democratic Caucus, some of his former colleagues protested,[88] partly arguing that the vice president was part of the executive branch and had no business presiding over a legislative meeting.[89] There were other reasons Democratic senators did not want the domineering Johnson chairing their meetings, but the dust-up reflected a new attitude regarding the constitutional status of the second office. It had moved.

Following Kennedy's assassination on November 22, 1963, Johnson became president, and his performance during the remainder of Kennedy's term suggested the importance of the vice presidency and focused attention on presidential succession and inability. In 1965, Congress proposed, and two years later the states ratified, the Twenty-Fifth Amendment to the Constitution, which addressed vexing problems of presidential succession and inability primarily by providing a means to fill a vice-presidential vacancy and procedures to handle presidential inability.[90] The amendment implicitly saw the office as an integral part of the executive branch. Whereas the original vice presidency had been deemed expendable, the Twenty-Fifth Amendment reflected the belief that the nation always needed a vice president.[91] It presumed that a president was entitled to choose a vice president with whom he was politically and personally compatible but also that Congress should be able to confirm (or not) the president's choice to provide democratic legitimacy.[92] In late 1967, the perceptive political scientist Paul T. David observed that "the Vice Presidency is in transition to a new institutional status in which it will be recognized as an office established predominantly in the Executive Branch, while retaining its constitutional prerogatives in the Legislative Branch."[93]

Johnson's four immediate successors, Hubert H. Humphrey, Spiro T. Agnew, Gerald R. Ford, and Nelson A. Rockefeller, increasingly operated from the Executive Office Building, a venue that represented their association with the executive branch. They discharged executive assignments like those Nixon and Johnson had handled—committee chairman, foreign emissary, administration spokesman, partisan warrior, legislative liaison. Johnson multiplied Humphrey's executive branch assignments, appointing him to chair presidential task forces or councils on the Peace Corps, space, equal opportunity, employment, youth opportunity, physical fitness, recreation, Indian opportunity, and natural beauty, among others.[94] Johnson sent Humphrey to Asia, including Vietnam, on several occasions and to Europe, Africa, and Latin America. Humphrey became a leading spokesperson for the Vietnam War. When Johnson elected not to run for reelection, Humphrey secured the 1968 Democratic nomination and overcame formidable obstacles to almost defeat Nixon.[95]

Agnew inherited some of Humphrey's domestic assignments, and some new ones such as chair of a new Office of Intergovernmental Affairs, a role William Rehnquist, then assistant attorney general for the Office of Legal Counsel, advised was appropriate. The vice president "occupies a unique position under the Constitution," Rehnquist wrote. Although the future chief justice thought for "some purposes" the vice president's "status in the Executive Branch is not altogether clear," Congress and different presidents had given the vice president various executive roles such that "his status may be characterized as Legislative or Executive depending on the context," and his "availability" to serve as an executive branch member and chair of the body seemed clear.[96] Beginning with Agnew, Congress added a line in the executive branch budget to support vice-presidential activities.[97] Agnew's most prominent role was as a political surrogate who vigorously attacked Nixon's critics. In this respect, his role mirrored that of Nixon in the Eisenhower administration, leading some distractors to disparage him as "Nixon's Nixon."[98]

From Nixon on, vice presidents rarely presided over the Senate. When Rockefeller appeared for parts of four consecutive days, Senate Majority Leader Mike Mansfield congratulated him on breaking Hubert Humphrey's recent record of three straight days.[99]

Yet the executive branch was changing even as the vice presidency moved toward it. The branch's expanded domain and size led to the creation in the 1950s and 1960s of new institutions to coordinate and control the expanding work entrusted to the president. The White House staff became larger and more specialized and grew to include new structures and expertise to help the president handle national security, legislative liaison, domestic policy, press affairs, and so on. This expanded personnel and apparatus gave the president greater capacity and an expanded court of loyalists but also created bureaucracies to manage, some of which had or developed their own agendas.[100] These developments impacted presidents, but they also posed challenges for vice presidents. The vice president lacked staff support to provide the expert analysis he needed to participate as an informed adviser or to administer programs. The president's expanded court typically viewed the vice president as a competitor.

By the 1960s, eminent men such as Johnson and Humphrey saw the vice presidency as a stepping-stone to the presidency.[101] The selection often followed a meeting with other party leaders, although sometimes those sessions provided the illusion of consultation regarding decisions already made.[102] For instance, in 1968, Nixon, not his putative advisers, identified Agnew as a prospective running mate.[103] The choice was typically made for political reasons, such as to balance the ticket ideologically or geographically, to placate a disgruntled faction, or to appeal to an important bloc of states. Kennedy chose Johnson to help carry the South; Barry Goldwater selected Representative William Miller because he was an aggressive campaigner who got under Johnson's skin; Nixon picked Agnew as acceptable in the South and border states but not controversial elsewhere. Notwithstanding the rising importance of the vice presidency, the running mate was generally chosen hurriedly at the end of the convention after the presidential nomination was decided. Occasionally, the choice followed some systematic examination of the pasts of various presidential options, as in 1964, when Johnson subjected Humphrey to intrusive questioning,[104] and in 1968, when Humphrey's friend Max Kampelman interviewed various prospects,[105] but generally no vetting occurred. In 1972, George McGovern selected Missouri senator Thomas F. Eagleton minutes before the deadline for making his choice after several prominent Democrats had rejected his offer but recommended Eagleton as a rising star. McGovern's campaign had been advised that Eagleton had been treated for depression but never asked Eagleton about his health until after he was selected. Eighteen days later, McGovern forced Eagleton from the ticket.[106]

Although the vice presidency had clearly grown and established itself in the executive branch, it remained limited. Much vice-presidential time was spent doing make-work in an office often more frustrating than influential.[107] Eisenhower tried to dump Nixon in 1956, suggesting that the vice president might better pursue his presidential ambitions from a Cabinet position. Nixon knew better. He understood the value of the vice presidency as a presidential springboard and knew that moving to the Cabinet would be perceived as a demotion, like that imposed on Wallace in 1944, and that, in the words of Eisenhower and Nixon biographer Stephen Ambrose, "the best possible place for [Nixon] was right where he was, one (damaged) heartbeat away from the Presidency."[108] Nixon remained on the 1956 ticket and became Eisenhower's heir apparent. Yet Eisenhower was unable or unwilling to design an ongoing substantive vice-presidential role that was acceptable to others in his administration.[109] Asked at an August 1960 press conference to identify some Nixon idea that had become policy, Eisenhower replied, "If you give me a week, I might think of one. I don't remember,"[110] a response damaging to Nixon, who was trumpeting his vice-presidential experience as a reason voters should prefer him to Kennedy.

Johnson had been a legislative master as Senate majority leader but was largely sidelined from those matters as vice president. He had thought that chairing the Senate Democratic Caucus and his relationship with Speaker of the House Sam Rayburn would establish him as a force on Capitol Hill. After seventeen Senate Democrats revolted against him chairing their caucus, Johnson discovered, as Nigel Bowles put it, that "the responsibilities of the vice-presidency were likely to be even fewer than he had supposed."[111] Kennedy ignored Johnson's requests for a White House office, an independent executive staff, and general supervisory power of various national security matters.[112] Kennedy made clear that his aide Lawrence F. O'Brien, not Johnson, handled legislative liaison. Johnson's ongoing assignments regarding race and space had symbolic importance, but he lacked the staff or agenda control to direct those areas. Watching Johnson, his associate Harry McPherson learned "one of the oldest lessons of American government . . . that the Vice Presidency is empty of power."[113]

Johnson promised a big role for his vice president yet ignored the suggestion that he bring the vice president into the White House.[114] Instead, he found ways to humiliate Humphrey. Early in their term, he excluded Humphrey from the American delegation to Winston Churchill's funeral. During a long and testy press conference answer, Johnson observed that "it had never occurred to me and I had never had it brought to my attention so vividly that it was the duty and the function of the Vice President to be present at all official funerals,"[115] a disingenuous response from someone who as vice president had led delegations to funerals of high-profile international figures. After Humphrey opposed bombing North Vietnam at a February 10, 1965, meeting while Soviet premier Aleksei Kosygin was in Hanoi and followed up with a memorandum to Johnson outlining the adverse political consequences of escalating America's involvement, the president admonished him against sending him written advice on the subject and ceased inviting Humphrey to sessions on Vietnam,[116] an exclusion that communicated Humphrey's diminished standing. Humphrey's numerous domestic assignments were mostly peripheral except the chairmanship of the President's Council on Equal Opportunity to coordinate programs relating to civil rights. Yet Johnson stripped Humphrey of even that role in September 1965. When liberals challenged Johnson's Vietnam policies, the president dispatched Humphrey to Southeast Asia in February 1966 with little advance notice and with LBJ loyalists as chaperones. Upon Humphrey's return, Johnson converted the too-compliant Humphrey into a principal salesman of his Vietnam policies, thereby exploiting his standing with liberals.

Nixon had contempt for Agnew. He scornfully rejected Agnew's request for a weekly meeting and rarely met with him.[117] Agnew had little substantive role other than as a political hit man. Nixon sometimes derided Agnew as his insurance policy against assassination. Agnew contributed to his problems by the obtuse manner in which he did his job and occasionally infuriated Nixon by opposing his positions at meetings with others.[118] Nixon wanted to replace Agnew in 1972 with former treasury secretary and Texas governor John Connally and explored various strategies to achieve that end before concluding that the costs exceeded the reward.[119] Agnew led early polls measuring preferences for the 1976 Republican nomination after the 1972 landslide reelection. During his fifth year in office, Agnew observed that "the President hasn't defined my role yet."[120] Implicitly, he had, and Agnew's diminished assignments made clear that he was not the preferred successor. Agnew's presidential ambitions and vice presidency ended with his resignation in October

1973 incident to a plea agreement to avoid indictment for allegedly having accepted bribes as governor of Maryland.

Agnew's resignation brought the first use of the Twenty-Fifth Amendment to fill a vice-presidential vacancy. Nixon wanted to nominate Connally, but legislative leaders advised that the former Democrat could not be confirmed and favored Ford.[121] The ongoing impeachment proceedings against Nixon increased the likelihood that the vice president would become president. Nixon nominated Ford, and the Republican House minority leader was confirmed, 92 to 3 in the Senate and 387 to 35 in the House, and sworn in on December 6, 1973, less than two months after his nomination.[122] Nixon involved Ford in legislation regarding agriculture and national security matters,[123] but Ford spent much of his ten-month vice presidency on the road, campaigning for Republican candidates in the 1974 midterm elections and staying as clear of Watergate as possible.[124]

Paul Light has, however, pointed out an underappreciated legacy of Agnew's vice presidency, the creation of a line in the executive budget for the vice president's office. Whereas vice presidents had previously been dependent on the budget of someone else, a task force, or their Senate allowance to pay aides, this new line item gave vice presidents resources to develop a larger staff. Whereas Nixon and Johnson had each scratched together a staff of about twenty, Ford had more than three times that many, mostly supported by the new executive line, which Ford persuaded friends in Congress and the executive branch to inflate, thereby allowing him to add a counsel, a national security adviser, speechwriters, and other personnel.[125]

Nixon's resignation on August 9, 1974, to avoid impeachment and removal brought the second instance of presidential succession in little more than a decade and the second use of Section Two of the Twenty-Fifth Amendment. This time, however, the nominating president, Ford, was himself a product of that amendment, not of a national election. Ford invited suggestions from legislators and party officials before narrowing the choice to Rockefeller, the four-term former governor of New York; George H. W. Bush, a former congressman who had held appointive positions under Nixon; and Donald Rumsfeld. He selected Rockefeller on August 20, 1974. Lengthy hearings focused on Rockefeller's immense wealth, his extravagant gifts to public officials, and other aspects of his political career and extended beyond the November midterm elections. On December 10, 1974, the Senate confirmed Rockefeller, 90 to 7, and nine days later, the House did, 287 to 128.[126]

Rockefeller came to office amid high expectations.[127] He had previously sought, or been a leading candidate for, the presidency three times and had declined the vice presidency on the Republican ticket in 1960 and the Democratic ticket in 1968.[128] Yet Rockefeller's vice presidency fell far short of predictions.

Ford liked Rockefeller and wanted him and his staff to feel welcome.[129] But little thought was given to how to structure Rockefeller's role, which was largely undefined even the day before his confirmation. Rumsfeld suggested giving Rockefeller a Cabinet department to run.[130] Ford aide Jack Marsh perceptively argued that Rockefeller's role would depend not just on his substantive responsibilities but on "operational and staff procedures" regarding his working relationship with the White House." The Office of the Vice President must be treated "more as insiders than outsiders." Marsh suggested including a Rockefeller aide at staff meetings and giving the vice president access to information from various offices.[131]

Ford ultimately gave Rockefeller a smorgasbord of assignments— vice chairman of the NSC and Domestic Council, studying whether the White House should have a science adviser, helping with the bicentennial celebration, and so on. He announced that Rockefeller could see him without an appointment and included Rockefeller's staff in White House meetings.[132] The Domestic Council role appeared significant, but many other assignments were not. A few weeks later, Ford named Rockefeller to chair a high-profile blue-ribbon commission exploring allegations that the Central Intelligence Agency (CIA) had engaged in domestic espionage.[133] No mention was made of the vice president serving as a general adviser or troubleshooter.

Rockefeller thought the Domestic Council role would confer power comparable to that which Henry Kissinger wielded in foreign policy, and accordingly he fought for that designation, which Chief of Staff Rumsfeld opposed. Rockefeller placed his aide James Cannon as executive director of the council, but Cannon reported to Ford through

Rumsfeld, an arrangement that minimized Rockefeller's significance.[134] And, shortly after Rockefeller and Cannon were installed, Ford approved a recommendation that no new domestic initiatives be pursued in 1975, a proposal from a senior staff meeting that neither Rockefeller nor Cannon had attended.[135] After canvassing unsuccessful efforts to use the vice president, eminent presidency scholar Stephen Hess called putting Rockefeller in charge of the Domestic Council "the worst failure of all."[136]

Rockefeller had a weekly private meeting with Ford for which he insisted on setting the agenda and often lectured Ford. When he left proposals behind, on whether the president should have a science adviser or for a $100 billion energy independence initiative, Ford's chiefs of staff circulated them to other aides for comment, which often came back with misgivings.[137] When other Ford advisers opposed Rockefeller's energy independence corporation proposal,[138] Ford had to choose between a Rockefeller pet project and orthodox Republican principles at a time when he faced Reagan's challenge for the Republican nomination. Ford's support for the energy program was portrayed as indicating Rockefeller's historic influence,[139] but the initiative went nowhere in Congress and presaged the end of Rockefeller's tenure.[140]

Rockefeller developed powerful White House adversaries, including Rumsfeld and Dick Cheney. In late October 1975, Rumsfeld and Cheney advised Ford that Rockefeller was a source of problems in the White House.[141] In November 1975, less than a year after Rockefeller had taken office, Ford asked the vice president to remove himself from consideration for the 1976 ticket.[142]

Rockefeller contributed to his own demise. He was anathema to the increasingly conservative base of the Republican Party but did little to strengthen his position with that constituency. Rather than speaking at party events, he preferred to remain in Washington, D.C., and New York.[143] Having spent most of his career as governor of New York, Rockefeller was accustomed to deciding, not advising. He did not operate well in situations where he was not the boss. He was not well suited to being number two.[144]

Conclusion

By 1976, the vice presidency had grown but remained limited. The office was attracting able men, largely because it had become a good presidential springboard. Vice presidents handled duties in the executive branch, but their portfolios tended to be peripheral and often demeaning, and their assignments were generally disjointed and episodic. Vice presidents often clashed with important administration figures, thereby limiting their influence. Robert Kennedy disliked Johnson and missed few opportunities to embarrass him. Johnson aides often were dismissive of Humphrey, Nixon's associates disliked Agnew. Rockefeller ran afoul of Rumsfeld and Cheney.

During the mid-1970s, the prominent historian and political activist Arthur M. Schlesinger, Jr., urged abolishing the office.[145] Kissinger, who had observed the vice presidencies of Agnew, Ford, and Rockefeller, also provided a dismal assessment of the office. The promised partnership almost never developed, he wrote. Presidents were uneasy with their vice presidents, "whose most exhilarating moment" would be provided by the president's own death. Because presidents could not remove their vice presidents, they did not give them meaningful assignments. The lack of staff support limited the vice president's utility as an adviser. Turf-conscious White House staffers saw the vice president as a competitor.[146] Former senator Eugene McCarthy had coveted the vice presidency in 1964 but fourteen years later described it as "the worst conceived and defined" constitutional institution. Someone qualified to be president should not be wasted on the second job, but someone not so qualified should not be the first successor. Eliminating the vice presidency would be a fitting memorial to Humphrey, McCarthy wrote, for he had been wasted in, and a victim of, that office.[147] Writing in 1976, Humphrey said that a vice president, "regardless of talent and the President's personality, has a choice between two relationships: acquiescence and hostility."[148]

Carter and Mondale were about to prove them all wrong.

3

Laying the Foundation

Although discussions of the Mondale vice presidency typically focus on the enhanced governing role of the vice president, Jimmy Carter and Walter Mondale were also associated with innovations in the vice-presidential selection process, campaign, and transition roles. The new selection system involved a lengthy, deliberative process that emphasized the presidential qualifications of a running mate. The campaign included the first vice-presidential debate and other less visible but significant new features that integrated the Mondale and Carter operations. The transition role involved the vice president–elect in constructing the new administration.

The four innovations—selection, campaign, transition, and duties—were interrelated and mutually reinforcing. The new selection process allowed greater scrutiny of, and reflection about, alternative vice-presidential possibilities. A presidential candidate who engaged in such a process was more invested in the choice, more likely to reach a comfortable decision, and more publicly associated with it. The vice-presidential debate gave greater visibility to the second office and its contestants and increased the incentive to choose a running mate of presidential stature. Participation in the transition increased the vice president's prospects for success. The new stature and possibilities of the office added incentives to choose a qualified running mate and enhanced its appeal to able persons.

Carter's role was indispensable to the changes, but Mondale also played an important part. His approach to his vice-presidential interview and his thoughts about the vice presidency reinforced Carter's belief in the potential of the office. His performance in the vice-presidential debate provided a model for others, helped secure Carter's victory, and strengthened Mondale's standing. His contributions during the transition foreshadowed his role in, and value to, the administration.

These changes contributed to Mondale's success in office. They also helped recast future vice-presidential selection, campaign role, and transition activity. They succeeded and became institutionalized because they were based on sound institutional engineering and were skillfully implemented.

The Mondale Selection

Carter conducted a far more intensive vice-presidential selection process than had previously occurred. Several factors led him to commit so much to the effort.

Lessons from Contemporary Events

Historical events encouraged Carter to treat his vice-presidential search seriously. He dared not repeat McGovern's haphazard 1972 process. McGovern clinched the Democratic nomination on the first night of the convention when he prevailed on a challenge to many of his California delegates, but he deferred seriously considering running mates, other than Senator Edward M. Kennedy, until his nomination became official two nights later. McGovern was so intent on persuading Kennedy that he did not identify a compelling available alternative.[1] When Kennedy repeated past refusals to run, McGovern belatedly began a frantic search that resulted in the offer to Eagleton minutes before the deadline after others had declined. McGovern's campaign hierarchy had heard reports of Eagleton's past health problems but never asked Eagleton about the subject before offering him the nomination.

Dissatisfaction with McGovern's process led the Democratic Party to consider reforming vice-presidential selection. Hubert Humphrey chaired a party commission to assess ways to focus earlier attention on the decision and to extend the time to make it. Other events also raised the saliency of the issue. Agnew's resignation in October 1973 after pleading no contest to tax evasion suggested the need for greater scrutiny of vice-presidential candidates. He had been selected and elected twice notwithstanding undetected criminal conduct. The Twenty-Fifth Amendment provided a model for scrutinizing prospective vice presidents. The Ford and Rockefeller confirmation proceedings gave the vice presidency greater prominence. Ford's succession marked the third time in little more than a decade that a sitting or former vice president had become president. The confirmations of Ford and Rockefeller, after Federal Bureau of Investigation (FBI) background investigations and extensive questioning, suggested inquiries that might be appropriate in vetting potential vice presidents.[2]

CONDITIONS CONDUCIVE TO CARTER'S PROCESS

Circumstances also created conditions conducive to a more intensive and deliberative process. Whereas many past presidential nominations had been decided at the convention, Carter essentially secured the prize on June 8, 1976, more than a month before the Democratic Party meeting began. That early resolution, an unanticipated consequence of changes in delegate selection, allowed Carter to consider his decision without the distraction of campaigning for the nomination.

In memoranda, Carter's top aide, Hamilton Jordan, had encouraged him to consider elevating the vice presidency and to choose a running mate whom he respected, had pointed out that his selection process would shape perceptions of him, and had argued that choosing a well-qualified vice-presidential candidate was prudent politically.[3] Jordan's suggestions found a receptive audience in Carter, who was disposed to take the decision seriously. As an engineer and a small businessman, he was accustomed to using available resources. He thought it wasteful to underutilize a vice president's talents, an attitude that encouraged him to choose the best person possible. He was sufficiently secure not to feel threatened by his vice president.[4] And Carter understood the hazards of an incompatible number two. His lieutenant governor, Lester Maddox, had frequently undermined him,[5] an experience Carter wanted to avoid repeating. Carter also recognized that a well-executed process might reassure those who feared a one-term former governor of Georgia lacked sufficient high-level governmental experience to be president.

Carter's early success allowed him to clarify running-mate options. As the party's new leader, Carter could assert himself in a manner that previously would have seemed presumptuous. Whereas Carter's rivals and their supporters would previously have felt inhibited from considering the vice-presidential nomination, it was now the best prize remaining. Carter's prospects for election made the second spot attractive. Mondale, Edmund Muskie, and Frank Church had rebuffed McGovern but sought Carter's invitation. Finally, Carter could choose a running mate without having to bargain over the vice presidency,[6] a luxury he shared with other modern nominees of both parties.

CARTER: CONSTRUCTING A PROCESS

In April 1976, campaign aide Hamilton Jordan presented Carter with a general outline of a running-mate selection process. Carter was later given a list of several hundred prospective running mates, including Democratic office holders, celebrities, and unconventional names.[7] Carter decided that his running mate had to be a member of Congress to compensate for his own lack of national experience[8] and reduced the list to about twenty names. He and his associates consulted with Washington insiders and other knowledgeable persons about prospective choices.[9] Polling regarding those on Carter's list produced inconclusive results given the wide disparity of familiarity with the candidates. Mondale finished near the bottom, probably because his name recognition was much lower (30 percent) than others such as Senator John Glenn, the first American to orbit the earth, and former presidential candidates Church and Muskie.[10]

Carter placed his confidante, Atlanta lawyer Charles Kirbo, in charge of the process. Kirbo interviewed possible running mates in Washington in late June 1976. Although some sessions were courtesies to stroke egos, most of those interviewed were serious possibilities.[11]

MONDALE: INTO THE PROCESS

Hindsight presents Mondale as a natural selection, but his inclusion in the pool was not inevitable. In spring 1976, Mondale's chief of staff, Richard Moe, prepared a memorandum to "put into focus some questions which had to be addressed in the next few months," specifically whether Mondale was interested in running for vice president. Moe outlined the advantages (best opportunity to be president, opportunity to influence the executive branch and to become involved in new policy areas, the emoluments) and disadvantages (loss of independence, the "unhappy" history of the office, loss of privacy). Moe thought Mondale closely fit Carter's likely running-mate profile and suggested ways Mondale could maximize his chances if he decided to pursue the vice presidency, as Moe thought he should. Moe thought Mondale should consider the "arrangement" he would want.[12]

Mondale initially had misgivings. "I was very happy in the Senate. I'd been there twelve years. I was hitting my sweet spot. I was working on issues I liked. I had some seniority. I was into my committee work. I was a happy camper."[13] Mondale had witnessed Humphrey's unhappy experience and loss of independence as vice president, which lessened the job's appeal.

Mondale's attitude changed after speaking with Humphrey in late May 1976. Humphrey told Mondale that notwithstanding the trials of having been Johnson's vice president, he was glad he had served and recommended that Mondale be open to it.[14] Humphrey's encouragement helped convince Mondale. Mondale had only met Carter in passing but admired his civil rights leadership in Georgia.[15] Still, Mondale retained some ambivalence. "Even after I agreed to do it, there was a part of me that wanted to stay in the Senate."[16]

Ultimately Mondale made Carter's short list along with six other congressmen—Senators Church, Muskie, Glenn, Henry Jackson, and Adlai E. Stevenson III and Representative Peter Rodino.[17] He initially was not high in Carter's ranking but apparently made cuts at various stages of the process, based largely on positive feedback from Senate colleagues.[18]

EXECUTING THE PROCESS
Carter's selection process included three primary components. First, Kirbo collected information on Carter's finalists. Kirbo's investigation included a questionnaire to each candidate inquiring about tax problems, finances, campaign contributions, lawsuits, divorces, arrests, health, and anything in the candidate's or a close relative's personal life that might embarrass the ticket if known.[19] Kirbo reviewed the information and

had other attorneys and accountants conduct further examination where necessary. He spoke with Mondale's doctor regarding Mondale's high blood pressure, sought medical advice regarding Mondale's medication, and investigated Glenn's business dealings.[20] Carter's due diligence, though rudimentary by later standards, was path-breaking in 1976.

Second, Carter introduced the vice-presidential job interview. Muskie, Glenn, and Mondale each met with Carter in Plains, Georgia, in early July.[21] Carter interviewed the other finalists in New York City prior to or during the Democratic convention. The sessions were announced in advance, lasted a few hours, and were followed by a joint press conference. They allowed Carter to interact with prospective running mates, most of whom he barely knew, and were a very important part of the process.[22]

The interview enhanced Mondale's prospects. He had studied the vice presidency, had reviewed briefing books comparing his and Carter's positions, and had read Carter's campaign book, *Why Not the Best?* and some of his speeches.[23] Moe's memorandum "The Conversation" summarized Mondale's strategy. Mondale viewed the vice presidency as "an arm of the presidency" and would be a "team player." Mondale was interested only if he would have a substantive role. He could help Carter politically and in governing due to his experience and relationships with Jews, labor, liberals, Democrats in Congress, the Washington media, and Humphrey. Moe's memo suggested answers to perceived vulnerabilities: Did Mondale's early withdrawal from the 1976 race suggest that he was lazy? Was he too liberal? Was he sufficiently strong on foreign policy? Other aides also provided memoranda, for instance, demonstrating Mondale's compatibility with Carter on busing and his foreign policy credentials.[24]

Mondale and his wife, Joan, traveled to Plains for his interview on July 8, 1976. During several hours of discussions, Carter was impressed by Mondale's preparation and ideas about the vice presidency and found him "personally compatible." "He was from a small town, as was I, a preacher's son, and shared a lot of my concerns about our nation."[25] The Carters "felt an almost instantaneous affinity" with the Mondales.[26] The interview resolved Carter's doubts that Mondale was too liberal, that he had focused on peripheral issues, and that his early withdrawal from the 1976 race indicated an aversion to hard work.[27] Mondale also felt good about the meeting.[28] He was impressed with Carter's thoughts about the vice presidency and was assured that Carter did not intend it to be merely a ceremonial position. As they reviewed the meeting on the flight home, both Mondales thought Mondale had "connected" with Carter and would be selected.[29]

Finally, Carter consulted broadly regarding his choice. He asked leading Americans to evaluate prospective running mates.[30] Church's prospects may have suffered when his interview with Kirbo went poorly[31] and because of relatively negative references from distinguished Americans.[32]

Some campaigned for the job. Church prepared talking points advocating his selection. Representative Carroll Hubbard sent Carter that document with his endorsement of Church; Henry L. Kimelman, a Church fund-raiser, and others contacted Carter aides on Church's behalf.[33] Mondale did little campaigning for the second spot, selling himself primarily through his performance at his sessions with Carter and Kirbo.

CRITERIA FOR AND CONSEQUENCES OF THE CHOICE

Ultimately, the choice narrowed to Mondale and Muskie. Carter made his decision on the convention's third day before calling Mondale at 8:30 on July 15, 1976, the convention's final day.[34] Mondale's participation in the process made his acceptance a formality.

In addition to seeking a running mate with national legislative experience, Carter articulated two primary criteria—competence and compatibility. "The overriding consideration," Carter said, "was how a person might perform the duties of President." Carter also "wanted to know how compatible we would be" during the campaign and in office.[35]

Yet Carter was not oblivious to political factors. Although not committed to any particular geographic balance, those interviewed came from outside the South—two easterners (Muskie and Rodino), three midwesterners (Glenn, Mondale, and Stevenson), and two westerners (Church and Jackson). Carter wondered whether he needed a Catholic running mate (Muskie or Rodino) but concluded that he did not.[36] He looked favorably on Muskie and Church, who had run for president.[37]

Mondale was helped by his liberal ideology, his strong ties to traditional Democratic constituencies where Carter was weak, and his connection to a midwestern agricultural state.

Carter changed his mind several times. Initially, he apparently favored Church, who had been tested in the primaries; had run well in western states where Carter did poorly; and was a foreign policy expert, an area in which Carter was weak.[38] Carter later gravitated to Glenn, then to Muskie.[39] Carter's closest associates were divided between Jackson, Glenn, and Mondale, although many apparently preferred the latter.[40]

In selecting Mondale, Carter achieved various conventional ticket balances. Mondale seemed likely to play well in competitive industrial and midwestern states and was an important bridge to liberal voters and organized labor, two Democratic constituencies with reservations about Carter. The selection of Mondale pleased the convention and party.[41]

A New Selection Process

Carter's performance created a new model for vice-presidential selection with the following features. Carter's process was deliberative. He signaled the decision's importance by investing considerable resources in it, particularly his and Kirbo's time. He systematically gathered information from multiple sources. The existence of the process and the names of those being considered were public. Transparency increased the likelihood that favorable and unfavorable information would surface. The postinterview press conferences suggested how the prospective nominee might behave on a national stage.

The process had a democratic component. The timing of the decision, right before the campaign, virtually dictated that Carter would weigh the electoral impact of alternative choices. Transparency allowed supporters and detractors to comment. Carter consulted widely.

The process occurred under optimal conditions. These included the early resolution of Carter's nomination, his strong standing in polls, and the design and execution of a process that showed him in a favorable light and allowed him to obtain and analyze information.

Carter removed most of the process from the convention. Although he interviewed four candidates there, he saw the leading options—

Muskie, Mondale, and Glenn—and conducted his investigation and consultation in advance. By speaking to party leaders individually, not in groups, he maximized his control.

Carter's criteria—qualifications to be president, compatibility, and Washington experience—coincided with governance considerations. A vice president would be most likely to contribute if he were a very able person who was compatible with the president and his associates and brought resources that the presidential nominee needed, essentially the considerations Carter identified.

Earlier presidential candidates had insisted that they sought the most qualified successor but sometimes made such statements incredible by picking someone with suspect credentials. Carter's conduct lent credence to his claims. His final list consisted of highly regarded public figures. The finalists, Mondale and Muskie, were among the party's most talented figures.[42]

The selection of Mondale also reinforced Carter's message of change. Like Carter (fifty-one), Mondale was young (forty-eight) and a fresh national figure. Carter related the ticket's appeal to "disaffection" with Washington and "the youthfulness of our ticket," which suggested the possibility of innovation.[43]

Finally, Carter recognized that the selection process tested his leadership and would communicate his decision-making ability and values. Carter understood that the process could enhance his image and acted accordingly.

Campaign Role

Carter and Mondale also took innovative steps in the campaign to raise the stature of the vice-presidential candidate and contribute to the success of the office.

COORDINATED CAMPAIGN
Carter and Mondale decided shortly after the convention to run a coordinated campaign.[44] Given the option of conducting the vice-presidential campaign from Washington, Minneapolis, or Atlanta, Car-

ter's headquarters, Mondale quickly elected Atlanta. The choice was a "no brainer"[45] but proved important.

From the outset, Carter treated Mondale as a partner whose participation was invited. Five days after Mondale's selection, Moe told Carter and his top aides that Mondale "would, of course, be willing to go anywhere and do anything that would be helpful." Moe wrote Mondale that "Governor Carter appreciated that, but indicated he wanted *your* ideas on your role when you come to Plains Sunday."[46] Carter communicated this inclusive approach in other ways. At a retreat to discuss the campaign, room assignments paired a Carter and a Mondale aide.

Mondale and his staff reciprocated by their willingness to play a supporting role. Mondale instructed his aides to work in a collegial manner with Carter's staff. More than a dozen Mondale aides, including Moe, Mike Berman, David Aaron, Robert Barnett, Bert Carp, and Eliot Cutler, worked in Atlanta in an integrated operation with Carter's team.[47] Working at the same headquarters and living in an adjacent hotel, the two staffs had regular communication. Some Mondale aides had participated in prior presidential campaigns and incorporated lessons from those experiences. The Carter staff was not averse to soliciting their help; for instance, it imitated Mondale's scheduling operation.[48]

VICE-PRESIDENTIAL VISIBILITY

Carter allowed Mondale greater visibility than prior vice-presidential candidates. Mondale occasionally appeared with Carter, and they conducted joint press conferences on defense and economic and foreign policy on three consecutive days in late July.[49] Although Carter took the lead, Mondale got substantial air time. Carter called on Mondale to offer reflections, both responded to questions, and Carter raised the possibility that he and Mondale "might disagree" on the B-1 bomber without that possibility bothering him.[50] The sessions allowed Carter and Mondale to discuss substantive issues and signified Carter's plans to elevate the vice presidency. They suggested that Mondale would be present for briefings and that his views were welcomed. They presented Carter as not threatened by sharing the stage or by disagreement.

Mondale's absence from Carter's briefings three weeks later drew attention. Vice-presidential involvement, long anomalous, was becoming expected. The candidates had mutually decided that Mondale's time was better spent campaigning, explained Carter. Mondale was familiar with the issues on that day's agenda from Senate hearings. His staff was there, and he and Carter spoke by phone.[51]

Roughly two weeks later, Carter and Mondale held another joint press conference. Both made opening statements before Carter took questions. Carter pronounced himself pleased with Mondale's campaigning. He emphasized the importance of compatibility and disclosed that they had exchanged speeches to learn from each other.[52] They campaigned together occasionally, and Mondale joined Carter for the campaign's closing rally in Flint, Michigan.[53]

VICE-PRESIDENTIAL DEBATE

The 1976 vice-presidential debate set a precedent that contributed to the growth of the second office. Although the idea of a vice-presidential debate predated 1976,[54] that campaign included the first such event as an adjunct to the presidential encounters.

The vice-presidential debate did more for the second office than the three presidential debates did for the first. Prior to the debates, 45 percent felt unfamiliar with Mondale and 50 percent with Ford's running mate, Kansas senator Bob Dole.[55] Ford and Carter would have received extensive coverage without debating. The vice-presidential debate moved Mondale and Dole to center stage for one Friday evening before an audience estimated at 43.2 million people,[56] about 50 percent of households,[57] less attention than the Carter-Ford sessions drew but more than vice-presidential candidates usually received.[58]

Having debated in the Senate, Mondale and Dole did not initially appreciate the perils of this new institution. Mondale's staff persuaded him to conduct a mock debate in his Senate office with aide Roger Colloff impersonating Dole. Colloff's effective performance helped Mondale anticipate how Dole might approach the unique format.[59]

Mondale and Dole presented different models of vice-presidential debate performance. Understanding that the debate would introduce him to the electorate, Mondale sought to demonstrate presidential characteristics. He emphasized three points:[60] (1) the economy suffered from eight years of Republicans in the White House; (2) Republican presidents had ignored basic problems; (3) America needed new leadership.[60]

In contrast, Dole had minimized the debate's importance, and "he came in looking jumpy and insecure," Mondale recalled. "He wasn't prepared. He hadn't thought it through. He didn't have themes."[61]

Dole performed traditional vice-presidential roles. He praised Ford as "a man of compassion and competence" and "of unparalleled decency and honesty and courage" among other accolades but devoted much of his commentary to attacking Carter and Mondale. He disparaged Carter as "very ambitious" and politically in sync with Mondale, "one of the most liberal Senators," who voted for "every inflationary spending program except in defense, when he votes for every cut." Carter and Mondale believed in "bigger government," which would exercise "more control and more interference with everyday lives." Dole criticized Carter for his comments about Ford, for tax deductions he had taken, for not disclosing his Cabinet appointees, for not having "a foreign policy," and for giving an interview to *Playboy* magazine. Mondale was subject to the control of organized labor. Whereas others, like Dole, had had to work for what they achieved, Mondale had been appointed to various offices.

Dole displayed his acerbic wit (Mondale would "still be in the Senate" when the election was over; labor leader George Meany was Mondale's "makeup man"; Carter got "the bunny vote") but not presidential quality. He belittled the vice presidency as "indoor work and no heavy lifting" and said if he won, he might not "do anything in the first hundred days, even the second hundred days." He even made fun of the League of Women Voters, the debate sponsor.

Dole's most significant gaffe came near the end of the debate when he twice labeled twentieth-century wars as "Democrat wars." Mondale knew Dole had made similar comments during the campaign[62] and answered that Dole had "richly earned his reputation as hatchet man" for making such a charge.

Mondale's debate performance boosted the Democratic ticket. After Dole listened to Ford extol his performance during their postdebate phone call, he said, "I wonder what *he* was watching."[63] Carter's pollster advised that the Mondale-Dole choice provided "a real ace in the hole" and urged Carter to exploit it.[64] Hamilton Jordan, Carter's closest adviser, opined that the Mondale-Dole debate gave Carter two or three points, "a huge impact" and was "decisive" for many voters who were indifferent as between Carter and Ford.[65] Dole later acknowledged that the "Democrat war" comment hurt "for at least a couple of weeks."[66]

The debate enhanced Mondale as a campaign asset. Whereas voters had preferred Mondale to Dole, 48 percent to 36 percent,[67] and Carter had previously mentioned Mondale when speaking to Mondale's natural constituents,[68] after the vice-presidential debate, Carter consistently invoked Mondale as a reason to prefer the Democratic ticket[69] and used Mondale in campaign advertising.[70] Carter argued that the "first responsibility" Carter and Ford had after their nominations was choosing a running mate. Carter would trust Mondale to be president "in a minute."[71] When Carter was accused in the final debate of failing to select able associates, he pointed to Mondale as the type of people he would bring to government.[72]

Mondale's schedule during the closing weeks reflected the campaign's perception of his value. He hopscotched between the electoral rich, competitive states of Ohio, Pennsylvania, New Jersey, and New York. By contrast, Dole's time was spent in farm states with relatively few electoral votes that figured to be safe Republican areas.

Mondale's presence helped Carter. An NBC News postdebate poll reported that Mondale was preferred as vice president, 51 percent to 33 percent.[73] A Harris Poll found that Carter's support rose 3 percent when Mondale's name was included.[74] A CBS News survey reported that 11 percent of voters listed the vice presidency as a factor in their votes, with 80 percent supporting Carter-Mondale.[75] In New York, 20 percent of Carter's voters cited Mondale as a factor in their decision.[76] Carter told Mondale several times that he helped elect them,[77] and Moe thought Mondale made "a huge difference" in Ohio, Wisconsin, and Minnesota.[78]

Mondale's campaign contributions made a significant vice presidency more likely. The campaign began a pattern of vice-presidential involvement. Mondale's performance enhanced his standing, and the two staffs became accustomed to working together.

Transition

Following the popular vote, Carter immediately made clear that Mondale would have a significant role. Although "no really good precedents" existed for including the vice president "in organizing and operating the government," Carter's transition memo assumed he intended to include Mondale "in important meetings" and "give him an advisory voice in major decisions."[79] Carter signaled Mondale's importance in multiple ways. He announced that Mondale would have a substantive role in the administration. He regularly included Mondale in important transition meetings. He consulted Mondale frequently. He engaged Mondale's staff in the transition. He praised Mondale in public statements. Many Mondale associates landed important administration jobs.

Mondale joined Carter in Plains immediately after the election. Carter publicly thanked Mondale for "a superb job" during the campaign, said he and Mondale had become close friends, and promised that Mondale would assume a "larger role" than any of his predecessors. Mondale would be "a full partner" in the transition and would be closely involved as Carter chose members of his administration.[80]

Carter reiterated these themes eleven days later at his second press conference. He referred to top officials who would serve with him and Senator Mondale. The selection process for high administration officials would resemble that which had produced Mondale, and Mondale would "work closely" with Carter. Carter would seek Mondale's recommendations for each position and would "consult" Mondale in evaluating those recommended and in evaluating program initiatives. Mondale would help Carter interview candidates for top positions. Although Mondale would operate primarily from Washington, he and Carter would meet often. Mondale would join Carter for separate briefings with Secretary of State Kissinger and the CIA.[81]

Mondale traveled to Plains the following day to help Carter prepare to meet with Democratic congressional leaders. He attended Carter's publicized meetings during the transition, including briefings by CIA director Bush and officials from the Pentagon;[82] sessions with sixteen prominent businessmen and economists and advisers on government reorganization;[83] a three-hour meeting with Senator Jackson;[84] and a discussion of New York City's precarious fiscal situation with the state's governor, Hugh Carey, and Mayor Abe Beame.[85] Mondale attended Carter's meetings to consider an economic package on December 27, 1976, and January 6, 1977,[86] and a meeting with Carter's top national security advisers on January 5, 1977.[87] He and Carter met with congressional leaders regarding an economic package.[88]

Mondale helped select the Cabinet.[89] He frequently spoke to Carter about appointments and became the first vice president–elect to sit through meetings with prospective Cabinet members and candidates for high-level positions.[90] Mondale helped persuade Carter to name Joseph Califano as secretary of health, education, and welfare and Robert Bergland as secretary of agriculture.[91] During a mid-December press conference, Carter said personnel decisions had been made "in an unprecedented way" through "a very tight and continuing partnership" with Mondale. They had conducted interviews together, which reflected how they would function in office. Carter would continue to depend on Mondale's "sound judgment and good help" and appreciated Mondale's "great work."

Mondale's staff also joined in the transition effort, thereby expanding Mondale's influence. Mondale aides knew scores of congressional staffers whom they evaluated for governmental positions. Aaron, Mondale's foreign policy assistant, was one of four named to focus on Carter's transition regarding international policy.[92] Moe was charged with identifying potential candidates for top economic slots.[93]

At Carter's request, Mondale prepared an agenda of issues for the initial Cabinet meeting in late December[94] and headed a process to establish priorities, events, and initiatives in the administration's early days.[95] Mondale worked with Carter on various policy areas, including the economic package, foreign policy, and the shape of the pardon Carter pledged to issue upon taking office relating to Vietnam War draft resisters. Mondale and his associates did not always prevail but participated actively in the transition.

Carter spoke frequently of Mondale's eminence. On December 22, 1976, he told reporters he planned to give Mondale a large policy workload.[96] The following day, he announced that he would give Mondale "unprecedented" responsibilities and called him the "top staff person."[97] At a meeting with his prospective Cabinet in late December 1976, Carter described Mondale as "my chief staff person" and told the White House staff that Mondale was their boss. Carter's spokesman, Jody Powell, announced that Mondale would be Carter's "principal adviser" on many issues as virtually an equal partner.[98] Carter told *Time* magazine that Mondale would "play a major role in governing," would be the "chief staff person," and would be "a constant adviser" and "constant partner" in decision-making.[99] A front-page headline in the *New York Times* the day after Christmas predicted Mondale would have "Real Power."[100]

The transition helped establish Mondale's role. It allowed Carter and Mondale to become better acquainted and cement their relationship by furnishing an opportunity for them to work together regularly. "Every time I met with Carter I felt better about being vice president. We had real discussions,"[101] said Mondale. It established Mondale's participation in decision-making, setting a precedent for once the administration took office. It developed similar patterns at the staff level and provided a further occasion for Mondale associates to demonstrate their value. Mondale's visible role signaled his access and clout, thereby communicating that he was a valuable ally. Finally, Mondale's success at placing friends in important positions enhanced his influence.

Conclusion

The seven months prior to Carter's inauguration were consequential for the vice presidency. During that time, Carter and Mondale established precedents that shaped the future of vice-presidential selection and the campaign and transition roles of the vice president–elect. Expectations and models they helped create have had a lasting impact, not only on these critical preliminary stages but also on the future of the vice presidency.

More immediately, these events established the foundations of Mondale's vice presidency. Carter had selected a highly qualified running mate who brought needed skills to his administration and with whom he was compatible. Carter engaged Mondale in campaign planning, and Mondale's campaign performance enhanced his standing with Carter's circle. Mondale's transition role foreshadowed his later activity and influence and enhanced his ability to contribute to the administration.

4

The Mondale Model:
Creating the Vision

The success of the Mondale vice presidency depended on Carter and Mondale creating a comprehensive and sensible shared vision of the office and identifying and committing the necessary resources. No prior president had integrated the vice president into the fabric of the White House. Many vice presidents had coveted a substantive role, but presidents had either not wanted or not known how to create one.

The Mondale model of the vice president as a close presidential adviser and troubleshooter has compelling logic, but important elements were not obvious in 1976. The vision emerged after months of study, consultation, and thought as Carter, Mondale, and their associates reimagined the office to rescue it from its normal low status.

The vision Mondale proposed, and Carter accepted, abandoned the conventional view that the second office was "standby equipment." That phrase may have described the office's principal remaining constitutional justification, but they concluded that it need not be the guiding rationale. Instead, the Mondale model emphasized the vice presidency as a contributing institution in the executive branch, not simply a national insurance policy. Whereas past vice presidents had envisioned using the job to maximize their ambitions, Mondale proposed a vision responsive to administration needs. In making the vice president a significant part of the administration, Mondale's proposal mitigated some traditional obstacles to a meaningful vice-presidential role while better serving the succession function.

Mondale's vision illuminates the White House vice presidency, but the creative process also offers lessons about institutional reform and the leadership necessary to promote it. The new vision emerged from a careful process whereby Carter, Mondale, and their associates analyzed a challenged institution, redesigned it in a novel and somewhat counterintuitive manner, identified the resources to sustain it, and obtained the necessary consensus for it.

Developing a New Vision

The Mondale model had its genesis in Mondale's vice-presidential interview with Carter on July 8, 1976. Carter and Mondale had each thought about the office, and the topic consumed much of their meeting. Mondale saw the vice presidency as an "arm of the Presidency" and sought a substantive role. He recognized that access to Carter could be the linchpin of such a role. Mondale was prepared to work in the background and pledge "loyalty and cooperation" in return.[1]

Encouraged by Jordan's memoranda,[2] Carter was predisposed to elevate the office. Following his July 5 meeting with Muskie, Carter had pledged to craft "a strong role" for his vice president in domestic and foreign affairs, including perhaps in government reorganization or congressional liaison or as a foreign emissary.[3] When Carter and Mondale met, "Carter jumped in ahead of me and described at Plains how he wanted to shape the office,"[4] Mondale recalled. Carter spoke generally of his intended "executivization" of the office.[5] Mondale made clear that he was interested only in a substantive role. Moe's June 21, 1976, memorandum had combined realism ("Who can remember the last happy VP?") with optimism ("but it doesn't have to be that way") and a prescription for success ("access and . . . a substantive role").[6] Carter and Mondale agreed that the office had been "a wasted asset" and that if Mondale were chosen and the ticket won, they would define the relationship after the election.[7] The conversation, though general, left Mondale "with enough confidence that we were talking about the same thing."[8]

In selecting Mondale, Carter promised to "put major responsibilities" on the vice president to an unprecedented degree. Mondale would have access to information, including military and security secrets. Nothing would constrain Mondale from "full communication" with, or expressing misgivings to, Carter.[9] And Mondale might relieve Carter of some presidential burdens—ceremonial, political, and substantive.

Notwithstanding Carter's good intentions, any effort to enhance the vice presidency faced seemingly intractable problems. History was discouraging, and, as chapter 2 indicated, some thoughtful people had abandoned hope for the vice presidency.

Mondale asked his former legislative assistant Robert B. Barnett to analyze the vice presidency in summer 1976. Barnett surveyed the literature and interviewed past vice-presidential staffers. His thirty-eight-page memo contained insights that helped shape Mondale's ultimate vision. Barnett outlined problems that had undermined past vice presidents—conflict between the two principals, between the two staffs, and between the vice president and presidential staff.[10] He traced interprincipal conflict to four sources—the president's perception of the vice president "as a potential competitor for attention"; the president's belief that the vice president's status was due to the president's elevation of him; the vice president's "macabre role" as potential successor, which made both uneasy; and the vice president's supreme "frustration" at his "subservient," and often empty, role. Even the vice president's ceremonial functions were those often unworthy of the president. Barnett concluded that interstaff conflict often arose because presidential staff refused to share information and access. Vice-presidential staffers resented their inferior status and being denied these essential tools. The interstaff conflict resulted also because the presidential staff saw the vice president as a competitor with the president for recognition and with them for access. "In short, probably the greatest problem faced by a Vice President is the lack of meaningful duties,"[11] Barnett concluded.

Barnett argued that "the most important determinant of the pleasure and success" of Mondale's vice presidency would be his relationship with Carter. A "close, personal relationship" with Carter would make Mondale "happier," cause Carter to solicit his advice, and give Mondale "substantive and satisfying duties." "No one can tell you how to establish this close, personal relationship. It is, however, probably the most important task you can assume," Barnett wrote. If Mondale could establish a relationship of "trust and confidence" with Carter, "many, but not all, of the problems which you will encounter will be eased."[12]

Barnett implied that the vice president's most useful role was "to serve as a sounding-board for the President," a role that depended on establishing this close personal relationship. If he had a "close, personal relationship with the President," Mondale could become a "Super Advisor." This status "more than anything else" would allow Mondale's "views to have a meaningful impact in policy-making." Barnett suggested that the vice president "should be one of the small group of persons to whom the President turns for important advice" and "should be one of the group who is present when the President makes important decisions."[13]

Barnett made two further points that Mondale apparently underscored with a felt-tip pen. Mondale should retain a personal staff but rely on Carter's advisers regarding specific duties to eliminate jealousies and give presidential staffers a role in shaping, and a reason to support, vice-presidential recommendations. Barnett also suggested that Carter's inexperience regarding Congress and its leaders created "an historical and practical vacuum into which [Mondale] might step." Mondale might act as Carter's legislative liaison either by heading the Office of Congressional Affairs or by involving himself "on a more informal and selective basis." Barnett added the "cautionary comments" that some vice presidents were uncomfortable advocating the president's legislative program either because it was awkward dealing with former colleagues or legislative staff or because they felt resented by their former peers.[14] As will be discussed later in this chapter, Mondale opted for an informal and selective role in legislative activity.

Barnett identified problems that had undermined Rockefeller as vice chair of the Domestic Council. Its staff was responsible to Ford, not him; Cabinet members preferred to report to Ford; and the Office of Management and Budget (OMB) was "a powerful adversary." If Mondale found these problems "insurmountable," he might conclude that his most "important input" on domestic matters might be through "informal contacts" with Carter. If given the role of "Super Advisor," Mondale could undertake "ad hoc assignments" in which he could rely upon the staffing and views of other administration officials. "Rather than interposing yourself between other administration officials and the President, you could work with them in the formulation of policy on a case-by-case basis."[15]

Barnett also made recommendations regarding the vice president's foreign policy role. He urged Mondale "to seek to be included in the flow of foreign policy information on a regular basis" and to "tie yourself into" the NSC staff by asking Carter to allow it to serve Mondale or by placing some Mondale people on it. Barnett encouraged Mondale to seek to make foreign travel "more substantive and targeted" than ceremonial.[16]

Rockefeller had sent Mondale a warm "Dear Fritz . . . Sincerely, Nelson" letter on November 3, 1976, congratulating him (twice in four paragraphs) on his election and pledging to help "in any way we can."[17] Two days later, Rockefeller sent Carter and Mondale a seven-page memorandum titled "Observations on the Relationship between the President and Vice President,"[18] which described the constitutional and statutory duties of the vice president, desirable staffing patterns, and special assignments Rockefeller had undertaken. Rockefeller stated that "the single most important responsibility" of the vice president was "to be prepared to assume on a moment's notice the duties of the Presidency," which depended on "a close and intimate working relationship with the President." This relationship required direct access to the president, weekly private meetings with the president based on an agenda the vice president prepared, inclusion of the vice president in all "important meetings" of various formal bodies and of the vice president's representative in daily White House staff meetings, and cooperation from executive branch personnel.

Rockefeller's memorandum, though helpful in some respects, had a different orientation from Mondale's ultimate vision. Rockefeller emphasized the vice president's formal roles and assignments, especially as potential successor, which he called the "single most important responsibility." Rockefeller recognized that the vice president could undertake certain assignments while standing by, yet, unlike Barnett's memo, gave little attention to any advising role. The vice president's close relationship with the president was necessary primarily to prepare him to succeed to the presidency and only secondarily to allow the vice president to serve as "a special source of informed, confidential and independent advice."

Rockefeller emphasized twelve formal assignments he had undertaken, primarily chairing or serving on various commissions, not advising. Rockefeller's orientation to formal arrangements rather than personal relations as a source of vice-presidential influence was evident even in his belief that the vice president should set the agenda for his meetings with the president.

Within days of the election, Mondale had a sense of the broad outline of his vision, and it differed substantially from that implicit in Rockefeller's memo. In a postelection interview, he expressed three fundamental ideas that became central pillars of the Mondale model. Mondale wanted to be a general adviser on "central issues"; he wanted to troubleshoot where he could be helpful; and he did not want an operational role.[19]

Mondale's vice-presidential vision was a radical departure. His predecessors had sought to enhance the office largely by identifying specific responsibilities as their own. Rockefeller's focus on heading the Domestic Council reflected this preoccupation. Mondale rejected a turf-based concept and embraced a quite different approach. He imagined a functional role as an adviser and operator without any executive branch portfolio. Mondale refined his vision during the month after the election. He spoke with Humphrey, Rockefeller, and some Humphrey aides about the office and explored the subject with his staff. Prior to the meeting with some Humphrey vice-presidential associates, Ted Van Dyk, a former Humphrey aide, sent Mondale a five-page memo, which Mondale gave to Moe after scribbling "Excellent Memo."

Van Dyk began with the "obvious" point that any vice presidency depended on the president's wishes. He anticipated that "pressures and misunderstandings" would ultimately challenge the Carter-Mondale relationship. Like Rockefeller, Van Dyk predicted that "being prepared" would be Mondale's major role. Van Dyk provided some valuable insights consistent with Barnett's earlier advice. Mondale's ability to sustain his relationship with Carter would depend on regular communication; such meetings would not simply benefit Mondale but would allow Mondale to give Carter "your unfiltered, candid views of congressional, public, governmental and political facts of life. This will be important for him because you are the only person in government, other than himself, who will be taking a broad overview of things." Mondale could become Carter's "personal sounding board and counselor, if a healthy relationship develops." Van Dyk urged Mondale to ration his time carefully. Mondale would need to accept ceremonial duties at Carter's request but should decline most others. Humphrey had expended much energy on trivial functions that distracted from more substantial matters.[20]

The day after Mondale's meeting with the Humphrey staffers, Moe gave Mondale a two-page, single-spaced memorandum regarding the developing vice-presidential vision. Moe urged Mondale "to mention several things more specifically than you have in the past" to demonstrate that Mondale had been thinking about the topic and to claim some areas "that otherwise might be pre-empted during the course of the transition."

Moe's discussion shared the premise of the Rockefeller and Van Dyk memoranda that "clearly" Mondale's "most important constitutional function" was "being prepared." "You can make a good case that everything is subordinate to this purpose." Consistent with Barnett's earlier memo, Moe suggested that Mondale request "at least one staff person" on the NSC and Domestic Council to help in this respect. Moe emphasized Mondale's "advisory role across the board" as something that Mondale had "already indicated to Carter" was his potential "greatest service" and encouraged Mondale to stress that role at "every opportunity." It would depend on access to information regarding foreign and domestic matters and an established time on Carter's weekly calendar for private conversation.

Moe's memorandum suggested that Mondale indicate interest in some specific areas that (1) did not intrude on anyone else's turf and (2) did not involve line assignments. Thus, with respect to the Domestic Council, Mondale might indicate interest in "a long range policy planning function that exists nowhere else in the government and yet one which . . . does not conflict with my straight line departmental responsibilities" and in advising on legislative prospects of various programs. Mondale might also suggest the possibility of a Hard Crime Task Force, a topic on which no work at the federal level was being done. Mondale might chair investigative commissions "when something pops up unexpectedly and fits in nowhere else in the federal structure." Mondale should reiterate interest in foreign travel (including perhaps an early trip involving "our principal allies") and political work but "continue to resist any line responsibilities for congressional relations for all the reasons" Mondale had previously articulated.[21]

The Vision Expressed: The December 9, 1976, Memorandum

In early December, Mondale and Moe met with Carter to discuss Mondale's role. Mondale outlined a vice-presidential role principally as an across-the-board adviser and troubleshooter. As the only other elected official and one not "encumbered" by an institutional bias or "specific responsibilities," Mondale reasoned that he was well positioned to advise on matters where Carter wanted his input or where Mondale had views he wished to advance.[22] Whereas other vice presidents had sought or received particular operational responsibility, Mondale said he wanted to avoid such roles. Mondale indicated that the advisory role could succeed only if he had unfettered access to Carter and the information he received.[23]

At Carter's request, Mondale committed his ideas to paper in a December 9, 1976, memorandum he asked Moe to prepare.[24] That eleven-page document largely defined his ultimate role. It began by recognizing the historical difficulties in "defining an appropriate and meaningful role for the Vice President" and mentioned the inherent problems, essentially those Barnett had identified months earlier. Mondale hoped his memorandum would "outline a set of relationships, functions and assignments that will be workable and productive for the administration." He stated his commitment "to do everything possible to make this administration a success." Mondale realized that his "personal and political success" was "totally tied" to Carter's and to the achievements of Carter's administration.[25]

Mondale suggested that his potential "most important contribution" was as a "general advisor" to Carter. As an adviser, the vice president could provide a useful and unique perspective. Mondale wrote, "Being the only other public official elected nationwide, not affected by the specific obligations or institutional interests of either the Congressional or Executive Branch, and able to look at the government as a whole, does put me in a unique position to advise."[26]

Recent presidents had suffered from insulation from competing, and often critical, viewpoints. Mondale suggested that he could "offer impartial advice and help assure" that Carter was not shielded from views he should hear. That role required the following:

1. Frequent, comprehensive intelligence briefings comparable to Carter's;
2. A "special relationship" with others in the executive branch, including their responsibility to respond to his requests for information;
3. Participation in key advisory groups;
4. A staff representative on the National Security Council and Domestic Council;
5. A relationship with the White House staff for him and the vice-presidential staff;
6. Access to Carter, including a regular weekly meeting and other access he needed.

Mondale suggested that he could also serve Carter as a trouble-shooter, responding to Carter's "direction" to explore particular problems of concern and mediating interagency disputes. Mondale proposed that he could "play a very significant role through foreign travel" to express Carter's interest in "selected foreign policy areas," providing an "additional presence abroad" and providing Carter with "a first-hand assessment of foreign leaders and situations." Mondale suggested that he could advise Carter regarding congressional relations and "become more operational" on behalf of Carter's major initiatives. Mondale could help with political activity and as a liaison to certain groups.[27]

The Vision's Innovations

Mondale's vision was innovative in four important respects. First, he saw his most important role as a contributing member of Carter's administration, not as standby equipment. Whereas Rockefeller saw all vice-presidential activity as derivative of the successor role, Mondale reversed the relationship. He did not mention the successor role until the end of his memorandum. Then, although recognizing that as "the most important constitutional obligation of the [vice presidency]," he said that the "relationship and assignments" he had suggested "were not focused on that obligation" but did "meet the test."[28]

Second, Mondale's vision responded to the question of how the vice presidency could help the president, not how it could enhance the vice president's position. Earlier drafts spoke of defining a mutually beneficial role ("helpful to you and meaningful to me"), a formulation dropped in Mondale's second draft, when the "workable and productive for the administration" language was introduced. Mondale's memorandum repeatedly emphasized his interest in helping Carter. "I am committed to do everything possible to make this administration a success," he pledged. Mondale's proposed role drew upon his talents and interests and recognized his stake in Carter's success. "I fully realize that my personal and political success is totally tied to yours and the achievements of your administration," Mondale wrote.

Mondale's focus on helping Carter succeed addressed some factors Barnett had identified as perennial sources of vice-presidential weakness. Mondale's emphasis on Carter's success gave Carter and his aides reason to see Mondale as a partner, not as a rival. Giving the vice president ongoing consequence subordinated the successor role and its ominous implications for the president and his inner circle. And Mondale converted his political dependence from a source of vice-presidential frustration to a reason Carter should give him a substantial role. Mondale's dependence deepened his investment in Carter's success, thereby offering further assurance of Mondale's loyalty and giving Carter further reason to enlist his help.

Third, Mondale's memorandum emphasized and sought to preserve and to capitalize on the vice-presidential uniqueness. The memorandum pointed out, "Being the only other public official elected nationwide, not affected by specific obligations or institutional interests of either the Congressional or Executive Branch, and able to look at the government as a whole, does put me in a unique position to advise." The vice president was distinctive because (1) he was an elected national politician who (2) could give unbiased advice because he was unencumbered by a duty to represent departmental objectives and (3) was free to focus on administration priorities because he was thus unconfined. Vice-presidential uniqueness offered opportunities for the administration but required that the vice president be treated differently from other advisers. Mondale's vision imagined a vice-presidential role that would add ongoing value, not duplicate existing capabilities, if the office's unique features were exploited and protected.

Mondale's conception had implications for the vice president's troubleshooter role, too. As the nation's second officer with a close relationship with the president, the vice president could help resolve interdepartmental disputes on an "assignment-by-assignment basis."[29] Since Carter's White House assistants would lack authority to dictate to Cabinet officers, someone needed to resolve interdepartmental disputes or Carter would become a frequent referee. Moreover, the vice president's stature allowed him to deal with foreign heads of state and legislative leaders in a way only Carter could surpass. Mondale's vision allowed him to use his experience and relationships to advance Carter's policies.

Finally, Mondale's approach was innovative in its aversion to ongoing operational assignments. Prior vice presidents had sought specific line assignments and broadcast them as evidence of their involvement. "A lot of Vice Presidents had tried to improve their importance by taking on a lot of tasks. I didn't think that helped very much,"[30] said Mondale.

Mondale concluded that specific operational roles would undermine his advising function. First, such assignments would consume the time of the vice president and his staff,[31] thereby diverting them from advising or significant troubleshooting. If the vice president were to help the president with the central problems facing the nation, he had to avoid responsibilities that would undermine his ability to focus on critical areas as they emerged. Mondale wanted to be able to roam the government and come to see Carter "when I had something to say."[32]

Second, line assignments often intruded on someone else's domain,[33] thereby putting the vice president in a turf war. Mondale wanted to avoid being "in the middle of bureaucratic jealousies" that would erode the goodwill he might otherwise enjoy. He wanted others in the administration to see him as a potential ally, not an intruder. "I tried to work with the agencies, not supplant them. I didn't want to have agencies trying to undermine me."[34]

Third, many line assignments "trivialized the vice presidency."[35] Presidents had typically assigned vice presidents tasks unworthy of their own time, fostering a perception that the vice president was peripheral.

Fourth, undertaking line assignments could jeopardize the vice president's general perspective. Responsibility for a particular program would give the vice president a vested interest in its success and create a perceived, and probably actual, conflict of interest regarding resource allocation. How could he be an objective, across-the-board adviser if he were responsible for one program? Moreover, an ongoing duty would compromise the vice president's uniqueness; he might be seen as just another department head with an agenda to advance, not as an unencumbered adviser who shared the president's holistic view.

Carter's Contribution to the Vision

Carter accepted Mondale's vision and agreed to give Mondale the resources the memo identified.[36] Mondale would serve as a general adviser and troubleshooter. He would have a private weekly lunch with Carter; would have the right to attend all meetings in the Oval Office; and would receive the Oval Office paper flow, including the president's intelligence briefings. Mondale's associates David Aaron and Bert Carp would serve on the NSC and Domestic Council, respectively, and Mondale aides would be included in White House staff meetings.

Carter also added other, crucial resources. Although Mondale had not requested a White House office in addition to the vice president's usual space,[37] Carter sent him a West Wing layout and invited him to choose any space (other than the Oval Office). Mondale selected the office between those generally occupied by the chief of staff and the national security adviser.[38]

The idea for a White House office was at least encouraged by a memorandum Stephen Hess, a presidential scholar and former Republican strategist, sent Carter on December 13, 1976, just four days after Mondale's memo. Hess traced past difficulties and stated the basic problem as "how then to take advantage of a vice president's wisdom in advising (without creating friction which came from giving him operational responsibilities) and how to prepare a vice president for possibly assuming the presidency (when the vice president is outside the orbit of responsibilities that draw people into the presidential circle)?" Hess suggested giving Mondale the office the chief of staff usually occupied (since Carter planned not to have such a person). Hess made other suggestions consistent with those in the Mondale memo—include Mondale on the distribution list for papers Carter received; include Mondale in Cabinet groups Carter chaired; use Mondale as a political surrogate and for foreign travel. Most importantly, Hess said, Mondale should not be given assignments Carter would not do himself "if he had the time."[39]

The West Wing office placed Mondale in the loop of White House decision-making. Physical proximity would make it easier for him to participate in formal and informal discussions. He could be in the Oval Office in a few seconds. West Wing visitors could drop by for scheduled or impromptu meetings. The West Wing presence helped Mondale and his staff monitor activities and participate in questions of interest. Finally, it symbolized Mondale's importance.[40]

Carter also acted to minimize the likelihood that friction with the presidential staff would undermine Mondale, as it had some of his predecessors. Carter admonished his staff to respond to Mondale's requests as if they came from Carter and that undercutting Mondale would cost them their jobs.[41]

Finally, Carter integrated Mondale and his staff into the White House. Moe, Mondale's chief of staff, became a member of Carter's staff, too, and attended its senior staff meetings and the morning meeting with Carter in Mondale's absence. The placements of Aaron and Carp as deputies at NSC and in the domestic shop, respectively, had symbolic and operational consequence. They made it "visibly impossible" to deprive Mondale of information that was a predicate of being effective.[42] Other Mondale aides would work with their counterparts on Carter's staff.

In agreeing to, and surpassing, Mondale's proposal, Carter demonstrated again that he wanted Mondale to play an important role. Carter saw such a role as consistent with good governance because it would use, rather than waste, Mondale's talents and prepare him to succeed if need be. Carter's action was also self-interested. He believed that establishing the White House vice presidency would enhance his administration.

Conclusion

The creation of the White House vice presidency was contingent on the development of a workable vision and the necessary resources. Mondale was able to offer a rational vision that made the vice president a present and significant administration figure—part of Carter's team, not a competitor. Not surprisingly, Mondale's approach resonated with Carter. The vision also succeeded because it exploited and protected the unique characteristics of the vice presidency. It rested on the premise that the distinctive attributes of the vice presidency—constitutional stature, electoral connection, perspective, and shared interest—gave the vice president unique value as an adviser and troubleshooter if those assets were preserved.

The substantive vision of the White House vice presidency emerged from an instructive process of constitutional reform. Carter and Mondale shared the objective to enhance the vice presidency. Rather than think in terms of discrete assignments, they attempted a general vision of the office. That required a careful examination to understand the problems and possibilities of the institution. Mondale drew from the past, and he and his associates thought about the office in new ways. In performing their analysis, they addressed the appropriate governance question: How could the vice president add value to government? That focus increased the likelihood that they would identify an approach helpful in governing and appealing to Carter and his associates. Having identified a role in which Mondale could add value, they identified resources he would need to succeed. Carter helped, not only by his commitment to the project but by adding resources beyond those Mondale suggested. Carter was predisposed to establishing a constructive arrangement, but Mondale enhanced the proposal's appeal by the manner in which he presented it.

The new vice-presidential vision offered a plan from which to build a new vice-presidential role. Whether the vision could succeed depended on its implementation, the subject of the next chapter.

Implementing the
Mondale Model

By the end of 1976, Carter and Mondale had placed several pillars of the White House vice presidency. Carter had committed to making the vice president a significant part of the executive branch. He had chosen a talented and compatible partner with relationships and experience that supplemented his own. Mondale had reimagined the office and been promised resources to support his vision. Carter's behavior toward Mondale added credibility to his promise to elevate the office, and their relationship and those at the staff level encouraged that development.

The final, but necessary, step was to convert promise to reality. For ultimately, the test of Mondale's vision was its workability over a sustained period. Implementing the vice-presidential design was among the challenges, and successes, of Carter's presidency. Mondale became an influential adviser and troubleshooter who contributed significantly. He did not always prevail or escape all frustrations of his office, yet he became a central White House player who helped shape and implement policy with unprecedented vice-presidential influence on a wide range of matters. And the successful execution of his vice-presidential vision demonstrated possibilities of the office and provided a model for replication.

Early Steps

Carter acted immediately after his inauguration to implement the new vision. He signaled Mondale's significance by sending him on a nine-day trip to Europe and Japan to meet with important allies. Carter directed Press Secretary Jody Powell to tell the media of "the particular importance" of Mondale's trip, and Powell described Mondale as Carter's "personal friend as well as a chief policy and political adviser."[1] Mondale's helicopter departed from the south lawn of the White House after a Sunday ceremony at which Carter declared that Mondale had his "complete confidence" and was his "personal representative." "To have a Vice President leave on a diplomatic mission this quickly after inauguration—on a diplomatic mission of this kind—is unprecedented in American history,"[2] Mondale observed.

Mondale discussed substantive issues, including the troubled European economies and Carter's approach to the Soviet Union, with important allies. Mondale assured North Atlantic Treaty Organization (NATO) nations of America's continuing involvement with Europe and Carter's commitment to pursue arms-reduction agreements in consultation with America's allies. He held substantive meetings with leaders of Germany, Italy, Great Britain, France, and Japan and with Pope Paul VI.[3]

Carter welcomed Mondale back on February 1, 1977, in a public ceremony, praising Mondale, twice, for "an absolutely superb job." Mondale had "engaged in the same kind of discussions on the same subjects and with the same depth that I would have if I had gone on the trip myself."[4] The following day, Mondale briefed Carter for one and one-half hours and held a White House press conference.[5]

Mondale's maiden trip gave him early, favorable visibility in a presidential context. It had an important substantive component, and the choice to send Mondale signaled his stature. Finally, the trip allowed Mondale to develop relationships with, and acquire information about, world leaders.

Mondale's subsequent schedule included unprecedented presidential access and wide-ranging substantive involvement. In February 1977, Mondale met with Carter on each of fourteen workdays that both were in Washington, D.C., generally several times daily, usually for extended periods. They lunched on February 3, 4, 7, 21, and 28; on seven occasions in March (four times alone and with labor leader George Meany, Federal Reserve Bank Chair Arthur Burns, and Secretary of Agriculture Bob Bergland); and six times in April. They frequently met three or four times daily; Mondale was with Carter five times on April 18 and six times the following day.[6] Mondale spent at least 20 percent of his office time with Carter during each of his first six months in office except April. Generally, Mondale spent at least 30 percent of his time with Carter during this period; in July, 48 percent of his office time.[7] Roughly one-quarter of Mondale's working time in Washington from 1977 to 1981 was spent with Carter.[8] Mondale's participation in so many Oval Office meetings during the first months established a pattern of enhanced vice-presidential involvement that signaled that he had access and was worth cultivating.

The part of Mondale's day away from Carter was also significant. During his first six months in office, Mondale held more than eighty meetings with foreign officials. He regularly conferred with ranking administration and legislative figures and was heavily involved in a range of domestic and economic issues.[9] Mondale played a leading role in developing Carter's electoral package, reforming America's intelligence agencies, and reformatting policy regarding Africa.

By word and deed, Carter repeatedly promoted Mondale. In swearing in his Cabinet, Carter referred to his choice of Mondale as having "set a standard of excellence." "It would be hard to equal what Fritz Mondale has meant to me," but he hoped to duplicate that relationship with his other associates.[10] In an early televised speech, Carter declared, "Vice President Mondale will be a constant and close adviser for me."[11] Carter told one media group of his "unprecedented . . . superb relationship" with his vice president. Carter and Mondale had "a natural compatibility," and Carter had given Mondale "tremendous responsibilities" and "a unique independence to make available to the Nation his superb qualities." Carter and Mondale spent "several hours together every day." Mondale received the same "secret briefings" as Carter and had a "permanent invitation to attend every conference" that Carter attended. Mondale could speak for Carter, and there was "a growing recognition" of that fact. Carter "benefitted greatly" from his relationship with Mondale.[12] In May, Carter declared that there had never been "a President and Vice President who have been bound together more closely with a common philosophical commitment, with a common belief and confidence in the quality of the American people, and a sharing of every possible problem and its potential solution." Mondale was "in almost every, way an equal partner" with Carter.[13] Carter's words and actions made the desired impression. Three months into their term, journalist Charles Mohr presciently wrote that elevating the vice presidency could be a significant legacy of Carter's first 100 days.[14]

In late September 1977, Carter was stunned to learn that some reporters questioned Mondale's role. He instructed Powell to rebut the rumors, and Carter telephoned White House correspondents Jack Nelson of the *Los Angeles Times* and Hedrick Smith of the *New York Times* to attest to Mondale's importance.[15] Nelson described Carter's action as "an extraordinary response."[16] Carter praised Mondale's abilities at a news conference and said, "There is no aspect of my own daily responsibilities as President that are not shared by the Vice President." Carter said he spent more time with Mondale than with the rest of his staff combined. "There is no one who would approach him in his importance to me, his closeness to me and also, his ability to carry out a singular assignment with my complete trust."[17] Carter's actions helped establish Mondale's significance. Berman wrote in February 1978 that Mondale's "role and relationship with the President are well known and he can thus command the attention and respect of the executive branch and the Congress."[18]

Mondale's assessment mirrored Carter's claims. Mondale wrote Carter on September 6, 1977, that he was "completely satisfied with the role that you have allowed me to play in your administration." Carter had treated him as "a full working partner," and they had "established a solid foundation for a fruitful personal and political relationship in the years ahead." Mondale had not experienced the frustrations common to his predecessors. His access to Carter and to "the critical information of government" and his "range of involvement" and relationship with others "have exceeded my expectations." Mondale attributed his contributions to "the complete latitude, access and support you have given me, all of which are unprecedented."[19]

Mondale's senior staff thought Mondale's first year had been "extremely successful"; his "excellent" relationship with Carter "exceeded all expectations"; he could not have "had a better first year."[20] Berman wrote that Mondale had "an unparalleled relationship with the President" and was "involved in issues and missions that matter."[21] Moe presciently observed, "You have broken new institutional ground which is bound to benefit your successors and which I believe will be regarded by historians as the turning point in relationships between the Presidency and the Vice Presidency."[22]

Mondale's Roles

Mondale functioned as senior adviser across the entire range of domestic, international, political, and personal issues and as a troubleshooter who handled significant assignments. The roles were interrelated and mutually reinforcing. Mondale's access as an adviser made him a credible troubleshooter; his troubleshooting enhanced his advice.

ADVISER

Mondale emerged as one of Carter's most significant advisers. Paul Light found that 100 percent of Mondale's staff and more than 80 percent of Carter's thought Mondale had influence; 82 percent of Mondale's staff thought he had "a great deal" of influence.[23]

Consistent with the design of his role, Mondale and his staff had full access to information that allowed him to be knowledgeable about issues being considered and their merits. He had easy and frequent access to Carter and others in Carter's inner circle. He had opportunities to offer advice privately as well as in meetings others attended. He and Hamilton Jordan were the only government officials with regular access to Carter who dealt with the full range of issues. His advice to Carter was candid and often critical.

Because others perceived that Mondale was influential, they brought problems to him. Powell and Jordan often went to Mondale to persuade Carter.[24] "His views were important to Carter, so if you were involved in a dispute, you wanted Mondale on your side," Bert Carp said.[25] In turn, Mondale's access to information increased his value to Carter. Access produced information, and information produced access in a cycle that generated its own momentum.

Mondale had multiple opportunities to influence policy. He could become involved on "any issue . . . at any stage, beginning, middle or end." He could put his views on any memorandum Carter received[26] or could weigh in verbally. Mondale's opportunities included (1) his weekly private lunches with Carter; (2) his freedom to drop in to see Carter privately; (3) his ability to submit written memos to Carter or have his views reflected on paper submitted to Carter; (4) his right to attend any meeting in the Oval Office; (5) his participation in recurring meetings, especially the Friday foreign policy breakfasts; (6) his regular interactions with Carter's other senior advisers; and (7) the regular interaction of his staff with other White House personnel.

Carter and Mondale met privately for lunch each week, usually on Monday, whenever both were in Washington. Mondale's staff scheduled around that appointment. "We have an easy relationship and discuss matters of the most personal and national importance without constraint," wrote Carter on August 29, 1977.[27] During these lunches, Mondale often raised the "really serious political problems, things you could not talk about in front of other people," Mondale said.[28] "It was the most valuable single time Mondale had with Carter,"[29] said Moe.

Carter and Mondale treated the private lunches as confidential, an arrangement that benefited both principals. Mondale could give, and Carter receive, Mondale's candid advice with little danger of leaks. Contrary to Rockefeller's suggestion, there was no agenda—certainly not one Mondale imposed. Moe prepared suggested topics and talking points for Mondale each week, which Mondale revised and drew from, generally scribbling cryptic prompts in the margins.[30]

The notes suggest some advice Mondale offered and topics discussed. Mondale scribbled "public works meeting" above and "water praise them" below "Congressional Relations" on the memo Moe prepared for the first lunch. Carter had opposed numerous water projects as congressional pork, thereby alienating many in Congress. Mondale sought to educate Carter about Congress and to guide Carter away from that fight.

Mondale's notes suggest that the April 11, 1977, lunch included discussion of Mondale's troubleshooting activities relating to South Africa, regulation of intelligence gathering, the election reform legislation package, and the agenda for Carter's early months as well as Carter's energy message (the topic of an Oval Office meeting Mondale attended later that day), Israeli leader Shimon Peres, and Hubert Humphrey, among other topics. Powell and his deputy, Rex Granum, joined Carter and Mondale for thirteen minutes, suggesting that a media issue may have arisen.[31] Lunch on August 22, 1977, apparently included discussion of a SALT Interim Agreement; Humphrey; the investigation and status of Carter's OMB director and close friend, Bert Lance; the desirability of involving Republican senators Howard Baker and Barry M. Goldwater as prominent supporters of the proposed Panama Canal treaty; and Mondale's review of his duties.[32] The following week, they discussed Lance and the Panama Canal treaties again as well as southern Africa, China, Israel, the American Jewish community, and individual senators.[33]

In 1980, Mondale repeatedly urged Carter to end his self-imposed policy of not campaigning while Americans were held hostage in Iran.[34] "When do you get out of W.H.," Mondale wrote in his February 27, 1980, notes.[35] "Hiding in W. House" and "Get out of WHouse?" Mondale scribbled on his talking points for his March 10, 1980, lunch with Carter.[36] "Get Out of WH," he wrote at the top of his notes for his March 25 lunch.[37] "Carter Must Get Out," Mondale wrote on this April 17, 1980, talking points.[38]

The lunches helped make private presidential–vice-presidential meetings White House routine. They allowed Mondale to share information with and give candid advice to Carter confidentially on all subjects. They allowed him to inform Carter of his activities to assure that they met with Carter's approval. They helped Mondale develop and protect his relationship with Carter. They symbolized Mondale's stature and helped make him a valuable ally for others.

Mondale's private access to Carter freed him from having to debate controversial matters in larger meetings where leaks might occur. Any disagreements could remain his and Carter's secret, thereby minimizing the chance of embarrassment to either principal. Mondale could implement presidential decisions without space perceived between his and Carter's positions. Mondale's circumspection in larger sessions also allowed Carter to receive a broader range of advice. Mondale feared that his full participation in such meetings would hinder debate because others might assume that his comments reflected Carter's views.[39] By listening, Mondale could help synthesize advice for Carter. Moreover, the practice protected Carter from having to choose between Mondale's publicly expressed advice and that of others. This arrangement also reinforced the vice president's elevated stature. Unlike others, Mondale attended larger sessions as an advisee, not adviser, thereby distinguishing his position.

Mondale could also drop in or phone Carter whenever he chose. Mondale generally preferred speaking to Carter rather than sending memos to permit an exchange and to allow him to gauge Carter's reactions. "I'd go in and out of the Oval Office several times a day. Carter had an open-door policy toward me,"[40] Mondale recalled. This privilege allowed him to participate in important meetings, to alert Carter to developments, and to weigh in on matters that were moving toward resolution before his next lunch.

For instance, early in the term, Mondale acted to change the administration's position in *Regents of the University of California v. Bakke*,[41] the landmark case on affirmative action in university admissions. The Department of Justice's initial brief restricted race-conscious admissions, contrary to the expectations of the civil rights community and commitments of the Carter-Mondale campaign. After Stuart Eizenstat, Carter's principal domestic affairs assistant, alerted him, Mondale approached Carter, who ordered the brief revised to support affirmative action but not quotas. At Carter's request, Mondale met with Attorney General Griffin Bell, Eizenstat, and White House Counsel Bob Lipschutz to discuss revisions.[42] Bell, unhappily, later described the *Bakke* brief as the "first civil rights case in which Mondale made the weight of his office felt."[43]

Mondale also intervened to change Vance's speech to the United Nations on the Middle East in late September 1978. After Mondale failed to persuade Vance and Brzezinski to soften the tone to avoid antagonizing Israel, he contacted Carter, who (unbeknownst to Mondale) had already approved the draft, reaching him at 9 p.m. while Carter was watching *Paint Your Wagon* in the White House movie theater with guests. Following a four-minute conversation, Carter left the theater, reread the speech, and ordered modifications to accommodate Mondale's concerns. Vance's speech was later praised by both sides.[44]

In March 1980, Mondale used his walk-in privileges to help Carter handle fallout from America's support of a UN resolution critical of Israeli settlement activity. Carter had authorized the American ambassador to support the proposed resolution after he had been advised that references to Jerusalem had been deleted and an American amendment incorporated. In fact, references to Jerusalem remained. Carter had agreed at Camp David that negotiations would resolve the status of Jerusalem and that the United States would veto or abstain regarding any UN resolution relating to the subject. Israeli Ambassador Ephraim Evron visited Mondale the following morning to express his government's unhappiness regarding this breach of America's agreement on an issue of great importance to Israel. Mondale and Jordan advised Carter "that the Israelis and the American Jews were extremely upset" and that the resolution mentioned Jerusalem six times.[45] Mondale lunched with Carter, met four more times that day with Evron, and met with Carter four times in less than two hours.[46] Carter accepted Mondale's advice that he announce that the United States had not changed its position regarding Jerusalem and that the earlier American vote had been based on the mistaken belief that references to Jerusalem had been removed from the resolution.[47]

Mondale participated in various meetings on Carter's schedule, including annual budget reviews, sessions with economic advisers, breakfasts with congressional leaders, and sometimes Carter's weekly intelligence briefing. He regularly attended Carter's morning meeting with his senior domestic staff. Mondale often joined Carter for special nonrecurring sessions—meetings with foreign leaders, for instance, or with labor leader George Meany.

The most important regular meeting Mondale attended was the weekly Friday foreign policy breakfast. It initially involved only Carter, Mondale, Vance, and Brzezinski but later included some other close advisers. Here "Carter tried to generate real debate and develop decisions in the meanest of foreign problems. President Carter was much more frank at these meetings. We had candid, even distasteful discussions without their content getting out of the room."[48] Mondale expressed himself freely at these sessions,[49] often addressing the political implications of foreign policy issues. Brzezinski called Mondale's "political judgment" his "most important substantive contribution." Mondale was "a vital political barometer" for Carter, who respected Mondale's "opinion on the domestic implications of foreign policy decisions." Since Carter rarely considered domestic aspects of foreign policy, Mondale "provided a needed corrective."[50] Others present lacked Mondale's political background and sensitivity. Moreover, Mondale had to convey foreign policy decisions in political arenas. "I was coming at foreign policy issues with the politics in mind as well. There's often a disconnect among high officials between policy and whether it will sell. I had to go out of the room and handle the politics and explain the decisions, on the campaign trail, on Capitol Hill."[51]

Mondale's interactions, and those of his staff, with Carter's assistants provided further opportunity to influence policy. Mondale began with, or developed, strong relationships with central figures in the national security, domestic, and political operations offices. Aaron helped keep Mondale abreast of national security developments and traveled with him abroad. Their conversations allowed Mondale to influence foreign policy, as did the interaction between Mondale's national security aide, A. Denis Clift, and Brzezinski's office.

Mondale forged important relationships with Eizenstat and Jordan. He and Eizenstat took a common approach to many domestic issues,[52] and their alliance was reinforced by the friendship they developed. Mondale's ability to influence political and personnel matters benefited from his relationship with Jordan.[53] "I consider I work for Mondale," Jordan declared publicly. "He's my second boss, the way Carter is my first boss."[54]

The location of Mondale's office between those of Jordan and Brzezinski encouraged communication with these Carter aides with principal responsibility for political and international matters, respectively. "We often popped in on each other," wrote Jordan. "When there was something to talk about, Fritz . . . would simply pop into my office, or I would stick my head into his,"[55] Brzezinski wrote.

Consistent with Barnett's 1976 memo, the White House staff supported Mondale. The NSC staff helped Mondale prepare for foreign travel, and Aaron and NSC area specialists accompanied Mondale on overseas trips as appropriate. When Mondale met with labor leaders,

Landon Butler, the Carter assistant with that portfolio, often provided support.

Mondale retained a personal staff of longtime associates and specialists in programmatic and political matters. His office received the White House paper flow in time to participate in policy formation.[56] Carter integrated Mondale's staff into overall White House operations, a step that followed the pattern set and benefited from the relationships established during the campaign.[57] Moe attended senior staff meetings, which helped keep the Mondale team in concert with Carter's operation, staffed various important presidential initiatives,[58] and played a principal role in ending the Kennedy challenge to Carter's renomination. Mondale's other aides worked with their Carter counterparts.[59] Paul Light found that 31 percent of Mondale's staff had daily, and 27 percent weekly, contact with their White House counterparts (compared with 7 percent and 14 percent of Rockefeller's aides). Most with daily contact were engaged on policy issues,[60] thereby enhancing Mondale's ability to affect policy. Possession of White House passes enabled them to move freely between the Executive Office Building, where most worked, and the White House and to interact with Carter's staff in the White House mess and otherwise.

Mondale gave Carter candid and critical advice. "What I tried to do with Carter, and he appreciated it, was to give him my best, often critical advice but not to be a pest. Once he made a decision, I supported it,"[61] Mondale said. Mondale, for instance, pushed Carter to budget more money for social programs, to be more sympathetic toward Israel, to be more accepting of congressional folkways, and to be more conciliatory to Kennedy. Mondale unsuccessfully favored the $50 tax rebate, a higher minimum wage, and higher farm supports during the first year. He opposed Carter's decision to commit to a deficit no larger than $30 billion.[62] He disagreed "strenuously" with Carter's decision to impose economic sanctions, including a grain embargo, on the Soviet Union after it invaded Afghanistan.[63] "Mr. President, we need to be strong and firm, but that doesn't mean you have to commit political suicide!"[64] When Carter decided to require draft registration, Mondale went into "a near-rebellion," a disagreement that Carter described as "much worse" than his opposition to the grain embargo.[65]

At times, Mondale questioned Carter's approach to the presidency. On April 3, 1978, he wrote Jordan that "the President is spending entirely too much time on foreign affairs and, even in the domestic area, too much time on detail and too little time out front in public events— in Washington, but particularly around the country." Carter needed to do more to win public acceptance for his goals and policies by spending more time discussing his programs in public forums. Carter's staff "should try a few speeches for the President in which we seek to crank in some eloquence."[66]

On April 19, 1978, Mondale sent Carter a seven-page memo titled "Observations on Your Presidency." Mondale's "most basic recommendation" was that Carter "should dramatically increase the degree to which you emphasize the public education role of your presidency." Carter should "undertake a much heavier speaking schedule." The administration needed to do a better job of defining its goals. Carter's speeches needed to be less descriptive and "more persuasive and eloquent."

Mondale also suggested steps to rebut the perception that Carter was a "weak" and ineffective president who was overcome with minutiae, reclusive, "preoccupied with foreign affairs," "a manager and not a leader," and served by a limited staff overpopulated by Georgia friends. Mondale thought the public perception was "in most instances . . . inaccurate" but needed to be addressed by the education effort he suggested, "by some vetoes and/or strong rhetoric," and by disciplining "disloyal persons" to stop leaks and "damaging statements." The Cabinet needed to become more politically engaged to serve Carter's goals.

Mondale thought "there is a good deal of validity to the argument" that Carter spent too much time studying staff memos and "not enough time in public giving speeches and appearing with people." America wanted "a leader," not "a manager." The element of Carter's presidency that most "cries out for correction," Mondale wrote, was his lack of sufficient attention to his "public role." Mondale suggested that he, too, should assume a larger "public education role" through increased domestic travel and speaking. Mondale thought much advice Carter received was not "helpful." Carter should meet regularly with some "wise and experienced" insiders for candid and confidential advice.

Mondale also criticized the administration's approach to foreign policy. There was "inadequate strategic political thinking in the development of our foreign policy," in part because Carter's foreign policy advisers resisted considering the domestic political environment in which foreign policy problems arose. And Carter became "too personally and too deeply involved in too many minor foreign issues."

Finally, Mondale sought to counter the rightward drift of the administration. Even those calling themselves "conservatives" wanted progressive governmental programs. The administration needed to address inflation, but not by sacrificing jobs. The contrary position was "insensitive."[67]

Mondale's most significant disagreement with Carter came in July 1979 after Carter abruptly canceled his energy speech and retreated to Camp David with close advisers to consider next steps. Carter and his Georgia advisers were captivated by pollster Patrick Caddell's analysis of a psychological crisis pervading the nation and favored a presidential address about it.

Mondale disagreed strenuously. He thought the problems were not psychological but economic. Rather than reprimand the public, Carter should be candid but should propose a specific energy program in a televised speech and build support for it in a speaking tour and other political activities. Mondale's criticism was so strong during a group meeting on July 5, 1979, that Carter adjourned the session and invited Mondale for a private talk.[68]

Carter welcomed Mondale's advice even when critical. "It says something about Carter. It didn't bother him. What he wanted was candor and confidentiality. As long as he knew he could trust me, he encouraged simple declarative sentences."[69]

Carter often took Mondale's advice. Mondale helped convince Carter to restore $2 billion of proposed social welfare reductions,[70] to have the *Bakke* brief rewritten, to intervene to save Indochinese boat people, to make America's intelligence agencies behave according to legal restrictions, and to support a boycott of the 1980 Olympics in Moscow to protest the Soviet Union's invasion of Afghanistan.[71] Mondale's influence was clear even when he did not prevail immediately or completely. In response to arguments from Mondale and Eizenstat, Carter toned down the discussion of national malaise and included specific energy recommendations in the July 1979 speech.[72] Carter finally agreed to end his self-imposed moratorium on campaigning during the hostage crisis. Mondale persuaded Carter to appoint a Middle East negotiator, to soften rhetoric about Israel, and to renounce the vote on the Jerusalem resolution. Mondale also influenced a number of personnel decisions in addition to the initial hirings of Califano, Bergland, Aaron, and Carp. To the dismay of Carter's more conservative attorney general, Bell, Mondale was able "to shape Administration policy to his way of thinking in important areas . . . in some instances" due to his West Wing presence and the placement of Aaron and Carp in their positions.[73]

TROUBLESHOOTER

Mondale's troubleshooting activity was extensive and consequential and was closely and reciprocally related to his advising role. Mondale could be more effective as a troubleshooter because others knew he was an important presidential adviser. Mondale's troubleshooting enhanced his advising role because it gave him information and insights and increased his capital within the administration.

Legislative Troubleshooting

Mondale was not responsible for legislative liaison work and did not intrude on the turf of Frank Moore, a longtime Carter associate, who assumed that portfolio. Nonetheless, Mondale played an important role in legislative matters.[74] Carter and his inner circle were unfamiliar with, and often insensitive to, Congress,[75] whereas Mondale had been a Senate insider and his principal aides had extensive legislative experience. He attended legislative leadership breakfasts and often Moore's congressional relations meeting after it was added to Carter's schedule in 1979.[76] Mondale engaged in several types of legislative activities.

Mondale was a conduit for information between the White House and Capitol Hill. His former colleagues "felt like they could talk to Fritz when they couldn't talk to Jimmy Carter or couldn't talk to Frank Moore or Hamilton Jordan,"[77] Moore said. They appreciated that he could speak to and for Carter. Mondale worked to maintain old, and establish new, relationships on Capitol Hill.[78] He often met congressional leaders, committee chairs, and Hill friends for breakfast or lunch and invited legislators to the Naval Observatory or elsewhere.[79]

Mondale's conduit work helped him as a legislative adviser and strategist. His meetings with members of Congress often suggested advice for Carter and his closest associates. Mondale advised Carter that the nomination of Paul Warnke as director of the Arms Control and Disarmament Agency was perceived "as a symbolic test vote on arms control policy" that could "set the domestic political and public relations tone for future negotiations." Mondale thought it important to produce at least sixty-seven votes for Warnke's confirmation, twelve to seventeen more than Mondale thought were on board in early February 1977. He proposed that he meet with undecided senators and that Carter speak to a handful of key members.[80]

Mondale discussed legislative matters with Carter over lunch. He often counseled Carter on how to approach legislative leaders.[81] When Mondale found the voter registration bill short of the votes needed, he urged Carter to compromise. "Fritz, I'll defer to your judgment. J," Carter scribbled on Mondale's memo.[82] At Carter's request, Mondale instructed Cabinet members to give Democratic congressmen advance notice of announcements affecting their states or districts.[83]

Mondale was an occasional lobbyist for administration positions, particularly on important matters such as ratification of the Panama Canal treaties.[84] In late August 1977, Mondale discussed the treaty with fourteen senators. He suggested a strategy that included military briefings and involvement of high-level Republican support[85] to secure the support of the undecided senators and to limit the impact of right-wing opposition. He helped dissuade Senator Dennis DeConcini from adding a potentially devastating amendment to the first treaty and helped to persuade California's conservative Republican senator, S. I. Hayakawa, to support the second treaty by encouraging Carter to respond favorably to Hayakawa's suggestion that he be given the opportunity to advise Carter on foreign policy.[86] Senator Thomas F. Eagleton largely credited Mondale with ratification of the treaties,[87] each of which passed with one vote to spare, 68–32. Mondale also lobbied for ratification of the SALT treaty, for legislation to create a Department of Education, and for the Equal Rights Amendment extension, among other projects.

Finally, Mondale worked to preserve a Democratic Congress. Mondale's office began planning for 1978 Senate races in the summer of 1977. Mondale's August 1, 1977, lunch notes reflected that twelve Senate seats were competitive and suggested that the administration work to recruit able candidates and bolster vulnerable incumbents. Mondale's staff had prepared an action plan in consultation with Carter's principal political aides.[88] Mondale campaigned actively for Democrats running for the House and Senate. During 1977, he appeared at events honoring Senators Robert Byrd, Richard Clark, Eagleton, Phil Hart, Floyd Haskell, Thomas McIntyre, Pat Moynihan, and Hubert Humphrey and for House candidates Peter Rodino, Ike Skelton, Leon Panetta, Ed Koch, Martha Keys, Michael Harrington, Frank Annunzio, and Tom Lukens in addition to various Democratic Party events in Georgia, Iowa, Arkansas, North Carolina, Illinois, Ohio, South Dakota, and New Hampshire. In 1978, Mondale appeared at more than 125 political events before election day. He devoted parts or all of more than fifty days to public campaigning. Not surprisingly, his activity intensified as the elections approached. In October 1978, Mondale spent part or all of fifteen days campaigning in fifteen different states and spent most of five of the first six days in November campaigning in six states, primarily for House and Senate candidates.

Mondale began focusing on the 1980 congressional campaign shortly after the 1978 elections. He first met with Democrats running for reelection to the Senate in early 1979. That year, he spoke at fund-raisers for Senators Jim Sasser, Gaylord Nelson, Alan Cranston, Frank Church, and Gary Hart and House candidates Joe Moakley, James Florio, Bill Green, and Tom Harkin. In spring and summer 1980, he attended breakfasts with Senate Democrats up for reelection.[89] With Carter's relations with Senate Democrats in shambles, senators used Mondale to convey their suggestions and requests.[90]

Mondale's legislative activities reinforced each other. His conduit work provided information, making him a more effective adviser. His access to Carter encouraged legislators to seek him out. His relationships with legislators and his influence at the White House made him an effective lobbyist, a role that was enhanced by campaigning for senators and representatives.

Foreign Travel

Some of Mondale's most significant troubleshooting activities involved foreign policy, of which foreign travel was the most visible aspect. Mondale visited thirty-six countries as vice president.[91] He also was an adviser, hosted foreign visitors, spoke on foreign policy, and lobbied Congress regarding such matters. As was true elsewhere, the various roles fortified each other.

Mondale's foreign travel generally took him with a substantive agenda to significant nations. He attended few funerals or inaugurations. He used foreign travel to force bureaucracy to address and often resolve bilateral issues.

Mondale followed his initial trip to Europe and Japan with one to Portugal, Spain, Austria, Yugoslavia, and Great Britain in May 1977, which included discussions with South African prime minister John Vorster regarding American policy toward South Africa, Rhodesia, and Namibia.[92] Frustrated by the slow pace in developing policy on South Africa, Carter asked Mondale to spearhead that review in March 1977.[93] Mondale worked with Vance, Brzezinski, Aaron, and United Nations Ambassador Andrew Young to develop American policy regarding South Africa, Rhodesia, and Namibia. Believing the Nixon and Ford administrations had mistakenly focused on minimizing the Soviet Union's influence in the region, Mondale prepared an action memorandum outlining a new approach that linked U.S.–South African relations to "a progressive transformation of South African society," including the end of apartheid and transition to majority rule. Mondale recommended pushing Vorster to support early majority rule in Rhodesia and Namibia. He conceded that this new approach would probably produce little in the short term but thought it would have a "constructive impact" on South Africa's future decisions.[94]

Mondale had extensive conversations with Carter before meeting Vorster. During several days of frank discussions, Mondale conveyed, privately and publicly, that America's future relations with South Africa were contingent on its moving away from apartheid and that the United States supported majority rule in Rhodesia and independence for Namibia.[95] "I felt comfortable kicking Vorster around the block because Carter said it was OK,"[96] said Mondale. At the end of his press conference, Mondale implied that the administration advocated "one person, one vote" for South Africa, prompting Vorster to accuse him of meddling in internal affairs. Mondale did not persuade Vorster to abandon apartheid but found that intransigence did not lead to a similar attitude regarding Rhodesia and Namibia. Mondale secured Vorster's endorsement of British-American efforts to facilitate an independence constitution for Zimbabwe. On balance, Mondale told Carter that his talks with Vorster had gone "as well as could be expected."[97]

Mondale's visits to Portugal and Spain supported the emergence of democracy in those two nations; his trip to Yugoslavia signaled the "importance" America placed on that nation's "independence, political unity, and territorial integrity."[98] Based on Mondale's recommendations, Carter directed the Departments of State and the Treasury to redo an unworkable loan agreement with Portugal and directed that the United States move ahead with a new Azores Base Agreement and develop "on a priority basis" ways to strengthen moderate trade unions in Portugal. Mondale's discussions with President Josip Broz Tito produced Carter's commitment to make an early decision on military equipment for Yugoslavia.[99]

Mondale concluded that his foreign trips could help overcome bureaucratic inertia that often stalled worthwhile initiatives. In preparing for trips, he tried to bring pending bilateral initiatives to the surface and press agencies to bring them to a resolution. In preparing for his April 1978 trip to the Philippines, Indonesia, Thailand, New Zealand, and Australia, Mondale asked six departmental or agency heads to suggest bilateral programs.[100] Mondale brought specific initiatives to each country,[101] and the resulting economic benefits and arms sales helped him achieve some human rights objectives.[102] Mondale told Carter that his trip produced "substantive discussions at each stage, a number of helpful results, and a number of issues requiring further attention by the Administration."[103] Mondale's "action forcing" initiatives achieved administration objectives while enhancing his standing with international leaders and within the administration.

Mondale played important roles regarding America's Middle East policy, including during the historic Camp David accords between Israel and Egypt. He advised Carter during private lunches and at meetings of Carter's foreign affairs team.[104] He assured American Jewish leaders of Carter's commitment to Israel. Finally, Mondale participated in direct talks with leaders of Middle Eastern countries to advance the peace process. As the American whom Israeli officials most trusted, he regularly communicated with them.[105]

Mondale traveled to the Middle East in late June 1978 to attempt to jump-start the peace talks.[106] His trip, which coincided with the thirtieth anniversary of Israel's statehood, was originally focused on the United States–Israel relationship[107] but expanded to include a stop in Egypt as regional tensions increased. The modified trip was designed to reinforce the bilateral relationship with Israel, emphasize the search for peace, and press Israel and Egypt toward compromise.[108] Israeli prime minister Menachem Begin later said that discussions with Mondale made him more optimistic about the peace process.[109] Mondale spoke at the Knesset, where he suggested that the land-for-peace formula should apply to disputed areas and pledged continued American military assistance for Israel.[110] Mondale elicited concepts from the Israelis and Egypt that contributed to the subsequent Camp David Accords, including President Anwar Sadat's agreement not to insist on Palestinian self-determination as a prerequisite to a treaty with Israel.[111] Mondale's report to Carter included the parties' agreement to send their foreign ministers to meet with Vance, Mondale's call for a political negotiator, and his recommendation that Begin and Sadat meet in a private setting.[112]

Carter initially asked Mondale to keep the government running in Washington while shuttling to the Camp David summit to join Carter and the two delegations.[113] Mondale regularly spoke with Carter and traveled to Camp David on September 7 and 10, 1978, for high-level meetings.[114] With the peace talks appearing destined for failure, Carter told Mondale to cancel his weekend appointments because "I needed him to come help me minimize the damage."[115] During the next three days, Mondale participated in meetings with Carter and negotiations with Israeli and Egyptian decision-makers.[116] Mondale persuaded Carter to drop a suggestion that Israel agree to a return to 1967 borders with "minor modifications."[117] Carter wrote that Mondale, along with Vance and Brzezinski, had provided his "best advice" in the negotiations.[118]

One of Mondale's most consequential roles occurred when he intervened to redirect U.S., and ultimately international, policy regarding the plight of the Indochinese boat people. Genocidal regimes were forcing refugees to sea in unseaworthy vessels in acts that smacked of ethnic cleansing. Assistant Secretary of State Richard Holbrooke called the problem to Mondale's attention in spring 1979. "He told me there was a real disaster going on and that we needed to develop a program. It was a vicious, racist thing; the communists were pushing the ethnic Chinese out to sea. The high commissioner was going along with it."[119] Internal differences in the American government had impeded an effective response.[120]

Mondale alerted Carter and, with his authorization, convened a meeting to develop options. The Mondale-guided process led the United States to fund refugee resettlement, send the navy on rescue missions, and increase the number of Indochinese refugees accepted to 14,000 per month.[121] Mondale was central to changing American policy. The next month Mondale represented the United States at the United Nations conference on the Indochinese refugees in Geneva as a last-minute substitute for Carter.[122] After a day of private meetings with representatives of leading countries,[123] Mondale gave an eloquent speech on July 21, 1979. "Some misery so surpasses the grasp of reason that language itself breaks beneath the strain. Instead, we gasp for metaphors. Instead, we speak the inaudible dialect of the human heart." Invoking the world's failure to rescue German Jews at the 1938 Evian conference, Mondale implored, "Let us not re-enact their error. Let us not be the heirs to their shame." Mondale outlined a seven-point plan that included increased responses from other nations in rescuing and accepting refugees and financing the effort in addition to America's commitment to accept an additional 168,000 refugees over twelve months. His words had greater impact because he had persuaded Carter to increase America's response. "Let us fashion a world solution. History will not forgive us if we fail. History will not forget us if we succeed," he concluded.[124]

Mondale's speech received enthusiastic ovations, the only address so honored.[125] He called it "one of the few speeches in my life where I thought I changed the outcome of people's lives."[126] The conference, largely due to Mondale's efforts, changed Vietnamese policy, saved lives, and culminated in an international program that resettled millions of refugees. Vance viewed it as "one of the most significant acts of the Carter Administration."[127]

Mondale spent nearly a week in China in late August 1979, a mission Vance described as "one of the most important and successful trips ever made by an American official to China."[128] Mondale had worked as part of a small team to normalize relations with China during the first years of Carter's presidency, and his trip helped that process.[129] Consistent with his practice, Mondale used his trip to force decisions on various matters regarding trade, intelligence, and security that had been stuck in the bureaucracy.[130] His trip produced a trade agreement granting China most-favored-nation treatment, aid to develop hydroelectric energy in China, an export-import bank credit arrangement for China of up to $2 billion over five years, and legislation extending incentives for American businesses to invest in China.[131]

The Chinese were sufficiently pleased that they accepted "with delight" Mondale's invitation for Premier Hua Guofeng to make a return visit and agreed to a civil aviation agreement and other bilateral ties.[132] Mondale became the first American leader to address the Chinese people directly when his Beijing University speech on August 27, 1979, was broadcast on Chinese television and radio and reprinted in Chinese newspapers. Mondale focused on the mutual benefits of improved bilateral relations but also articulated Carter's human rights message. "Governments are coming to understand not only the necessity, but also the fundamental wisdom and decency of protecting the rights of their people through law." His optimistic speech sounded some themes he had urged Carter to adopt ("The Americans are an historically confident people. . . . My country is blessed with unsurpassed natural resources. Moreover, we also have unparalleled human resources"). He offered China assurances vis-á-vis the Soviet Union ("Thus any nation which seeks to weaken or isolate you in world affairs assumes a stance counter to American interests") and announced steps to foster closer economic ties between the two nations.[133]

Constituency Outreach

Mondale worked with core Democratic constituency groups, an activity that matched a Mondale strength with a Carter need. Mondale was a frequent emissary to labor leaders and speaker at national and state labor meetings. His nine-month effort helped repair the rupture in relations between Carter and Meany.[134] Mondale helped produce a management-labor agreement as a prelude to the Chrysler bailout plan.[135]

Mondale had strong ties to African Americans, and his calendar included regular meetings with civil rights leaders and members of the Congressional Black Caucus. Planning of his trip to western Africa recognized its domestic impact and included some influential black Americans.[136] Mondale was also a frequent emissary to Jewish groups to defend Carter and to gauge that community's response to Carter's Middle East proposals.[137]

Spokesman
Mondale gave frequent speeches to support Carter's programs. The index of his vice-presidential speeches exceeds fifty pages.[138] Significant speeches already discussed include those at the Israeli Knesset, at the refugee conference in Geneva, and at Beijing University. Mondale drew the challenging assignment of defending Carter's economic policies at the Democratic Midterm Convention in December 1978 in Memphis. The midterm elections had gone poorly for the Democrats, Carter's popularity within the party was sinking, and many preferred Kennedy. While Kennedy loudly championed progressive social policies, Mondale defended the administration's focus on combating inflation. Society would "suffer terribly" if inflation were not solved, Mondale warned. Democrats would be turned out of office,[139] and Democratic ideals and policies would be destroyed. Mondale gave a forceful and widely acclaimed speech to the convention. Mondale frequently defended the administration's anti-inflation effort.

Mondale traveled domestically to explain administration policies. A January 1978 four-day tour to seven western states demonstrated administration interest in the region.[140] Although Mondale had opposed Carter's postponement of his July 1979 energy speech, he explained that action when he substituted for Carter at the National Governors Association on July 8, 1979. Elements of Mondale's optimistic speech found their way into Carter's later address.[141] One week later, Mondale took a four-day trip to California, Oregon, Kansas, Nebraska, South Dakota, Tennessee, and Pennsylvania to promote the SALT II treaty. Mondale had previously conducted SALT briefings for legislators but now took his message to states represented by uncommitted senators.[142] Mondale's trip included seven major speeches to World Affairs Councils and at universities and numerous press conferences, television interviews, and meetings with editorial boards.[143] Mondale also delivered the administration's messages through regular media interviews. During 1979, he had at least fifty sessions with political reporters in Washington, D.C. He appeared on two network morning television shows the day after the vote on the final Panama Canal treaty. As the energy crisis worsened, Mondale went on *Meet the Press* on July 1, 1979, to defend Carter's policies.

Renomination in 1980

Mondale was the campaigner-in-chief for the reelection of the Carter-Mondale ticket, a role that became demanding because Carter faced serious challenges for renomination from Kennedy and California governor Jerry Brown, and Carter had promised not to campaign while Iraq held Americans hostage. Disenchantment with Carter was sufficiently strong that some advanced Mondale as an alternative candidate,[144] a chorus strong enough that Mondale felt compelled to issue a statement repeating his "hope" that Carter would seek reelection.[145]

Mondale spent several days a week in late 1979 and early 1980 campaigning in the caucus and primary states of Iowa, New Hampshire, Florida, and Illinois. He spent more than 50 percent of the first three months of 1980 campaigning in 20 states, giving more than 100 speeches, attending 75 receptions, and holding 125 news conferences on other main events. His performance was widely acclaimed.[146] Mondale's effective work mobilizing traditional constituencies was helpful to Carter's renomination.[147]

Line Assignments

Consistent with his vice-presidential vision, Mondale avoided line functions. The few such assignments he handled were time-limited or based on extenuating circumstances. For instance, Mondale chaired the agenda-setting process in the White House. Carter's staff saw that function as necessary to give order and coherence to Carter's program by setting priorities among, scheduling, and determining Carter's level of involvement in departmental programs. Mondale's staff warned that a "high degree of sensitivity" would be required to avoid "the appearance or the reality" that Mondale was serving as White House chief of staff. "Nothing could be more disruptive" of Mondale's relations with Carter's staff than the idea that he would enforce deadlines or expose mistakes; that must be a committee, not vice-presidential, role. Moreover, "special caution" was required that Mondale's staff not set the agenda for committee meetings lest resentment result.[148] The agenda-setting role did not take a substantive area from another office. Carter's White House offered no alternative chair, and Mondale coordinated the work closely with Jordan's office and with Eizenstat and Brzezinski to establish a productive operation.

Mondale's direction of the youth employment initiative more directly deviated from his "no line assignments" policy. Indeed, in announcing Mondale's role, Carter conceded that the assignment represented "one of the rare times that I've asked the Vice President to take a specific assignment of this kind. Ordinarily he helps me with more general subjects and is kind of an assistant President."[149] The program required interdepartmental collaboration, seemed likely to attract much of the available new resources for domestic programs,[150] and appealed to Mondale's traditional allies.

Finally, Mondale convened a task force on the District of Columbia consisting of representatives of the executive and legislative branches and the D.C. government. Although the task force was the sort of activity that had marginalized Mondale's predecessors, there were reasons for Mondale's involvement. It was meaningful to African Americans, an important Democratic and Mondale constituency. The issue had no departmental home, and the task force would "not be a decision-making group," words Mondale underlined on Moe's memo to him, but rather a "consultative vehicle for a continuing dialogue" among the White House, Capitol Hill, and the D.C. government. Mondale would remain involved only until "the proper relationships have been established" and then withdraw. He assigned a lower-level staff aide to the project.[151]

The Bad Part of Being Vice President

Notwithstanding his influence, Mondale did not escape all the frustrations of the second office. Carter and Mondale served in stressful times, and Mondale disagreed with some of Carter's substantive decisions and his operational style. He understood that he had forfeited his political independence in accepting the vice presidency and sometimes regretted that loss despite the advantages his position provided.[152]

During early 1979, Mondale became despondent at his predicament. Inflation, exacerbated by a sudden shortage of foreign oil, created economic hardships that hurt the administration's public standing. To combat inflation, Carter cut social programs Mondale valued. Mondale disagreed with Carter's approach to addressing their political problems. He became less engaged and spent less time at the White House during early 1979.

Mondale's staff shared the perception that things were not going well. Moe wrote, "I sense that this kind of agony is the real purgatory of the vice presidency; you're so close, and yet you're not. It's inherent in the office, and it takes a lot of getting used to."[153] Al Eisele, Mondale's press secretary, concluded from the 1979 staff memos that "the only common denominator that emerges is the feeling that neither the Vice President nor any of us is very happy with the role he is now playing in this administration." Like Moe, Eisele thought the "very nature" of the vice presidency made it "a real purgatory." Yet Eisele voiced the more optimistic conclusion that the office had "really unlimited possibilities."[154]

Historian Steven Gillon has written that Mondale considered resigning as vice president or not seeking another term.[155] Mondale and his closest vice-presidential aides confirm that he was dispirited. Mondale has said he was simply venting his frustrations and never would have resigned.[156] Of course, Mondale did not resign. On the contrary, he resumed a high level of activity in mid-1979. Although some tensions developed between the Carter and Mondale camps after the July 1979 Camp David meetings, the following period was a productive part of Mondale's vice presidency as he intervened to save Indochinese refugees, took his highly successful trip to China, served as a central figure in Carter's reelection campaign, and continued as a close and candid adviser and troubleshooter.

Carter's commitment to preserving Mondale's role continued throughout the administration. When Mondale forcefully disagreed with Carter's advisers during the July 1979 Camp David meetings, Carter adjourned the session so that he and Mondale could speak privately.[157] When anonymous White House aides made disparaging comments about Mondale, Carter rebuked his staff and threatened to fire anyone who criticized Mondale publicly.[158] Carter never retreated from the arrangement set forth in the December 9, 1976, memorandum. Carter's reelection committee filed papers as the Carter-Mondale Presidential Committee; including the vice president's name was an unprecedented gesture.[159] In reaffirming that Mondale would be his running mate, Carter said on October 9, 1979, "Fritz Mondale and I have a very good partnership, and I have no plans whatsoever to change it."[160] Two weeks later, he referred to Mondale as "the finest Vice President, perhaps, that ever served this country." Mondale had been involved in every decision as "a full partner" of Carter, and accomplishments attributed to Carter could not have been achieved without him.[161] In announcing his candidacy, on December 4, 1979, Carter called Mondale "the most effective Vice President in the history of the United States" and repeated his desire to run again with Mondale.[162] Asked by Dan Rather in August 1980 if there was "any chance that he would consider replacing" Mondale on the ticket, Carter replied, "No, none at all. I think Fritz Mondale is not only the best partner that a President ever had in this . . . office, but also the . . . best Vice President."[163] Mondale was Carter's "secret weapon," Carter told the Democratic National Committee. Traditional Democratic groups trusted Mondale to articulate their priorities, Carter recognized.[164]

As their term ended, Carter sounded the same theme. He told a postelection press conference that "no President" had ever had a "better Vice President" and that he and Mondale were almost like "brothers."[165] Carter "could not possibly think higher" of Mondale than he did. Carter said his relationship with Mondale "constantly improved" and that he never doubted Mondale's "competence, his loyalty or his friendship."[166] Carter told a Mondale biographer that "the closest that I ever felt to Mondale" was immediately after Reagan's inauguration as they rode together with their wives to Andrews Air Force Base. Carter felt an "extraordinary closeness" with Mondale that "never wavered" during their four years in office. There had never been "any reticence about an absolutely frank discussion, even on issues where we might have disagreed."[167]

To a degree never before achieved, Mondale exercised vice-presidential influence in the executive branch. He helped shape domestic and foreign policy as a trusted and unique adviser and, as a troubleshooter, helped Carter address critical problems the nation faced.

Yet what was most significant of the Mondale vice presidency was not the activities of its four years. Rather, its larger importance came in the example it established for future administrations and the lessons its impact offers regarding American government. "Your unique relationship with the Vice President will also serve as a model for your successors," Moe wrote Carter roughly two weeks after the 1980 presidential election.[168] He was right.

Why It Worked

The Mondale vice presidency was not easily created, and its success cannot be attributed to any single factor. Rather, it represented a triumph of institutional imagination, engineering, and execution. It depended on envisioning a new vice presidency, developing a supportive structure, and implementing that design. The elements were interdependent and operated in a changing political environment.

Identifying the relevant variables helps expose the complicated dynamic that produced the Mondale vice presidency, an exercise that gives a fuller appreciation of the magnitude of the accomplishment and the leadership involved. Unlike its successors, the Mondale vice presidency, as the first White House vice presidency, lacked the benefits provided by the precedents it established. Mondale had to create what others, to varying degrees, found in place. Mondale's experience also offers lessons about institutional reform and suggests some factors that may affect future vice presidencies.

The Components of Success

The factors that contributed to Mondale's vice presidency can be classified in different ways, and each ingredient was itself a composition. Yet the following discussion not only suggests some of the elements of Mondale's success but also provides a checklist for future vice presidents.[1]

CONTEXT

Like all political figures, Carter and Mondale acted in a context with discouraging, as well as encouraging, aspects. The rise of the office during the twentieth century and its migration toward the executive branch, particularly during the prior quarter century, provided some foundation on which to build,[2] as did the development of necessary staff support.[3] Nonetheless, the vice presidencies of Johnson, Humphrey, Agnew, and Rockefeller had exposed limits of the office and pitfalls of particular approaches and arrangements. The change in rules governing presidential selection accelerated Carter's nomination, thereby providing him with the opportunity to conduct his innovative vice-presidential search.[4] Finally, Carter had less experience in national government than any president since Woodrow Wilson, a deficiency that created opportunity for Mondale. These contextual factors allowed the development of the Mondale vice presidency but did not make it inevitable. Some factors had existed earlier without producing an enhanced institution.

CARTER'S COMMITMENT

The White House vice presidency would not have occurred without Carter's commitment, which preceded his vice-presidential interviewing in July 1976 and continued until he left office four and one-half years later.[5] Intellectually, Carter was convinced of the merit of an enhanced vice presidency, and his self-confidence allowed him to make space for someone else near the top of the governmental pyramid. "He did it out of the strength of personal security, even though I was a troublesome partner. He could accept that because he thought it would provide benefits," said Mondale.[6] Moe thought Carter's "own inner security, self-assurance" was critical. A reason the Carter-Mondale relationship succeeded was that Carter welcomed a "strong assertive Vice President playing a strong assertive role."[7]

Mondale's successful vice presidency could not have occurred without Carter's dedication, but that disposition was not enough to expand the vice presidency. After all, Ford had wanted to make his vice president significant, and he, too, could share the stage, but Rockefeller's term had been unsuccessful. Unlike their predecessors, Carter and Mondale understood *how* to translate desire into reality and worked effectively and persistently to make it happen.

COMPATIBILITY

That Carter and Mondale were personally compatible also contributed to the success of Mondale's vice presidency. There was, Michael Berman observed, "symmetry to their backgrounds." Carter was a born-again Christian, Mondale a minister's son. Both came from small towns— Carter from Plains, Georgia, Mondale from places even smaller.[8] They connected during their first meeting, and their relationship deepened during the years they worked together in the 1976 and 1980 campaigns, in the transition, and especially in the White House. Their personal compatibility encouraged Carter and Mondale to treat each other well, and that reciprocal conduct no doubt preserved and enhanced their mutual regard.

Carter and Mondale were also sufficiently compatible philosophically to make the relationship work. To be sure, Carter was much more conservative than Mondale,[9] yet their differences did not "rise to the level of such profound moral importance as to become insupportable," observed Eizenstat.[10] They shared commitments to civil and human rights and to greater government transparency. Their philosophical differences were manageable, and both sought to manage them.

Personal and political compatibility helped yet were insufficient to explain the success of the Mondale vice presidency. Although Ford and Rockefeller liked each other, Rockefeller's tenure had failed, in part because of policy differences but also due to other shortcomings in the design and execution of his vice presidency. Compatibility would not have made Mondale significant had the office been poorly imagined or structured, had Carter or Mondale approached it the wrong way, or had Mondale had little to offer.

THE VISION

Mondale's vice-presidential vision maximized the likelihood that he could contribute to the ongoing work of the Carter administration and minimized the risk that he would repeat his predecessors' mistakes. Mondale and his associates reimagined the vice presidency based on history's lessons. As discussed in chapter 4, Mondale's vision made the vice president an integral contributor to the administration, not primarily a national insurance policy; designed the vice presidency to assist the president, not aggrandize the vice president; and sought to add value, not create redundancy. Not surprisingly, it appealed to Carter and his inner circle. "Because I was Vice President, I could move in and out. I had the right stature to do things that only he could do," said Mondale.[11]

VICE-PRESIDENTIAL RESOURCES

Reimagining the vice presidency was essential, yet the right vision would have been insufficient without the necessary resources. In abstract terms, they included access to decision-making, information, and expertise as well as presidential support. Mondale's access to Carter gave him the opportunity to influence decisions and increased his importance to others. Access to information allowed him to know what issues were percolating so he could decide when and how to intervene and could do so in an informed way.[12] Access to expertise enabled Mondale to carry out his advising and troubleshooting roles. Presidential support enhanced Mondale's standing with others and encouraged cooperation with him. These abstract resources came from more tangible goods Carter provided, such as the West Wing office, Mondale's regular private meetings with Carter, his right to attend presidential meetings, his timely receipt of paper going to the president, his ability to enlist administration personnel to support his activities, the positions Aaron and Carp held, and the integration of Mondale's able staff into daily White House activities.

Carter's continuing support was a vital Mondale resource. "The relationship I had with Carter, being in on every meeting, being able to go to meetings, the way he insisted that the rest of the government saw me as his representative, made a huge difference," Mondale said.[13] Carter's early, frequent, and continuous praise of Mondale and his consistent actions conveyed an important message. As Berman put it:

Washington is a city in which symbols mean a great deal, no matter how many times the President might say that Mondale was to be treated as he was treated, Mondale would not have been taken seriously if at the same time it appeared that the President and his staff were not treating the vice president with the respect to which he should be entitled.

The fact that he was the first vice president with an office in the West Wing, the fact that Mondale entered and left the President's meetings at will, the fact that he was provided all the facilities of office and that the President used him on matters of importance were symbols that told the rest of the government that Mondale was for real and not to be trifled with or treated lightly.[14]

A Presidential Vice President

Mondale's vice presidency succeeded because Mondale brought quality to the office. He was able to offer useful advice that integrated political and substantive considerations. Carter and others involved Mondale because he enhanced deliberations and helped implement policy. Carter said he rarely rejected Mondale's advice "because Fritz tries to put himself in the role of a president and not just to espouse a fairly radical argument, one way or the other, in an irresponsible way." When Mondale spoke, Carter said, "everybody listens to him, because they know that he's approaching the point of making the judgment from the same perspective as if he were president."[15] Mondale was an effective legislative operator, a credible spokesman, and an able diplomat. Unlike many others, "Mondale never embarrassed Carter," a performance that enhanced their relationship, David Rubenstein, Carter's deputy domestic adviser, observed.[16] Carter's political advisers viewed Mondale as an ally and an important source of guidance because he was a good politician.

Political Capital

Mondale's political capital contributed to his success. His impressive performance in the 1976 campaign strengthened his position. He preserved his standing through his strong favorability ratings and never became a political liability. He maintained strong relationships with government officials, Washington journalists, and core Democratic constituencies such as blacks, Jews, labor, liberals—relationships that were helpful in governing, in meeting Kennedy's challenge for the 1980 nomination, and in unifying the Democratic Party after it.

THE MESH BETWEEN PRESIDENTIAL NEEDS AND VICE-PRESIDENTIAL RESOURCES

Mondale provided assets Carter needed. Whereas Carter lacked experience with Congress and in Washington, D.C., and was weak with core Democratic constituencies, Mondale had many friends in Congress, especially in the Senate, and was well regarded by Beltway insiders and the Washington press corps. Mondale could provide perspectives otherwise lacking in Carter's inner circle and credibility and relationships with groups suspicious of Carter and his Georgia associates. Mondale could explain this world to Carter and defend Carter to it.[17] Brzezinski, who often clashed with Mondale, observed that Mondale "complemented Carter both as a person and as a politician," so they were more effective together than either would have been alone.[18] Mondale's strength came not simply from his possession of assets Carter needed but from Carter's recognition that Mondale and his staff helped compensate for presidential weaknesses.[19]

PRESIDENTIAL LEADERSHIP STYLE

Carter's decision-making style enhanced Mondale's role. He centralized decision-making in the Oval Office, which gave an advantage to those such as Mondale with easy access to him. Carter also welcomed frank counsel, and an adviser's failure to persuade him in a particular instance did not diminish future influence.[20] These presidential traits made it easier for Mondale to advise Carter candidly.

Carter's belief in Cabinet government and his lack of a chief of staff for the first two and one-half years of his term created opportunities for Mondale, especially because neither Jordan nor Powell wanted a major operational role in the West Wing. Mondale became the logical candidate for certain mediating and coordinating functions, like the agenda-setting role.

Carter gave most associates discrete assignments and expected them to stay within their lanes. This structure helped assure Mondale a distinctive role since only he and Jordan had latitude to range across the issues the administration encountered.

Carter's leadership style accordingly made room for a vice president with Mondale's strengths and disposition to advise and troubleshoot.

Mondale had greater opportunities under Carter than he would have under a less engaged chief executive or one who relied on a strong chief of staff or one who preferred that his vice president assume specific on-going roles.

A VICE-PRESIDENTIAL VICE PRESIDENT

Mondale's success was also due to his ability to operate as vice president. He could follow as well as lead. He could accept that Carter, not he, was president, he had considerable interpersonal skills, and was strategic in his conduct.

Mondale had often operated in Humphrey's shadow during Mondale's twelve years in the Senate and was capable of deference.[21] Mondale gave Carter candid, often critical, advice, but accepted Carter's right to decide administration policy and to direct his activities. Mondale tended to save his advice for significant matters. He did not exhaust his welcome by often rearguing resolved matters. He would not troubleshoot without receiving Carter's clearance.

Mondale also acted strategically to protect Carter's, and his own, interests. By not joining debates in large meetings, he minimized leaks and protected Carter from having to choose between Mondale and a cabinet member. Mondale's hidden-hand advising, through his silence at large meetings, the confidentiality of his discussions with Carter, the circumspection of his staff, and his ability to use Aaron and Carp to advance ideas in larger sessions, protected his reputation for influence while insulating him from visible battles.[22]

Mondale's tact was evident in other ways. Offered a choice of West Wing offices, Mondale took the smaller, middle office, leaving the larger, corner office for Jordan. Carter had agreed that Mondale could avoid supporting administration positions that he saw as violating his principles, but Mondale never publicly distanced himself from Carter or his policies. He was circumspect even among friends. Mondale often camouflaged disagreements with Carter by explaining Carter's thinking and objectives rather than stating his own views. When asked if the Camp David meetings before the "malaise" speech "marked a turning point for the administration" Mondale responded that the question was really whether "it was a turning point for the country." He then explained Carter's thinking without revealing his doubts.[23]

Mondale took on difficult tasks. He volunteered to give speeches or take trips to ease Carter's burdens. He bore the brunt of the Carter-Mondale reelection campaign. Such an effort would have won any vice president credit but Mondale's role was distinctive. He repeatedly resisted suggestions that he, not Carter, should be the Democratic nominee and defended Carter to the Democratic base against Kennedy, a friend and liberal hero.

Mondale structured and implemented his vice presidency to avoid unnecessary conflict. He resisted ongoing responsibilities that intruded on the turf of others. He avoided appearing to pursue his own political agenda. He resisted staff advice in 1978 that he give speeches identifying himself with some major substantive area to enhance his personal prominence for fear that such activity might be resented by those around Carter.[24]

Mondale's skillful discharge of his relationships with Carter and other administration figures was critical to its success. Carter and his associates saw Mondale as an ally, not a competitor, because he conducted himself that way.

STAFF INTEGRATION AND INTERACTION

Positive interaction between the Carter and Mondale staffs contributed to Mondale's vice presidency. Carter structured his White House in a manner designed to include, and take advantage of the skills of, Mondale's staff. He appointed longtime Mondale aides Aaron and Carp to high-level positions on his NSC and domestic policy staffs, respectively, and gave Moe, Mondale's chief of staff, a second appointment on his staff. At Carter's direction, his aides regularly included Mondale's office in the White House paper flow and Mondale's staff in deliberations.[25] His aides supported Mondale's work as well as his own. These moves promoted cooperation and minimized interstaff rivalry. Carter's actions and admonitions set the tone for the White House staff. "The President confided totally in Mondale, so I knew I could be open with him,"[26] wrote Jordan.

Mondale's staff was also predisposed to cooperate. Mondale's staff worked to win the confidence of their counterparts during the 1976 campaign[27] and that effort continued in the White House. Carter's beleaguered legislative liaison, Frank Moore, found Mondale and his associates "very, very helpful, and very supportive of me."[28] When Jordan was under attack, Mondale extolled him to a reporter close to Jordan, and Mondale's press staff advised Powell of Mondale's actions. When Carter named Mondale to chair the Executive Committee to coordinate long-term planning, Mondale's staff noted the need to avoid "the appearance or the reality" that Mondale was becoming de facto chief of staff.[29] Mondale's staff worked for Carter's success.

Carter's principal aides saw Mondale as an ally in their effort to persuade Carter to consider the political ramifications of his decisions. "They wanted me to succeed," said Mondale of Carter's senior aides such as Jordan, Powell, and Eizenstat. "I was the political guy in the White House. These guys had worked with [Carter] for years. They knew Carter's tendency to be unpolitical. I was sort of a good-news guy for them because I was trying to get something solved politically. I was bringing something the Carter people wanted brought there. I often worked with them. I could get their candid advice, which made me more sure-footed."[30]

Lessons from the Mondale Vice Presidency

The success of Mondale's vice presidency depended on the structure Carter and he put in place, the relationship they developed and sustained, and Mondale's ability to perform. Carter's leadership was necessary, both in understanding what was needed to make his vice president a substantial contributor and in executing that understanding. Mondale's leadership was also essential. The vice presidency would not have grown as it did without Mondale's conception of the office, the value he added, and his skill in discharging his duties on a continuous basis.

Selection matters, and Carter chose well. Mondale was presidential, vice presidential, and compatible, and he added value by bringing needed experience and relationships. Although it is possible to imagine an able vice president succeeding without contributing distinctive experience and relationships to the administration, those attributes increased

Mondale's value. It is inconceivable that a vice president could succeed without being presidential, vice presidential, and compatible with the president. A poor vice-presidential selection would have prevented the accomplishment, notwithstanding Carter's initial commitment.

The factors presented here were interdependent and interrelated in ways both obvious and obscure. For instance, Carter's initial commitment to an engaged vice presidency continued, in part, because he saw that Mondale added value through the quality of his advice and troubleshooting activities and the political capital he contributed, all of which helped respond to administration needs. Carter and Mondale sustained their relationship; Mondale was vice presidential; and Mondale and his staff worked well with Carter's staff. Mondale added value in part because he was presidential and vice presidential and had political capital and resources that meshed with administration needs but also because the vice-presidential vision made sense and allowed him to contribute. The integration of Mondale's staff into White House operations helped Mondale exercise influence, but the ability and loyalty of Mondale's staff further encouraged their involvement. Mondale worked well with Carter's associates because of his interpersonal skill but also because Carter wanted them to cooperate with Mondale and they saw that Mondale added value.

It is not necessary to sketch all of these feedback loops to demonstrate the interrelated influences that accounted for Mondale's success. The Mondale vice presidency succeeded in part because Carter, Mondale, and their associates took a holistic view of it. The various factors interacted to compound the success of Mondale's vice presidency.

In addition to their interdependence, the various factors operated in a dynamic, not static, context. The political world that existed at the Carter-Mondale inauguration did not exist six months or a year or two years or four years later. External events reshaped the political environment—Carter's attempt to cut water projects, the energy crisis, the Lance resignation, the Panama Canal treaty fights, the Camp David accords, inflation, the "malaise speech" and Cabinet shakeup, the Kennedy challenge, the hostage crisis, and many more. Less-visible changes also had impact. Carter and Mondale had different experiences and perceptions as they moved from event to event. They worked together and saw each other's strengths and weaknesses, similarities and differences, likes and dislikes. They knew each other better after working together for six months or a year than on inauguration day. Their relationship changed as they experienced more together and more of each other.

Carter and Mondale understood the vice presidency differently and presumably better—as their service continued—than they had, for instance, when they considered Mondale's December 9, 1976, memorandum. The new vice presidency became more entrenched over time. Patterns of dealing became routine, not novel. As time passed, Mondale conducted some aspects of his vice presidency differently. He attended fewer meetings with Carter, in part because the prerogative was established, in part because some meetings could be skipped. Carter and Mondale saw how the vice presidency could address problems confronted by the administration. Mondale undertook foreign missions, patched up administration disputes with constituent groups, and traveled domestically to improve the administration's standing. They also faced new challenges from the political calendar, such as midterm elections and their reelection campaign, and from unanticipated events such as the Kennedy challenge and the Iran hostage crisis.

Over time, Carter and some of his aides gained some experience with the national government and the Beltway, thereby diminishing some of the distinctiveness of what Mondale and his associates initially offered. However, this development did not make Mondale and his staff irrelevant. Greater experience was not necessarily synonymous with understanding or skill, nor did it replace Mondale's relationships. Events presented new challenges. Carter's relationship with Meany ruptured and needed to be repaired—by Mondale. Legislators became frustrated with Carter and his team, requiring Mondale's intervention. Time may have diminished some of Mondale's initial advantages, but it did not eliminate them, and events produced new challenges and opportunities.

Moreover, performance won Mondale and his associates greater responsibility as deeper relationships developed and their credibility grew with Carter and his team. Carter appreciated Mondale's loyalty and service; Mondale recognized that Carter had fulfilled his commitments regarding Mondale's role and had far exceeded Carter's predecessors in doing so. Mondale's diplomatic successes revealed new skills. The departure of Lance, a rare Carter intimate who was the president's contemporary, created a void. The Kennedy challenge enhanced Mondale's value to the administration. The various factors that contributed to the success of the Mondale vice presidency were not constants but varied in response to external events and to reactions in the White House.

The dynamic nature of the Mondale vice presidency suggests a further point, one implicit in the prior discussion. Implementation of the vision was crucial, and it necessarily occurred on a continuing basis throughout their joint service. Notwithstanding Carter's desire to put his vice president to work, his initial friendly feeling for Mondale, their vice-presidential vision, Mondale's capital, and so forth, the experiment would have failed had Carter abandoned his commitment to the enterprise or had Mondale not conducted himself throughout the term in such a way as to add value and remain in Carter's favor. As Carp put it, "The magic" was not in their "initial arrangement" but "in how they managed to sustain it."[31]

The interplay of those factors made Mondale's term as vice president more productive than those of his predecessors. There were bumps along the road, but Mondale's influence and involvement far surpassed those of prior vice presidents.

More importantly, Mondale's service established the White House vice presidency. It created a new set of expectations regarding the office that have survived and indeed grown; it offered a model for vice-presidential contribution. The next chapters discuss how his successors have benefited from, and built on, the Mondale model of the White House vice presidency.

7

The White House
Vice Presidency:
Bush to Gore

The Mondale model vice presidency could have disappeared when Mondale left office. Its creation had been personal to Carter and Mondale, and no legal requirement compelled its continuance or precluded their successors from reverting to earlier arrangements. The precedents from Mondale's term were significant, but four years' experience of an administration rejected at the polls could not automatically erase 188 years of alternative versions of a less robust office. Yet Carter's and Mondale's successors did not turn back. Instead, they continued, and expanded, the White House vice presidency. Though not exact replicas of Mondale or each other, Vice Presidents Bush through Biden acted as senior presidential advisers and troubleshooters supported by the Mondale resources.

For Vice Presidents Bush, Quayle, and Gore, the advising role became regularized; vice-presidential troubleshooting was adapted to serve each president's needs and each vice president's talents; and ongoing portfolios became part of the job, beginning with Bush and expanding with Quayle and especially with Gore. The development of the White House vice presidency did not skip the twelve years between Mondale and Gore, as some suggest, but continued during the Bush and Quayle terms. And notwithstanding the institutionalization that occurred, the White House vice presidency was sufficiently flexible to allow variation as each occupant put an individual gloss on the institution.

Bush

Ronald Reagan announced in his victory statement that he and George H. W. Bush would have "a true partnership and a true friendship in the White House,"[1] but Bush's precise role was undetermined, and Reagan's early expressions were untested by performance. At the Republican convention, Reagan had said the vice presidency was "a very real position" with "very real duties" but then discussed the anachronistic role as president of the Senate, an emphasis that could not have cheered Bush. Bush did little better. He suggested that the vice president should be loyal but seemed to view the main role as taking over should misfortune befall the president.[2]

Bush joined Reagan and his closest associates after the 1980 election to discuss administration jobs.[3] When Alexander Haig was recommended for secretary of state, Bush alone predicted that Haig would create problems.[4] Reagan chose Haig, but Bush's concerns proved prophetic, and Haig lasted only about a year. Bush, a former CIA director, recommended that the position go to an intelligence professional,[5] but Reagan selected his campaign chair, William Casey, who had little, and remote, relevant background. Bush maintained a low profile, working to place supporters, often in the Department of Commerce, where his friend Malcolm Baldridge became secretary.[6]

During the transition, Bush met with Mondale regarding the vice presidency. Sessions with Mondale convinced Bush of the value of the West Wing office, the right to invite himself to Oval Office meetings, and other resources Carter had given Mondale. The transmission occurred at the staff level, too. Mondale's associates exposed the new Bush team to operational aspects of the job as Moe, Berman, and their colleagues took pains to educate their counterparts on Bush's incoming staff.[7] Although Reagan and Bush had just ousted them from office, Mondale was a frontrunner for the 1984 Democratic nomination, and Bush would probably be on the opposing ticket, Mondale and his associates "totally submerged" these personal or political considerations to instruct Bush's team, "often with the zeal of missionaries," regarding the contours of the new-model vice presidency,[8] said Chase Untermeyer, executive assistant to Vice President Bush. By the time he took office,

Bush regarded the Mondale approach as "a very good model" and one he hoped to follow.[9] A few months later, Bush reported that he and Reagan were following the Carter-Mondale agreement whereby the vice president had access to the president, was included in his meetings, and could be heard in policy discussions.[10]

Bush became an important presidential adviser, a role that grew over time. He had extensive access to Reagan, retained Mondale's West Wing office, and routinely attended Reagan's daily national security briefing and his chief of staff meeting. He often joined Reagan's meetings with foreign dignitaries or congressmen or topical sessions, especially regarding foreign and national security matters. His staff attended interagency national security meetings to keep him informed. Bush spent less time in the West Wing than had Mondale, dividing his time between it and his Executive Office Building office, which was less "constrictive" and closer to his staff.[11]

Bush's weekly lunches with Reagan were his "most productive sessions"[12] and helped him establish a relationship with the president. Bush tried not to burden Reagan and often brought jokes to lunch. Reagan regarded the lunches as "pleasant,"[13] but the sessions were not entirely social. Reagan and Bush discussed a wide range of topics,[14] "from affairs of state to small talk."[15] Bush felt free to raise topics and offer opinions[16] but did not use the lunches to advance agendas of others[17] and kept the discussions confidential. Bush advised Reagan on foreign policy at lunch[18] and in memos he sent Reagan when he traveled.[19]

Bush generally refrained from stating his views in meetings, even small sessions, with Reagan's other senior advisers,[20] preferring to share his views privately with Reagan. Although some disparaged Bush's practice,[21] his silence did not signify lack of, or failure to exercise, influence. Although Bush thought his role was primarily to assist in articulating policy, he often posed questions, offered information or observations,[22] or arranged meetings for Reagan to hear different viewpoints.[23]

Reagan insiders thought Bush very influential. Robert McFarlane, Reagan's third national security adviser, said Bush "often" was "the decisive influence on Reagan" and affected his attitude toward the Soviet Union.[24] When Secretary of State George Shultz requested a presidential audience to air complaints about the NSC, he asked that Bush attend, presumably because of his influence.[25] Nancy Reagan enlisted Bush to advise her husband about the Soviet Union.[26] Reagan "let Bush in. He considered him as a full partner, across the board. He liked Bush,"[27] said Kenneth Duberstein, Reagan's legislative liaison and fourth chief of staff. Craig Fuller, who worked for Reagan, then Bush, said, "When [Bush] chose to assert influence, the relationship with Ronald Reagan was such that he had considerable influence. He didn't assert that influence that often. He didn't see the office as Vice President as one where he should be shaping policy as much as making sure the President has the information to make decisions."[28]

Bush's most controversial advising role related to Reagan's decision to sell arms to Iran to obtain the release of American hostages held in Lebanon. Bush attended meetings in summer 1985 in which McFarlane briefed Reagan, and Bush reportedly voiced doubts, although less vehemently than Secretary of Defense Caspar Weinberger and Shultz.[29] Shultz said Bush was present but silent on January 7, 1986, when Shultz and Weinberger voiced strong opposition.[30] In August 1986, an Israeli counterterrorism expert told Bush that the transfer of military equipment for hostage releases involved radical elements in Iran.[31] Although Bush conceded during legal proceedings that he had been regularly advised of events relating to the arms sales to Iran, he denied knowing of the diversion of funds to the contras in Nicaragua.[32] After the scandal broke, Bush advised Reagan on damage control, telling him the American people would not accept his explanation that he had not traded arms for hostages[33] and discussing a response to the Tower Commission report.[34] He urged Reagan to meet with his foreign affairs advisers to allow them to air their differences and to stop self-serving leaks.[35]

In 1988, Bush became unhappy that the administration was negotiating with Panama leader Manuel Noriega, offering to drop his drug indictment if he surrendered power. The initiative posed problems for Bush's presidential campaign. At one meeting, Reagan and Bush went "toe-to-toe"; at another, Bush and his ally Secretary of the Treasury James Baker "were adamant and cutting in their opposition to the president."[36] Bush's approach "was very unusual" for him, and he left one meeting "somewhat upset."[37] In May 1988, Bush publicly stated that as president he would not negotiate with drug dealers.[38] Significantly,

Bush's willingness to disagree with Reagan in government councils and publicly first occurred during the 1988 campaign and after Bush had paid a price for silent loyalty in the arms-for-hostages affair. Even then, Bush was uncomfortable with publicly separating himself from the president and did so in an understated way.

Bush spent considerable time interacting with friends in Congress, at the House gym and elsewhere on Capitol Hill,[39] inviting legislators to the Naval Observatory or on *Air Force Two* when he visited their states. These encounters helped Bush receive information and gauge congressional attitudes so he could advise Reagan and his legislative team.[40] "Members confided with the Vice President because oftentimes it's easier to tell a Vice President something. You don't horse-trade in the Oval Office with the president of the United States. You tell the vice president, 'It would really help me if you'd look at X.' Bush was terrific at being the train conductor on stuff like that,"[41] said Duberstein. Bush made numerous calls to advance Reagan's legislative priorities.[42]

Bush's major troubleshooting involved foreign policy. A skilled diplomat, he made forty-one foreign trips,[43] often to significant places — the Soviet Union, China, Europe, and the Middle East — on substantive missions. Fuller judged Bush as "extraordinarily valuable" to Reagan as a foreign emissary, both "as a reliable communicator" of Reagan's views to world leaders and "as a very reliable reporter" who communicated personally with Reagan.[44] Bush wrote cables directly to Reagan, conveying his impressions of foreign leaders, reporting their concerns, and addressing bilateral issues. This practice enhanced Bush's effectiveness with foreign leaders, who could speak freely to Bush with the understanding that he would report directly to Reagan.[45]

Bush's relationship with Chinese leader Deng Xiaoping from his time as trade liaison representative to China accounted for Bush's China trip in May 1982 when the Chinese were upset over proposed American arms sales to Taiwan. Bush told the Chinese of Reagan's interest in, and emphasized the mutual benefits of, better relations. Bush defended and explained the Taiwan arms sale yet was treated "warmly" and returned with new overtures from China.[46] He reported China's misgivings regarding America's relations with Taiwan, a topic on which Reagan was unyielding.[47] Bush's trip contributed to the signing of the third joint communiqué with China, in which the United States pledged to reduce arms sales to Taiwan and China promised to seek a peaceful resolution with Taiwan.[48]

Bush's China trip illustrated the interrelated nature of his vice-presidential work. In addition to the diplomatic and advising components, he spoke publicly regarding America's interest in furthering relations with China while selling arms to Taiwan[49] and replied to a "frank and candid" letter from Senator Barry M. Goldwater, a leading Taiwan supporter. Bush assured Goldwater that he had told the Chinese that Reagan wanted improved relations while fulfilling commitments to Taiwan, a course Goldwater would complicate by saying publicly what his letter hinted. Bush told Goldwater that America's allies wanted the United States to improve relations with China, partly to counterbalance the Soviet Union, and solicited Goldwater's help.[50] Bush returned in October 1985 to China, where he was greeted warmly despite concerns over Taiwan and proposed protectionist measures.[51] He worked to preserve a delicate balance between China and Taiwan.[52]

Bush took a twelve-day, seven-nation tour of western Europe in February 1983 to counter growing opposition to American deployment of nuclear weapons there.[53] At the trip's outset, Bush presented Reagan's letter offering to meet Soviet leader Yuri Andropov to ban intermediate nuclear weapons. Bush spoke to the United Nations Disarmament Committee, met with the Soviet negotiators, consulted with allies, and spoke publicly to influence public opinion.[54]

Bush attended numerous inaugurations and funerals ("You die, I fly," he said) and made ceremonial travel productive. Funerals provided "useful opportunities" to meet with world leaders.[55] Bush led America's delegation to funerals of three consecutive Soviet leaders, assignments that allowed him to meet each new successor. Bush's account of his meeting with Konstantin Chernenko at Yuri Andropov's funeral[56] inclined Reagan to want to meet the new leader, a project that engaged Bush.[57] Thirteen months later, Bush was even more optimistic after meeting Mikhail Gorbachev at Chernenko's funeral.[58]

Bush went to Poland in 1987 to help move it from the Soviet bloc. While there, he announced an exchange of ambassadors, spoke on Polish national television, signed an agreement for scientific cooperation, and met with Solidarity leader Lech Wałęsa. The trip improved relations between the United States and Poland.[59]

Rockefeller[60] and Mondale[61] had advised Bush of the perils of assuming line responsibilities, and Bush basically accepted Mondale's conception of the vice president as a generalist.[62] But Bush thought the vice president should be a senior adviser "with portfolio,"[63] a view consistent with, and perhaps responsive to, Reagan's belief that the vice president, "like a vice president in a private corporation . . . should be an executive with duties and functions."[64]

Bush accordingly assumed several line assignments that were structured to mitigate the concerns Mondale had identified. The roles generally involved interagency efforts that required some high-level interdepartmental coordination to provide a more effective governmental response.[65] The vice president's stature and relationship to the president made him an appropriate coordinator, and the interdepartmental nature of the work minimized the intrusion on others' turf. The assignments associated Bush with important, though not defining, issues and ones of concern to the Republican base, were generally time-limited, and did not absorb much vice-presidential time.

Two days after their inauguration, Reagan named Bush to chair a Task Force on Regulatory Relief to review past and pending regulations.[66] Reducing federal regulation was important to Reagan's agenda. Reagan claimed that Bush's work had reduced regulations by more than 25 percent, had cut more than 300 million hours of paperwork, and would produce public savings of more than $150 billion over ten years.[67] The task force disbanded in August 1983, claiming the executive branch had done what it could.[68] Reagan reestablished the task force in December 1986 to propose reductions in regulatory burdens to improve productivity and competitiveness.[69]

Two months into his presidency, Reagan named Bush to chair crisis management in the event of a foreign or domestic emergency. Bush would coordinate the federal response, engage in planning, and chair meetings in Reagan's absence.[70] The White House had rejected Haig's solicitation of that role,[71] prompting Haig to threaten resignation.[72] The group met following various crises, such as the conflict in the Falkland Islands, America's invasion of Grenada, and a suicide attack that killed 241 marines in Lebanon.

Bush also chaired Cabinet-level task forces to combat drug flow into southern Florida beginning in January 1982[73] and to address terrorism beginning in June 1985.[74] Regarding the latter, after working with federal agencies and American allies, Bush gave Reagan a classified report in December 1985 and a public version on March 6, 1986, with recommendations, including the need for a management system that assigned responsibility for combating terrorism, for bilateral and multilateral cooperation, and for improved intelligence.[75] At Reagan's request, Bush reconvened the task force after the Iran-contra scandal[76] and reported that the earlier report was appropriate and being implemented.[77]

As an administration spokesperson, Bush aggressively defended Reagan and his policies. He traveled frequently — eighty-nine domestic trips during his first two years as vice president[78] — and his foreign travel and task force work often afforded topics for speeches upon his return. For instance, on December 3, 1986, Bush said Iran's strategic importance made engagement imperative, and intelligence suggested that pragmatic elements were emerging with whom the United States could deal. Reagan was concerned about the hostages. Once Reagan learned of "possible improprieties," he immediately disclosed the problem, authorized an investigation, and created the Tower Commission to study NSC operations. Bush said that America had an important foreign policy agenda, and "a forgiving American people" should rally around "this strong and honest President."[79] The following month, Bush defended the administration's antiterrorism strategy at a Washington conference. Reagan believed he had not traded arms for hostages and had strenuously combated terrorism, Bush said. Bush vigorously denied that America had made "concessions to terrorists" or acted in a manner to "encourage future terrorism."[80]

Bush was an important political surrogate. During his first year, he made twenty-two trips outside Washington for partisan Republican events. He campaigned for Republican candidates, made political appearances across the country,[81] and raised more than $3 million for the party and its candidates.[82] On October 19, 1982, Reagan noted approvingly that Bush had been campaigning for Republican candidates virtually full time.[83] Bush continued to shoulder much political work, especially in 1984 and 1986.

Bush had frequent access to Reagan and advised him, especially on foreign affairs. He was particularly engaged in foreign travel and in work as a legislative liaison, party surrogate, and administration spokesperson. He handled several line assignments to coordinate the work of multiple agencies to advance Reagan's agenda regarding some important issues without occupying much of Bush's time. Bush's access to Reagan enhanced his value in legislative liaison and diplomacy.

Quayle

Contrary to common assumptions, Dan Quayle's vice presidency did not retreat to earlier patterns. Quayle functioned as an important and effective presidential adviser and troubleshooter with the resources of his immediate predecessors. Quayle was very much engaged in the George H. W. Bush administration, and his tenure consolidated developments that Mondale had begun and Bush continued.

Quayle was among the senior advisers who regularly met with Bush during the transition regarding appointments and policy. Some conservatives sought positions through Quayle.[84] He urged the appointments of Jack Kemp, John Tower, and William Bennett and later recommended Dick Cheney.[85]

Quayle retained essential resources, including the West Wing office, weekly lunch, and presidential access. He attended Bush's daily national security briefing and remained for a second meeting with Bush and his chief of staff. These two small sessions took an hour or more each morning and covered the full range of national security, domestic, and political matters.[86] Quayle also attended meetings of the Cabinet and National Security and Domestic Policy Councils and meetings on the budget and with congressional leaders and heads of state, among other sessions.[87] He participated in Bush's two U.S. Supreme Court nominations.[88] Quayle met with Bush more often, and longer, than did any other staff members except National Security Adviser Brent Scowcroft and Chief of Staff John Sununu.[89]

Quayle used his lunches to brief Bush on legislative developments, his foreign travels, and other assignments.[90] He recognized the lunches' value in developing a relationship with Bush.[91] Unlike Bush, Quayle acceded to requests from Cabinet members and other personnel to raise matters with Bush and reported the president's responses to the request-ers.[92] The practice enhanced Quayle's standing with others, who would often approach him with some issue before a lunch.

Quayle joined meetings of Bush's foreign policy advisers but appar-ently was not among the most influential voices in the room. Bush and Scowcroft mention Quayle only ten times in their lengthy foreign pol-icy memoir, generally to note his attendance without reciting any con-tribution. Bush identified his principal foreign policy advisers as Baker, Cheney, Scowcroft, the CIA heads William Webster and later Robert Gates, and Powell, and he described Quayle and Sununu as "two other important individuals, though involved mainly in domestic policy" who "contributed to our foreign policy team." Bush described them as "bright" and "very interested in arms control" and considered their advice "extraordinarily helpful."[93]

Still, Quayle was part of the small group of eight or fewer in the room when Bush addressed the most vexing national security issues. He expressed himself, sometimes contrary to Bush's inclination.[94] He was skeptical of Gorbachev's efforts to reform the Soviet Union[95] and was perceived as more sympathetic to Israel than some others on Bush's national security team. Israeli leaders often reached out to Quayle to ex-press their views through "side communications," which he shared with others in Bush's inner circle.[96] Regarding the possibility of reform in Russia, Quayle viewed it as his role, in part, to ensure that proposals re-ceived "serious discussion."[97] Often Quayle raised political implications of foreign policy choices where his insights added to the discussion.

Quayle was an important legislative and political adviser. Sununu described Quayle as "the go-to guy" for difficult problems with Con-gress. Quayle became engaged and "said the hard things" in "tough po-litical discussion[s]."[98] Untermeyer admired Quayle's "superb political knowledge and political sensitivity" and his ability to interpret political and legislative trends.[99] Quayle pushed Bush to seek authorization from Congress to use force against Iraq[100] and unsuccessfully urged Bush to propose an earned income tax credit for lower-income workers rather than simply opposing the minimum wage.[101] He opposed raising taxes and unsuccessfully tried to persuade Bush to withdraw from the budget deal that included tax increases.[102] Quayle urged Bush to use political capital after the Persian Gulf War to advance a domestic agenda.[103] He advised Bush to attack Democrats, not primary rival Pat Buchanan; to adopt a Rose Garden strategy in 1992; and to make his speeches less negative and more programmatic.[104]

Quayle contributed significantly through legislative work. Unless traveling, he generally spent two afternoons (six to eight hours) each week on Capitol Hill. He typically attended the Tuesday lunch for Republican senators, the conservative or moderate Senate Republican lunch on Wednesday, and the House Republican strategy session. Quayle had many friends in each house and in both parties. He considered himself a conduit for communications with Congress because members shared information with that him they would not mention to Bush's legislative team.[105] Bush thought Quayle "extraordinarily effective" as a bridge between the White House and Congress.[106] When House Republicans stopped speaking with Sununu and OMB director Richard Darman after Bush broke his "no new taxes" pledge, Quayle became the only channel for communications.[107] Although he had opposed the tax increases, Quayle defended Bush to livid conservatives. He maintained good relations with many Democrats. When Senator Edward M. Kennedy asked Quayle to consider "a coordinating role" in discussions between the administration and Congress on education, Quayle promised to "keep an eye on things" and instructed his staff to "make sure we do something on this."[108]

Quayle helped in various battles. He lobbied for Tower to be secretary of defense, for confirmation of Judge Clarence Thomas to the Supreme Court, for the 1989 minimum wage, for upholding Bush's veto on legislation restricting the development of the FSX fighter plane, for the 1990 budget deal, and to fund the space station, among other legislative efforts.[109] Quayle led the administration's efforts for legislation to send arms to help Prince Sihanouk gain power in Cambodia,[110] to fund the B-2 Stealth bomber and the Strategic Defense Initiative ("Star Wars"),[111] and to obtain authorization to use force to remove Iraq from Kuwait in 1991.[112] He made lobbying calls while abroad, which signaled the importance of the issue. Quayle and Sununu often worked a "good cop/bad cop" lobbying routine.[113] Whenever the White House got "stuck legislatively," Quayle went to Congress to round up the necessary votes.[114]

Quayle visited forty-seven countries, with his travel focused on Latin America and Asia. Although Quayle aspired to be a policy-maker for Latin America, the State Department discouraged that role. Still, Quayle made seven trips to the region, attending inaugurations and other events to support democratization and to compensate for Bush's and Baker's relative absence.[115] Many of the trips discharged important ceremonial functions, providing a high-level presence in important countries to which Bush and Baker gave less attention. They also communicated concern regarding human rights or democracy. During Quayle's second week in office, he reprimanded senior El Salvador officials regarding human rights abuses, demanded that they investigate the killing of ten peasants and hold the guilty parties accountable, and linked continued aid to improvement.[116] In March 1990, Quayle warned Chilean dictator General Augusto Pinochet not to interfere with the newly elected democratic government.[117] Quayle traveled frequently to Asia to show the flag, develop commercial relations, and discuss American military base arrangements with host countries. During the Persian Gulf crisis, Quayle visited Venezuela to persuade it to increase its oil production and to Saudi Arabia, where he met with King Fahd; Sheik Jabbar al Ahmed al Sabah, the exiled emir of Kuwait; and American troops.

Quayle identified his role in suppressing a coup in the Philippines in November 1989 as among his major contributions. While Bush, Baker, Scowcroft, and Sununu were flying to a summit with Gorbachev, Quayle spoke to President Corazon Aquino several times, questioned officials regarding how the United States might neutralize rebel planes, and conferred with Scowcroft and Sununu. Quayle wrote that he "was the one asking the questions, seeking the options and pushing for a consensus."[118] Bush aide Fred McClure thought Quayle was very effective.[119] Yet Colin Powell, then chairman of the joint chiefs of staff, claimed that he, not Quayle, asked the central questions; Powell and Scowcroft credited Powell with devising the plan to use American aircraft to ground rebel planes and suggested that Quayle's calls confused matters.[120] Cheney operated from his home (either because he was sick or did not want to deal with Bush through Quayle) and also spoke with *Air Force One*.

Quayle was an important envoy to the Republican right wing. He frequently met with or spoke to conservative activists, associated Bush and the administration with conservative themes, and defended the administration to conservative congressmen and opinion leaders. His May 1992 "Murphy Brown" speech attributed urban problems to "a poverty of values," including the disintegration of the nuclear family, and called for dismantling the welfare system and replacing it with other approaches. It criticized television character Murphy Brown for glorifying permissive values by having a child out of wedlock and suggested that renewing "our public commitment to our Judeo-Christian values" would help address the problem.[121] Some other significant speeches spoke to wider audiences, such as his important justification for the Persian Gulf War.[122]

As political surrogate, Quayle visited all fifty states, often handling invitations that merited attention but that Bush could not accept. Quayle observed that "the burden of political campaigning falls to the vice president the majority of the time."[123] He traveled extensively in 1990, campaigning and raising money for candidates and the Republican Party.[124]

Line assignments, though they had been peripheral to Bush's vice presidency, were a focus of Quayle's service. Quayle's assignment to head the Competitiveness Council, the first significant ongoing operational role for a White House vice president, "became a power center."[125] Bush created the council on April 4, 1989,[126] as a successor to Bush's regulatory task force, although refocused on competitiveness, a Quayle interest from his Senate service. The move raised the profile of work important to business and conservatives, was a reminder of Bush's credentials in the area, and gave Quayle a visible role to demonstrate executive talent.

The council had impressive membership—the attorney general, the secretaries of treasury and commerce, the White House chief of staff, the director of OMB and chair of the Council of Economic Advisers (CEA)—but its initial impact was unclear because it was not a decision-making body, lacked independent staff, and was limited to "review regulatory issues and such other matters" bearing on competitiveness upon Bush's referral. Sununu thought the council should not seek "exotic or exciting" issues, because "most important issues are dull" and should address things such as "the fact that most degrees in math and science are given to foreign students and the problem of dropouts." Attorney General Richard Thornburgh thought it should prepare reports showing policy differences between the United States and other countries affecting competitiveness. Quayle stated such themes as projecting America's position by 1992 regarding competitors and biotechnology,[127] a topic that occupied the council for a year.[128]

To combat criticism of growing regulation, Bush expanded the council's jurisdiction on June 15, 1990, by strengthening its regulatory review authority[129] and instructing departments to assist to prevent "reregulation."[130] The fortified council identified four goals—reducing regulatory burdens, developing human resources, eliminating governmentally imposed burdens on scientific innovation, and promoting free flow of investment capital. Quayle asked Cabinet members to propose deregulatory initiatives and directed agency heads to submit for review any "agency policy guidance that affects the public," including strategy statements, guidelines, policy manuals, and the like, and to conduct a cost-benefit analysis for each major rule.[131] The council met five or six times per year. Between meetings, Quayle's staff worked to resolve issues.

Bush preferred not to umpire agency disputes with the council, and few appeals went to him,[132] a pattern that enhanced Quayle's power. On the rare occasions when an agency head did appeal to Bush, Quayle made certain he would win by learning Bush's views in advance so he could compromise if Bush did not favor his position.[133]

In several instances, the council eased environmental restrictions regarding recycling or wetlands.[134] In November 1991, Quayle announced a reformed drug approval process that reduced development and review time, allowed nongovernmental entities to handle some matters, and permitted greater data exchange with other nations.[135] The council incubated domestic initiatives such as an "Agenda for Civil Justice Reform in America," which Quayle unveiled at the 1991 annual meeting of the American Bar Association. Quayle argued that America's legal system impeded competitiveness and suggested expanding alternative methods of dispute resolution, controlling discovery, and capping punitive damages.[136] Bush issued an executive order applying some of these recommendations to federal agencies.[137]

Quayle's council became controversial as critics complained that it undermined the regulatory process and favored corporate interests.[138] Seven congressional committees investigated it.[139] In July 1992, twenty-six Democratic senators accused it of acting "secretly" and "hijacking the public regulatory process" to undermine public health and safety, consumers, and the environment and asked that the council's funding be withheld.[140] While Democrats excoriated,[141] Republicans defended[142] Quayle and the council.

Bush reestablished the National Space Council on April 20, 1989,[143] and charged his "right-hand man, our able Vice President, Dan Quayle," to lead it to define goals in space exploration.[144] In addition to representing the "frontier," space impacted national security, foreign policy, and economic and technological issues. Quayle established a blue-ribbon commission to examine the future of the National Aeronautics and Space Administration (NASA). It assigned low priority to the space station and space exploration, which Bush had emphasized. In response to objections, Quayle revised the report to preserve the space station and accommodate Bush's views.[145] Quayle encountered suspicions at NASA due to his interest in the Strategic Defense Initiative and also encountered turf issues with Baker over who would negotiate a U.S.-Russian space agreement.[146]

In essence, Quayle participated in the full range of high-level meetings and contributed significantly, especially as a legislative and political adviser and troubleshooter. His work on the Competitiveness Council involved a significant and continuing assignment that advanced the conservative agenda and limited federal regulation. He undertook important, though sometimes ceremonial, diplomatic work and was an important link to the Republican base. His service further consolidated patterns of the White House vice presidency that Mondale and Bush had established.

Gore

Al Gore became a significant across-the-board presidential adviser and assumed important operational roles. His portfolios organized much of his activity, contributing to his advising role and generating other assignments. He focused on his presidential race the last two years of his vice presidency. Bill Clinton supported him enthusiastically, but Gore and Clinton became estranged due to campaign-related tensions and Gore's revulsion over Clinton's affair with White House intern Monica Lewinsky.

Gore participated actively in significant transition events in 1992–1993.[147] Gore and aide Roy Neel were among the small group who regularly met with Clinton to consider who should be appointed to important administration positions.[148] Gore was a "force" in these sessions.[149] Gore's associates Carol Browner, Kathleen McGinty, and former senator Timothy Wirth became director of the Environmental Protection Agency (EPA), director of the Council on Environmental Quality, and undersecretary of state, respectively, and Gore's brother-in-law, Frank Hunger, became an assistant attorney general.

Gore's transition role grew four years later. He interviewed Cabinet contenders, and Clinton often deferred appointments until after he could confer with Gore. Gore helped place Madeleine Albright as secretary of state and former senator William Cohen as secretary of defense[150] and choreographed moving Federico Peña from Transportation to Energy[151] and the appointments of allies William Daley (Commerce) and Andrew Cuomo (Housing and Urban Development).

After initially competing with Hillary Clinton, Gore emerged as Clinton's closest, across-the-board adviser for most of their period of service. Clinton and Gore discussed developments at weekly lunches, and Gore advised Clinton candidly.[152] Clinton credited the lunches with helping maintain their relationship.[153] Gore typically brought a fairly detailed agenda of issues to discuss.[154] He had unfettered access to Clinton and regularly attended Clinton's daily CIA/NSC briefing; policy meetings; and Clinton's press conference preparation, where he sometimes used humor to redirect Clinton from angry, counterproductive responses.[155]

Clinton referred to Gore's "extraordinary role"[156] as vice president. George Stephanopoulos wrote that "[a] president has no real peers, but Gore was getting close" by 1995.[157] John Podesta, Clinton's fourth chief of staff, called Gore Clinton's "first advisor in chief" across the board.[158] Clinton solicited Gore's comments, and when Gore spoke, Clinton was "absolutely riveted," Mike McCurry, Clinton's press secretary, recalled.[159] Clinton treated Gore "like a full partner in policy discussions,"[160] Albright wrote. He was the "key member" of Clinton's foreign policy team, whom Clinton relied on extensively.[161] "Everyone wanted to get Gore on his side. If you could get Gore on your side you could increase your chances of the outcome you wanted," said McCurry.[162] Gore was more willing than many of his recent predecessors to offer advice with others present.[163] When Clinton once complained to aides about events and asked what he could do, Gore replied, "You can get with the goddamn program"[164]—words not routinely spoken to presidents. Clinton's staff often enlisted Gore to introduce order into decision-making or to bring matters to a resolution. Gore could "deliver a message" to Clinton in a way staff members could not.[165]

Gore advised on a full range of domestic, foreign, personnel, and political matters, often encouraging the sometimes indecisive Clinton to decide and move on.[166] Gore helped deficit hawks prevail,[167] helped persuade Clinton to intervene in Bosnia,[168] and participated in Clinton's two Supreme Court nominations.[169] He helped convince Clinton to offer a balanced budget proposal and successfully pushed Clinton to take a hard negotiating line with Republicans in budget negotiations in 1995[170] and supported Clinton in signing welfare reform legislation.[171] Clinton followed Gore's advice in a range of matters relating to reinventing government, the environment, and telecommunications.[172] Other administration figures regarded him not simply as another Clinton adviser but as a coprincipal.[173] When Secretary of State Warren Christopher had trouble getting time on Clinton's calendar, he scheduled a weekly meeting with Gore. Gore successfully encouraged Clinton to make difficult personnel decisions, even those involving close Clinton associates.[174]

Gore's staff enhanced his advising role. His chiefs of staff were also presidential assistants, and Leon Fuerth, his national security adviser, served on the principals and deputies committees of the NSC and National Economic Council. The highly respected Fuerth[175] was a "full partner"[176] in deliberations with Anthony Lake and Sandy Berger, Clinton's top national security aides, with the understanding that his views would not be attributed to Gore while the process was working to a recommendation. This arrangement avoided skewing policy formulation by an early statement of Gore's position, given Gore's influence. Fuerth and Gore shared a common approach, however, and Fuerth's engagement assured that Gore's likely inclinations would inform recommendations.[177] When the West Wing was dysfunctional in 1993, Clinton asked Gore to allow Neel to serve as Clinton's deputy chief of staff. Jack Quinn, Gore's second chief of staff, later became Clinton's counsel.

Although Gore functioned primarily as Clinton's senior adviser, he also undertook more line assignments than any other White House vice president. These assignments involved significant matters, provided a focus for his activity, and spawned numerous troubleshooting responsibilities.

Clinton named Gore to lead the National Performance Review, later the National Partnership for Reinventing Government (NPR or REGO), on March 3, 1993.[178] Clinton described Gore's mission as "reinventing the role of the Federal Government" and "examining everything we do from top to bottom."[179] Gore had planned to avoid line responsibilities aside from environment and telecommunications, but after Hillary Clinton was placed in charge of health reform, REGO gave Gore a comparable assignment to rebut the perception of a diminishing role.

REGO seemed turf-invading work that could antagonize administration figures, congressional leaders, and other stakeholders. Clinton called it a "risky adventure,"[180] a columnist termed it "the domestic equivalent of being sent to a funeral in Thailand,"[181] and the *New York Times* buried the announcement in a dismissive story on page 23.[182]

Yet REGO was important to Clinton, who sought to replicate nationally a gubernatorial initiative. He launched REGO at a well-attended event, described it as a "historic step" and as part of the "change" he represented, directed Cabinet members to assign "their best people to this project,"[183] and frequently mentioned it. The specter of bureaucratic conflict was reduced because many assistant secretaries were not in place.

In addition to Elaine Kamarck from his office, Gore commandeered about 250 career civil servants and others to review departmental performance. He held town hall meetings in various agencies and around the country,[184] hosted a reinventing government summit in June 1993, and met with agency heads.

Gore presented the initial report at the White House on September 7, 1993. Its 384 recommendations promised to eliminate 252,000 government jobs by 1998 and save $108 billion.[185] Over the next four days, Clinton and Gore appeared together at REGO events in Virginia, Ohio, California, and Texas,[186] a significant presidential commitment, especially given the demands of various foreign policy events during that period. Clinton issued orders implementing Gore's recommendations, praised Gore's work repeatedly, and stressed REGO's importance. The assignment gave Gore visibility in a popular cause; in addition to events with Clinton, Gore appeared on high-profile television shows.[187]

After Republicans won Congress in the 1994 elections by attacking government, REGO became a marquee Clinton program to demonstrate commitment to reducing government. Clinton's 1995 State of the Union address highlighted REGO.[188] In February 1995, Clinton credited Gore's REGO work with cutting the federal workforce by more than 100,000 people and saving $63 billion, with reductions in numerous departments and agencies.[189] In September 1995, Clinton called REGO "an exceptional achievement," unprecedented "in the history of modern American Government," and Gore announced more than 180 additional proposals with projected savings of $70 billion over five years.[190] By August 1996, Gore's third annual progress report claimed savings of $118 billion.[191] Clinton used REGO as a prime argument for his reelection. In his memoir, Clinton wrote that "Al Gore's highly successful initiative confounded our adversaries, elated our allies, and escaped the notice of most of the public because it was neither sensational nor controversial."[192]

Gore headed several bilateral commissions with other countries. In this "fascinating role," Albright said Gore "almost served as a prime minister" to handle substantial foreign policy issues.[193] Gore assumed a major role regarding relations with Russia as cochair of the Gore-Chernomyrdin Commission, which Clinton and Boris Yeltsin agreed to establish in early April 1993. Russian foreign minister Andrei Kozyrev had suggested such a commission to institutionalize, and engage more Russian officials in fostering, the relationship, and the Clinton administration saw it as a hedge against "President Boris Yeltsin's erratic streak."[194]

Beginning in September 1993, the commission met twice annually and involved much of Clinton's Cabinet and their Russian counterparts. It sought to create an enduring peace based on mutually beneficial projects.[195] Working groups promoted investment opportunities and cooperative ventures in environment, energy, space, and other matters. The sessions served as the "boiler room" of the bilateral relationship to force action to resolve bilateral issues and implement commitments.[196] The commission worked to safeguard nuclear materials in the former Soviet Union[197] and became the venue for disclosures regarding nuclear armaments.[198]

Gore's rapport with Viktor Chernomyrdin and relationships through the commission provided alternative channels as Yeltsin's ailments and lifestyle compounded his political vulnerability.[199] Strobe Talbott, Clinton's deputy secretary of state, said "Gore-Chernomyrdin" was "a synonym for our ability to get attention and action" from Russia on "hard issues."[200] Clinton said the Gore-Chernomyrdin relationship "played a major role in the continued strengthening of our partnership with Russia"[201] and allowed the countries to work together in Bosnia, to reduce nuclear weapons, and "to do a whole range of things."[202]

Gore and Egyptian president Hosni Mubarak chaired the U.S.-Egyptian Partnership for Economic Growth and Development beginning in September 1994 to promote economic reform in Egypt. In October 1994, Clinton and South African president Nelson Mandela announced a commission chaired by Gore and Deputy President Thebo Mbeki to enable the two governments to effectively use American aid, develop business relationships between the two countries, and support South Africa's development.[203] The Gore-Mbeki Commission met twice each year and created six working groups involving Cabinet-level officials in ongoing discussions on a range of issues. Leaders of both countries cited its importance.[204] Gore also cochaired bilateral groups with Kazakhstan and Ukraine.

Gore assumed general responsibility for environmental issues, a role strengthened by the placement of Browner and McGinty.[205] Clinton's 1993 Earth Day speech, pledging to protect a range of species and act to combat global warming, was seen as reflecting Gore's influence over contrary arguments of Secretary of the Treasury Lloyd Bentsen and Secretary of Energy Hazel O'Leary.[206] Gore frequently spoke on environmental issues and announced environmental initiatives, and Clinton acknowledged Gore's environmental "leadership."[207]

Gore helped salvage the Kyoto negotiations on climate change when, in December 1997, he flew to Kyoto; met with representatives of key countries; and, after urging Clinton to authorize increased American negotiating flexibility,[208] announced that shift in his speech. Gore handled other high-profile environmental missions. He headed America's delegations to a world conference on population in Egypt in 1994, where he helped foster agreement on an international right to birth control, and to a sustainable development summit in Bolivia in December 1996.[209] With the Chinese premier, Gore cochaired a United States–China Policy Forum on Environment and Development to foster sustainable development.

Gore was also responsible for telecommunications. He was the administration's principal spokesperson regarding information-age technology and formulated its legislative proposals on telecommunications.[210] In signing the Telecommunication Act of 1996, Clinton acknowledged Gore's leadership.[211] Gore worked to make the V-chip a standard feature in new televisions so parents could regulate their children's viewing options, and he advocated a television rating system similar to that used for movies.[212] Gore pushed to increase competition in telecommunications and for the E-Rate to make the Internet accessible to most American schools.[213]

Gore headed a Cabinet-level Community Enterprise Board (later named the Community Empowerment Board) to focus on providing federal support, and implementing local initiatives, for economic development of distressed urban and rural communities.[214] Clinton asked Gore to develop a plan to use government contracting to reward businesses located in empowerment zones.[215]

Gore performed numerous high-profile troubleshooting assignments, some relating to his various portfolios. In early November 1993, Gore challenged Ross Perot, the 1992 third-party presidential candidate and opponent of the proposed North America Free Trade Agreement (NAFTA), to a televised debate about NAFTA at a time when the treaty was in trouble.[216] The debate, Gore's idea, was questioned by some Clinton staff,[217] but Gore's performance helped turn opinion in favor of NAFTA and suggested how politicians could defend NAFTA to constituents.[218] "The case for NAFTA could not have been made more forcefully or eloquently than it was by Vice President Gore,"[219] Clinton said.

As the NAFTA debate and Kyoto speech suggested, Gore was an important administration spokesperson on a range of topics. When the administration lacked an effective foreign policy voice during the first term, Gore assumed the role. He effectively presented REGO in appearances in nationally televised shows. He often announced new administration initiatives regarding the environment, telecommunications, or other matters.

Gore emerged as an important Clinton defender following allegations about Clinton's affair with Lewinsky. Gore praised Clinton's leadership throughout 1998. When Clinton confessed after having lied about the relationship, Gore issued a statement from his vacation expressing pride in Clinton, a friend, who had courageously admitted a mistake and was a great president.[220] A month later, Gore stated that the independent counsel's report was no reason to upset the elections of 1992 and 1996.[221] After Clinton was impeached, Gore publicly defended him as a great president.

Gore's line assignments generated numerous troubleshooting responsibilities. After Yeltsin publicly lectured Clinton in Budapest in early December 1994 regarding the perils of expanding NATO, Gore used that month's Gore-Chernomyrdin Commission meeting to reassure Yeltsin and urged Clinton to consider that NATO should defer expansion to avoid a rupture with Russia, advice Clinton was disposed to accept.[222] Gore met with Chernomyrdin to devise a strategy regarding NATO's bombing in Yugoslavia[223] and played a "key role" in putting together the partnership between Chernomyrdin and Finland president Martti Ahtisaari, whose diplomatic work produced the cease-fire.[224] Gore helped control the nuclear weapons of the former Soviet Union. He represented the United States in an agreement whereby Kazakhstan agreed to dismantle its nuclear arsenal, led negotiations with Ukraine whereby it surrendered its nuclear weapons, and helped negotiate an agreement for uranium to be brought to the United States from Kazakhstan for safeguarding. Gore traveled to Ukraine three weeks after the installation of President Leonid Kuchma to show his support for Kuchma's economic reform agenda and urge him to abandon nuclear weapons.[225]

Gore's REGO work produced other troubleshooting assignments. Clinton often enlisted Gore's help in departmental problems as they arose, such as airline safety or immigration reform. Clinton named Gore to head the Ounce of Prevention Council in 1994 to help state and local governments address causes of criminal behavior, a project Clinton tied to Gore's work on REGO and the Community Enterprise Board.[226] Gore found synergies between his telecommunications portfolio and his work regarding empowerment zones and crime prevention when he proposed that the telecommunications industry donate 50,000 cell phones to assist neighborhood watch groups.[227]

Gore helped reposition Clinton for the 1996 campaign. He participated in senior strategy sessions in the White House residence and conferred privately with Clinton and his political guru, Dick Morris. Gore was an active fund-raiser for Clinton's reelection. He was the star attraction at thirty-nine fund-raising events that produced nearly $9 million, hosted twenty-three White House coffees for major donors, and attended eight more with Clinton. He phoned fifty-two donors, producing $800,000.[228] Gore played an active role campaigning in the 1998 midterm elections. He spent much of the fall traveling the country to support Democratic candidates for the House and Senate, often using partisan rhetoric to rally the Democratic base.[229]

Despite his sixteen years of service, Gore was not a man of Congress, nor was he particularly popular with his former colleagues. Outside his portfolio, Gore did not focus on legislative work as Mondale, Quayle, Biden, or even Bush did. Gore was often used to make public statements torpedoing Republican ideas, a role he relished. But since Republicans disliked him, his presence on the Hill tended to attract opposition.[230]

Conclusion

The White House vice presidency survived and became deeply entrenched during the Bush, Quayle, and Gore tenures. Each functioned as a presidential adviser and troubleshooter supported by resources Mondale had obtained for the office. Unlike Mondale, each accepted ongoing operational responsibilities. Bush assumed several peripheral assignments for finite periods. Quayle handled two portfolios, one of which, the Competitiveness Council, was central to his work. Gore assumed numerous continuing and significant assignments that helped define his vice presidency.

Bush clearly became someone on whom Reagan relied, especially as their service together strengthened their relationship. Quayle contributed importantly in specified areas. Gore seemingly exercised the most influence as an adviser over a broad array of topics.

The three vice presidencies demonstrated the inherent flexibility of the White House vice presidency. Although all were advisers and troubleshooters and assumed portfolios, their terms were quite different. Bush served as a legislative adviser and troubleshooter, but his most significant contributions came as a foreign affairs adviser and diplomat. Quayle traveled abroad, but his principal roles were as a legislative and political adviser and troubleshooter, in running the Competitiveness Council, and as a link to the Republican right. Gore advised and had influence across the board, yet various portfolios organized much of his work. Gore had served in Congress longer than Quayle and Bush but spent less time on Capitol Hill than they did.

Despite the individual variations, the White House vice presidency developed under each of the three. As significant as they were, no one suggested, rightly or wrongly, that they dominated the administration. That was about to change.

8

The Triumph of the Vice Presidency: Cheney to Biden

The Dick Cheney and Joe Biden vice presidencies were quite different, but both symbolized the transformation of the office. Each man sacrificed much to become vice president. Cheney gave up millions of dollars in salary, bonuses, and stock options as the chief executive officer of Halliburton to become vice president, though his health history might have cautioned him against undertaking such stressful service. Whereas his predecessors saw the second office as a presidential springboard, Cheney credibly denied that he had presidential aspirations. He wanted to be vice president—period. Biden was less definitive about his presidential ambitions, yet his age (sixty-six) when first inaugurated and Hillary Clinton's likely 2016 candidacy lessened his then-apparent prospects. And Biden loved the Senate, where he had great influence and had been his own boss for thirty-six years. Why surrender clout and independence to serve a much younger, less-experienced man?

Cheney and Biden were no doubt motivated in part by a sense of civic duty and partisan loyalty. Yet they both apparently thought the vice presidency offered opportunity for important service. Their perceptions can be traced to their recent predecessors' experiences and their sense that the presidents they served contemplated an influential vice presidency.

They were right. Each became an extraordinarily consequential presidential adviser and made important operational contributions. Their terms illustrated the diversity of vice-presidential performance and the dynamic nature of vice-presidential influence.

Cheney

TRANSITION ROLE

After having directed Bush's vice-presidential search, Cheney assumed a second unprecedented role in running the 2000–2001 transition (see chapter 10). Cheney operated from Washington with a few close associates even while courts resolved the election. He formulated short lists for high-level positions and, along with designated chief of staff Andrew Card and personnel director Clay Johnson, met with Bush to consider them.[1] Cheney escorted those being interviewed for Cabinet positions to sessions with Bush.[2]

Cheney influenced the selections of his friends Donald Rumsfeld (secretary of defense), Paul O'Neill (secretary of the treasury), and Spencer Abraham (secretary of energy) to Cabinet positions. Other Cheney associates landed important departmental or White House roles[3] — Paul Wolfowitz as Rumsfeld's deputy, Sean O'Keefe as deputy director of OMB, Stephen Hadley and Zalmay Khalizad at the NSC, and John Bolton at the Department of State, although Wolfowitz and Hadley had been advising Bush independently of Cheney. Cheney also successfully sponsored candidates for various domestic Cabinet and sub-Cabinet positions who shared his aversion to government regulation.[4] Cheney's transition role strengthened his position. Many kindred spirits landed important White House and departmental positions, and had reason to feel indebted to him in view of his role in staffing the administration. And his transition role confirmed yet again Bush's reliance on Cheney.[5]

Cheney's transition role was much more modest four years later. Bush took Card and NSC aide Condoleezza Rice, but not Cheney, to Camp David after the 2004 reelection to plan the second term. Bush named Rice secretary of state without consulting Cheney, and the vice president played no role in shaping Bush's second inaugural address articulating second-term themes.[6]

INFLUENTIAL ADVISER

Cheney established an unprecedented level of vice-presidential influence during Bush's first term. Bush associates resisted the suggestion that Cheney was president or copresident,[7] and their arguments fit with other evidence suggesting that Cheney's influence, though historic during Bush's first term, was as vice president, not de facto president. Bush was, as he insisted, the decider who occasionally rejected Cheney's counsel, even on national security matters. Peter Baker was closer to the mark in concluding that Bush initially viewed Cheney "as his consigliere guiding him through a hostile and bewildering capital."[8]

Cheney functioned primarily as an adviser who could become involved in any issue and attend any meeting.[9] Cheney, Joshua Bolten said, was a "true counsellor, not a decision-maker or manager."[10] Cheney kept the advice he gave Bush confidential,[11] which enhanced his influence. Much of Cheney's power, his biographer Stephen Hayes rightly observed, was invisible and reflected his talent at operating behind the scenes, especially when alone with Bush, as he often was.[12] Cheney was knowledgeable, credible, and persuasive and understood Bush, and it is not hard to imagine him being persuasive in their private discussions.

Cheney began each day with an early-morning CIA briefing at the Naval Observatory to prepare for a similar 8:00 a.m. session with Bush. The dry run helped Cheney to influence Bush's briefing and to probe areas that might not immediately interest the president. Cheney often requested more information, thereby creating a stream of communications with intelligence agencies, and often joined Bush's briefing remotely when he traveled.[13] Bush and Cheney also met with the FBI director regularly to review domestic threats. And "after that, it's whatever [is] hot."[14]

Bush and Cheney continued the weekly lunch, which allowed Bush "to hear whatever Dick had on his mind." Cheney was the only Bush adviser whose meetings were regularly scheduled. Bush distinguished Cheney from his other senior advisers because he was an elected official, and Bush wanted Cheney to be familiar with the issues Bush faced because "it could become his at any moment."[15] Notwithstanding Bush's characterization of the sessions as succession preparation, they were designed to help Bush, not Cheney, succeed. Cheney usually brought several matters to discuss; occasionally Bush had something to raise. Cheney felt uninhibited about addressing policy or personnel matters.[16]

Cheney frequently joined Bush's meetings, at least 75 percent of the time, according to one informed estimate,[17] including when Cheney's old friend, Federal Reserve Chair Alan Greenspan, lunched with

Bush.[18] Cheney saw Bush multiple times on days when both were in Washington.[19]

Although some recall Cheney as being quiet in larger meetings,[20] he participated actively in sessions with principal advisers such as the weekly meeting of Powell, Rumsfeld, and Rice (or their second-term successors). Robert Gates described Cheney as "open about his views," which he presented "forcefully."[21] In NSC meetings, he asked questions to sharpen discussions[22] and expressed preferences[23] but did not put Bush "in a corner or take away his options."[24] Cheney regularly joined meetings of the National Economic Council, which familiarized him with competing views before advising Bush.[25]

Cheney clearly was influential, especially early on. When Bush learned that American planes had bombed Iraqi sites to enforce a no-fly zone in February 2001, he called Cheney for reassurance.[26] Shortly after hearing of the attacks on 9/11, Bush instructed his aides to put him in touch with Cheney and repeatedly spoke to the vice president throughout the day.[27] During British prime minister Tony Blair's September 2002 visit, Cheney attended all Bush-Blair meetings, including one restricted to the two principals.[28] After Bush's national security team advised Bush to initiate war against Iraq by attacking a compound where intelligence sources placed Saddam Hussein, Bush excused everyone else from the Oval Office to confer privately with Cheney, who urged him to order the attack. Bush did.[29]

Cheney's access and Bush's reliance on him enabled Cheney to obtain presidential approval of important initiatives without respecting normal channels. Early on, Bush signed a letter drafted by Cheney's office retreating from Bush's campaign pledge to reduce power-plant emissions and abandoning the Kyoto treaty on climate change without the input or knowledge of interested senior officials.[30] Cheney obtained Bush's signature right before Bush met with EPA director Christine Whitman, who would have opposed it. Rice was "appalled" that Cheney was allowed to issue the letter without clearance from Powell or her, given its diplomatic implications.[31] Cheney persuaded Bush to assert executive prerogatives to deny Congress information about Cheney's energy task force.[32] He advised Bush against compromising the 2001 tax cut[33] and helped construct the 2003 tax cut.[34] When Cheney grew impatient with an interagency effort on handling detainees, he spearheaded an alternative process that excluded Powell, Rice, and the military.[35] His counsel, David Addington, produced an executive order creating military commissions that Bush signed on November 13, 2001.[36] Powell learned of it from CNN, and Rice and other leading officials were also not consulted.[37] Cheney persuaded Bush to insist publicly that talks regarding North Korea's nuclear program be based on complete and irrevocable dismantling without advising the State Department, which was heavily engaged in the issue.[38] Cheney advised Bush to authorize the CIA to use enhanced interrogation techniques.[39] After 9/11, Cheney urged Bush to have the Pentagon give priority to planning for military action against Iraq. He received periodic briefings on the military planning, played a crucial role in the decision to go to war in Iraq, and was briefed daily about it.[40]

Cheney did not engage in issues such as education and stem-cell research. Whereas Bush was responsible for all policy, Cheney focused on areas important to him or where he could have an impact, such as policy regarding national security, foreign affairs, the economy, taxation, energy, the environment, and judicial appointments. As Paul Kengor pointed out, Cheney was a specialist, not a generalist, who came "with a niche"[41] or, perhaps more accurately, a number of niches, some of them quite substantial.

Cheney's influence was reinforced by his staff's integration into White House operations.[42] His chief of staff and national security adviser, Lewis "Scooter" Libby, was an assistant to Bush, as was political/communications adviser Mary Matalin. Addington worked closely with Bush's White House counsel, Alberto Gonzales, whom he often dominated with his greater experience, knowledge, and ideological commitment, especially after 9/11. Addington was often present when Gonzales considered important legal matters.[43] Cheney assembled a large team of national security advisers[44] who represented him at interdepartmental meetings,[45] where they would "flummox the process" to prevent initiatives they opposed.[46] Cheney's staffers were aggressive, able, and influential, the latter quality enhanced by Cheney's perceived clout.[47] Rice characterized Cheney's staff as "ultra-hawkish" and "determined to act as a power center of its own."[48] Libby was among the most powerful people in the administration and was a rare nonprincipal included at meetings of the NSC and its principals' and deputies' meetings. Addington became an architect of the legal strategies to support the war on terror. White House arrangements gave Cheney multiple chances to prevail—through staff interactions, at principals' sessions, or alone with Bush.[49] His views on pressing issues were forcefully and effectively presented and, especially during Bush's first term, often followed.

Yet Cheney's advice did not always prevail on matters important to him even during the first term. He would have been less conciliatory after an American reconnaissance plane collided with a Chinese plane.[50] He would have attacked Iraq sooner [51] and without asking Congress to authorize force and the United Nations for another resolution.[52] Cheney disagreed with Bush's decision to repudiate the suggestion in his State of the Union address that Iraq had tried to purchase uranium from Niger.[53] He opposed intervening in Liberia to address human rights violations in 2003.[54] During the 2004 campaign, Cheney thought same-sex marriage should be left to the states, whereas Bush endorsed a constitutional ban.[55]

After 9/11, Cheney sometimes worked at an "undisclosed location" such as Camp David or the Naval Observatory. Physical absence was an inconvenience although mitigated somewhat by Cheney's ability to participate in important meetings remotely by videoconference. When Cheney was away, Libby or Deputy Chief of Staff Dean McGrath represented him. That period was relatively short-lived, and more often than was revealed, Cheney and Bush were together in the West Wing.[56] Moreover, Cheney traveled less often than other recent vice presidents.

During the Bush-Cheney second term, Cheney's influence diminished significantly. Bush emphasized exporting democracy, not promoting American national security, as a foreign policy objective.[57] Bush nominated Harriet Miers for the Supreme Court over Cheney's opposition.[58] He replaced Cheney's friend Rumsfeld without seeking Cheney's input[59] and refused to pardon Libby after he was convicted on several charges of perjury and obstruction of justice, notwithstanding Cheney's strenuous lobbying for that relief.[60] Cheney was less influential regarding Iraq, and Bush took softer approaches to North Korea and Iran[61] and rejected Cheney's advice that the United States bomb Syria's nuclear reactor,[62] although he sided with Cheney in not deterring Israel from doing so.[63] Bush agreed with Rice over Cheney in calling for a cease-fire in Lebanon in 2006.[64] He rejected Cheney's advice that the administration ask Congress to strip the courts of jurisdiction regarding military commissions in response to an adverse Supreme Court decision.[65] Cheney declined to head a task force dealing with Hurricane Katrina's devastation of New Orleans and the Gulf Coast because he realized that the assignment was simply symbolic.[66] Cheney opposed Bush's decision to disclose and limit some CIA detention and interrogation procedures.[67] As president of the Senate, Cheney joined an amicus brief urging a stronger progun position than had the administration in a case before the Supreme Court, thereby prompting a rebuke from Chief of Staff Josh Bolten.[68] Cheney became "increasingly isolated" in the administration's senior ranks and often prefaced remarks by noting that others disagreed with him.[69]

Even with his influence diminished, Cheney remained a presence and a factor. He retained his access to Bush and his right to participate. At his insistence, the White House threatened to veto proposed legislation to ban torture in interrogations of terrorists.[70] Bush gave Cheney's ally John Bolton a recess appointment as UN ambassador and asked Cheney to search for Greenspan's replacement.[71] Cheney supported the Iraqi surge, although he was not its architect.[72]

EARLY OPERATIONAL ROLES

Bush relied heavily on Cheney in the early days of the administration. In response to California's energy crisis in early 2001, Bush named Cheney to head a task force on energy policy on January 29, 2001.[73] The assignment consumed less than 10 percent of Cheney's time during its four-month life[74] yet became controversial owing to the perception that energy producers had vast influence while environmentalists had little and to the secrecy surrounding its work. The energy policy, which Bush unveiled in May 2001, focused on expanding oil drilling, "clean" coal, use of natural gas, and nuclear power as well as conservation.[75] Cheney became the point person on the 2001 tax cut. On May 8, 2001, Bush announced that Cheney would oversee an effort to protect America from an attack involving weapons of mass destruction.[76] Cheney's office recommended steps to improve intelligence gathering and regarding responses to such an event.[77]

LEGISLATIVE OPERATOR

Cheney was an important conduit for communications, especially with Republican members of Congress. In addition to his Senate office, House leaders provided Cheney space,[78] an unprecedented recognition of his role and his former position on the House leadership ladder. Cheney generally attended the Senate Republican policy lunch, which allowed him to take the pulse of that body.[79]

Cheney set the early legislative tone of the Bush administration when he rejected the counsel of moderate Senate Republicans that the administration be open to compromise, insisting instead on pursuing its conservative platform notwithstanding the narrow 2000 election result.[80] His aggressive position ultimately played a role in the Republicans' loss of control of the Senate in May 2001, when James Jeffords left the party.[81] Cheney played a major role in negotiating the 2001 and 2003 tax cuts.[82] His intervention on the latter was critical after House and Senate Republicans stopped communicating.[83] Cheney lobbied key legislators to support the war against Iraq.[84] He briefed congressional leaders regarding the warrantless surveillance program.[85] He tried, unsuccessfully, to convince Senator John McCain of the merits of enhanced interrogation methods to deter his legislative response.[86] Cheney lobbied legislators to support Secretary of the Treasury Henry Paulson's plan to bail out the American economy in fall 2008.[87]

THE WAR AGAINST TERROR AND IRAQ

In the moments after two hijacked planes crashed into the World Trade Center as part of Al-Qaeda's terrorist attack on September 11, 2001, Cheney took operational command of the situation. As news of the attack spread, and with Bush in Florida, key White House figures congregated in Cheney's office until he was evacuated to the Presidential Emergency Operations Center amid fears of an attack on the White House.[88] Bush spoke to Cheney before addressing the nation that morning and thought it important to include in his short statement that "I have spoken to the Vice President."[89] Cheney spoke repeatedly with Bush, Rumsfeld, and others and worked to ground planes. Cheney urged Bush to deviate from his publicly announced plan to return to Washington due to security concerns.[90] Bush delayed his return but told the nation that "I've been in regular contact with the Vice President and other national security officials."[91]

At one point, Cheney ordered military planes to shoot down nonresponsive commercial planes. Bush and Cheney later claimed that Cheney's action implemented Bush's prior decision. None of that day's many records, official or not, documented such a conversation. After Cheney gave the order, Bolten urged Cheney to confirm it with Bush, which Cheney did without objecting that Bush had already agreed to that course. Many, including the 9/11 commission, questioned the Bush-Cheney explanation.[92] In any event, with Bush away and handicapped by poor communication, Cheney exercised some presidential prerogatives. When Bush returned to Washington that evening, he met with Cheney as part of the National Security Council, then with him as part of a smaller group, then with Cheney alone.[93] They lunched together the next day.

Cheney was an architect of policies related to the war on terror, including those regarding military commissions, enhanced interrogation, and warrantless surveillance,[94] and became their prime defender.[95] Following conversations with heads of intelligence agencies, Cheney encouraged development of a program to allow more intrusive electronic surveillance; Addington worked on the legal framework. The program required renewal every thirty to forty-five days based on recommendations from various officials, including the attorney general. Addington prepared the reauthorization orders and took them to each signatory.[96] In early 2004, the new head of the Office of Legal Counsel, Jack Goldsmith, rejected the legal reasoning supporting the program and persuaded his superiors to oppose reauthorization. Cheney and Addington negotiated unsuccessfully with the Department of Justice,[97] but Bush apparently was unaware of the problem until March 10, 2004, the day the program would end.[98] Bush reauthorized the program nonetheless, only to learn on March 12, 2004, that Deputy Attorney General James Comey and FBI director Robert Mueller planned to resign in protest.[99] Bush then instructed that the program be amended to accommodate their complaints and told his "advisers" he did not want "to be blind-sided like that again."[100]

Cheney's office was instrumental in developing policies for enhanced interrogation of suspected Al-Qaeda and Taliban detainees. Addington prepared an executive order holding the Geneva Convention inapplicable to Al-Qaeda detainees, which Cheney got Bush to sign in early February 2002. Cheney zealously defended that position in public statements and in conversations with congressmen.[101]

Cheney was a principal architect of the war on Iraq. In addition to advising Bush to instruct the Pentagon to prepare contingency plans for a war with Iraq,[102] Cheney pursued intelligence regarding Iraq's efforts to obtain nuclear weapons and the connections with terrorism,[103] often traveling to CIA headquarters to review raw data and confer with analysts. Some implied that Cheney's interest in connecting Iraq and Al-Qaeda was obsessive and led him to credit unreliable information[104] or that it pressured analysts to exceed evidence to find a connection.[105] Cheney worked on creating an Iraqi government in anticipation of the fall of Saddam Hussein.[106] He spoke publicly on the danger Iraq presented, at times getting in front of administration policy, most notably in August 2002, when he publicly disparaged sending weapons inspectors to Iraq while Bush was considering that approach.[107] The same speech stated that Iraq would obtain nuclear weapons soon, a prediction that was unsupported by available intelligence.[108] Later Cheney was charged with telling Prince Bandar bin Sultan, the powerful Saudi ambassador to the United States, that Bush had decided to attack Iraq.[109] Cheney remained a proponent of the war even as others lost faith. In December 2006, he insisted that Bush continue to speak in terms of victory and supported a surge of American troops.[110]

Cheney undertook less foreign travel than many other recent vice presidents.[111] His diplomatic work was generally substantive, often involving the war on terror or against Iraq or other significant matters. Other than a speech in Canada, he did not leave the United States until March 2002, when he made a ten-day trip to Britain and eleven Middle East countries to discuss a possible war in Iraq and the Israeli-Palestinian conflict.[112] Upon returning, Cheney appeared on Sunday political talk shows, where he reported that Arab leaders worried that Saddam Hussein would obtain weapons of mass destruction and pushed Palestinian leader Yasser Arafat to renounce terrorism.[113]

Cheney made several trips to Iraq and Afghanistan. He traveled to Iraq in December 2003 and in May 2007 for an unannounced visit at the beginning of a mission to the United Arab Emirates and Jordan. In December 2004, he conferred with Hamid Karzai while attending his inauguration in Afghanistan.[114] Cheney returned to Afghanistan several more times and to Pakistan[115] in February 2007 to warn of consequences if it did not more aggressively combat Al-Qaeda.[116] Cheney made several trips to Saudi Arabia, where he had long-standing relationships. Cheney returned to the Middle East in March 2008 to visit Oman, Saudi Arabia, Israel, the West Bank, Turkey, Iraq, and Afghanistan. The agenda included the wars in Afghanistan and Iraq, Iran's nuclear ambitions, and the Israeli-Palestinian conflict.[117] The Iraq stop allowed Cheney to trumpet recent successes there.[118]

Cheney traveled to Japan, China, and South Korea in April 2004 for talks regarding the North Korean nuclear threat[119] and to Australia and Japan in February 2007. He went to Lithuania, Croatia, and Kazakhstan in spring 2006 to meet with eastern European leaders at the Vilnius conference and deliver a speech criticizing Russia's treatment of its neighbors. Cheney minimized ceremonial travel but attended King Fahd's funeral in Saudi Arabia and ceremonies in Poland marking the sixtieth anniversary of the liberation of the Auschwitz concentration camp.[120]

SPOKESPERSON AND PARTISAN ACTIVITY

Although Cheney initially made few appearances in order to rebut suggestions of a Cheney-dominated administration,[121] he emerged to give major speeches outlining the administration's energy policy in spring and summer 2001[122] and became a spokesman for Bush's policies regarding the war on terror and in Iraq. Five days after 9/11, Cheney appeared on *Meet the Press* to discuss America's response. During that appearance he articulated the need to work "the dark side . . . in the shadows in the intelligence world," often "without any discussion, using sources and methods" available to intelligence agencies.[123] During the first half of the first term, Cheney did other lengthy interviews on high-profile shows, where he discussed the war on terror and Iraq. Cheney's role as a spokesman changed as his popularity declined. During the second term, his appearances largely focused on conservative media and institutional settings with less frequent interviews with general media until the end of his term, when he appeared more often. He vigorously defended the national security policies he had helped set in place regarding the war on terror and Iraq, including the use of waterboarding in the fight against terrorism.[124]

Cheney probably spent less time on political matters than other vice presidents, but his partisan engagement was striking. By August 2002, Cheney had already campaigned in thirty states for Republican candidates, had raised $12 million, and was scheduled to make two political trips per week during the midterm campaign.[125] In 2006, he appeared at at least 120 events, many for Republican congressional candidates, with victory rallies in Montana, Idaho, Colorado, and Wyoming during the last few days. Prior to the 2004 Republican convention, Cheney had raised $15.4 million at forty-five Bush-Cheney events and $5.6 million at fourteen national party events.[126] During the 2004 presidential campaign, he made political appearances on at least nine days in August, sixteen days in September, nineteen days in October, and the first days in November before the election.

OTHER ROLES
Cheney led a small group to consider prospective Supreme Court nominees.[127] It interviewed potential nominees at the Naval Observatory and made recommendations to Bush for the vacancies he filled. Cheney preferred Judge Michael Luttig over John Roberts as a more "dedicated conservative jurist," although Roberts was on the small list Cheney's group approved, as was Samuel Alito.[128] Cheney also chaired a five-person Budget Review Board to consider departmental appeals of OMB decisions of budget issues. The stature of those on the board deterred Cabinet secretaries from appealing adverse decisions to the president.[129]

CONCLUSION
Cheney's vice presidency was distinctive. He renounced presidential ambitions and spent less time than his predecessors on political activities. Unlike Bush, Quayle, and especially Gore, he avoided long-term line responsibilities. He did not engage in all issues Bush addressed but

was centrally involved in the defining issues of the Bush administration, especially those relating to national and homeland security, Iraq, and the economy, where he was an influential adviser who often acted in an operational fashion. During the first term, he was more powerful than his predecessors. For the first time, some analysts questioned whether the vice presidency was too powerful. His influence declined during the second term. Even so, as he prepared to leave office, Cheney said that he had "loved being Vice President. It's been a great job." Bush had kept his word that Cheney would be "a major part of his team," and Cheney had remained "actively engaged."[130]

Biden

The day after the 2008 election, Biden and his transition directors, Edward (Ted) Kaufman and Mark Gitenstein, met with Barack Obama and his top advisers to begin creating the new administration. During the next few months, they met to select personnel and consider major initiatives. Biden participated in interviews for key positions, and many whom he recommended were selected.[131] In January 2009, Biden went on a Senate trip to Iraq, Afghanistan, and Pakistan, which positioned him to advise regarding that region.

Biden retained the Mondale resources, including the West Wing office, weekly lunch, the right to attend Obama's meetings, and inclusion in the paper flow. Biden wanted to be the "last person in the room" to advise Obama and to retain flexibility to dedicate his time to its "highest and best use," an arrangement Obama accepted.[132]

Biden spent considerable time with Obama. When both were in Washington, Biden joined Obama's regular intelligence briefing and often attended Obama's meetings with Secretaries of State Hillary Clinton and John Kerry; of Defense Robert Gates, Leon Panetta, and Chuck Hagel; and of the Treasury Timothy Geithner and Jack Lew and occasionally with other Cabinet officials. He often participated in Obama's meetings with foreign leaders.[133]

Although Biden saved some advice for his private sessions with Obama, unlike some predecessors, he spoke freely in meetings of Obama advisers,[134] partly because Biden liked to be heard and Obama preferred that views be subject to discussion. Biden frequently stirred debate by raising questions and challenging assumptions. "The President likes to listen to argument and decide. It helps the President get to better decisions if the Vice President is stirring things up and he is hearing different points of view," said Ron Klain, Biden's first chief of staff.[135] Obama told Biden to express himself candidly and ask tough questions.[136] Biden also often was a harbinger of bad news. "People want to tell the President good news. That's human nature," Klain said. "The Vice President is willing to give him bad news."[137] Obama credited Biden with "truth-telling" notwithstanding the common institutional impediments to such candor.[138]

The Obama-Biden lunches were free-wheeling, two-way exchanges of information and opinions. Both principals raised matters for discussion. "The most important part of the lunch was just spending time together," said Bruce Reed, Biden's second chief of staff. "The President and Vice President are both always busy with their own itineraries, and it is important for their relationship to spend a little time alone together, no matter what they talk about."[139]

Biden played an important role in discussions regarding policy on Afghanistan. His preinauguration trip to Afghanistan, itself a significant symbol of his role in the administration, left him with doubts regarding the progress and objectives of America's war effort.[140] Whereas many of Obama's national security advisers favored sending additional troops to Afghanistan, Biden advocated a more limited role and pushed Obama's advisers to define strategic goals.[141] He argued that the war in Afghanistan lacked support in America[142] and strongly and repeatedly opposed the surge in troops that the Pentagon advocated.[143] Obama encouraged Biden to challenge arguments advanced by other national security advisers and said the vice president played "an enormously useful function."[144] Although Obama ultimately sent additional troops, Biden was credited with making certain that Obama heard discussions of a full range of options, helping define parameters of American policy and introducing political considerations into the discussion.[145] Although Biden questioned the administration's strategy, he defended it publicly while continuing discussions with Obama. Ultimately, Obama decided to withdraw 30,000 troops by summer 2012, consistent with Biden's counsel.[146]

Biden advised on the full range of issues. During deliberations regarding whether to attempt the U.S. Navy SEALs assault on the residence where Osama bin Laden was believed to be living, Biden pushed Obama's advisers to make definitive recommendations. Biden also emerged as an important presidential adviser regarding legislative matters ranging from the passage of the recovery act to the various budget and tax deals to the Strategic Arms Reduction Talks (START) treaty. Biden interviewed the finalists for the first Supreme Court vacancy and advised Obama on the appointment. During meetings on the bungled health care rollout, Biden was often tougher on the responsible officials than Obama in an effort to bring the program into operation.[147] In December 2013, after five years in office, Obama said Biden had been "at my side in every tough decision that I have made . . . you name it, he's been there."[148]

Biden assumed significant ongoing portfolios during Obama's first term on disengagement from Iraq, implementing the Recovery Act, and as chair of the Task Force on Middle Class Working Families. Each was a major administration undertaking, involved interdepartmental issues, and was time-limited. In contrast to Gore's continuing portfolios, Biden preferred assignments with a "sell-by date."[149]

In summer 2009, Obama asked Biden "to provide sustained, high level focus from the White House on Iraq."[150] Handling the disengagement from Iraq was a natural vice-presidential role because it involved diplomatic and military issues and required dealing with Iraqi politicians, a role better suited to Biden than the national security adviser. White House Chief of Staff Rahm Emanuel had suggested Biden for the responsibility, and others embraced the idea.[151]

Biden traveled to Iraq seven times during his first term, regularly spoke to a range of Iraqi leaders by phone, and conducted Cabinet meetings on Iraq. He retreated from that role during the second term, although he continued to interact frequently with Iraqi leaders.

Obama named Biden to oversee the implementation of the Recovery Act on February 23, 2009, a role many Democratic senators had proposed,[152] after Biden had submitted a memorandum describing the intricate managerial and political tasks involved. In a nationally televised address to Congress, Obama acknowledged the magnitude of the undertaking and said he had asked Biden "to lead a tough, unprecedented oversight effort" since "nobody messes with Joe."[153] Obama announced that Biden would work closely with his Cabinet and with governors and mayors to discharge the assignment.[154]

Implementing the Recovery Act involved coordinating the work of federal agencies and interacting with state and local officials. Assigning the job to the vice president made sense because of its magnitude and the skills and stature needed given the intergovernmental, interdepartmental, and political nature of the undertaking.

Biden called a Cabinet meeting every month or six weeks regarding recovery issues. Cabinet secretaries or their deputies typically attended. In the meetings he communicated information on best practices and focused on implementation, not policy. Biden encouraged discussion of problems, which he tried to resolve. During the first two years of implementing the Recovery Plan, Biden called nearly two dozen Recovery Act Cabinet meetings, had fifty-seven phone meetings with governors and mayors, and traveled to more than forty Recovery Act sites. Governors and mayors were asked to identify problems; Biden's staff was instructed to contact the official within twenty-four hours with a resolution or an approach to resolving it.[155] The Recovery Act was well implemented with a minimum of fraud and waste. *Time* credited Biden with having "set the tone" and having stopped 260 projects that "flunked his smell test."[156] Biden relinquished the role after two years in mid-February 2011.

Obama created the White House Task Force on Middle Class Working Families on January 30, 2009, with Biden as its chair and Biden's economic adviser, Jared Bernstein, as executive director.[157] Including eight Cabinet members and four high-ranking White House officials, it coordinated and amplified agency work regarding programs helpful to those in or aspiring to the middle class. The task force involved Biden in domestic initiatives including health care, making college affordable, job creation, retirement security, workplace safety, and work/family balance. By meeting regularly during Biden's first term, it allowed the administration to maintain focus on programmatic issues even when otherwise preoccupied with the economic and national security challenges. The task force provided an umbrella for much of Biden's domestic, nonpolitical travel during the first term.

Its inaugural meeting on February 27, 2009, in Philadelphia considered the impact of green technologies on middle-class jobs. Participants included six Cabinet officials, two high-level White House aides, and state and local officials. The following month, four Cabinet members and Senator Amy Klobuchar attended a task force town hall meeting in St. Cloud, Minnesota, on how the Recovery Act could help middle-class families. On April 17, 2009, the task force met in St. Louis regarding making college affordable. On May 26, 2009, in Denver, Biden called for the Council for Environmental Quality to report to the task force in ninety days on proposals for ways to expand opportunities through a green economy. On July 16, 2009, he led discussions on how health care reform would help older Americans in Alexandria, Virginia. On July 10, 2009, Biden and other officials held a roundtable discussion of rising costs of health care. On September 9, 2009, he held a meeting at Syracuse University on making college affordable. This partial list illustrates the range of Biden's activities under this umbrella.

Biden participated actively in legislative efforts. He often met with legislators or lobbied them as part of administration efforts, such as on the Affordable Care Act. At times, Obama gave Biden substantial responsibility for particular legislation, such as securing Senate passage of the Recovery Act or START treaty. For the former, Biden focused on a few Republican targets who he concluded might be amenable to supporting the measure. He repeatedly called his friend Senator Arlen Specter, by some accounts as many as fourteen times, as well as a half-dozen other Republican senators. Ultimately, three Republican senators agreed to support the measure.[158] Biden spoke repeatedly to Senators Kerry and Richard Lugar to plot strategy on the START treaty as well as to key senators such as Bob Corker and Johnny Isaakson[159] and had at least fifty contacts with senators to secure ratification of the treaty. Based on his conversations with a dozen Republican senators during the day or two before the vote, he persuaded dubious White House officials that the necessary two-thirds of the senators would vote for ratification.[160] During the summer of 2015, Biden was positioned to play a major role in persuading members of Congress to support the controversial agreement with Iran regarding its development of nuclear weapons.

Biden became the administration's principal negotiator on a series of critical legislative deals. In December 2010, he negotiated with Senate Minority Leader Mitch McConnell and Speaker of the House John Boehner to extend the Bush-era tax cuts in exchange for tax breaks for low- and middle-class taxpayers and other concessions.[161] The follow-ing summer, Biden again negotiated the deal to prevent the federal gov-ernment from defaulting on its obligations.[162] After others were unable to reach a resolution to avert a "fiscal cliff" crisis, Biden became engaged as the point person who negotiated an agreement with McConnell at the end of 2012.[163]

In addition to his travel to Iraq, Biden's other diplomatic missions were also deeply substantive. Less than three weeks into the first term, Biden outlined the administration's approach to foreign policy in a speech at the Munich Conference on Security Policy.[164] The trip al-lowed Biden to hold bilateral meetings with leaders of Russia, Ger-many, France, Great Britain, Poland, Ukraine, Georgia, and NATO. Biden made at least twenty-one trips abroad in the first term. He vis-ited Iraq, Russia, China, Japan, Israel, Afghanistan, Georgia, Ukraine, Egypt, Kenya, South Africa, Canada, Mexico, Chile, Costa Rica, Bel-gium, Spain, Italy, Bosnia and Herzegovina, Serbia, Kosovo, Finland, Moldova, Mongolia, Greece, Turkey, and Honduras. At the beginning of the second term, he returned to Germany, France, and the United Kingdom and later visited Italy, Brazil, Tobago, Trinidad, Columbia, India, Singapore, Panama, Mexico, China, Japan, and South Korea. Biden spoke at the Conference of the Americas in May 2013 to ar-ticulate the administration's approach to South America, a region he traveled to five times in the first five years and which was a continuing focus during the second term.

Biden also took an active role regarding Asian policy. On September 11, 2009, he hosted Wu Bangguo, chair of China's National People's Congress. In August 2011, Biden visited China as part of a nine-day trip that included stops in Mongolia and Japan. Biden was the guest of China's vice president Xi Jinping, who made a reciprocal visit to the United States. Xi Jinping was in line to become China's president, and the Obama administration thought Biden could develop a helpful rela-tionship with him. On July 19, 2013, Biden articulated the administra-tion's vision for its rebalance toward the Asia-Pacific region.[165] Biden thereafter traveled to India and Singapore in July 2013. In India, he conducted talks focused on economic relationships, energy and climate, and defense and regional cooperation. In Singapore, he addressed trade and security issues as well as maritime disputes in the South China and East China Seas[166] and met with Japanese prime minister Shinzo Abe.[167] He returned to China, Japan, and South Korea in late 2013 at a time of tension in the region owing to China's claims regarding the East China Sea.

Biden also became heavily involved in matters regarding Ukraine and other former republics of the USSR as well as Turkey, Cyprus, and other Balkan countries. He frequently spoke by phone to leaders of these and other countries.

Following the Newtown, Connecticut, tragedy in which twenty children and six faculty members were killed in a school shooting in December 2012, Obama charged Biden with leading an initiative to propose new gun-control measures.[168] Biden spearheaded an effort that included 22 meetings with 229 organizations[169] and spoke to 31 elected officials before presenting proposals to Obama at a White House meeting on January 14, 2013. Obama issued 23 executive orders that Biden's group proposed to reduce gun violence and called for legislation to eliminate loopholes, expand background checks, and ban small weapons.[170] Although legislation for background checks had majority support in the Senate, a largely Republican filibuster blocked a vote. As national legislation seemed remote, Biden disengaged from the role, which no longer constituted the "highest and best" use of his time.

Biden undertook a major campaign role for Democrats in 2010 and 2014 and for the ticket's reelection. The activity, of course, goes with the job, but Biden genuinely enjoyed campaigning, and Democrats wanted him in their districts and states because they perceived him to be effective. Biden campaigned for numerous Democratic candidates during both midterm elections.

Conclusion

Cheney and Biden both played consequential roles as White House vice presidents, yet they differed from each other and from their predecessors. Cheney's significance related largely to his influence as a presidential adviser and White House operator, especially regarding national security matters. He did not always prevail; no presidential adviser ever does. Yet by all accounts, Cheney was extremely influential, especially during Bush's first term. Cheney pushed for certain outcomes, and first-term administration policy generally followed directions he favored in areas of interest to him, especially regarding national security. He minimized foreign and political travel and avoided long-term line assignments, all of which allowed him to focus his energies on policy formulation.

Biden played an important role as an adviser, too. His contributions came in the advice he provided, although his value sometimes related to his ability to stir the debate to help expose all aspects of a problem for Obama. Whereas Cheney's legislative value came primarily from working with the Republican caucuses and conducting briefings on national security matters for bipartisan legislative leaders, Biden played a different and probably more important legislative role than did any of his predecessors. Unlike Gore and Cheney, Biden was trusted by members of Congress on both sides of the aisle. He frequently worked with legislators on a bipartisan basis. He worked with Democratic members of the Senate and House but also played a critical role in negotiating major legislation with opposing leaders that was unique in the history of the vice presidency.

Biden also was deeply engaged in foreign policy, as a foreign traveler and as someone who stayed in close touch with foreign leaders on a regular basis, especially regarding particular trouble spots such as Iraq, Ukraine, and Nigeria and areas of administration focus such as Latin America.

Biden managed three central efforts of Obama's first term—implementing the recovery plan, disengaging from Iraq, and the Task Force on Middle Class Working Families. As such, his approach fell somewhere between Mondale's aversion to line assignments and Gore's continuing embrace of many. Unlike Gore's portfolios, Biden's involved the principal issues facing the administration, were time-limited, and invariably involved interdepartmental matters.

Biden's presidential ambitions were less evident than those of Mondale, Bush, Quayle, and Gore, yet unlike Cheney, he did not issue an early Sherman statement. As had recent vice presidents other than Cheney, Biden engaged actively in political and other domestic travel, yet, unlike Bush and Gore, his second term was not consumed with seeking the presidency.

Each of Mondale's successors faced different challenges and responded differently. The contexts they encountered and their responsive behavior is the topic of the next chapter.

9

Determinants of Vice-Presidential Role: Bush to Biden and Beyond

Mondale's successors each performed as senior advisers and trouble-shooters, each retained the Mondale resources, and most assumed ongoing portfolios. These recurring activities and features reveal some contours of the White House vice presidency as it has developed over the past four decades and as it now exists. Continuities are readily apparent, and they suggest expectations and patterns of behavior associated with the office.

Yet the vice-presidential terms of Mondale's five successors, as described in chapters 7 and 8, also presented distinct variations. Each vice president entered the office Carter and Mondale had created, yet each vice presidency differed from Mondale's and from those of the other White House vice presidents. Institutionalization has not imposed uniformity; regularity has not brought rigidity.

The persistence of variety within the White House vice presidency is not surprising. Each vice president encountered a distinct context. Each vice president faced different opportunities and constraints; each had different interests, strengths, and weaknesses; and each served a president with different needs, styles, and desires. Not surprisingly, each vice president pursued a different mix of activities and functioned differently. The specific work and relative success of each vice presidency has turned on contextual factors and the way each president and vice president responded to them. Although the White House vice presidency has become institutionalized, circumstance and responsive choices shape behavior and success in office. Many of the same factors that contributed to Mondale's success have helped account for the influence of his successors. This chapter sketches the constraints faced by each of Mondale's successors and the way each responded to that context.

Bush

Bush entered office needing to establish credibility with Reagan and his inner circle. In addition to the inherent challenges of the relationship, Bush alone of recent vice presidents had competed against the president in a way that left scars. Ronald and Nancy Reagan harbored misgivings about Bush from the 1980 primary campaign.[1] Some Reaganites questioned Bush's commitment to Reagan's principles;[2] resented his confidant, James Baker, being Reagan's chief of staff; and feared that Bush associates would claim spoils of victory.[3] The administration included many Reagan conservatives, surrounding Bush with skeptical coworkers.

Reagan's leadership style also affected Bush's advising opportunities. Reagan believed in certain guiding principles while delegating much authority to White House staff and certain Cabinet members. This approach probably lessened Bush's ability to influence policy during private time with Reagan. Reagan spent less time in the West Wing than had other presidents, and Bush, perhaps accordingly, used his other spaces more than had Mondale.

Bush also entered office with advantages. He benefited from resources Carter and Mondale had created that Reagan agreed to continue. Although Reagan lacked Carter's zeal to elevate the vice presidency, he was predisposed to involve Bush because he "had always believed that Vice Presidents in our system of government were relegated to a kind of just standing and waiting position," which he considered "a waste of talent."[4] Reagan also gave associates the benefit of the doubt, so Bush's relations with Reagan began on a positive note.[5] In late autumn 1981, Reagan asked Barbara Bush if her husband was happy and insisted she tell him if ever he was not.[6]

Baker's presence as chief of staff during Reagan's first term also helped. He included Bush in meetings and helped him develop relationships,[7] for instance, sending Cabinet secretary Craig Fuller to brief Bush on departmental matters once or twice a month.[8] Baker placed Bush people in the administration and the Republican National Committee.

Bush succeeded, too, because of his presidential capabilities. Unlike Reagan, he had national security and foreign affairs experience. Whereas Haig undermined his own position by self-aggrandizing behavior and national security adviser Richard Allen had diminished rank compared to others who held that position before and after his tenure, Bush could handle significant diplomatic assignments and advise on national security matters. And he brought needed resources, including experience in the national executive and legislative branches, with the national party and relationships on Capitol Hill, and with Republicans who were not part of Reagan's constituency.[9]

Bush adopted a modest conception of his office. He gave priority to developing a relationship with Reagan based on reciprocal respect and trust. His guiding principles were to recognize the limitations of his office, remain loyal, not leak information, speak only on the record, and give Reagan advice based on his best judgment.[10] Shortly after their election, he wrote the Reagans pledging loyalty and support, stating his desire to help Reagan, and promising to abide by Reagan's decisions even when he disagreed with them.[11]

Bush worked to demonstrate his loyalty to, and develop rapport with, Reagan. He reserved policy comments for their private meetings,[12] which he kept confidential. He viewed his office as "a support mechanism to the president," an articulator, not formulator, of policy. Bush publicly supported Reagan's decisions, did not push his own agenda, and told his staff it could help him by helping Reagan. He brought jokes to his weekly lunches and seasoned memos to Reagan with light touches. One cable ended by describing Bush's experience sitting naked in a sauna with four Finnish strangers.[13] After meeting Gorbachev, Bush wrote that the "Gucci comrade" was not as well dressed as Reagan aide Michael Deaver, "but he beats the hell out of the Penney's basement look" of earlier Soviet leaders.[14] Humor was not their only bond. Upon hearing Reagan promise German leader Helmut Kohl that he would honor a commitment to visit a cemetery where some Nazis were buried, Bush wrote Reagan of his pride in Reagan and offered to take some of the "heat." Touched, Reagan taped Bush's note to his diary.[15] Bush shouldered unpleasant tasks such as negotiating Donald Regan's departure as chief of staff.[16] Reagan later said Bush had "been heart and soul in support of everything that we're trying to do, and I am convinced of his sincerity in supporting all of those measures."[17]

Ultimately, Reagan and Bush established a warm relationship.[18] Deaver thought Reagan saw Bush as the only person other than Nancy Reagan with whom he could talk confidentially and called their relationship "superb."[19] Anticipating the 1988 Republican presidential nomination battle, Reagan wrote that although he had always thought the party should choose the nominee, neutrality would be "tough" because his "heart" would favor Bush,[20] a preference Reagan implicitly conveyed to others.[21] When Bush told Reagan he would understand if Reagan helped his close friend Paul Laxalt in 1988, Reagan replied that he would "remain absolutely neutral."[22] Nancy Reagan did not share her husband's affection for Bush[23] but recognized Bush's influence with her husband and sometimes enlisted his help.[24]

Bush behaved in a circumspect manner. His conduct following the Reagan assassination attempt provided an early, conspicuous example and impressed Reagan's team.[25] Bush abstained when Weinberger, Edwin Meese, and Deaver pushed competing candidates to be secretary of the air force.[26] He admonished his first-term staff not to discuss a future Bush presidential race.[27] When the *New York Times* criticized Reagan, Bush called its publisher to complain. When Justice Thurgood Marshall called Reagan a racist, Bush contacted Marshall to attempt a meeting.[28]

Bush used his interpersonal skill to develop relationships with administration personnel. He tried to avoid confrontation with Haig by traveling to countries Haig had already visited or that were outside his interests. He cultivated Haig's successor, George Shultz, who could influence Bush's diplomatic work, by inviting him for lunch when he was named secretary of state and by supporting him against hard-line critics.[29] After a briefing by Ambassador Max Kampelman, Bush invited Kampelman to continue the conversation in his office.[30] Bush's greeting of Colin Powell on his first day as deputy national security adviser made Powell feel "like a bonus-baby rookie welcomed by one of the club owners."[31] After Reagan named Frank Carlucci as his national security adviser, Bush discussed Carlucci's new position with him. He later told Carlucci that Reagan was concerned with the number of personnel changes Carlucci was making and suggested he write Reagan about it.[32]

Bush structured his staff to minimize friction with Reagan's people. His first-term staff was not political or aggressive, but aides like Admiral Daniel Murphy and Donald Gregg were well connected in national security communities and interacted with Reagan's staff to keep Bush current and represent his views.[33] During the second term, Bush overhauled his staff in anticipation of a presidential race with politically savvy figures such as Craig Fuller who were well regarded in Reagan circles.

Although Bush deferred to Reagan's right to set administration policy, he found opportunities to influence Reagan through skillful hidden-hand advising. He used his diplomatic talent, interpersonal skill, and relationships to add strength in areas of administration weakness. Ever loyal, he won the respect of Reagan and his circle. As some Reagan loyalists moved on, Bush remained, with an ever-improving relationship with Reagan. That culminated, as chapter 14 will suggest, in Reagan's tacit support of Bush for the 1988 nomination and his effective work in helping Bush become the first sitting vice president to be elected president in 152 years.

Quayle

Quayle faced unique challenges among the White House vice presidents. After the Bush campaign bungled the rollout of his selection and Quayle experienced a rocky 1988 campaign, as chapter 12 recounts, he entered office amid lingering questions about his fitness to be president. His poor poll numbers at the outset made him a political liability.[34]

Although Quayle's primary interest was foreign and national security policy, his opportunities were constrained relative to those of recent vice presidents. Bush began his term with far more experience, relationships, and interest in foreign and national security policy than any other recent president and accordingly was less dependent on his vice president. The composition of Bush's national security team further inhibited Quayle's opportunities. Baker was Bush's close friend of thirty-five years, his past and future campaign manager, and a Quayle detractor. Other formidable figures—Scowcroft, Cheney, Powell, Lawrence Eagleburger, and Robert Gates—held major national security positions, reducing the value of Quayle's expertise. Quayle favored the Strategic Defense Initiative ("Star Wars"), which found little support in Bush's inner circle. Baker kept Quayle from traveling to some desired spots.[35]

Quayle, however, served a prior vice president who understood the second office, having spent eight years in it.[36] Bush was predisposed to model Quayle's role on his own vice presidency. He would "welcome [Quayle's] advice" and give Quayle assignments, but Quayle would be a "generalist," as he had been.[37] Bush understood the indignities associated with the job[38] and empathized with Quayle. He praised Quayle for doing "a first-class job" and being "superb" and complained he was "getting the most unfair rap from his critics of anybody that's been in this job." When reporters asked why comedians targeted Quayle, Bush emphasized that "it just goes with the territory" and praised Quayle's work.[39]

Quayle acted to rehabilitate his standing. He maintained tangible resources that Mondale and Bush had associated with the office, including regular presidential access. He assembled a highly competent, very conservative, and aggressive staff, including William Kristol, who soon became chief of staff; Spencer Abraham, later a U.S. senator from Michigan and secretary of energy; David McIntosh, later a representative from Indiana; Allan B. Hubbard, later director of the National Economic Council; and national security advisers Carnes Lord and Karl Jackson, among others. The Office of the Vice President became an enclave for Reaganites. Quayle rejected the advice of counselors that he undertake a speaking tour to restore his standing, preferring to concentrate on loyally serving Bush.[40] Finally, Quayle identified niches where he could contribute.

Quayle spent a lot of time on Capitol Hill, gathering information to aid his advising role and using his popularity and knowledge to become the go-to guy on legislative matters. He reached out to Democratic friends as well as Republican members. He was a regular emissary to conservatives, an important role given that faction's concerns regarding

Bush.[41] Quayle was also an astute political strategist. These three roles—legislative, conservative, and political—contributed to a White House somewhat lacking in those areas.

Whereas Bush had focused on demonstrating loyalty as vice president, Quayle needed to overcome perceptions regarding his qualifications. He tried to shape policy, even when sometimes advocating positions different from Bush's. In October 1989, he criticized the Soviet Union and Gorbachev while Baker was making conciliatory speeches. Quayle may have been out of step, or his remarks may have been designed to placate the Republican right,[42] a group important to Bush and Quayle.[43] Occasionally, Quayle went too far. In March 1991, Quayle said the United States should not have stopped fighting in Iraq when it did. "It doesn't help Quayle with me and it doesn't help him at all," an irritated Bush wrote.[44] Yet Bush also recognized that Quayle was extremely loyal to him, as demonstrated when Quayle vigorously defended to his conservative constituency Bush's decision to abandon his pledge not to raise taxes, even though Quayle had strenuously opposed that decision.

Quayle's appointment to head the Competitiveness Council served both Bush and Quayle. It allowed Bush to demonstrate commitment to issues of concern to Reaganites and permitted Quayle to develop a record on matters important to his base. Quayle avoided the perception that he was intruding on departmental turf by letting agencies take the lead, as he did when Solicitor General Kenneth Starr headed the legal reform effort while using Quayle's involvement to heighten its visibility.

Quayle worked well with Bush's principal chiefs of staff. He formed a natural alliance with fellow conservative Sununu, who frequently suggested Quayle for political assignments helpful to the vice president and encouraged his involvement in deliberations.[45] Samuel Skinner was also a Quayle friend; indeed, Quayle rebutted suggestions that conservatives might oppose Skinner as Sununu's successor.[46] Quayle tried to strengthen his relationship with Scowcroft by bringing in a national security adviser, Karl Jackson, with close ties to him.

Notwithstanding efforts to improve his public image to prepare for 1992 and beyond, Quayle was unable to overcome earlier perceptions. Bush's health problems in May 1991 resurrected questions about

Quayle's fitness to be president.[47] A year later, the "Potatoe" incident (when Quayle prompted a twelve-year-old to add an "e" to "potato" in a school spelling exercise) derailed Quayle's efforts to reestablish his identity. Quayle was relying on a cue card the teacher had provided,[48] but the episode reinforced unflattering perceptions. As Bush's ratings declined, some urged Bush to drop Quayle from the 1992 ticket. Quayle remained and performed ably during the campaign yet never overcame the image developed in 1988.

Quayle's ability to contribute was limited by his public image and the administration's strength in national security. Yet Quayle found important areas in which to add value. He was a valuable and insightful political and legislative adviser and operator who filled administration voids. He used his sense of Congress and relationships there and with conservatives to help Bush. Quayle preserved his standing with conservatives and the party base by his attention to those groups. He campaigned actively for Bush's nomination when the president was challenged from the right by Pat Buchanan. The Competitiveness Council incubated some domestic initiatives and helped Bush with conservatives. Quayle was more outspoken than Bush had been as vice president but remained loyal to the president. Although he did not make all of the foreign trips he would have liked, he contributed through travel to Latin America and Asia.

Gore

Whereas Quayle never overcame perceptions of him from the 1988 campaign, Gore began his service with a boost from the 1992 campaign. As chapter 12 recounts, Gore was an electoral asset, especially in joint appearances with Clinton where his presence emphasized admirable Clinton traits. Frequent campaign bus trips allowed Clinton and Gore, and their spouses, to develop relationships that carried forward into the administration. Gore also impressed many Clinton insiders. His chief aide, Roy Neel, developed rapport with Clinton personnel during the campaign.

Gore also faced challenges. First Lady Hillary Clinton also had a West Wing presence, and her status positioned her to have the last word with Clinton in a way that even the Mondale-legacy resources could not match. Media attention encouraged speculation that Gore would be a lesser player. Clinton's inclusive and unstructured management style[49] gave numerous aides access in large meetings, thereby reducing Gore's comparative advantage and pushing him to participate in large meetings as just another adviser, not a second principal. Unlike other recent vice presidents, Gore was not inclined to spend much time on the Hill, nor did he excel there.[50] Moreover, Clinton aides sometimes suspected that Gore's presidential ambitions colored his advice.

Clinton was, however, willing to create opportunities for Gore. He recognized Gore's talent and expertise and thought it "smart" to give Gore significant work.[51] After speaking with Mondale's chief aides,[52] Neel used Mondale's December 1976 memorandum as a model for the Clinton-Gore arrangement.[53] When Moe told Gore at a reception during the 1992–1993 transition of the importance to Mondale's success of Carter's two admonitions to his staff (treat vice-presidential requests as presidential requests, and do not badmouth the vice president), Gore took Moe to Clinton and prompted him to repeat the message to the president-elect.[54] The day after the Clinton-Gore inauguration, Clinton opened his Cabinet meeting by reaffirming Gore's role and telling the senior members of his administration to treat and respond to Gore as if he were Clinton and Gore's staff as if they were the president's aides.[55]

Gore brought presidential quality and talents that meshed with administration needs. Clinton credited Gore's experience in national government and in Congress with saving Clinton from numerous mistakes in their early years.[56] Gore's substantive strength in national security, the environment, and telecommunications supplemented Clinton's different expertise.

Clinton and Gore shared a common ideology and were personally compatible, at least until the last years of the administration, when Clinton's Lewinsky affair and their differences regarding Gore's 2000 candidacy strained their relationship. Both were intelligent Southern centrists of the baby-boom generation with a shared interest in public policy. Clinton "enjoyed immensely" discussing policy and politics with Gore,[57] whom he recognized as a significant asset. Although some degree of "brotherly rivalry"[58] colored the relationship, they recognized their common interests. Gore's different temperament also helped. Clinton's longtime friend and secretary of labor, Robert Reich, thought Gore "the perfect complement" to Clinton due to their differences. Gore was "methodical," "linear," and "cautious" where Clinton was "haphazard," "creative," and "impetuous." "The two men need one another, and sense it."[59] Gore sometimes pushed Clinton to conclude lengthy discussions with a decision. White House aides often looked to Gore to introduce organization and focus in administration operations.[60] Gore was able and willing to speak bluntly to Clinton.

During their first year, Gore seized opportunities to demonstrate his value. His knowledge of foreign policy allowed him to contribute, as an adviser and a spokesman, as Clinton initially focused on domestic problems. REGO was not Gore's preferred assignment, but he made it an enormous political asset. Gore's debate with Ross Perot in November 1993 boosted NAFTA's prospects and enhanced Gore's standing because NAFTA was a critical Clinton foreign policy goal.[61]

Any president would have found that the demands of the job in the 1990s far exceeded his available time, but Clinton probably felt that disparity acutely given his interest in policy, his tendency toward long meetings and broad accessibility, and an undisciplined policy process, especially during his first years in office. Clinton needed help, and Gore's performance demonstrated that he could provide it. Initially, Gore's vice presidency largely followed the Mondale model, but his weighty line assignments soon supplemented his advising function to give his vice presidency a very different look. In addition to the environment and telecommunications, Gore soon collected REGO and the Gore-Chernomyrdin Commission, each of which spawned other assignments. REGO made Gore a bureaucratic expert and a logical referee for other interdepartmental issues; the bilateral-commission model generated requests for imitation. Gore's personality may have disposed him to a more structured vice presidency, or he may have responded to Clinton's preference and circumstance. Gore soon found himself managing relations with Russia, Egypt, and South Africa as well as much of the former Soviet Union and handling a host of matters relating to the federal bureaucracy in addition to the environment and telecommunications.[62] Concurrently, Gore was advising Clinton across the board and campaigning actively for Democrats, for the Clinton-Gore reelection, and to position himself for the 2000 presidential election. It was a heavy load for anyone, and perhaps the burdens cost Gore time to reflect or to rest.

Clinton's and Gore's shared first-term interests made them natural partners as they considered together how to rescue the administration after the disastrous 1994 midterms,[63] a challenge that no doubt strengthened their bond. Gore's access to Clinton enabled him to withhold opinions in large meetings, thereby positioning himself as more like Clinton than a subordinate.

In addition to the significant portfolios and access, Clinton enhanced Gore's stature with speaking roles at joint events and frequent and effusive public praise. "I will never be able to convey publicly or privately the depth of gratitude I feel for the partnership that we have enjoyed," he said on one occasion. "I know that one of the most important factors [in the administration's success] was the unique and unprecedented relationship I have enjoyed with this fine, good man."[64] Gore's vice presidency would be "a model for future administrations of both parties, because it seems to me rather foolish to not make the most of the incredible potential that you now know the office of the Vice President has because of the way that Vice President Gore has filled it."[65] Gore, in turn, was loyal. Clinton aide John Hilley recalled that Gore would voice his views but then defend Clinton's programs, even those he knew would be unpopular in 2000.[66]

By their second inauguration, Clinton and Gore had shared two electoral successes and had established a strong working relationship. Whereas many longtime Clinton associates returned to private life, Gore remained, with enhanced stature, especially as heir apparent and given his role in constructing the second-term administration.

Gore's preoccupation with his own presidential run during the second term consumed a considerable portion of his time and introduced some divergence between Clinton's and his interests. Whereas Clinton would never again face voters and had only four years to seal his presidential legacy, Gore weighed how policies would impact Democratic primary voters in 2000. As heir apparent, Gore became a target of Republicans focused on 2000 and Democrats with presidential ambitions.

Gore's fund-raising activities for the 1996 reelection were widely attacked, causing his favorability rating to plummet, in one poll by 20
percent to only 29 percent in six weeks by mid-March 1997.[67] Although
Gore was exonerated of wrongdoing, the episode left a mark. After it
became clear that Gore would not be prosecuted, the Lewinsky scandal
broke in January 1998, constituting a cloud on Clinton's presidency. As
a presidential candidate, Gore felt compelled to emerge from Clinton's
shadow and to distance himself from Clinton's ethical lapses. He described Clinton's affair with Lewinsky as "inexcusable" and avoided the
White House for months.

Nonetheless, Gore made significant contributions as an adviser and
handler of consequential operational assignments. Clinton and Gore
were politically and personally compatible for most of the time; when
they separated, it was Gore who imposed the distance. They brought
the vice presidency to new levels of influence. Gore became a less-
important adviser as the second term wore on, in part because Clinton's
confidence grew, in part because Gore was often away focused on his
own campaign,[68] in part due to the rift that developed between them
owing to the Lewinsky affair. Gore was looking to governing in the
future, not in the present.

Cheney

Cheney began his term with more influence than any vice president before or since. Cheney himself,[69] some of his colleagues,[70] and academics[71] have attributed his power to his lack of presidential ambition. Since
he was not interested in seeking the presidency, the argument goes, his
only agenda was helping Bush achieve his objectives.[72] Cheney's advice
was not colored by calculations of how policies would impact his presidential candidacy but reflected his best judgment. Accordingly, Bush
and his associates had no reason to second-guess Cheney's motives or
to see him as a competitor. The administration avoided the "traditional
kind of splits"[73] between the presidential and vice-presidential offices.
Cheney's counsel thus became more credible, and normal tensions
between presidential and vice-presidential staffs were eliminated. Al-

though that unique situation probably played some role, its impact has been exaggerated.

Cheney's lack of presidential ambition removed one conflicting motivation from his calculus but did not necessarily commit him to Bush's agenda. Ideology or other influences could still have caused Cheney to pursue different policies or priorities than Bush. Presidential ambition is not fatal to vice-presidential power; other White House vice presidents have been influential and loyal without issuing Sherman statements. And one would have expected a vice president's lack of presidential ambition to elevate influence most during the second term because the president and vice president share a first-term interest in reelection, and the remoteness of a vice president's presidential run should cushion conflict in the early years. Yet Cheney's influence was significantly reduced during the second term, suggesting that other factors explained his early eminence and subsequent decline.

Cheney's lack of ambition contributed to his influence not so much by enhancing his credibility as by protecting his time and resources. He did not need to cultivate party activists around the country or spend time in Iowa and New Hampshire or elsewhere. He spent less time campaigning than other vice presidents, preserving more time for governing. He was around more. He allocated fewer staff positions to political work, reserving more slots for policy, especially regarding national security.

Other reasons largely explained Cheney's influence. He entered an office that had been an integral part of the White House for nearly a quarter century and had achieved enhanced visibility during Gore's service. Cheney was the beneficiary of the expectations and resources that accompanied his office. In addition to this favorable inherited context, Bush and Cheney generated other vice-presidential advantages.

Bush had thought extensively about the office[74] and wanted someone to help him govern. That inclination was consistent with his business background, which informed his leadership style. Bush was a manager and decision-maker who was comfortable setting a vision and priorities and relying on Cheney and others for implementation.[75] Bush had relatively little knowledge of many national and international issues at the outset of his term and was disposed to instinctive decision-making rather than immersion in detail. Someone with Cheney's expertise and orientation to detail provided a helpful counterbalance. Finally, Bush enjoyed the political aspects of his job. This disposition enhanced the value of a vice president who would mind the White House. Cheney's preference for behind-the-scenes governance roles complemented Bush's public orientation.[76]

Cheney was unique among White House vice presidents in entering office with an established relationship with the president, one developed and tested during the vice-presidential search and 2000–2001 transition. These roles provided test-drives of the Bush-Cheney operating relationship and gave Cheney credibility with Bush of a sort that other vice presidents needed to develop in office. They also communicated Cheney's standing, something Bush underscored by telling senators Cheney spoke for him.[77] Moreover, Cheney's transition role allowed him to place allies in important positions.

Cheney also was distinctive in his knowledge of, and experience in, the executive branch and the White House. He alone of the White House vice presidents had served in inner-circle administration positions. As Ford's deputy chief of staff and chief of staff and George H. W. Bush's secretary of defense, Cheney had observed the White House, the presidency, and the vice presidency at close range and knew how to operate and protect his position. Cheney had served in both political branches and, alone in the Bush White House, had been in Congress.[78] Cheney had long-standing relationships with influential figures in the administration, Congress, and elsewhere.

Cheney's role began large and expanded after 9/11 raised the value of a former defense secretary. Cheney's knowledge and credibility were huge administration assets, and during the first term, he exercised substantial influence over national security policy.[79] His close relationship with and access to Bush, his expertise on the subject, the reinforcement Rumsfeld and others gave his views, and the lack of rapport between Bush and Powell enhanced his role.[80] Bush and Cheney shared a similar worldview that made the president receptive to the vice president's advice.[81]

Cheney's staff enhanced his reach. Libby was among the most powerful people in the White House, with access to Bush as well as Cheney and inclusion at various levels of the NSC apparatus. Addington's influence with the White House counsel and Office of Legal Counsel helped establish legal rationales for responses to 9/11. Cheney's staff included numerous people with national security expertise, allowing it to make Cheney's presence felt over a full range of foreign and military matters.

Cheney's influence declined in the second term. There is more reason for confidence in that conclusion than in pinpointing a cause. Bush grew more confident as his knowledge increased and after winning reelection with a popular-vote majority. Bush surely realized that some Cheney judgments had been flawed. Iraqis had not greeted Americans as liberators, weapons of mass destruction never were found, American lives and treasure had been lost, and increasing public doubts about the war eroded Bush's standing. Bush must have recognized that Cheney's lack of political sensibility presented perils, especially after Cheney managed the reauthorization of the warrantless surveillance program in a way that almost produced a mass Department of Justice exodus in spring 2004.[82] Whereas Cheney's approval and favorability ratings exceeded 50 percent for much of the first term, they plummeted during the second term,[83] thereby lessening his utility as a spokesperson, except to the Republican base.

Two unusual second-term events hurt Cheney's standing. The criminal trial of Libby, Cheney's closest aide, embarrassed the administration. Cheney and Libby had attempted to rebut false reports that Cheney's office had orchestrated a CIA decision to send Ambassador Joe Wilson to Niger to investigate whether Saddam Hussein had sought to obtain uranium, as Bush had claimed. To discredit Wilson, Libby reportedly suggested to some journalists that Wilson's wife, Valerie Plame, a covert CIA employee, had had a role in sending Wilson. Federal law prohibited disclosing the identity of a covert official, making Libby potentially vulnerable. Libby denied revealing information about Plame's identity but was charged with perjury in late October 2005 and convicted in March 2007 after a trial embarrassing to the administration and Cheney.

On February 11, 2006, Cheney accidentally shot Harry Whittington while they were duck hunting together in Texas. Cheney did not issue a public statement about the incident or respond to calls from Bush's aides for hours. The next day Cheney's host disclosed the event to a local reporter. Cheney refused to speak to the press for days until Bush's and Cheney's staffs persuaded him to give an interview to a friendly reporter at Fox News.[84] As Cheney's popularity plummeted, he became more problem than solution.

Cheney's lack of presidential ambition had been seen as mitigating the competition that undermined some president–vice president relationships. Yet the perception that Cheney was running the government ultimately bothered Bush. Bush considered replacing Cheney in 2004 to show that he was in charge.[85] He described his lunches with Cheney as valuable to prepare Cheney to succeed,[86] which obviously was not their purpose. While interviewing Gates for the secretary of defense appointment, Bush volunteered that Cheney was "a voice, an important voice, but only one voice."[87]

Personnel changes also worked against Cheney. Whereas Powell never established a rapport with Bush, his successor, Rice, was personally and professionally closer to Bush than was Cheney. As the second-term secretary of state, she pushed for more-diplomatic approaches, and her access to, and relationship with, Bush trumped Cheney's. Libby's resignation on October 28, 2005, cost Cheney a highly effective and trusted associate.[88] Josh Bolten, who replaced Card as Bush's chief of staff in 2006, provided an effective counterweight to Cheney. Rumsfeld's departure in 2006 cost Cheney his closest senior ally; Gates was effective and frequently differed with Cheney.[89] Henry Paulson, the new secretary of the treasury, took control of economic policy and moved meetings from the White House, where it had been easy for Cheney to participate, to the Treasury. A new White House counsel, Fred Fielding, was able to withstand Addington more effectively than Gonzalez or Harriet Miers could.[90]

Cheney did not act to protect his public standing by engaging with media or in public appearances. He became a less-effective spokesperson and an easy mark for critics. He pursued unpopular policies that he could not effectively sell. When Martha Raddatz of ABC News commented that large majorities opposed further war in Iraq, Cheney, replied, "So?" And when Raddatz asked whether Cheney cared what Americans thought, Cheney cautioned against paying much attention to polls.[91] In January 2007, Senator John McCain was quoted as saying

Bush had "listened too much" to Cheney and had been "badly served" by him,[92] comments Cheney claims he later repudiated. Later that year, nearly all Republican presidential contenders publicly distanced themselves from Cheney.[93]

Cheney exercised enormous influence during Bush's first term. Bush's organizational style and personality made him receptive to an active vice president, and Cheney's credibility with Bush, experience, knowledge, skill, and reputation enhanced his position, especially after 9/11 brought Cheney's expertise to the fore. Ultimately, Cheney conducted himself more as a national security specialist than a political generalist. Rather than seeing the field as Bush did and offering insights from that perspective to help Bush think through the decisions facing him, Cheney increasingly became another pleader with an agenda to advance. When Cheney vigorously, but unsuccessfully, sought a presidential pardon for Libby, he was not trying to see the problem from Bush's perspective, much less pursuing the president's agenda. The Libby episode was, of course, distinctive because of Cheney's relationship, yet it illustrated the evolution of Cheney's position. As Cheney became less politically attuned and as his standing eroded, his usefulness diminished. Whereas most White House vice presidents saw their influence grow during their service, Cheney experienced the opposite trajectory in rather dramatic form.

Biden

Biden faced distinctive challenges, both from the political context and regarding his relationship with Obama. Whereas prior White House vice presidents had benefited from institutional turf their predecessors had won, Biden faced some erosion from perceived abuses during Cheney's vice presidency. Cheney critics had complained of an imperial vice presidency, a perception that prompted calls for institutional reform rather than simply viewing the Cheney vice presidency as anomalous. Whereas Libby had been assistant to the president as well as vice-presidential national security adviser, his Biden counterpart, Anthony Blinken, was relegated to deputy assistant status.

Biden was nineteen years older than Obama, who belonged to Biden's sons' generation. Biden had served thirty-two more years in the Senate and had chaired the Senate Foreign Relations Committee, where Obama had been a very junior member. Now their relationship was inverted. That circumstance had proved problematic for Kennedy and Johnson. Biden had been his own boss for thirty-six years and, as chair of two powerful Senate committees, was accustomed to leading. Now he was to follow Obama. Stylistically, the two men were quite different. Obama was cerebral, disciplined, and on message; Biden extroverted, spontaneous, and gaffe-prone. These Biden qualities seemed ill suited for the vice presidency; predecessors Mondale, Bush, Gore, and Cheney were known for their self-discipline. The differences caused stresses, and Biden's occasional campaign gaffes frustrated Obama.[94] Biden's advice was not invited regarding campaign strategy. Rather, he was given daily assignments by Obama's top staff.[95] Initially, Obama seemed less inclined than his recent predecessors to praise his vice president publicly to signal his importance.

Early on, Obama twice publicly displayed annoyance with Biden, first when Biden made a joke about Chief Justice Roberts bungling the presidential oath and then at a press conference when Obama expressed bewilderment about a Biden statement. Biden raised the subject with Obama at lunch, pointing out that such comments would undermine Biden's ability to contribute, and Obama apologized.[96]

Yet Biden brought strengths to the job. He had a clear vision of the vice presidency, influenced by discussions with Mondale and with Biden's first chief of staff, Ron Klain, who had served Gore in that position. Biden sought to emphasize the advising role while being open to a small number of time-limited portfolios, an intermediate approach between Mondale's and Gore's.

Biden also brought expertise, skill, and relationships in critical areas. He was a man of the Senate with a keen sense of where competing sides could find common ground. He had many friends in Congress, especially in the Senate, on both sides of the aisle. Hillary Clinton called Biden "a master Senate operator."[97] Biden also knew foreign policy and many world leaders. His understanding of politics and politicians and his interpersonal skills proved helpful in navigating life in the White

House and in dealing with other foreign and domestic political figures. Secretary of Defense Gates often disagreed with Biden and questioned his judgment but said Biden was "simply impossible not to like."[98] Other Republicans liked and praised Biden, a valuable credential in an increasingly partisan age.

Biden worked to demonstrate loyalty to Obama and his inner circle. During the 2008–2009 transition, Biden praised Obama publicly and emphasized his comfort working for Obama and that the ticket was in the right order. He tried to minimize his mistakes, and his associates worked to persuade Obama's staff that Biden's candor was an administration asset.

During policy discussions, Biden helped Obama obtain necessary information. He often challenged other advisers to elucidate policy options during debates on Afghanistan and the Osama bin Laden raid, playing a role Obama appreciated.[99] Biden was willing to play the "bad cop," for instance, in sessions to discuss the bungled rollout of the health care program.

Biden loyally defended Obama. When Representative Anthony Weiner attacked Obama during a meeting between Biden and House Democrats, Biden cut him off and declared that he would not listen to such talk.[100] In his acceptance speech at the 2012 Democratic convention, Biden lavishly praised Obama's courage in ordering the successful mission against bin Laden. On occasion, Biden illustrated Obama's wisdom by arguing that most of his advisers, including Biden, had counseled against the mission.[101]

Obama demonstrated confidence in Biden by giving him consequential portfolios, especially the Iraq disengagement and implementing the recovery plan. These two roles associated Biden with central international and domestic administration undertakings and gave him authority to convene Obama's national security and domestic advisers, respectively. Biden's troubleshooting was equally consequential. He became the administration's point person for crucial negotiations over tax or budget policy, where he was able to broker compromises because Obama and congressional Republicans trusted him and he was able to see the area in which a compromise might occur. Such assignments communicated Biden's significance and gave him opportunities to prove his value.

Biden was helped by friends in other key positions. Tom Donilon, the deputy and later national security adviser, was a longtime Biden associate whose wife and brother worked for Dr. Jill Biden and the vice president, respectively. Biden had good relationships with key Obama aides, including Emmanuel, William Daley, and David Axelrod. Biden and Hillary Clinton, an old friend, breakfasted weekly at the Naval Observatory for "frank and confidential conversations."[102] Second-term officials such as John Kerry and Chuck Hagel were also friends.

Biden's staff was deeply involved in White House operations. Its members often assumed responsibility for presidential programs as Obama and Biden integrated their operations. "If the best person to do something is in the OVP, they should do it. Same thing for the vice president. He should be staffed by a presidential person,"[103] said Klain. Thus, Cynthia Hogan, who had handled several Supreme Court confirmations as Biden's counsel in the Senate Judiciary Committee, took responsibility for the confirmation of Sonia Sotomayor. Biden people moved to positions on Obama's staff. Klain was influential and managed Obama's debate preparations in 2012 and served as Ebola czar in 2014. Jay Carney, Biden's original press secretary, became Obama's press secretary. Bruce Reed, Biden's second chief of staff, was a key figure in the 2011 budget negotiations, which consumed much time, as did supervising policy development for Obama's 2012 State of the Union address. Blinken, Biden's original national security adviser, became Obama's deputy national security adviser and then undersecretary of state during the second term. Blinken and Jake Sullivan, Biden's national security adviser at the beginning of the second term, played important roles in negotiations with Iran.

Ultimately, Obama and Biden grew to like each other. Each appreciated the skills the other had. Obama valued Biden's loyalty and political sense. Biden recognized that Obama had kept their agreement regarding Biden's role and access.[104] Some White House staffers were upset when Biden supported same-sex marriage before Obama took that position, but Obama was forgiving and instructed his staff to stop criticizing Biden.[105] Obama and Biden forged a strong relationship, which Emanuel referred to as their "deep bond of trust."[106] The depth of that relationship was suggested during the funeral for Biden's son, former

Delaware attorney general Beau Biden, in June 2015, when Obama de-livered a principal eulogy in which he declared himself "a Biden."[107]

Although Obama's chief of staff ordered polling to determine whether Hillary Clinton would be a stronger running mate than Biden in 2012, there is no evidence that Obama ever considered replacing Biden. In-stead, Biden played an important role in the 2012 campaign. His per-formance in the vice-presidential debate helped stop the ticket's decline after Obama's disastrous first debate.

Obama's second-term administration looked quite different from his first. Whereas some Cabinet and White House positions turned over, Biden remained in place. Unlike Cheney, he preserved a presidential campaign as an option, yet, unlike Bush and Gore, he was not an heir apparent given Hillary Clinton's early dominance of the field. Whereas Biden's first term had featured some long-standing line assignments, Biden more closely followed the Mondale model during the second term. He served as a general adviser to the president and a troubleshooter who worked on a range of important foreign and domestic problems as they arose and remained politically engaged.

Conclusion

Mondale's five successors each benefited from the inherited expecta-tions and resources of the White House vice presidency. Those features became more entrenched with each occupant, providing a structure through which vice presidents could contribute as advisers and in oper-ational roles. Each so contributed.

The presidents under whom they served all faced complex challenges and saw the virtue of a robust vice-presidential role. Some, such as George W. Bush, had thought a lot about the job and had integrated it into their leadership approach. Others, such as Reagan, were predisposed to some vice-presidential role or, in the case of George H. W. Bush, had experi-enced it. All were certainly open to it. Once in office, they recognized that they needed high-level help and welcomed vice-presidential involvement.

Each vice president needed to establish and maintain a compatible relationship with the president, to respond to the context presented him, and to demonstrate that he could add value. All recognized the importance of building relationships with the president and his inner circle, and each succeeded, at least most of the time. Some, such as Bush, Quayle, and Biden, were extroverts, skilled in interpersonal relationships. They seemed to sustain, and even improve, their relationships with their presidents during their terms. Gore shared some common experiences with Clinton, and he and Cheney had attributes their presidents lacked but apparently appreciated, although in each case the relationships diminished during the second term. All vice presidents recognized the importance of demonstrating loyalty, respecting confidences, and deferring to the president even while giving him candid advice.

Such a relationship also depends on political compatibility. Each vice president was comfortable with the general direction of the administration. George H. W. Bush was less conservative than Reagan or Quayle, but the differences were manageable. Gore, Cheney, and Biden did not always agree with their presidents but almost always accepted their decisions. That Bush and Cheney diverged more often during the second term contributed to Cheney's reduced role.

Defining a role depended on the vice presidents showing they added value. George W. Bush began with an appreciation of Cheney's abilities and his likely role, although he could not have anticipated that 9/11 would make security the preoccupation it became. Over time, he saw that Cheney had weaknesses that made Bush less deferential to his advice. The others saw their roles expand as they increasingly showed that they added value. The emphasis of their work, advising and operational, varied, but each found niches where they deployed their talents to serve administration needs. Needs provided opportunities but often arose in unanticipated areas, making flexibility a vice-presidential virtue.

Flexibility was critical, too, because context changes. The vice presidents had to adjust to the demands of the political calendar, personnel moves, and other changed circumstances, including the presidents' development and different attitudes. Second vice-presidential terms were different from the first four years. Bush did a better job than Gore or Cheney of adjusting to the latter differences, although his adverse circumstance (the Iran-contra scandal) presented different challenges from those Gore or Cheney faced.

Vice-presidential success also depended on protecting political capital. Most vice presidents recognized that their ability to contribute was affected by their public approval and relationships and worked hard to preserve them. Quayle's relatively low favorability ratings hurt him, but he retained the respect of the Republican base and conservatives where George H. W. Bush had needed help. Cheney's indifference to his standing impaired his influence.

Ultimately, vice-presidential success depended on a range of factors. Mondale's successors began with structural advantages provided by the White House vice presidency. How each exploited those advantages and preserved his position depended on each president's continued commitment to the vice-presidential role and each vice president's ability to understand and respond to the challenges of the context he encountered.

10

The Vice-Presidential
Selection Process

Vice-presidential selection has changed dramatically due largely to innovations of 1976. The modern process bears little resemblance to 1952–1972 and even less to prior practice. Decision-making that formerly consumed less than a day, had little structure, and received scant public attention now stretches for months, involves recurring features, and is a media spectacle. The manner of choosing running mates continues to evolve, as some aspects originated after 1976 and each selection varies somewhat. Vice-presidential selection now (1) allows more investigation of options under conditions more conducive to deliberate choice; (2) shifts control further from party leaders toward presidential nominees; (3) focuses attention on the vice presidency for a longer period; and (4) furnishes greater incentive to choose a running mate who is a plausible president.

The new process and the White House vice presidency reinforce each other. The process focuses attention on the office. It identifies the presidential candidate more closely with the person chosen and increases the likelihood that vice-presidential candidates will be very able and become an integral part of the administration. In turn, the White House vice presidency has added importance to the process, encouraged able people to participate, and given presidential candidates more reason to choose wisely.

The dynamic that has reshaped the selection process resembles that which transformed vice-presidential work. In 1976, Carter, and to a lesser extent Ford, introduced new practices in vice-presidential selection. Some innovations were later modified to address defects revealed by experience. Others were developed or expanded. Many became institutionalized through repetition in later cycles.

Although the process has become institutionalized, three features lend variety to each choice. First, the process is dynamic as candidates remedy problems of prior selections while imitating successful features. Campaigns have expanded vetting to include new subjects, have adjusted the timing of selection to maximize impact, and have managed the process to produce more favorable perceptions. Second, each process occurs in a unique context that may encourage distinctive behavior. Finally, the idiosyncrasies of each presidential candidate and his associates introduce different values, perspectives, and characteristics.

The refinements of the process reduce, but do not eliminate, the possibility of mistakes. Human beings collect, consider, and act on the information. Context narrows options and often complicates the decision. Although the current process improves on past models, it remains subject to error, especially in challenging environments. There are no guarantees.

The Prior System

Before 1976, vice-presidential selection occurred almost entirely at the convention. Presidential candidates typically secured nomination near the convention's end. Prior to 1940, they had little role in running-mate selection. Thereafter, most addressed that subject only after their success was assured. Amid celebrations, a tired candidate hurriedly considered options. The decision was typically announced on the convention's final day so delegates could approve the choice and hear the acceptance speeches.[1] In assessing vice-presidential selection from 1952 to 1972, William G. Mayer concluded that "there was no vice presidential selection *process.* There was simply a decision that had to be made."[2]

That pattern changed in 1976. McGovern's haphazard process, Agnew's election twice despite criminal activity, and the extensive scrutiny of Ford and Rockefeller under the Twenty-Fifth Amendment in 1973 and 1974 suggested that more intrusive vetting was appropriate. These events stimulated reform efforts, some of which proposed varying the convention calendar or deferring the vice-presidential selection to allow presidential candidates more time to consider the choice.[3] Although not then apparent, events had rendered such proposals obsolete. The growth of primaries and caucuses made preconvention resolution of presidential nominations likely.[4] Since 1976, every presidential nomination but one has been determined well before the convention.

The Carter, Ford, and Reagan Selections of 1976: A Study in Contrasts

Three major candidates chose running mates in 1976, and they illustrated old and new patterns. In designating Senator Richard Schweiker, Reagan followed the relatively obsolete strategy of using the second spot to entice delegate support for the presidential nomination. Ford's selection blended old and new; like Carter, he vetted possibilities, but he deferred deliberation to the convention's end after securing the nomination. Carter introduced a new model.

FORD'S SELECTION: VETTING WHILE COMPETING

Unlike previous examples between 1976 and 2012, Ford's selection process was the only time an incumbent president chose a new running mate,[5] was not his first presidential decision, and followed the only presidential nomination resolved at the convention. Ford initiated a selection process while competing with Reagan. He charged Edward C. Schmults, deputy White House counsel, with conducting background checks on prospective nominees.[6] Ford's associates prepared a questionnaire based on inquiries directed to prospective presidential appointees. Each potential candidate agreed to provide Ford, and, if selected, to make public, financial statements, tax returns for the previous ten years, and a physician's report. In addition, they were asked for basic biographical and family information and about past residences, organizational memberships, foreign countries visited, employment history, litigation, arrests, and mental health, among other topics. Open-ended questions were designed to discover controversial utterances and information that could be a "possible source of embarrassment" to the prospective candidate or to Ford.[7] Candidates were promised that only Ford, Cheney, White House counsel Phil Buchen, and Schmults would review the material, which would be returned (except that regarding Ford's designee). The vetting was performed in roughly the two weeks before selection.

Ford asked delegates and alternates to send him at least five ranked choices.[8] Senator Barry Goldwater wrote that without John Connally on the ticket, victory was "practically impossible."[9] White House aide Robert Hartmann favored Rockefeller,[10] as did Ford's friend, former Secretary of Defense Melvin Laird.[11] William Casey thought Secretary of the Treasury William Simon could help "on the pocketbook issues"; with Catholic, ethnic, and Reagan voters; and with those opposed to "Nixon-Kissinger style detente."[12] Businessman Robert O. Anderson favored Anne Armstrong.[13] Senator Charles Percy provided five preferences but offered to discuss a Ford-Percy ticket confidentially.[14]

REAGAN'S SCHWEIKER GAMBIT

About three weeks before the convention Reagan, a conservative hero, made the shocking selection of Schweiker, a liberal Republican. Reagan's campaign was stalled.[15] Reagan and Schweiker had a positive meeting,[16] and Reagan hoped the move would attract delegates by demonstrating his receptivity to a range of views and by constructing an attractive ticket for the general election campaign. Reagan's gambit backfired and gave some conservative delegates reason or excuse to back Ford.[17]

Reagan also proposed Resolution 16(c) to require all candidates (i.e., Ford) to designate a running mate before the presidential balloting. Reagan hoped disclosure of Ford's choice would alienate some delegates who favored another or were offended by the selection.[18] Resolution 16(c) lost, 1,180 to 1,069, and Ford was nominated by virtually the same vote.

FORD'S EARLY-MORNING SELECTION

Ford was "tired and wanted to go to bed" after winning the nomination, but he needed to choose a running mate. Ford met with Reagan around 1:00 a.m. on the convention's final day and solicited his view on six options—Simon, Connally, Robert Dole, Howard Baker, Elliot

Richardson, and William Ruckelshaus. Reagan replied positively about Dole.[19] Ford had agreed not to ask Reagan to join his ticket, a condition Reagan's camp had imposed.[20] Ford also did not want Reagan as his running mate. Years later Reagan said he would have accepted had Ford asked him to be his running mate.[21]

After his session with Reagan, Ford held a lengthy meeting that ultimately included Rockefeller, Senators Robert Griffin and John Tower, Melvin Laird, John Marsh, Hartmann, Bryce Harlow, Cheney, Stuart Spencer, and Robert Teeter. Ford had previously reviewed the vetting information. The group considered the names given Reagan plus Armstrong and a few others. The choice narrowed to Armstrong, Baker, Dole, and Ruckelshaus. Some pushed Ruckelshaus, a midwesterner with a positive public image; others thought he lacked the credentials. Ford seriously considered Armstrong as a historic choice who might help him overcome his huge deficit in the polls. The meeting adjourned around 5:00 a.m. without a decision. Some Ford advisers feared an effort to draft Reagan for the second spot or that a floor fight would ensue if Ford chose Ruckelshaus or someone perceived as liberal.[22] The group reconvened at 9:20 a.m. and reached consensus on Ford's choice, Dole.[23]

CARTER AND THE NEW SELECTION PARADIGM

Carter's quite different vice-presidential selection process was discussed in chapter 3 and will be simply sketched to highlight contrasts. Since Carter clinched the nomination five weeks before the convention began, he was better positioned than Ford to create a new selection process. His nomination secured, he commenced the most elaborate vice-presidential selection process to that time with the following features: (1) Carter's closest confidante, Charles Kirbo, headed the process, signaling its importance; (2) Carter and Kirbo solicited advice from party luminaries; (3) Carter created a short list of seven; (4) Kirbo gave the short listers a questionnaire seeking personal, financial, medical, and other information, and he and others then investigated the finalists; (5) Carter met individually with the seven; (6) those interviews were publicly announced and followed by a press conference. Although Carter did not finalize his decision until the last day of the convention, his public process lasted for five weeks. The process helped establish Carter as the party's leader, exhibited him as a decision-maker, publicized those Carter was considering, and projected transparency.

LEGACIES OF 1976

Nineteen seventy-six was a watershed in vice-presidential selection. Ford and especially Carter introduced preselection vetting, a practice not dependent on, but certainly helped by, the early resolution of the presidential contest. Once the presidential nomination was determined, the vice-presidential choice became the premier story. This change raised the visibility of the vice-presidential selection and made the presidential nominee's role more conspicuous, thereby increasing the stakes of an improvident process or choice. Early resolution allowed presidential candidates to choose from a larger pool. Time allowed tensions from the nominating contest to subside, thereby encouraging a more rational assessment of options. Unsuccessful presidential candidates and their supporters could recalibrate their ambitions. Presidential candidates became more dominant as vice-presidential consultations took place outside the convention in a context the nominee controlled. The early resolution also allowed preconvention selection, a topic discussed in chapter 12.

The New Process in Action

The new vice-presidential selection process involves several tasks. These include identifying prospective candidates, collecting and analyzing information about them, and deciding on a nominee.

LEADERSHIP

Following Carter's and Ford's examples, presidential candidates typically establish a structure for vice-presidential selection before or once they have secured the nomination. They usually designate either a close associate, often without independent standing in the party;[24] an experienced party insider;[25] or a committee[26] to conduct the search or at least the vetting. Some search leaders helped identify prospective candidates, conducted or oversaw the vetting, and influenced the decision. Kirbo, John Reilly (1984), Paul Brountas (1988), Warren Christopher (1992 and 2000), Cheney (2000), James Johnson (2004), and Beth Myers (2012) were among those who met with party luminaries to solicit suggestions and information and participated in the ultimate decision-making. Republican designees (except Cheney and Myers) have generally investigated prospective running mates but not built the pool or made political judgments. In recent cycles, Christopher and Johnson brought in Washington lawyer James Hamilton to head or cohead the vetting.

BEGINNING THE PROCESS

The vice-presidential selection process must begin early enough to allow full investigation and consideration of alternatives yet produce a choice responsive to the context of the fall campaign. Circumstances change, so judgments that seem compelling in the spring may lose their logic by July or August.

Like Carter, most candidates begin their process shortly after clinching the nomination, but variation exists. Gore and Christopher prepared a list of about twenty-five possible running mates and a longer list of people to consult in February 2000.[27] John Kerry met with Johnson to discuss the process on March 3, 2004, after his Super Tuesday victories and John Edwards's withdrawal.[28] Whereas Clinton engaged Christopher in 1992 to head his vice-presidential search in the early spring even *before* securing the nomination,[29] George H. W. Bush waited until late July 1988, about three weeks before the convention, to contact prospective running mates.

There is reason to defer the process while competing for the presidential nomination. The selection process requires concentrated attention from the candidate and generally from his closest advisers. Accumulating delegate support preoccupies the campaign hierarchy. A presidential candidate cannot identify all vice-presidential options or obtain all information from them until the presidential nomination is resolved. Finally, delaying the decision may allow the political context of the fall campaign to crystallize.

Still, some preliminary work can occur such as thinking about criteria; deciding on a structure for, and identifying leaders of, the process;

constructing a long list; beginning profiles on prospective candidates from public information; and establishing guiding principles.

FORMING THE POOL

The Long List

Presidential candidates generally form their pool of potential running mates from an internally constructed list and outreach efforts. Brountas visited 50 congressional leaders beginning in mid-June 1988 and solicited suggestions from 200 other people.[30] He interviewed dozens to determine their interest in being Michael Dukakis's running mate and to obtain recommendations.[31] Kerry spoke with Democratic leaders, including senators and members of the House of Representatives.[32] Outreach efforts help make the process inclusive and provide information. Six of the last fourteen major party presidential nominees were governors who often considered members of Congress they did not know well.

The initial long list routinely draws from current and recent office holders and some outside-the-box ideas. Clinton's 1992 "eclectic" list of thirty-eight possibilities included journalist Bill Moyers and Apple Computer executive John Sculley.[33] In April 1996, Dole gave Robert Ellsworth twenty-five names to consider against a preferred profile. The list included some Republican luminaries such as James Baker, Cheney, and Rumsfeld; some eventual short-listers such as John Engler and Connie Mack; some unconventional choices such as businessman Norman Augustine, Justice Antonin Scalia, and General Norman Schwarzkopf; and some rising stars such as George W. Bush and John McCain. It included five women, one African American (Powell), and a Democrat (Sam Nunn) but not the eventual selectee, Jack Kemp.[34]

Conversely, George H. W. Bush began his process in late July 1988, about three weeks before the 1988 Republican Convention, when he contacted more than a dozen prospective running mates to gauge their interest. Those called included two primary rivals (Dole and Jack Kemp), two women (Senator Nancy Kassebaum and former secretary of transportation Elizabeth Dole), five governors (James R. Thompson, John Sununu, Thomas Kean, George Deukmejian, and Caroll A. Campbell, Jr.), two former governors (Lamar Alexander and Richard Thornburgh), and five senators (John Danforth, Pete Domenici, William Armstrong, Alan Simpson, and Quayle).[35]

Campaigns typically prepare reports on those on the long list from publicly available information as well as from any outreach efforts. This work is often performed by volunteer lawyers associated with the political party. The reports often reveal reasons why some on the longer list would be an unsuitable running mate. Clinton initially instructed Christopher to give priority to fifteen of the names on his list:[36] six senators (Gore, Bill Bradley, Bob Graham, John Kerry, Nunn, and Jay Rockefeller); four current or past governors (Ann Richards, Barbara Roberts, Roy Romer, and Bruce Babbitt); Representative Lee Hamilton; Mayor Maynard Jackson of Atlanta, Georgia; Moyers; Sculley; and Powell.[37] On May 11, 1992, Christopher began interviews to obtain advice, ascertain interest in being selected, and assess interviewees. Some—Bradley, Powell, and Rockefeller—declined to be considered.[38] Christopher reported to Clinton on the fifteen top candidates on May 26, 1992, while Clinton campaigned for the Ohio primary; a week later, Christopher delivered profiles of the other candidates and discussed other prospective interviewees. Five days later, Clinton directed Christopher to focus on Gore, New York governor Mario Cuomo, Hamilton, Senator Harris Wofford of Pennsylvania, and former senator Paul Tsongas. After Cuomo and Tsongas withdrew, Clinton added Senator Bob Kerrey (Nebraska) and Graham (Florida) to his list.

On April 1, 2012, Mitt Romney reduced a list of two dozen to eleven options. These consisted of senators or former senators Kelly Ayotte, John Coryn, Bill Frist, Rob Portman, and Mario Rubio; Representative Paul Ryan; and governors or former governors Chris Christie, Mitch Daniels, Mike Huckabee, Bob McDonnell, and Tim Pawlenty. After considering write-ups on these eleven options a month later, he settled on a short list of five.[39]

Presidential candidates with a reasonable chance generally find many prominent figures interested in being on the ticket. The increased stature of the office, its involvement in White House decision-making, and its value as a political springboard enhance its appeal. Many formidable figures who have forgone a presidential race have made themselves available to be the running mate, including Mondale and Edmund Muskie (1976),

Lloyd Bentsen (1988), Gore (1992), Kemp (1996), Cheney (2000), and Paul Ryan and Chris Christie (2012). Whereas a presidential race requires years of nonstop campaigning and fund-raising and winters in Iowa and New Hampshire, a vice-presidential campaign is a two- or three-month, high-profile sprint.

Nonetheless, some seemingly attractive candidates remove themselves from consideration. Some are deterred by the nature and risks of modern campaigning, the lifestyle consequences, the vetting process, or a ticket's poor prospects. Mondale's 1984 process might have looked different if Cuomo, Nunn, and Senator Dale Bumpers had agreed to be considered.[40] Yet those candidates also withdrew in years when prospects seemed brighter. In 1988, Bradley, Nunn, and Representative Thomas Foley disclaimed interest in joining Dukakis's ticket.[41] Bradley, Jay Rockefeller, Tsongas, and Cuomo declined to be considered in 1992.[42] William Bennett removed himself in 1996. Senator Connie Mack, the 1996 runner-up, refused to be considered in 2000, as did Powell and McCain.[43] Cross-party running mates (Powell, 1992, and McCain, 2004) generally are unavailable (although Joe Lieberman was willing to join McCain's ticket in 2008), as are former presidents (Ford, 1980) and presidential candidates (Gore, 2008).

The long list sometimes omits the ultimate choice. Kemp was not on Dole's long list; Palin was a very late addition to McCain's list; and Cheney was not among those vetted, although apparently in Bush's mind.

Constructing the Short List

Presidential candidates usually narrow their list to three to six finalists, a group that generally supplies the nominee. The outside-the-box ideas generally do not make it into the box from which the running mate is drawn.

Some candidates populate their short list with those with some essential quality they seek in a running mate. For instance, many governors have included mostly, or only, Washington insiders. Other presidential candidates have preserved options with more eclectic lists. Ford's final four included one woman (Armstrong), two senators (Dole and Baker), and one former office holder (Ruckelshaus). Armstrong and Baker were from the South or Southwest, Dole and Ruckelshaus from farm states. Bush in 1988 narrowed his list to Quayle, Bob or Elizabeth Dole, Kemp, Peter Dominici, and Alan Simpson. All were Washingtonians, but they presented an assortment of possibilities. Kemp and Quayle were from the Reagan wing of the party, Elizabeth Dole was a woman, Quayle a baby boomer. Those on Clinton's short list—Gore, Graham, Hamilton, Kerrey, and Wofford—were all members of Congress, but the list included regional, ideological, and age diversity. George W. Bush said his "finalists" included four current or former governors (Alexander, Tom Ridge, Frank Keating, and Engler); five current or former senators (Danforth, John Kyl, Chuck Hagel, Bill Frist, and Fred Thompson); and, of course, Cheney. Obama carefully considered choosing his chief rival for the nomination, Senator Hillary Clinton, but his finalists were Biden, Senator Evan Bayh of Indiana, and Governor Tim Kaine of Virginia. Bayh and Kaine were men of Obama's generation; Biden was much older. Bayh and Kaine came from competitive states; Biden did not. Kaine was a newcomer to the national scene, whereas Biden was a familiar face. Romney's finalists were Ryan, Christie, Tim Pawlenty, Rob Portman, and Marco Rubio.[44]

Reducing the list helps make the process manageable. It is easier to vet, interview, and consider fewer candidates. Yet the short list comes at a price. If spots are used for symbolic purposes or to reward allies, a nominee may have limited real options, especially if vetting reveals concerns regarding some. A candidate who shortens the list too early or who adjusts priorities may foreclose or abbreviate the vetting and/or consideration of candidates. Kemp, Cheney, and Palin all emerged late in the process.

THE VETTING PROCESS

Modern presidential candidates follow a vetting process for short-listers that builds on those introduced by Kirbo and Schmults. It seeks to ferret out information about prospective candidates to minimize unwelcome surprises. The information may persuade against selecting a running mate with a problematic past, or at least allow the campaign to prepare for, and minimize damage from, unhelpful revelations. The inquiry must be sufficiently wide-ranging to produce comprehensive portraits and flexible enough to address the diverse issues that different candidates present.

The vetting process typically begins by obtaining the prospect's agreement to participate and cooperate. The vettee is generally asked to designate a contact person; to complete a questionnaire; and to provide documents within a specified period, although sometimes the questionnaire is answered verbally. Although confidentiality and discretion are promised, vettees are sometimes cautioned to assume that information may become public.

Campaigns have used intrusive and lengthy questionnaires as vetters add inquiries suggested by prior vetting experiences. Modern questionnaires dwarf Kirbo's nineteen-question document, with 50 to 100 questions not uncommon. The vetting process addresses a wide range of personal, financial, health, and political matters. Residences and employment since age eighteen, extramarital affairs, memberships, speeches and writings, tax returns, military service, and medical records are covered. Business associates, clients, and friends are fair game; whether a candidate has ever paid for an abortion has been asked. The investigation includes family members as well as the candidate and candidate's spouse. Gifts received, promises of employment to the candidate and family members, controversial tenants or associates, security clearances or firearms permits sought and/or denied, and controversial foreign visits or honors are among the subjects probed. "You look at every aspect of someone's life because you don't want to miss something that will be an embarrassment to the presidential candidate or the vice-presidential candidate," James Hamilton said.[45] Hagel described the questionnaire as "essentially everything about your life."[46] Lieberman compared it to "having a colonoscopy without anesthesia."[47] Responding takes time. Alexander devoted two vacation weeks to Bush's 2000 form.[48] Hagel invested a similar amount of time in completing the questionnaire and involved business associates, accountants, lawyers, doctors, staff, and family.[49] Materials are generally submitted with the understanding that they will be treated confidentially and often with the promise that they will be returned or destroyed.[50]

Since prospective candidates present different potential trouble spots, the scrutiny must address diverse areas. Mondale, Muskie, and Dukakis presented relatively simple financial pictures; Dianne Feinstein, Geraldine Ferraro, Bentsen, Cheney, and Danforth, among others, did not. Kerrey's lifestyle, Graham's notebooks, and Sarah Palin's family presented unique challenges. Lieberman had issued more than eight hundred opinions as Connecticut's attorney general.[51] John Edwards had an extensive law practice, Cheney had had three heart attacks, and Biden had suffered an aneurism.

Timing is critical, as Mondale's 1984 process suggested. Its inquiry into the financial backgrounds of prospective candidates began only one week before the convention, when such information was sought from Mayor Diane Feinstein of San Francisco, Mayor Henry Cisneros of San Antonio, Dukakis, and Ferraro.[52] James Johnson spent an hour with Feinstein, the original favorite; then two Mondale attorneys spent four hours with her and fourteen hours at her husband's office. Meanwhile, Mondale associates Michael Berman and Tony Essaye vetted Dukakis in Boston. They were unexpectedly dispatched to New York to meet with Ferraro and her husband, John Zaccaro, on July 10, 1984. Berman and Essaye completed Ferraro's questionnaire from information provided to them and examined Ferraro's tax returns and her husband's business relationships but had little time to perform their check. The Ferraro and Feinstein vetting introduced a new feature of vice-presidential screening—the review of the financial activities of the prospective running mate's affluent spouse. Zaccaro, not Ferraro, reviewed the handwritten answers because many questions related to his activities.[53]

Most subsequent candidates have dispatched the questionnaire sooner and often to a wider group of prospective running mates. Dukakis's questionnaire went to seven semifinalists—Bentsen, Glenn, Gore, Dick Gephardt, Lee Hamilton, Graham, and Jesse Jackson.[54] James Hamilton, who headed (2000 and 2004) or coheaded (2008) Democratic vetting, says two weeks are needed to vet a candidate.[55]

Whereas Kirbo and Schmults operated essentially alone in 1976, campaigns now engage teams in the vetting process. Six lawyers performed background checks on Bentsen. They interviewed more than fifty people and reviewed public records, including forty-five years of microfilmed newspapers.[56] Former deputy attorney general Jamie Gorelick headed an eight-person team that vetted Lieberman in 2000. The investigation reviewed Lieberman's writings, including undergraduate editorials for the *Yale Daily News* in the 1960s; his wife and ex-wife were interviewed.[57] Recent Democratic vets generally assign about ten lawyers per vettee, supplemented by specialists to review tax returns and medical records.[58] Those involved often have previously participated in vetting prospective vice-presidential nominees or candidates for other high governmental positions.

The vetting process generally includes a meeting (or meetings) with short listers for follow-up and intrusive questions. Dukakis's options and their spouses were asked whether anything in their background could embarrass the campaign.[59] Quayle had several sessions with Robert Kimmett, including the weekend before his selection was announced.[60] Arthur Culvahouse met for hours with McCain's finalists, generally accompanied by the person who had prepared the initial report on that candidate and perhaps a specialist. During those sessions, he explored areas the answers suggested and additional matters, including some standard questions to test "vice-presidential mettle" (e.g., why they wanted to be vice president, whether they could use nuclear weapons, whether they would risk innocent civilians' lives to kill bin Laden).[61]

In addition to thoroughness, confidentiality, and expedition, James Hamilton identifies "respect" as a fourth hallmark of vice-presidential vetting. "You've got to realize that the people you're vetting have reached the pinnacle of American life. They are distinguished people, and you are asking them the most invasive type of questions. You have to do it in the most respectful manner."[62]

BACKSTOPPING THE CAMPAIGN'S VETTING PROCESS

Three additional strategies may reduce the risk of making a poor selection. Presidential campaigns can gain some assurance by focusing on prospective running mates who have previously been scrutinized. These include serious presidential candidates who participated in at least some primaries and caucuses; incumbent vice presidents; high-level executive appointees; those who have long been nationally prominent; and perhaps those who ran competitive races in large states, although Larry Sabato rightly points out that state and local press are generally far less probing than the national media.[63]

The first three categories account for thirteen of the twenty selections since 1976. Of the remaining seven choices—Mondale and Dole in 1976, Ferraro in 1984, Quayle in 1988, Lieberman in 2000, Palin in 2008, and Ryan in 2012, four (Mondale, Dole, Lieberman, and Ryan) were prominent national figures. The others—Ferraro, Quayle, and Palin—produced postselection stories that embarrassed the campaigns, although sometimes based on information vetting had already discovered.

The likelihood of a beneficial vice-presidential choice probably increases when presidential candidates know the running mate. The presidential and vice-presidential candidates on six of the fourteen first-time tickets since 1976 had served or worked together (Ford and Dole, Bush and Quayle, Gore and Lieberman, Bush and Cheney, Kerry and Edwards, and Obama and Biden). Four pairs had campaigned against each other (Reagan and Bush, Dole and Kemp, Kerry and Edwards, and Obama and Biden). Eleven presidential candidates held formal interviews or discussions of the vice presidency (Carter and Mondale, Mondale and Ferraro, Dukakis and Bentsen, Clinton and Gore, Dole and Kemp, Gore and Lieberman, Bush and Cheney, Kerry and Edwards, Obama and Biden, McCain and Palin, and Romney and Ryan).

Presidential campaigns can generate information by leaking a short list in order to elicit negative information about, or reactions to, prospective running mates (as well as to flatter those mentioned and suggest that the presidential nominee is considering a range of choices). How and when leaking occurs affects the quality of information produced. A leaked long list may diminish the incentive to divulge because the perceived likelihood of any particular selection is small. Timing also matters. A leaked list can produce information only if those interested in exposing a candidate, such as the media or other prospective choices, have sufficient time. Revealing a short list is unlikely to uncover ammunition from the opposing political party; it will hold such information until the running mate is announced.

A campaign that places a high priority on surprise is less likely to leak to obtain information. A leaked story right before the 1988 convention that Quayle was one of six finalists with "surprisingly strong support"[64] came too late and was insufficiently focused to produce much response. In view of Quayle's youth and relatively low profile, Republican consultant Stuart Spencer thought Bush's selection process was "criminal" for not leaking Quayle's name perhaps four or five weeks in advance to elicit feedback.[65]

Bringing damaging information to the surface early may inoculate, rather than disqualify, a prospective running mate. Negative information may have less impact if it emerges before a choice is announced so that the public can assimilate it. Moreover, negative information often seems most consequential if the presidential candidate seems inept for missing it, a perception that disappears when the disclosure precedes the decision.

Those new to the national scene are more likely to have unreported embarrassing information and are probably more vulnerable to its disclosure. The media are more likely to subject such candidates to "microscopic inspection,"[66] and when damaging disclosures emerge, the public has less other information to provide a sheltering context.

Campaigning for Vice President

Some campaign for the vice-presidential nomination, often discreetly to preserve deniability.[67] Such campaigns may prove counterproductive if the presidential candidate feels pressured and sees that behavior as a harbinger of an unpleasant relationship. Moreover, a visible vice-presidential campaign raises the cost of nonselection. As Quayle put it, strategies exist for a politician to be included "on the available chart," but ideally without much "fanfare" to avoid a visible failure.[68]

Quayle mounted a well-devised effort for the 1988 Republican vice-presidential nomination. He began positioning himself after Bush won the New Hampshire primary. Quayle's assets included his compatibility with Bush, youth, midwestern roots, ideology, and relations with Democratic constituencies. Quayle raised his visibility by Senate addresses, press releases, and op-ed articles, speaking at Senate Republican lunches that Bush attended, visiting Bush's office, and conferring with friends in Bush's campaign. Quayle addressed strategic issues, such as devising an alternative to Democratic plant-closing legislation and ratifying the Intermediate-Range Nuclear Forces Treaty, a project important to Bush. He lobbied Bush to encourage Reagan to veto the defense budget on the grounds that it cut too much from the Strategic Defense

Initiative.[69] Quayle demonstrated deference. Unlike others, he initially did not reveal being contacted about the vice presidency so was omitted from an early story listing fifteen people Bush had called.[70] Quayle thereafter sought permission to divulge that he had been called,[71] a move that communicated discretion and loyalty.

Quayle had friends who advanced his name. Kenneth Adelman wrote an op-ed urging Quayle's selection. A conservative group objected to some moderate prospects but listed Quayle as an acceptable choice.[72] George Will arranged for Quayle to appear on a Sunday talk show along with Dole and Kemp.

In 2000, Lieberman engaged attorney Jonathan Sallet in part to "figure out ways to present positive reasons to choose me." They emphasized the compatibility between Gore and Lieberman's Senate records. Lieberman reached out to Democratic constituent groups with whom he had differed—trial lawyers, teachers, unions, organized labor—to minimize their opposition and enlisted Senator Chris Dodd to contact those groups on his behalf.[73] Four years later, Edwards increased his prospects by becoming a willing Kerry surrogate who made many appearances for Kerry.[74]

Presidential candidates invariably disclaim interest in the second spot in the early stages of a race in order to preserve the viability of their presidential campaign. That does not mean that some are not pursuing the second prize. Frank Church, for instance, seemed interested in the second spot on Carter's ticket even as he campaigned for the presidency in the relatively few states he entered.[75] Edwards enhanced his vice-presidential prospects by his presidential campaign. Conversely, a poor showing can be devastating, as Graham learned in 2004.

CANDIDATE INTERVIEWS

Like Carter, every Democratic presidential candidate since 1976 has interviewed short listers, but the interviews have become less visible. Republican presidential candidates interview selectively.

Mondale's 1984 process resembled Carter's approach. Seven candidates—Bentsen; Ferraro; Governor Martha Layne Collins; and Mayors Thomas Bradley, Henry Cisneros, Feinstein, and Wilson Goode—had publicized meetings with Mondale at his Minnesota home between June

21, 1984, and July 6, 1984. Mondale's process was panned.[76] Whereas Carter met with only three candidates in Plains, Georgia, and the others at the convention, where those events did not dominate the news, Mondale's process was protracted and reminded the public of Mondale's association with the Carter administration.[77] Whereas Carter interviewed six senators and one famous member of the House, Mondale saw a less prominent group—only one senator, one newly elected governor, a congresswoman, and four mayors—and its composition exposed him to the criticism that he was catering to Democratic interest groups.

No subsequent candidate has announced interviews or followed them with press conferences. Dukakis disclosed interviews generally after they occurred,[78] and subsequent Democrats have conducted interviews secretly. To avoid reporters in the hotel lobby, Clinton associates brought some prospective candidates to their interviews through the garage in a sports utility vehicle and took freight elevators to meet Clinton in a suite reserved under another name, a level of precautions Lee Hamilton compared to meeting Libyan leader Colonel Mu'ammar Gadhafi in a bunker.[79] Obama's 2008 interviews occurred at hotels around the country, with the interviewees being sneaked in via a car with tinted windows.[80] Republican candidates have interviewed less often. Dole met with Kemp at a Watergate apartment; George W. Bush spoke with Danforth in a Chicago hotel for several hours; McCain and Palin spoke the day before the announcement. Romney met with Ryan.

Interviews may be less important when the presidential candidate knows those on the short list. Even so, one or more meetings may help evaluate those under consideration, gauge compatibility, and discuss the anticipated relationship and vice-presidential role. Interviews of Mondale, Bentsen, Gore, Kemp, Edwards, and Palin contributed to their selections, as did Cheney's interaction with Bush.

The Cheney Selection

The most unique recent process occurred in 2000, when Cheney, the vice-presidential vetter, became the choice. Cheney had declined to be considered in March 2000 but subsequently agreed to direct Bush's search process.[81] Bush never abandoned the thought of Cheney on his ticket. Cheney began with an expansive list before reducing it "to the truly viable candidates" whom he called to determine their interest.[82] In May and June 2000, Cheney sent questionnaires to prospective candidates. The questionnaire included close to 200 questions and sought documents, including ten years' worth of tax returns, medical records, speeches, books, videotapes of television appearances, credit reports, and FBI files. Attorneys supervised by Cheney's son-in-law, Philip J. Perry, reviewed the materials.[83] Cheney frequently briefed Bush.[84] Bush identified nine finalists by early summer—Alexander, Frist, Thompson, Danforth, Ridge, Kyl, Keating, Engler, and Hagel—and discussed options with a few advisers.[85]

At some point, Cheney began to entertain the idea of joining Bush's ticket. He had tried, unsuccessfully, to persuade Bush to consider Cheney's close friend Rumsfeld, notwithstanding long-standing tensions between Rumsfeld and Bush's father.[86] Cheney's advocacy of Rumsfeld might suggest that Cheney thought Bush needed someone with a profile similar to his own—a senior conservative with national security, White House, and congressional experience. The *New York Times* reported that Cheney told Brent Scowcroft, a close friend of Bush's father, in June 2000 of his openness to the vice presidency and that Scowcroft told George H. W. Bush, an account the older Bush and Scowcroft denied.[87] George W. Bush told Cheney multiple times that he was "the solution to my problem."[88] On July 1, 2000, while returning from a weeklong hunting trip in South America with his daughter, Mary, Cheney asked for her reaction to his running for vice president, a topic he had "given a lot of thought to."[89]

On July 3, Cheney and Bush reviewed vice-presidential options. After hearing Cheney's "final report," Bush said, he had decided that Cheney was the ideal running mate.[90] Cheney agreed to explore the necessary steps to become a candidate.[91] At a July 4 dinner, journalist Bob Woodward tried to "pump" Cheney for information. Woodward correctly sensed "a big story" but did not imagine that Cheney was the choice.[92] Cheney continued vetting others[93] while acting to qualify as Bush's running mate. He told Halliburton he might join Bush's ticket.[94] He underwent a medical examination on July 11 in Washington, D.C. Bush advised Cheney on July 12 that Bush's medical consultant had concluded that Cheney's heart problems were not disqualifying.[95] Bush associate Joe Albaugh considered Cheney's voting record and public history while Bush reviewed Cheney's finances, although Cheney did not complete the questionnaire or forward documents that the others submitted.[96] On July 15, 2000, Cheney met with Bush and Karl Rove, Bush's campaign strategist. Cheney and Rove argued against Cheney's selection, citing his health, arrest record, association with the oil industry, Texas residency, and conservative voting record and the fact that his native state, Wyoming, offered only three safe electoral votes.[97] On July 18, 2000, Cheney flew Danforth and his wife, Sally, to Chicago to meet Bush. Cheney attended the first part of the three-hour meeting.[98]

Cheney's name appeared in public speculation on July 20, but Bush declined to say whether Cheney was a possibility.[99] The following day, Cheney changed his voter registration to provide evidence of Wyoming residency and thereby allow Texas electors to vote for both Bush and him.[100] Cheney was now publicly identified as the favorite.[101] Although Bush normally conducted personal interviews for major appointments,[102] the only person he really interviewed, other than Cheney, was Danforth.[103]

Selection of the search leader as the running mate will likely remain an anomaly. Working with Cheney provided Bush with information regarding how they might interact in the White House, but the unorthodox process denied Bush other information because Cheney was not subject to conventional vetting. Bush probably took comfort in Cheney's prior record, stature, and George H. W. Bush's recommendation. Still, the episode signaled Bush's willingness to abandon normal process in decision-making.

THE PALIN SELECTION

John McCain's 2008 vice-presidential selection process was unusual for picking someone as obscure as Palin. McCain said in early April 2008 that his list was large and "embryonic" and that he wanted to complete the process as early as possible because he was "aware of enhanced importance of this issue given my age."[104] A. B. Culvahouse, Jr., his vetter, was a distinguished Washington lawyer who had been White House counsel to Reagan and had helped others navigate such processes and confirmations.

McCain began with about two dozen names. Culvahouse and about thirty lawyers, then or formerly at his law firm, prepared forty- to fifty-page reports on each from public materials. The campaign identified a short list of Mayor Michael Bloomberg of New York, Lieberman, and Governors Charles Crist of Florida, Tim Pawlenty of Minnesota, and Mitt Romney of Massachusetts, to each of whom Culvahouse sent seventy-four written questions. Culvahouse and associates interviewed all of the candidates. The comprehensive written and oral questions probed predictable areas, but Culvahouse also posed a few questions to test the interviewee's depth. To preserve confidentiality, Culvahouse did little outreach to people outside the process.

McCain wanted to choose Lieberman but belatedly concluded that the selection was impossible. Lieberman had taken positions unpopular with the Republican base, especially his support for abortion rights, which McCain's campaign feared might make Lieberman vulnerable to a floor fight. Moreover, some key states had "sore loser" statutes designed to prevent candidates from running on the other party's line. If applicable to federal campaigns, they would complicate a race with Lieberman on the ticket. They would also provide ammunition for Lieberman's detractors in any convention battle over his nomination. In the aftermath of the 2000 election, few wanted to risk a choice that might send the 2008 race to the Supreme Court. McCain's political advisers feared that choosing Lieberman would divide the party and force McCain to spend precious time shoring up his base.[105]

Shortly before her selection, Governor Sarah Palin of Alaska was added to McCain's long list and a report was prepared from public sources. She was added to the short list on August 24, 2008, and received the questionnaire, necessitating an accelerated vet. She flew to Phoenix on August 27, 2008, to meet with McCain the following day. She was interviewed for three hours by phone by Culvahouse and two colleagues. During this call, she revealed the pregnancy of her unmarried teenaged daughter. She spoke also with two high-ranking McCain aides. The next morning, August 28, Culvahouse briefed McCain and advised him that Palin was a "high risk high reward" option. Culvahouse told McCain that Palin would not be ready to be vice president on January 20, 2009, but praised her capacity.[106] McCain and Palin then met for an hour or so. After some brief consultation with his wife and a few aides, McCain chose Palin and announced the choice the next day.

The Palin selection illustrated how late additions can create problems. Even if the candidate is fully vetted, the campaign may lack the time or disposition to consider the information objectively. McCain and his strategists wanted to select Palin before Culvahouse or McCain met with her. Although the vetters uncovered relevant information, commitment to the outcome may have skewed McCain's analysis. As Dan Balz and Haynes Johnson nicely put it, "If there was a breakdown it appears not to have been in the vetting but rather in a decision made without a deeper understanding of whether Palin would be judged ready to sit a heartbeat away from the presidency."[107] Late additions may reflect poorly on the standard-bearer by making the process appear undisciplined, especially if new information becomes publicly known after the selection.

Sometimes a late entry is defensible. Kemp did not figure in Dole's early thinking but became a serious possibility about a week before he was chosen. Dole had reached a compromise with social conservatives on an abortion plank on August 7, 1996, so did not need to use the vice-presidential selection to appease that part of his base. Dole campaign manager (and former Kemp aide) Scott Reed met with Kemp that day, and Dole and Kemp met that night. News that Kemp was under consideration leaked on August 8, and Dole and Kemp sealed the deal the next day.[108]

Cheney, too, was a late addition and posed some challenges. Yet Kemp and Cheney, unlike Palin, had been national figures for decades. Roderick DeArment had little time to vet Kemp and relied in part on a discussion with Bob Kimmett, who had vetted him eight years earlier for Bush.[109] In addition to that earlier vetting, Dole and his associates had known Kemp for years; Kemp had been confirmed for the Bush cabinet in 1989 and had run for president in 1988. Cheney had served in leadership positions in the White House, in the House of Representatives, and as secretary of defense; had been considered as a vice-presidential and presidential candidate; and had been working with Bush. First raising candidates of the stature of Kemp and Cheney late in the process was far less risky than introducing Palin at the eleventh hour.

Controlling the Process

The increased length and greater visibility of the selection process present new management challenges. Reagan lost control of the process in 1980 by initiating negotiations with Ford at the Republican convention. Ford had refused to run as vice president when he and Reagan met on June 5, 1980, in Palm Springs, California. He and Reagan both lived in California, which posed a problem, and moving elsewhere would appear unseemly.[110] Reagan attempted to persuade him during an hourlong conversation upon arriving at the convention.

Reagan enlisted Ford's former secretary of state, Henry Kissinger, and Alan Greenspan to persuade Ford, and national party chair William Brock convened a breakfast meeting of Republican leaders, most of whom expressed enthusiasm. Other Republican luminaries had misgivings. Haig thought it "a prescription for trouble" and called Kissinger to oppose "this bizarre idea."[111] Cheney thought it a "dumb idea."[112]

Ford's and Reagan's representatives met periodically on convention Wednesday. Reagan's representatives presented a document suggesting that Ford would have power to supervise the NSC, OMB, and CEA,[113] an arrangement Cheney later described as "a co-presidency."[114]

Ford retained serious misgivings and thought the proposal unworkable. He feared friends would call him rather than Reagan, thereby creating the perception that Ford was overstepping, and worried that staff conflict would undermine any arrangement.[115] Cheney thought Ford never intended to join the ticket but made excessive demands that he expected Reagan to reject.[116]

Reagan wanted Republicans to appeal to Ford's party loyalty, which made the convention an auspicious setting for the discussions. Yet that venue compressed negotiations and made them very transparent. When CBS's Walter Cronkite mentioned a "co-presidency" during a televised interview with Ford, the former president's comments were construed as not rejecting the idea.[117] The Cronkite interview, and a later session with ABC's Barbara Walters, left the impression that a Reagan-Ford ticket was inevitable and that Ford would exercise unusual authority.[118] Recognizing that the situation was out of control, Ford and Reagan agreed that the "dream ticket" would not work.[119]

The frenzy over the Reagan-Ford ticket did not present Reagan well. His apparent willingness to delegate such extensive authority suggested confusion regarding the presidency. Reagan regained control by appearing at the convention to squelch the speculation and to announce his selection of Bush.[120]

MAKING THE DECISION

The process each time shapes the ultimate decision. Vice-presidential selections are not preordained. Rather, they emerge as the presidential candidate and close associates collect and sift information about available options measured against their perceived needs.

Presidential nominees often change their minds during the process, either because a preferred candidate becomes unavailable or less appealing or because events or strategic considerations make the eventual choice relatively more attractive than was originally the case. Carter changed his mind from Church to Glenn to Muskie to Mondale. Reagan pursued Ford before selecting Bush. Feinstein, not Ferraro, was Mondale's original preference. Clinton's interview of Gore was crucial. Dole pursued Bennett before Kemp. McCain wanted Lieberman before settling on Palin. The process can be educational for the presidential nominee. A longer process may allow a presidential candidate to reach a comfort level regarding the eventual nominee, as occurred with Kerry and Edwards in 2004, or to conclude that a preferred choice will not work, as McCain determined regarding Lieberman.

The final decision-making process varies from candidate to candidate. Some candidates discuss the idea in a structured meeting with key aides before deciding. Dukakis met with his wife, Kitty; Brountas; campaign manager Susan Estrich; and Jack Corrigan around his kitchen table to review the finalists before deciding to call Bentsen.[121] Clinton met with Hillary Clinton, Christopher, Mark Gearan, and Bruce Lindsey for several hours on the evening of July 8. He discussed the five alternatives, called some other advisers, and late that evening stated his decision to ask Gore.[122] Eight years later, having committed to announcing a running mate by August 8, 2000, nearly one week before the opening of the Democratic convention, Gore met with Christopher; his campaign chair, William Daley; his campaign manager, Donna Brazile; and his brother-in-law Frank Hunger beginning on the afternoon of August 6 and reached a decision after midnight.[123]

The structure and participants in the process may affect the outcome. The process George H. W. Bush used probably enhanced Quayle's chances. Bush met with his inner circle of Lee Atwater, Craig Fuller, Robert Teeter, Roger Ailes, Robert Mosbacher, and Robert Kimmett to discuss the choice[124] on August 6 and 12, 1988. Baker was absent but claims he told Bush that Dole and Quayle were the most logical choices.[125] Other accounts report that he had discouraged the selection of Quayle.[126] Bush asked his closest aides to rank their top three choices. Several were predisposed to Quayle, including Ailes and Teeter, who had worked for him, and Fuller. Others favored Dole but not Kemp, or vice versa, but also listed Quayle. Quayle was often listed on ballots of Bush's top advisers even if not first.[127]

To protect confidentiality, Bush directed Kimmett to share vetting information only with him.[128] Bush's political advisers lacked the opportunity to discuss possible problems that the background material might suggest. The compartmentalization of the process meant that the political implications of some information was not fully discussed. Bush may have overlooked the potential sensitivity of Quayle's service in the national guard due in part to the fact that his son, George W. Bush, had also served in that manner. Kimmett, an able government lawyer but not a political strategist, may have underestimated the impact of the issue. Teeter and Ailes presumably knew of the issue but probably took comfort in the fact that it had not prevented Quayle from being twice elected senator from Indiana. The information was certainly not disqualifying, but as chapter 12 suggests, Quayle was hurt because the Bush campaign was unprepared to handle the allegations.

Conclusion

The new vice-presidential selection process developed as presidential candidates responded to a changed political context. New arrangements that led to an earlier resolution of presidential nominations encouraged a more thorough vetting process. Carter modeled a more protracted deliberative process that relied on a trusted point person, consultation, due diligence, interviews, and visibility. Subsequent candidates adapted Carter's process.

The new process allows the presidential candidate to consider the vice-presidential choice over a longer period under conditions favorable to a deliberative decision. The lengthier process focuses attention on the office and prospective choices. Greater visibility provides added incentive to choose wisely. Even as presidential candidates no longer match Carter's transparency, the process allows extensive consultation and public discussion of alternatives.

Vice-presidential selections still encounter diverse problems, some of which are caused by human error. Information not shared sufficiently with advisers may not be fully considered. Late additions to a short list present perils. A rushed vetting process can miss relevant information or prevent its proper processing. It is probably wise for the presidential candidate to defer a decision until necessary. A later choice is more likely to reflect the context in which the campaign will be waged. It is important for the candidate to remain neutral until he or she has collected and considered all information. A presidential candidate who commits too soon may assess important information in a biased fashion.

A good process helps, but it cannot guarantee a good result. Ultimately, the outcome turns heavily on the presidential candidate's identification of and commitment to appropriate selection criteria and ability to choose a running mate who meets those standards, the topic of chapter 11.

Criteria for Selection

It matters who becomes vice president. A vice president who is presidential, vice-presidential, and politically and personally compatible with the president and who adds strength is likely to enhance an administration. One who lacks any of these qualities will probably make a less significant contribution.

Yet timing complicates choosing such a person. Vice-presidential candidates are selected in anticipation of a presidential campaign and election, not simply of a new administration. The administration occurs only if the campaign succeeds. This reality gives presidential candidates incentive to emphasize political considerations in choosing a running mate. They want to choose someone who will discharge campaign assignments effectively. They want the process to unite the party. They want a running mate who will help them win or at least not make defeat more likely.

The inevitable preoccupation with election does not mean governance gets ignored. Generally, it does not. Political considerations give most presidential candidates reason to value governance qualities. The vice-presidential selection sends messages regarding the presidential candidate's judgment and values and gives most nominees reason to choose an able and philosophically compatible running mate. In addition to choosing a running mate who emerges from the vetting process without disabling baggage, most recent presidential candidates weigh heavily whether prospective running mates are presidential, whether they are plausible partners, and whether they strengthen the ticket.

Such a running mate is also likely to contribute as a White House vice president. Presidents are more likely to involve a qualified vice president who shares their governing vision and adds strength to the administration.

Of course, these patterns do not describe every decision. Few contend that Sarah Palin was presidential or that John Edwards was vice-presidential. The normal tendencies sometimes yield to circumstances. Different individuals make the selections, the pool varies, each presidential candidate perceives distinctive needs, and people make mistakes.

The available pool obviously shapes the choice. Presidential candidates choose among real-world alternatives who may present some, but rarely offer all, of the traits of the dream running mate. Although the office now attracts able persons, the selector cannot always get whom he wants. Ford was unavailable to Reagan in 1980, McCain rejected Kerry in 2004, and Powell and Dale Bumpers refused to consider the second spot several times. Some pools are deeper than others.

In addition, each presidential candidate is distinctive. They see their interests differently depending on their temperaments, experiences, and objectives. They assign different priority to qualities such as compatibility, loyalty, and excellence and assess options differently. George H. W. Bush selected Quayle, but Ford or Reagan or George W. Bush or McCain may not have. George H. W. Bush passed on Dole and Kemp, whom Ford and Dole, respectively, chose. Mondale could have selected Bentsen but did not; four years later, Dukakis did instead of, among others, Gore, whom Clinton chose the next cycle. Gore passed on Edwards in 2000, whom Kerry selected in 2004. Obama picked Biden, whom several predecessors did not select. The different selectors were not the sole explanations, but they cannot be discounted.

Finally, circumstances shape the choices presidential candidates make. A highly credentialed candidate such as Mondale, George H. W. Bush, Gore, or McCain has different needs than a Washington neophyte such as Carter, Clinton, George W. Bush, or Obama. The seventy-three-year-old Senate Majority Leader Dole did not require Cheney's gravitas in 1996 and could not carry his health history; George W. Bush did and could. Reagan did not need help with the conservative wing of the party in 1980, but Bush did in 1988. Conversely, Bush did not need help from the Ford wing from which Reagan sought a running mate. A candidate perceiving an uphill race, such as Mondale in 1984, McCain in 2008, and perhaps Bush in 1988, may be more inclined to a high-risk, high-reward choice than one whose prospects seem more promising.

Patterns exist, but vice-presidential selection remains idiosyncratic. George H. W. Bush wrote in 1987 that vice-presidential selection was "one of the most unpredictable rituals of modern American politics."[1] Even so, generally, presidential candidates choose accomplished running mates.

Vice-Presidential Vision

The selection is affected by the general vision that the presidential nominee has for a running mate and vice president. Carter's commitment to making the vice presidency a substantive position influenced his process and criteria. Twelve years later, Brountas wisely encouraged Dukakis to consider his vice-presidential model before focusing on the selection process.[2] Christopher, too, recommended tailoring the selection process to the desired vice-presidential role and encouraged Clinton to choose the most-qualified person, to adopt a "Mondale plus" model, and to forge "a true partnership" such that the vice president would enjoy Mondale's access and undertake "meaningful policy assignments that would draw on his special talents."[3] George W. Bush and his associates attributed his choice of Cheney to governance, not political, considerations.[4]

Yet vice-presidential vision can only guide selection generally. Few presidential candidates foresee their vice president's precise role. That vision evolves as the presidential candidate proceeds through the search, as the president-elect structures the administration, as the two individuals interact, and as circumstances unfold.

Moreover, presidential *candidates* select running mates and accordingly weigh political considerations.[5] Ford told delegates he sought (1) "a person of character and experience, capable of leading the country"; (2) a candidate who "must articulate and support" Republican principles and be compatible with Ford; and (3) someone who would be "an asset" in the campaign and in governing.[6] Bush explained that Quayle was "qualified," that they agreed on "fundamental" issues, and that he would help politically because he understood the importance of planning for the future and was an excellent campaigner.[7] Ford was clearly qualified to be president, but Reagan pursued him because polls showed the former president would help politically.

Surviving the Vetting Process

A prospective candidate for vice president will be chosen only if he or she emerges from the vetting process without the discovery of disabling baggage. No presidential candidate wants a running mate's past to distract from projecting the ticket's message or to impugn the presidential candidate's decision-making ability.

Perfection is neither required nor attainable. Baggage is not disabling; as Cheney put it, "Everyone has negatives."[8] The question is, can it be carried? Does the burden imposed outweigh the benefits conferred relative to other options? Bush had derided Reagan's economic program as "voodoo economics." Lobbyists paid substantial sums to breakfast with Bentsen; some disparaged the practice by labeling him "Eggs Mc-Bentsen." Cheney had suffered three heart attacks, and Biden had had a brain aneurism and was prone to gaffes. Ryan was associated with his controversial economic plan. These problems were not disqualifying; the choices performed ably as candidates, and three of the five became vice president. Previously publicized flaws often are easier to handle because they already affect the prospect's standing and may have less impact than new revelations.

Vetability has adversely affected some widely mentioned candidates. Reagan's close friend Paul Laxalt was from Nevada, which engendered some concern that his associates might have ties to gambling.[9] Bob Kerrey, as a divorced man who had dated an actress, was a less likely choice in 1992. Bob Graham was hurt because he maintained an extraordinarily detailed diary recording mundane aspects of daily life. Romney's vetters reportedly found numerous red flags about Christie, who was also deemed uncooperative.[10] Vetting probably would disqualify as running mate some who became presidential nominees. In 1992, Bill Clinton would have had difficulty getting through a vice-presidential vet due to rumors of past infidelity.

Selection Criteria: The Critical Role of Competence

SOURCES OF VICE-PRESIDENTIAL NOMINEES

All recent running mates and virtually all serious contenders have had experience in a few offices: vice president, senator, governor, high executive branch positions, or the House of Representatives. Since 1976, eight of the twenty vice-presidential candidates were senators, six were incumbent vice presidents, three were former high-level executive officials, one was a governor, and two were members of the House of Representatives. That profile resembles the prior quarter century, when the thirteen major-party vice-presidential candidates included two vice presidents, seven senators, one governor, two high-ranking executive officials, and one representative.

Several patterns are striking. Since 1976, all but three vice-presidential candidates held public office at the time chosen, and the exceptions (Bush, Kemp, Cheney) had previously served in Congress and the executive branch. Democratic presidential candidates choose senators more often than do Republicans. Since 1952, 70 percent of Democratic vice-presidential candidates were sitting senators, whereas only 18 percent (three of sixteen) of the Republicans came from that body. Governors are rarely chosen. Whereas six of the twenty-six (23 percent) vice-presidential candidates from 1900 to 1948 were governors, only two governors (7 percent) have run for that office since then, and only one since 1976. Candidates perceived as national leaders (Nixon and McCain) chose the governors (Agnew and Palin).

PRESIDENTIAL VICE PRESIDENT

During the past three decades, competence has increasingly emerged as a threshold criterion. Modern presidential candidates have incentive to choose a running mate who, as Dukakis put it, "really shines as a potential president."[11] The increased importance of the presidency since the New Deal and World War II focused greater attention on the first successor. The greater visibility and expectations of the vice presidency, especially since the Mondale term, reinforced this development. As the vice president's importance grew, running-mate qualifications assumed additional significance. Most presidential candidates understand that the public expects able vice-presidential candidates and will judge the selector partly by the choice made.[12]

Moreover, presidential campaigns now subject vice-presidential candidates to greater scrutiny. In the information age, statements of vice-presidential candidates receive wide dissemination. New events, such as the preconvention rollout and vice-presidential debate, which are discussed in chapter 12, place the vice-presidential candidate center stage. The specter of an unimpressive figure a heartbeat away from the presidency may cost some support. A gaffe-prone vice-presidential candidate may distract from the ticket's message and sacrifice the advantages of a polished spokesperson.

Although a vice-presidential candidate's ability has become more important, Karl Rove's statement that recent vice-presidential selections are "more about governing and less about politics" is misleading because it implies that politics no longer dominates the selection.[13] Rather, picking a highly qualified running mate has become a political requisite. The vice-presidential selection measures the presidential candidate's decision-making ability and values,[14] and those who ignore governance considerations pay a price.

Of course, competence did not first become important in 1976. Other than Agnew, vice presidents during the prior quarter century—Nixon, Johnson, Humphrey, Ford, and Rockefeller—were formidable leaders. But the significance of competence has grown since 1976.

Defining a Plausible President

No objective measure exists to determine whether someone is presidential. A number of familiar measures suggest themselves, such as experience, prior consideration for president or vice president, subsequent consideration for those positions, and record of performance, but they involve, to varying degrees, subjective judgments and are imperfect gauges.

Experience, for instance, does not perfectly predict presidential aptitude. Abraham Lincoln served only a single term in the House of Representatives a dozen years before winning the Republican presidential nomination, whereas James Madison, John Quincy Adams, John Tyler, and Herbert Hoover had extensive governmental service yet were unsuccessful presidents. When Quayle equated his experience in 1988 with John Kennedy's·in 1960,[15] Bentsen famously replied, "You're no Jack Kennedy." Bentsen's retort rejected the premise that length of service, even in the same jobs, was dispositive. That implicit judgment has continued resonance.

Quantifying experience presents other problems. What positions are relevant, and how should they be weighed? Experience in traditional vice-presidential feeder positions seems most relevant,[16] although some draw the category more broadly.[17] But how does one compare Bush's time at the United Nations and in China; Mondale's, Dole's, Lieberman's or Edwards's years in the Senate; and Palin's time as governor of Alaska? How does the congressional service of Quayle, Gore, or Ryan compare with the executive experience of Bush or Kemp? Is the service of a small-state senator equivalent to that of a senator from a large state? Should service as governor of Maryland or Alaska count the same as service as governor of New York? Even if it is plausible to weigh the experience of legislative leaders (Cheney or Biden) more than that of their back-bench colleagues, no metric exists to compare such service. Finally, focusing just on governmental experience excludes nongovernmental work. Bush and Kemp spent four, and Cheney eight, years as respected former officials before their vice-presidential campaigns. Cheney's work as CEO of Halliburton and as a Republican luminary was surely more relevant than his time as a congressional aide more than a quarter century earlier.

Prior consideration for the presidency or vice presidency provides another basis for assessment. Mondale, Bush, Bentsen, Gore, Kemp, Cheney, Edwards, Biden, and Ryan had been considered presidential timber. This measure helps, but it involves subjective judgments and reflects elite bias. Mondale, Bentsen, Cheney, and Biden all withdrew from presidential races early. Should they receive points for having been considered or lose them because of the poor outcome?

Subsequent consideration for president or vice president provides another indication. Yet a vice-presidential race itself boosts recognition, thereby biasing the analysis. Agnew became a 1976 presidential front-runner until his forced departure. Does this success suggest his qualifications or the advantages of incumbency? Nixon was a dominant figure from the late 1950s to the mid-1970s, winning two of three presidential races, once in a landslide. Does that mean he was presidential timber when first chosen in 1952?

Finally, past performance might suggest presidential quality. Yet prior electoral success is not sufficiently discriminating because many frequently reelected politicians are not presidential or vice-presidential timber, and some figures who clearly were, such as George H. W. Bush, primarily held appointive positions. Finally, it is hard to compare electoral success in races of different stature. Congressional contests are generally quite different from statewide races, and running statewide in Idaho is not the same as doing so in Pennsylvania. No objective markers exist to measure performance in office. And a record in one office may not predict performance elsewhere. Johnson, Humphrey, Dole, Bentsen, and Biden were better senators than John Kennedy, but it is not clear that they were or would have been better presidents.

Determining whether someone is presidential is more art than science. The absence of more reliable criteria makes the four factors—experience, past consideration, future consideration, and record—frequent measures of vice-presidential qualification notwithstanding their imperfections. They suggest that those selected as vice-presidential running mates since 1976 have generally been presidential figures.

Table 11-1 shows that most first-time vice-presidential candidates had impressive experience in high governmental office before being chosen. Indeed, eleven of the fourteen first-time vice-presidential candidates had served for at least ten years in high office. The average period of service in these positions was 14.44 years. Many had held leadership positions.

Of the fourteen first-time vice-presidential candidates since 1976, all but five (Dole, Ferraro, Quayle, Lieberman, and Palin) had previously been considered for president, vice president, or both. Bush (1980) and Edwards (2004) had been runner-up for the presidential nomina-

Table 11-1 Service in High Public Office before Initial VP Selection

Candidate	Years of Service	Positions Held
Mondale	12	Senator
Dole	16	HoR (8), Senate (8), National GOP chair
Bush	10	HoR (4), UN ambassador, GOP chair, China liaison, CIA director
Ferraro	6	HoR
Bentsen	24	HoR (6), Senate (18)
Quayle	12	HoR (4), Senate (8)
Gore	16	HoR (8), Senate (8)
Kemp	20	HoR (16), secretary of HUD (4)
Lieberman	12	Senate
Edwards	6	Senate
Cheney	16	Deputy WH chief of staff and chief of staff (2), HoR (10), secretary of defense (4)
Biden	36	Senate
Palin	2	Governor
Ryan	14	HoR

Source: Much of this information, in modified form, appeared in Chart 1 in Joel K. Goldstein, "Veep Speculation Is Just That," Sabato's Crystal Ball, November 3, 2011, http://www.centerforpolitics.org/crystalball/articles/jkg2011110301/.

tion, and Gore and Kemp (1988) had lasted long in earlier races. Six others—Mondale, Bentsen, Cheney, Edwards, Biden, and Ryan—had been widely mentioned or had run, less successfully, for the presidential nomination. Seven (Mondale, Bush, Bentsen, Gore, Kemp, Cheney, and Edwards) had previously been seriously considered for their party's vice-presidential nomination. Most vice-presidential candidates have been perceived as presidential when chosen. From 1992 to 2008, Gallup found that more than 50 percent of registered voters considered vice-presidential nominees except Quayle and Palin qualified to be president.[18] Most vice-presidential candidates since 1976 have figured in subsequent presidential speculation. Four (Mondale, Dole, Bush, and Gore) of the fourteen vice-presidential candidates were later presidential nominees, three (Quayle, Lieberman, and Edwards) sought their party's nomination, and four (Bentsen, Palin, Ryan, and Biden) were widely mentioned as future candidates. Cheney and Kemp disclaimed further interest. Ferraro never became a presidential candidate. Several later distinguished themselves in other ways (Dole as Senate majority leader; Bentsen as secretary of the treasury; Mondale as ambassador to Japan; Gore as a winner of the Nobel Peace Prize; and Ryan as House speaker).

On balance, Mondale, Dole, Bush, Bentsen, Gore, Kemp, Cheney, and Biden were among the outstanding leaders of the period. Lieberman was a respected legislator when chosen, later ran for president, and was almost chosen for vice president by the other party's nominee. Edwards, though relatively new to national politics, was the runner-up for the 2004 presidential nomination, previously made Gore's short list for vice president, and later ran a credible race against Obama and Hillary Clinton (although subsequent revelations impeached his character and judgment). Quayle was an able young senator who was establishing a reputation as an effective member of Congress.[19] Ryan is a respected legislative leader.

The fact that presidential candidates have generally selected qualified running mates suggests that ability is valued. This conclusion is reinforced by looking at others considered in recent vice-presidential selections. In 1976, Carter decided between Mondale and Muskie and Ford between Dole and Howard Baker. That the choices narrowed to such talented people suggests quality was important. Other instances where the finalists suggest an emphasis on quality are Reagan (Ford, Bush, and Baker), Dukakis (Bentsen, Glenn, Gephardt, and Gore), Clinton (Gore, Lee Hamilton, Graham, Kerrey, and Harris Wofford), Dole (Kemp and Mack), Gore (Lieberman, Kerry, Edwards, and Evan Bayh), Bush (Cheney and Danforth), Kerry (Edwards, McCain, Gephardt, and Governor Tom Vilsack), Obama (Biden, Bayh, Tom Kaine, and Hillary Clinton), and Romney (Ryan, Rob Portman, Pawlenty, and Christie). The two instances where the vice-presidential candidate's credentials were most modest when chosen were Ferraro and Palin. In 1984, there were no Democratic women senators and only one governor. Although

Mondale gave priority to considering members of traditionally excluded groups, whereas McCain did not, both probably minimized plausibility because they faced uphill races and sought a game-changing vice-presidential selection.

The Importance of Compatibility

Many presidential candidates also emphasize their compatibility with prospective running mates. This criterion has two dimensions—personal and philosophical compatibility. The creation of the White House vice presidency gives presidential candidates greater reason to seek running mates with whom they can work and with whom they share a general governance vision. These attributes also have value during the campaign, where a running mate who resists assignments or goes off message poses problems.

The fortunes of some prospective vice-presidential candidates soared because a presidential candidate judged them to be compatible. Mondale's interview allowed Carter to overcome misgivings. Clinton and Gore apparently found much common ground, as their scheduled one-hour interview lasted three times that long. Impressed with how Cheney handled the vice-presidential selection process, George W. Bush became convinced they could work together.

Some chose running mates despite misgivings. Reagan's preferred running mate in 1980 was "ABB—Anybody but Bush,"[20] James Baker later wrote. Yet after negotiations with Ford collapsed, Reagan concluded that Bush made the most sense. Reagan sought Bush's assurance that he would support the party platform, including the anti-abortion plank. Dole selected Kemp even though they had long disparaged each other and embraced rival economic strategies and Kemp had endorsed Dole's opponent, Steve Forbes, only days before Forbes ended his campaign.[21] After meeting with Kemp, Dole made the choice.

Others rejected running mates as incompatible. Scars from the primaries were too fresh for Ford to select Reagan. Bush resisted Dole and Kemp, doubting either would be sufficiently loyal. Romney may have cooled on Christie, who was uncooperative during the vetting.[22]

All else being equal, a presidential nominee will prefer a personally compatible running mate. But all things are never equal, and candidates make trade-offs. The less-compatible option may have other assets. Selectors weigh compatibility differently or have varying levels of confidence in their abilities to achieve it. Reagan's pursuit of Ford and then Bush may have reflected security in his ability to work with others. Dole, having dealt with senatorial personalities, may have been more willing to choose a challenging partner than was Bush after eight years as a loyal vice president. A presidential nominee such as Carter or George W. Bush who truly intends to put the vice president to work may place greater emphasis on compatibility.

Ticket-Balancing

Ticket-balancing, though now less dominant,[23] has not disappeared. The practice is, of course, relational and requires considering both ends of the ticket.[24] The presence of balance does not confirm its influence because it may have been inadvertent. Nonetheless, ticket-balancing influences some selections.

TYPE OF GOVERNMENTAL EXPERIENCE

Presidential candidates who are Washington outsiders invariably select running mates with substantial experience in the nation's capital. Each of the six (former) governors nominated as presidential candidates since 1976 chose a Washington insider as a running mate. The short lists of Carter, Reagan, and Clinton consisted entirely of Washington insiders, as did Dukakis's (except Jackson). Bush included some fellow governors in 2000, but finalists Cheney and Danforth had extensive Washington experience. Governors choose Washington running mates for their expertise, real or apparent, regarding international issues and/or national government.

Washington insiders generally choose insiders, too. Since 1976, every insider except McCain chose an insider running mate, and McCain selected Palin only after concluding that Lieberman was not an option.

This pattern of outsider-insider and insider-insider tickets antedated 1976. The last outsider-outsider ticket paired New York governor

Thomas Dewey and California governor Earl Warren in 1948. From 1952 to 1972, the only outsider nominees, Eisenhower and Stevenson (1952), ran with senators, and every insider except Nixon (1968) chose an insider running mate. At least six of the eight first-time insider nominees since 1976 (all but Mondale and McCain) primarily considered insider running mates. Insiders prefer insider running mates due to the importance of national and international issues, the difficulty of being a successful governor, the longer terms and service of senators, and the greater opportunity insiders have to know other insiders.

GEOGRAPHIC BALANCE

Geographic ticket-balancing, although less prevalent than other issues, remains a characteristic of vice-presidential selection. Eleven of the fourteen first-time tickets combined candidates from different regions, the only exceptions being Ford-Dole, Clinton-Gore, and McCain-Palin. And geographic considerations influenced Ford's selection of Dole, a choice designed in part to help in farm states.

Geographic ticket-balancing is sometimes inadvertent. If the nation consists of four regions, a random process would produce geographic diversity 75 percent of the time. During much of the period since 1976, eastern Democrats were more liberal than southern Democrats, and western Republicans were more conservative than eastern Republicans. The Reagan-Bush ticket was balanced geographically, but Bush was chosen because he was associated with the moderate wing of the party, not because he voted in Texas. Dole chose Kemp because he was a conservative icon, not a former Buffalo congressman.

Still, geography remains a filter. Most candidates exclude those from their own region even if they do not seek any particular geographic balance. Carter interviewed no southerners and Dukakis none from the Northeast. Reagan considered only one westerner, his close friend Laxalt, who was hurt by geographic and ideological similarity.[25] Mondale's and Dole's short lists included no midwesterners. Clinton chose Gore only after satisfying himself that two southerners could run together. Kerry considered candidates from the South, Midwest, and West but not from the Northeast.

Geographic balancing has declined owing to the nationalization of American presidential campaigns. Vice-presidential candidates no longer limit campaigns to a single region. The decline of the convention as a decision-making body somewhat reduces some sources of geographic balance. Nonetheless, geographic ticket-balancing still sometimes affects vice-presidential selection.

IDEOLOGICAL BALANCE

Similar factors have lessened ideological balancing. Moreover, three other causes are also at work: (1) the increased role of presidential candidates in choosing their running mates encourages ideologically compatible tickets; (2) the White House vice presidency counsels against a philosophically incompatible running mate; (3) the greater ideological coherence of both parties reduces ideological balancing.

Still, ideological balancing is not obsolete. Presidential candidates generally seek philosophically compatible running mates but not necessarily ideological clones. By selecting a philosophically diverse, though compatible, running mate, presidential candidates try to unify their party, broaden their appeal, and suggest receptivity to other perspectives. Including instances where choices were designed partly to appeal to unenthusiastic segments of the party, ideological balance appears to have influenced at least nine of the fourteen first-time selections: Carter-Mondale, Ford-Dole, Reagan-Bush, Dukakis-Bentsen, Bush-Quayle, Dole-Kemp, Gore-Lieberman, McCain-Palin, and Romney-Ryan.

The desire for party harmony limits ideological balancing regarding issues where orthodoxy is expected. No presidential candidate wants an unhappy convention at which disgruntled party figures broadcast complaints. Candidates avoid choices likely to provoke convention controversy. Republican presidential candidates have invariably disqualified prochoice running mates in order to avoid an angry convention.

CROSS-PARTY BALANCE

Candidates occasionally consider the ultimate ticket-balance, a running mate from the other party. Clinton associates approached Colin Powell about the second spot in 1992, but Powell disclaimed interest.[26] Kerry seriously considered McCain, who ultimately decided against the idea.[27] Four years later, McCain wanted to choose Lieberman until associates convinced him that the Republican base would not accept that choice and "sore loser" statutes in competitive states might present another impediment.

Demographic Balancing: Gender, Race, and Ethnicity

Before and since 1976, virtually all serious vice-presidential contenders were white men. The absence from, or underrepresentation in, traditional feeder positions of women and racial minorities partly explained this fact.

Gender and, to a lesser extent, race have recently emerged as new ticket-balancing factors. Two quite different, indeed inconsistent, considerations explain these developments. The novelty of choosing a woman or racial minority makes such a selection historic, brands the selector as bold and pioneering, and perhaps confers political benefit. Ford wrote that choosing Armstrong would have been "the sort of dramatic announcement that would electrify the country." He came "very close" to selecting Armstrong but shied away from the risk—"What a gamble it would be!"[28] Not until 1984 did women and minorities figure in vice-presidential discussion when Mondale interviewed three women, two African Americans, and one Hispanic American and chose between two women, Feinstein and Ferraro. Since then, only four women and no minorities have made (or come close to) a vice-presidential short list. Of the women—Elizabeth Dole (1988), Jeanne Shaheen (2000), Hillary Clinton (2008), and Sarah Palin (2008)—only Palin was chosen, and none other came close. Mayors Bradley, Goode, and Cisneros in 1984 constitute the racial minorities who were seriously considered, although Powell would have been a strong candidate several times had he not removed his name. Faced with a difficult race against Reagan, Mondale thought choosing Ferraro might provide the needed boost. McCain hoped choosing Palin would reshape the election and attract women voters.

Conversely, women, and perhaps some racial and ethnic minorities, will figure more prominently in future vice-presidential selection as increasing numbers hold offices that typically produce running mates. Gender balance will lose novelty, but women will figure in vice-presidential discussions because of their expanding role in high public office. African American running mates will probably play a lesser role than women in future ticket-balancing. Relatively few African Americans hold traditional feeder offices, and the pattern of black voters tending to lean heavily Democratic may reduce the likelihood of African American vice-presidential candidates on the Democratic side. On the other hand, prospective Hispanic running mates may figure in future speculation, particularly given the concentration of that ethnic group in swing states and its less predictable voting patterns.

RELIGION

Presidential nominees considered religion during the Nixon-to-Mondale period. John Kennedy's associates argued that a Catholic running mate could help Stevenson in 1956, and from 1964 to 1972 one candidate in each race chose a Catholic running mate—William Miller, Edmund Muskie, Thomas Eagleton, and Sargent Shriver (the latter two both in 1972).[29]

Since then, religion has played little role. Mondale considered a Catholic (Ferraro) and a Jew (Feinstein), but religion was not a dominant consideration. Dole considered, but did not choose, two Catholics (Mack and Engler). Although several tickets have included religious diversity—Mondale-Ferraro, Dukakis-Bentsen, Gore-Lieberman, Kerry-Edwards, Obama-Biden, Romney-Ryan—except, perhaps, in Gore's choice of Lieberman, religion was not a factor.

AGE

Candidates occasionally assign priority to balancing age, especially if a presidential candidate is unusually young or old. Older presidential candidates have adopted either a "generational" or "succession" approach regarding running-mate age. A "generational" strategy seeks to offset the presidential nominee's older age with a youthful running mate, such as McCain's (seventy-two) selection of Palin (forty-four). Yet choosing an inexperienced running mate may exacerbate concerns regarding the presidential candidate's health. Under a "succession" approach, an older presidential candidate chooses a running mate in the prime of his or her career, thereby compensating for age by offering a presidential successor. Recent examples include Reagan (sixty-nine) with Bush (fifty-six) and Dole (seventy-three) with Kemp (sixty-one), although Reagan was prepared to run with Ford in 1980 when both were approaching seventy.

Younger presidential candidates have not been consistent, either. Clinton (forty-six) chose Gore (forty-five), thereby enhancing his theme of change. Obama (forty-seven), however, selected Biden (sixty-six) instead of Bayh (fifty-two) or Kaine (fifty), opting for generational balance. Clinton, having served almost twelve years as governor, may have felt freer to select a young running mate (especially because Gore had served sixteen years in Congress and run a credible presidential race) than did Obama, who had been a senator less than four years. Obama may have thought he already represented change.

The one time a running mate's age influenced a candidate in his prime occurred when George H. W. Bush (sixty-four) selected Quayle (forty-one). Quayle was the first baby boomer on a national ticket, something Bush thought would appeal to a new generation and show commitment to the future. "He's different from me. I'm 64 and he's 41 and that's good." Bush thought Quayle's "message of hope and opportunity" and "record of job creation" would appeal especially to "younger people."[30] Quayle was "a young leader," "a forceful voice in preparing America's workers for the labor force of the future," born midcentury and in mid-America and "holding the promise of the future."[31] Sometimes a large age gap may be coincidental. Romney (sixty-five) and Ryan (forty-two) were as far apart in age as Bush and Quayle, yet Romney was not perceived as old, and Ryan was apparently not picked for his youth.

Two Contrasting Selections

The choices of Bentsen and Gore ostensibly demonstrated different selection models. Dukakis-Bentsen seemed a classic ticket-balance of an eastern liberal governor and a southwestern moderate-conservative senator, whereas Gore reinforced Clinton's qualities. In fact, both choices were more complicated and, in some respects, similar.

Dukakis's short list suggests he valued ticket-balancing. All seven interviewees brought geographic balance, and all but Jesse Jackson brought experiential and ideological balance. Those Dukakis interviewed (except Jackson) were members of Congress. None provided as much balance as Bentsen.

Yet Dukakis took seriously the requisite to select a presidential running mate. Many whom he considered were plausible presidents. Glenn had been on Carter's short list and a presidential candidate in 1984. Hamilton was a widely respected twelve-term congressman and chair of the House Foreign Affairs Committee. Gore and Gephardt had run for president in 1988 and were emerging national leaders. Dukakis ultimately decided between four of the most plausible—Bentsen, Glenn, Gore, and Gephardt. Bentsen had served in Congress for twenty-three years and chaired the Senate Finance Committee. Mondale had considered him in 1984. During the 1988 campaign, he was the most popular national candidate.

Clinton's selection of Gore represented a reinforcing strategy. Although Gore had extensive Washington experience, as did some others on Clinton's short list, he resembled Clinton in that both were southerners, baby boomers, and Democratic centrists with Ivy League educations. As Clinton put it, "We were the same age. We were from the same part of the country. We both spoke without an accent. . . . It didn't make any sense. It violated all the conventional ideas."[32]

Reinforcement was not Clinton's inevitable strategy. No other option resembled him in so many ways. Graham was from Florida, but Wofford, Hamilton, and Kerrey were from the Northeast or Midwest. Kerrey was a baby boomer, but Graham, Hamilton, and Wofford were ten to twenty years older. Wofford and Kerrey were liberals, but Graham and Hamilton were moderates.

And Clinton did not ignore balancing. Whereas Clinton was attacked as a draft dodger and alleged philanderer, Gore had enlisted in the military and served in Vietnam and was a model family man. Whereas Clinton had equivocated regarding the Persian Gulf War, Gore had voted to authorize the use of force. Gore's expertise on environmental issues supplemented Clinton's interests and appealed to voters whom Clinton might not otherwise reach. Temperamentally Gore differed from Clinton, too.[33] Finally, Clinton apparently thought Gore's ability would help in the campaign and beyond.

Certainly, Dukakis wanted to court voters who shared Bentsen's views, but Bentsen was also an enormously accomplished legislator who probably was Dukakis's most presidential option. Gore reinforced some Clinton characteristics, but he also provided important balances and was probably Clinton's most presidential option.

SENDING MESSAGES ABOUT THE PRESIDENTIAL CANDIDATE

As Dukakis and Clinton demonstrated, vice-presidential selection allows presidential candidates to send messages about themselves and their values. By selecting Bentsen, Dukakis suggested openness to viewpoints other than his own. A ticket of two young, southern, small-town, photogenic centrists provided a visual image of Clinton's promise of change. By rejecting traditional balances, Clinton signaled that he would decide based on the national interest, not political expediency. Sometimes candidates use the choice to emphasize an issue. In 1996, Dole decided to refocus the election by emphasizing either moral or economic issues. William J. Bennett, a former Reagan and Bush Cabinet officer, was associated with the former, Kemp with the latter. Bennett declined to be considered, and Dole emphasized his tax-cut proposal by selecting Kemp.[34] Some candidates use the choice to display a disposition. Reagan hoped choosing Bush would answer fears that he would govern from the far right. Bush hoped choosing Quayle would show interest in the future of younger voters. By choosing Cheney, George W. Bush signaled that he would surround himself with seasoned figures to compensate for his inexperience.

By contrast, Mondale hoped a historic choice would project him as bold and creative.[35] Gore used the selection of Lieberman, an Orthodox Jew and the first Democratic senator to criticize Clinton over the Lewinsky affair, to emphasize his commitment to values and to separate from Clinton.[36]

Selection decisions sometimes need to avoid emphasizing vulnerable aspects. Dole's age made Cheney "a complete non-starter" because of his history of heart attacks.[37] McCain's inability to state how many homes he owned made it unlikely that he could select Romney, who also owned multiple residences.

Candidates sometimes must decide between alternative messages. Obama determined that he did not need to reinforce the message of change but needed gravitas and blue-collar appeal, considerations that favored Biden over Kaine or Bayh. In Palin, McCain courted the Republican base and reinforced his maverick image but undercut his emphasis on experience and his slogan "Putting America First."

Other Considerations

CARRYING A STATE

Presidential candidates almost never select running mates to carry one important state.[38] A running mate who is popular in a large, competitive state may help, but pursuit of a home-state electoral dowry yields to other factors. In view of the nationalization of campaigns and the advent of an information age, a presidential candidate cannot afford to choose a running mate who will help in one state but hurt elsewhere.

A review of home states of recent vice-presidential candidates suggests the insignificance of that factor. Table 11-2 shows that since 1976, vice-presidential candidates have come from twelve states, with electoral votes shown in parentheses.

If anything, the table overstates the impact of state size. The candidates from New York (Ferraro and Kemp), Texas (Bush), and Wisconsin (Ryan) had never been elected outside their congressional districts. Most were not expected to have broad home-state appeal.

Three represented states—Alaska, Delaware, and Wyoming—have among the very smallest populations, and Kansas and Connecticut are in the bottom half. Several candidates came from uncompetitive states—Alaska, Wyoming, and Indiana.

Presidential candidates since 1976 have often passed on running mates from large states. Carter chose Mondale (Minnesota, ten electoral votes), not Glenn (Ohio, twenty-five) or Stevenson (Illinois, twenty-six). The runner-up was Muskie (Maine, four). Ford chose Dole (Kansas, seven) over Armstrong and Connally (Texas, twenty-six), Baker (Tennessee, ten), and Ruckelshaus (Indiana, thirteen). Clinton chose Gore (Tennessee, eleven), not Graham (Florida, twenty-five) or Wofford (Pennsylvania, twenty-three). Bush chose Cheney (Wyoming, three) over Danforth (Missouri, eleven). Obama chose Biden (Delaware, three), not Bayh (Indiana, eleven), Kaine (Virginia, thirteen), or Hillary Clinton (New York, thirty-one), and McCain chose Palin (Alaska, three), not Bloomberg (New York, thirty-one), Crist (Florida, twenty-seven), or

Table 11-2 Home States and Electoral Votes of Running Mates

1976	Minnesota (10)	1996	Tennessee (11)
	Kansas (7)		New York (33)
1980	Minnesota (10)	2000	Connecticut (8)
	Texas (26)		Wyoming (3)
1984	New York (36)	2004	North Carolina (15)
	Texas (29)		Wyoming (3)
1988	Texas (29)	2008	Delaware (3)
	Indiana (12)		Alaska (3)
1992	Tennessee (11)	2012	Delaware (3)
	Indiana (12)		Wisconsin (10)

Source: Much of this information, in modified form, appeared in Chart 1 in Joel K. Goldstein, "Veepwatch Part 1: The Swing State Selection Myth," Sabato's Crystal Ball, April 5, 2012, http://www.centerforpolitics.org/crystalball/articles/veepwatch-part-1 -the-swing-state-selection-myth/.

Pawlenty (Minnesota, ten). Romney chose Ryan (Wisconsin, ten) over Portman (Ohio, eighteen) or Christie (New Jersey, fourteen).

Since 1976, only Dukakis's selection of Bentsen plausibly suggested a home-state influence. Yet Bentsen was not expected to carry his home state because Bush, also of Texas, was the competing presidential candidate. Glenn seemed more likely to tip Ohio's twenty-three votes to Dukakis.

It only makes sense to allow home-state considerations to influence running-mate selection if the prospective choice is likely to bring a basket of electoral votes to the ticket and that gain outweighs related other losses. A presidential candidate who appears to choose a partner just because that candidate is from a large, competitive state may tarnish his or her own image; a running mate from a large state has to be clearly presidential to be a palatable choice. As the field of competitive states narrows, a running mate who seems likely to help in an important swing state may have appeal, but only if he or she is presidential and will not cause offsetting harm elsewhere.

THE PRESIDENTIAL RUNNER-UP AND ALSO-RANS AS RUNNING MATE

Presidential candidates rarely select presidential primary opponents as running mates. This rule applies to the runner-up and to also-rans. Since

1976, sixteen of the twenty nominations have been seriously contested. Only runners-up Bush and Edwards became vice-presidential nominees, and only after the first choices (Ford and McCain) declined. Only three other runners-up (Hart, 1984; Dole 1988; and Hillary Clinton, 2008) were seriously considered.

Also-rans are even less likely to be selected. Biden is the only vice-presidential candidate who competed in primaries and finished lower than second. Some other also-rans received serious consideration for the second spot (Church, 1976; Baker, 1980; Gephardt, Gore, and Kemp, 1988; Kerrey, 1992; Gephardt, 2004; Romney, 2008; and Pawlenty, 2012). It may be difficult to explain selecting an also-ran over the runner-up. The perceived insult to Jackson may have been greater had Dukakis selected Gephardt or Gore. Yet Obama selected Biden, who received less than 1 percent of the votes in the Iowa caucus and then withdrew, not Clinton, who essentially ran an even race with Obama.

Campaigning Ability

A prospective running mate's campaign ability may impact the decision. Vice-presidential candidates must be able to make a convincing case for their party's standard-bearer and against the other ticket. Dole's attractions included his campaigning ability. Dole could attack Carter while Ford remained presidential. Edwards was perceived as an exciting campaigner who could communicate effectively with voters. Kemp was seen as the ideal person to help Dole sell his economic package.

Of course, even an accomplished campaigner may experience difficulty transitioning to a national campaign. Quayle, for instance, had rarely spoken to large audiences and generally used three-by-five note cards rather than a text. The teleprompter was a new experience for him. Finally, a running mate must learn the presidential nominee's positions in all their nuances, a problem that becomes more acute when he or she is chosen, as Palin was, late in the summer. An inexperienced running mate may have insufficient time to prepare.

Who Goes First

The other party's choice may influence selection. In 1976, 1988, 2000, and 2008, both parties chose new running mates. The party in the

White House held its convention (and designated its vice-presidential candidate) second and accordingly could respond to the other party's decision.

In 2000, for instance, Bush's selection of Cheney probably enhanced the chance that Gore would choose Lieberman, not Edwards, because Bush's decision meant Gore's choice would be "measured by a standard of seriousness."[39] Conversely, in 1988, Bush elected not to match Bentsen's gravitas with Dole, perceiving an opening to court baby boomers with Quayle. Finally, Obama's decision not to choose Clinton may have encouraged McCain to believe Palin might attract some Clinton supporters.

Dumping Vice Presidents

Incumbent vice presidents are rarely denied renomination. The vice-presidential selection system makes the president responsible for the initial choice and promotes compatibility between the two top officers. The White House vice presidency better positions the vice president to become an administration asset and to win favor with the president's inner circle just as the vice president's political role allows him to court party activists. The new presidential selection system increases the vice president's utility as a campaign surrogate for the president's reelection. George S. Sirgiovanni correctly observed that "vice presidents, the nation's human insurance policy, now have acquired a bit of coverage themselves."[40]

Since 1945, Rockefeller is the only vice president dumped by a president seeking nomination. Rockefeller's unpopularity with the Republican base jeopardized Ford's nomination against Reagan's challenge. Ford asked Rockefeller to withdraw to enhance Ford's prospects against Reagan.[41] Some Rockefeller detractors within Ford's inner circle thought Rockefeller's presence would prevent Ford's nomination.[42] Ford later regretted dropping Rockefeller.[43]

Since 1976, Quayle faced the strongest opposition to his renomination. As Bush's popularity dropped, Quayle's position became more precarious as the "Dump Quayle" chorus came from multiple directions. Kansas senators Dole and Kassebaum approached Powell about replacing Quayle.[44] James Baker passed to campaign strategist Teeter an associate's idea that Powell replace Quayle and supervise the domestic agenda. Teeter "loved the idea" and thought the three former Republican presidents (Nixon, Ford, and Reagan) might ask Quayle to step down.[45] Ford and Nixon urged Bush to drop Quayle,[46] as did high-ranking campaign officials.[47] Cheney thought Quayle should go,[48] as did Republican pro Ed Rollins,[49] conservative columnists William F. Buckley, Jr., and George Will, and various Republican members of Congress.[50] The speculation that Powell would replace Quayle was sufficiently intense that Powell contacted Quayle to disclaim designs on his job.[51]

Although polling suggested Bush would do better with undecided and non-Bush voters if he replaced Quayle,[52] Republicans favored retaining Quayle, 54 percent to 39 percent.[53] Dumping Quayle risked offending Bush's base, would suggest panic and raise questions about Bush's initial judgment,[54] and subject him to criticism as disloyal.

To prompt Quayle's withdrawal, some Bush allies leaked stories about the campaign's misgivings.[55] "What was needed was to persuade the vice president to remove himself from the ticket and exit gracefully, stage right," wrote Baker, who said Bush "would have accepted" Quayle's decision to withdraw.[56] But Bush would not initiate a move to remove Quayle, either because of the political cost, because he empathized with Quayle,[57] or due to his loyalty to Quayle. Bush and Quayle discussed the matter on two occasions. After the second session, Quayle's camp reportedly leaked that Quayle had offered to withdraw but Bush had asked him to remain, a story Bush supposedly claimed was not true.[58]

Some suggested that Bush dump Cheney in 2004. In mid-2003, Cheney offered to step down on three occasions. Bush dismissed the idea twice before considering it for a "few days" but rejecting it.[59] Bush presented a single offer and reported discussing with several advisers replacing Cheney with Senator Bill Frist. Cheney had "become a lightning-rod for criticism," and replacing Cheney would demonstrate that Bush, not Cheney, was "in charge."[60] Bush campaign aides were divided about replacing Cheney.[61] Bush valued Cheney's contributions, and Cheney's public standing apparently counseled against the move. Although Cheney's favorable and unfavorable ratings were essentially even, Gallup later found in July 2004 that 59 percent overall (up from 51 percent in late October 2003) and 71 percent of Republicans thought Bush should retain Cheney.[62]

Obama campaign aides conducted polling to determine whether replacing Biden with Hillary Clinton would help Obama in 2012. The polls found that the move would not significantly benefit Obama.[63] Obama never considered the idea, nor was it taken seriously, according to his close associates.[64]

The subject of dumping the vice president often engages political pundits but rarely represents a plausible course of action. Proponents tend to emphasize the perceived benefits of a change while ignoring the costs. Even before the advent of the White House vice presidency, the vice president's ability to curry favor with the party base made the course precarious. The White House vice presidency has decreased even further the likelihood that a president will replace a vice president who wishes to remain. The president's increased responsibility for the initial selection will expose his judgment to criticism if he implicitly concedes that the decision was an error and makes a change. Moreover, a White House vice president's central administration role increases the likelihood that he will retain political strength as well as some loyalty from the president and his other close advisers.[65]

Conclusion

Vice-presidential selection cannot be reduced to mechanical formulas. Each selector is unique and chooses from a different pool in a different context. Presidential candidates may envision an ideal running mate but ultimately must choose between real-world options with strengths and weaknesses. A presidential candidate faced with an apparently competitive race may be risk-averse in vice-presidential selection, whereas one whose chances seem extremely strong or weak may follow a different path, emphasizing governing criteria in the former situation or a high-reward, high-risk strategy in the latter.

Yet the transformation of the vice-presidential selection process since 1976 has been accompanied by an adjustment in the criteria for the choice. Running mates must be able to survive the vetting process without any disabling disclosure. Moreover, most presidential candidates choose running mates who are presidential and who are plausible partners. A running mate who does not appear presidential or who differs from the standard-bearer on fundamental issues is likely to make election more difficult. Presidential candidates also look for running mates who supplement their appeal by bringing different skills, knowledge, or perspective to the ticket. Balancing is far from obsolete.

Governance factors have political significance. The selection sends messages about the selector, a fact that provides reason for candidates to choose well. These incentives enhance the likelihood that running mates will be equipped to be effective White House vice presidents.

12

Vice-Presidential Campaigns

Vice-presidential campaigns have changed since 1976. Whereas presidential nominees formerly disclosed running mates on the convention's final day in an event overshadowed by the standard-bearer's acceptance speech, that announcement is now a significant, preconvention, multi-day event. Whereas the vice-presidential acceptance speech used to be shoehorned into the convention's crowded final day, it now generally highlights the prior day. And the vice-presidential debate, a Carter-Ford creation, provides a campaign focal point. Consistent with the White House vice presidency, these innovations have made running mates more visible and important. And consistent with that new governing institution, vice-presidential campaigns are better integrated into the presidential campaign.

In addition to these new central features of vice-presidential campaigns, recurring tendencies characterize the behavior of many vice-presidential candidates. Since most voters decide based primarily on the competing presidential candidates, campaigns generally highlight the standard-bearer, not the running mate. Accordingly, most contemporary vice-presidential candidates, like their predecessors, play supporting roles in which they celebrate the presidential candidate, sound campaign themes, and denounce the opposing ticket, often in less glamorous venues.

Yet vice-presidential campaigns are not all the same. Depending on circumstances, some vice-presidential candidates are emphasized, either by original design or campaign dynamics, whereas others perform more-modest services. The roles of vice-presidential candidates vary depending on the dynamics of the race, the needs of the ticket, and the perceived strengths (and weaknesses) of the running mate. Vice-presidential campaigns can impact the ultimate outcome and also help set the stage for the governing role that follows.

Standard Structure of Modern Vice-Presidential Campaigns

The modern vice-presidential campaign centers around three prominent events—and everything else. And sometimes the "everything else" matters.

THE VICE-PRESIDENTIAL ROLLOUT

The convention's traditional role in determining the presidential nomination formerly caused the vice-presidential choice to be deferred until the gathering's end except when presidents retained their first-term vice president. The move to presidential caucuses and primaries accelerated the resolution of presidential nominations and allowed an earlier vice-presidential choice. Although several presidential candidates (Carter, Reagan, and George H. W. Bush) secured nominations before the convention but delayed their choice, either to create convention drama or in reflexive adherence to tradition, presidential candidates ultimately realized that accelerating the decision provided additional opportunity for the presidential candidate to receive beneficial coverage and refocused the convention from the bottom of the ticket to celebrating the standard-bearer and deriding the opposition. This epiphany responded to experiences showing benefits of earlier announcements and perils of convention choice.

In 1984 Mondale became the first nonincumbent presidential nominee to announce his running mate before the convention when he identified Ferraro four days before it began. Mondale's selection process had been criticized as pandering to various interest groups, some of which were pushing their favorites in a way not helpful to his interests. For example, women's groups were insisting that Mondale choose a woman running mate and threatening a floor fight or to withhold support if he did not.[1]

Mondale's announcement in St. Paul, Minnesota, changed the narrative. It presented him as looking toward the future, not mired in his association with Carter's administration.[2] The choice was described as "historic," "bold," and "exciting." Mondale called it a metaphor for his message that the American dream should work for all.[3] Party leaders praised Ferraro; women's groups were ecstatic.[4] A *New York Times/CBS News* poll on July 12, 1984, found that 25 percent had a favorable and 10 percent an unfavorable opinion of Ferraro. Although some voters questioned her ability to handle an international crisis, Mondale gained 6 percent among younger voters. Whereas that poll showed no immediate overall change in the race, *Newsweek* found that the Democratic ticket now trailed by only 6 percent and led, 49 percent to 41 percent, among women.[5] The ticket campaigned at Mondale's boyhood hometown of Elmore, Minnesota, the next day. Ferraro challenged Bush to debate and accused Reagan of not being a good Christian because his policies were "unfair,"[6] a controversial charge she soon abandoned.[7] After a joint vacation, Mondale and Ferraro were welcomed to the convention in San Francisco in two large rallies.[8]

Four years later, Dukakis announced his choice of Bentsen six days before the convention. The selection commanded a banner headline and three front-page stories in the *New York Times*, with analogies to the Boston-Austin, Kennedy-Johnson combination and references to ideological and regional inclusiveness. Those helpful messages were muted by media attention to a perceived snub of Reverend Jesse Jackson, the runner-up for the presidential nomination and one of those purportedly under consideration to be Dukakis's running mate. In pre–cell phone days, the call notifying Jackson of Bentsen's selection reached his hotel after he left, and Jackson first heard of the decision from a reporter upon arriving in Washington, D.C. Dukakis's apologies did not mollify Jackson. Although the Bentsen selection allowed Dukakis to emphasize that he valued a vice president who would challenge his views (an implicit dig at Bush), media coverage of the feud with Jackson diminished Dukakis's ability to use his choice to attract swing voters and raised questions regarding his campaign's competence.[9]

The Ferraro and Bentsen rollouts, though generally successful, suggested two lessons. First, a running mate new to national politics may stumble, as Ferraro did in questioning Reagan's faith, especially if thrust into the spotlight of a national campaign with little preparation. Second, logistical mistakes, such as the missed call to Jackson, can lessen an otherwise effective rollout. Both types of problems recurred, to a much greater extent, in Quayle's rollout, which the Bush campaign, nearly flawless in other respects, totally botched.

After Bush revealed to associates on convention Tuesday that he had decided on his running mate without disclosing his choice, the campaign elected to accelerate the announcement by two days to that very afternoon to prevent a leak and to silence critics of Bush's process. The decision to expedite the announcement allowed no time to plan the rollout, prepare Quayle for his national debut, or even furnish appropriate advance work for Quayle's arrival.

Quayle was instructed to be dockside when Bush arrived in New Orleans via boat[10] and was admonished that secrecy was essential. Quayle, his wife, Marilyn, and aide Tom Duesterberg arrived at the Spanish Plaza in the August New Orleans afternoon heat. Lacking a security detail, they tried to force their way through the large crowd.[11] When Quayle reached the vessel, he was no doubt excited by the news and his exertion. Onstage, Quayle seemed hyperactive, not presidential.[12]

Since Quayle was relatively unknown and a surprising choice, early impressions were critical in shaping his image. Yet the Bush campaign was unprepared for the rollout. It had not enlisted leading Republicans to extol Quayle. Lacking a current Quayle biography or talking points for media distribution, it used a less-than-flattering third-party profile. Surprised party luminaries made unhelpful comments. Quayle was not well-prepared for early appearances. Quayle was separated from his Senate staff as the Bush campaign assumed responsibility for his appearances. It provided a staff of savvy Republican operatives, but its members lacked a relationship with Quayle or knowledge of his strengths and weaknesses.

The surprising choice generated questions. Why had Quayle enlisted in the national guard rather than serving in Vietnam? Had family influence procured preferential treatment? Had he propositioned Washington lobbyist/*Playboy* pinup Paula Parkinson during a golfing trip she had taken with several congressmen? Since Bush's communications personnel lacked vetting information, the initial response was ineffective. Ultimately, no evidence impugned Quayle on these scores (and some of the accusations had been discredited previously),[13] but the impact of the charges outlived the later rebuttals.

Little time was spent preparing Bush and Quayle for a press conference on the convention's third day, and most attention addressed questions anticipated for Bush.[14] The first three questions challenged Quayle's qualifications to be first successor, as did later questions. Quayle's recitation of executive experience during his twenties was unconvincing. He responded poorly when asked about Parkinson and the national guard.[15] He was unprepared for interviews that evening with network television anchors, telling NBC's Tom Brokaw that "phone calls were made" to get him into the national guard[16] and CBS's Dan Rather that his worst fear was "Paula Parkinson."[17] Baker dispatched two campaign aides after midnight to quiz Quayle about the circumstances leading to his national guard service.[18] Rumors spread that Quayle would be dropped, a course the Bush campaign quickly rejected.[19]

Bush's impressive acceptance speech rescued the convention. The rollout continued after the convention with joint Bush-Quayle appearances in Quayle's native Midwest. After Bush and Quayle spoke in Quayle's hometown of Huntington, Indiana, Quayle engaged in an impromptu press conference broadcast to the 12,000 supporters present. The crowd's boisterous support of Quayle and hostility toward the media intimidated the latter.[20] Bush and Quayle appeared together the following day in West Carrollton, Ohio. Some Republicans lamented that the controversy had diverted attention from Bush's themes,[21] whereas others criticized the choice.[22] During a twelve-day period, the three television networks devoted ninety-three stories to Quayle.[23]

The Quayle rollout demonstrated some hazards of a convention announcement. The initial plan for a late convention announcement diverted attention from Bush and his campaign themes to vice-presidential selection. The belated decision to accelerate the announcement left little time to prepare. That, coupled with the convention setting and the surprise nature of Quayle's selection, created an uncontrolled dynamic as the congregated media went into a feeding frenzy that the Bush campaign was unprepared to address.

The experience confirmed the advantages of a preconvention announcement. Moreover, it suggested that the value of surprise must be weighed against the readiness of the campaign and running mate for the rollout. Media material must be prepared; endorsers lined up with talking points, especially when the choice is unknown or controversial; and a campaign team put in place. The running mate must be prepared to speak and answer questions, and vetting information must be analyzed so that effective responses are ready to rebut attacks. Finally, an unknown candidate is particularly vulnerable because any adverse disclosure will shape public knowledge disproportionately and may suggest inadequate vetting.

The Quayle rollout presented a cautionary tale. In 1992, Gore associates congregated in Carthage, Tennessee, a few days before Clinton's anticipated decision to prepare for Gore's possible selection. They made sure appropriate statements were prepared and anticipated questions, such as on policy differences between Clinton and Gore.[24]

Post-Quayle, every first-time vice-presidential candidate has been chosen from two (Kemp and Biden) to twenty (Edwards) days before the convention.[25] The rollout runs for a day or so to weeks, with events involving one or both ticket partners. It provides a widely covered event in which the ticket receives favorable publicity in contexts set by the campaign.

Often the announcement introduces a newcomer to national politics. Most voters had not heard of, or lacked an opinion about, Palin, Ryan, Lieberman, or Biden when each was announced.[26] The rollout also seeks to communicate positive impressions about the presidential nominee. It emphasizes that the standard-bearer is the leader by furnishing a subordinate. It also identifies the nominee with certain values associated with the running mate. When both parties have new running mates (1976, 1988, 2000, and 2008), the rollout of the party in power (whose convention is second) may be used to divert attention from the opponent's convention. Gore named Lieberman five days after the Republican convention to shift the narrative; McCain blunted Obama's convention bounce by announcing his selection the day after Obama's Thursday-evening acceptance speech, thereby making Palin, not Obama, the weekend focus.

Although announcements usually occur within a week of the convention, candidates challenging an incumbent president may announce their choice earlier to attract needed attention. The Kerry-Edwards rollout began July 6 with an announcement and rally in Pittsburgh and continued for four days of campaigning through Ohio, Florida, New York, and Edwards's home state of North Carolina. Romney announced Ryan's selection on August 11, 2012, in Norfolk, Virginia, sixteen days before the Republican convention. The following day, Romney and Ryan appeared in North Carolina, another swing state, and Wisconsin, Ryan's home state, and did a joint interview for CBS's *60 Minutes* before Ryan campaigned solo at the Iowa State Fair on day three and in Colorado the next day. Following the announcement, Ryan's favorability rating jumped 15 percent generally and more than 20 percent among conservative Republicans.[27] Romney's selection of Ryan was less favorably received than most [28] but made 36 percent of Republicans more likely to support Romney.[29]

The candidates often appear in one or both of their hometowns or birthplaces. Dole announced Kemp's selection in Russell, Kansas, the day before they appeared in San Diego, the convention's site and a city where Kemp had played as a professional quarterback. Kemp's selection received three front-page *New York Times* stories when it leaked and again when announced the next day. Gore disclosed Lieberman's selection in Nashville on August 8, 2000, and they campaigned in their hometowns of Carthage, Tennessee, and Stamford, Connecticut, on August 9; in Atlanta on August 10; and in Bridgeport and Philadelphia on August 11. The *New York Times* gave three front-page stories to the Lieberman selection when the news leaked and two more the day following the formal announcement. On August 13, Lieberman appeared on five Sunday talk shows.

The event can be transformative, as Clinton's rollout of Gore demonstrated. Its impact became evident when Clinton, Gore, and their young families appeared in Little Rock on July 9, 1992, and presented an electrifying picture.[30] "No one could have predicted the enthusiasm that greeted the choice of Gore," wrote Christopher.[31] Clinton and Gore appeared together the following two days in Arkansas, then in Gore's hometown. The Gore rollout was a "pivotal moment" of the

1992 campaign[32] and triggered Clinton's surge. "Clinton and Gore together changed the way people viewed Clinton" such that the candidates' "common traits" dominated while Clinton's shortcomings were obscured.[33]

McCain used the Palin announcement in Dayton, Ohio, to emphasize campaign themes. Palin would help him "stand up to those who value their privileges over their responsibilities, who put power over principle, and put their interests before your needs." Palin had fought corruption and waste, had "great tenacity and skill," and was from "a decent, hardworking, middle-class family." Palin's sixteen-minute speech identified her with ordinary Americans; celebrated McCain as a profile in courage; and courted women, including Hillary Clinton supporters.[34] Thirty percent of Republicans became more and 5 percent became less likely to support McCain, but only 39 percent thought Palin qualified to be president, significantly lower than every running mate since 1992 except Quayle.[35]

The rollout presents risk for a newcomer to presidential politics. Public appearances begin immediately. Whereas presidential nominees have honed their message for months and become accustomed to the scrutiny of a national campaign, the new running mate debuts in a highly visible event. The McCain campaign sheltered Palin from the media for weeks. A remedy is to choose prepared running mates or to give them advance notice so they can get ready, as Romney did with Ryan.[36] A longer rollout, like those Edwards and Ryan experienced, allows the other side to brand the running mate. Democrats emphasized Ryan's controversial budget plan. Ryan became better known during the ten days following his announcement as those with no opinion about him dropped more than 30 percent to 26 percent. Yet his unfavorable ratings rose more than did his favorable ones.[37]

The rollout may be affected by the quality of the vetting and whether its fruits are shared with campaign decision-makers. The campaign may fail to respond effectively if potential problems are missed, underestimated, or kept from campaign operatives. Issues first publicized after the announcement, as occurred with Palin's selection, may impeach the competency of the selection process and the presidential candidate. Accordingly, some issues are best disclosed prior to the announcement.

Presidential candidates hope their vice-presidential pick will boost their campaign by confirming their decision-making ability. Generally, they do. The selections of Edwards, Lieberman, Cheney, and Gore were judged overwhelmingly to reflect well on the selectors. Bush's choice of Quayle was not.[38]

Although in surveys taken shortly after the vice-presidential choice is announced 60 to 80 percent of registered voters generally say the running-mate choice will not affect their votes, many report the comparison will influence them, generally in a positive direction. Clinton's choice of Gore in 1992 made 33 percent of voters more and 8 percent less likely to support Clinton. The selections of Kemp, Bentsen, Edwards, and Lieberman had positive margins of 12 percent to 18 percent, whereas those of Palin, Biden, Ryan and Cheney had single-digit positive margins. Bush's choice of Quayle had no initial effect in 1988 and made voters less likely to support Bush four years later.[39]

Although the data are not entirely consistent, presidential candidates generally receive some boost from the running-mate announcement. One study found that Clinton's choice of Gore provided an 11 percent gain, the largest measured bounce. Lieberman, Cheney, and Kemp provided 6 percent to 8 percent bounces, although about 3 percent of Lieberman's and Cheney's disappeared by the convention. Edwards provided little bounce.[40] Gallup found that the seven preconvention vice-presidential announcements from 1996 to 2012 produced bounces of −2 percent (Biden) to 9 percent (Kemp) with a 3 percent average. Recent selections (Biden, Palin, and Ryan) received smaller bounces.[41]

Moreover, voter reaction following the rollout provides simply a snapshot of public opinion in July or August, often when little is known about the running mate. A favorable reaction then can be helpful, as it was for Clinton in 1992, but what ultimately matters is how voters feel in November.

ACCEPTANCE SPEECH

The vice-presidential acceptance speech is the second major vice-presidential campaign event. When the choice was made at the convention, the running mate had little time to write and practice the speech, got little air time, and received slight media coverage. Since the 1996

Democratic convention, the preconvention announcement has allowed vice-presidential acceptance speeches generally to move to the prior night, when it is usually the main event, although perhaps for a smaller audience, rather than being a warm-up act. There is time to prepare and rehearse, and the remarks are longer and receive greater attention.

The vice-presidential acceptance speech serves several functions. In addition to sounding campaign themes, it often introduces a newcomer to national politics. Ferraro offered herself as evidence that "America is the land where dreams can come true for all of us" and said, "There are no doors we cannot unlock." Ferraro was a "daughter of working Americans" and "the daughter of an immigrant from Italy."[42]

Palin's forty-minute acceptance speech assumed unusual importance because she was unknown, had little government experience, had been shielded from the media, and was controversial. Her successful speech celebrated McCain for his service, courage, and leadership and introduced her as a citizen who had gone into public life "to serve the people," not to cater to elites, and as a mother of a son in military service and another with special needs. She had cut government waste by saying "thanks, but no thanks, on that Bridge to Nowhere." She disparaged Obama for tailoring his image to his audience, as a cultlike leader who had written two memoirs but no major laws, and as a weak commander-in-chief and spend-happy chief executive.[43] After Palin's well-received convention speech, her presence on the ticket made 29 percent of registered voters more and 21 percent less likely to vote for McCain. Some 55 percent thought the choice reflected well on McCain's decision-making, but 40 percent disagreed.[44]

Gore's 1992 speech recited a litany of failures of Bush and Quayle with the refrain "It is time for them to go." He praised Clinton for balancing eleven budgets, keeping taxes low, and creating jobs in Arkansas, and connected Clinton and himself to basic American values and to small-town America because Hope, Arkansas, and Carthage, Tennessee, were places "where people do know about it when you're born and care about it when you die."[45]

Cheney played a different role in 2000. Having served closely with Presidents Ford and Bush and concurrently with Reagan, he could present Bush as a leader with "the courage, and the vision, and the goodness, to be a great president." Cheney praised Bush as a successful governor who led in a bipartisan way. In a highly partisan speech,[46] Cheney attacked Clinton (Bush "will restore decency and integrity to the Oval Office"). Gore would try "to separate himself from his leader's shadow. But somehow we will never see one without thinking of the other." "It is time for them to go," he said repeatedly, borrowing Gore's 1992 refrain.[47]

The acceptance speech may also be important for an incumbent vice president. Although they have high name recognition, the absence of a rollout generally makes the acceptance speech their first high-profile campaign event. As White House vice presidents, they are well positioned to extol the president's leadership. After the bitter Carter-Kennedy primary, Mondale's 1980 acceptance speech sought to reunify the party by appealing to Kennedy supporters, celebrated Carter's progressive and enlightened leadership, and portrayed Reagan as an extremist by invoking popular programs that Americans supported, "but not Ronald Reagan," borrowing Hubert Humphrey's rhetorical device from his 1964 acceptance speech attacking Senator Barry M. Goldwater.[48]

Quayle devoted the first part of his 1992 speech to bolstering his image. He linked himself to traditional middle American values, discussed his work heading the Competitiveness Council, attacked Clinton and Gore ("Well, if they're moderates, I'm a world champion speller"), and celebrated Bush as a leader of character.[49]

Biden's 2012 speech praised Obama's leadership from the vantage point of someone who was with him regularly. Biden spoke of the progress of the prior four years, of the "enormity" of Obama's heart and his empathy for struggling Americans. Obama had rescued the American auto industry and authorized the successful mission against bin Laden, notwithstanding contrary advice. Biden contrasted Obama's and Romney's policies.[50]

THE VICE-PRESIDENTIAL DEBATE

The debate, the third marquee event of the vice-presidential campaign, has made vice-presidential candidates more visible and shows them under pressure. Vice-presidential debates have attracted anywhere from an estimated 26.6 million (Gore-Kemp) to 69.9 million viewers (Biden-Palin). The audience is generally smaller than for the presidential debates although the Palin-Biden debate drew a larger viewership than any of the Obama-McCain encounters and all but two presidential debates.[51] Whereas the rollout and acceptance speech occur early in the campaign, debates take place in October, usually within a month of election day.

Vice-presidential debates are unique. Whereas presidential candidates (other than incumbent presidents) have debated during the nomination campaign, vice-presidential candidates often have not experienced anything like these events. Whereas presidential candidates have been formulating replies for months, vice-presidential candidates generally have spent much less time packaging campaign issues in debate answers. Whereas presidential candidates are well known, the vice-presidential debate helps introduce many and may shape perceptions of whether or not they are presidential. Prior to the 1988 vice-presidential debate, two polls found that 40 percent to 55 percent essentially lacked an opinion of Bentsen or Quayle.[52] Some 30 percent reported no opinion or had not heard of Cheney a few weeks before the 2000 debate.[53] The stakes are substantial, especially because vice-presidential candidates debate only once.

Vice-presidential debates are not principally about the candidates on-stage. Savvy vice-presidential candidates do not focus on their counterpart but concentrate on extolling their partner, attacking the opponent, and sounding campaign themes. For instance, in 1988, Quayle relentlessly portrayed Dukakis as a tax-and-spend liberal. In his second answer, Quayle twice referred to the "liberal Governor" with "liberal policies." Five consecutive sentences associated Dukakis with tax increases, calling him "Tax-Hike Mike" from "Taxachusetts." Dukakis was "the most liberal national Democrat" to seek the presidency "since George McGovern." Dukakis was "simply out of step with mainstream America." Quayle lambasted the "Governor of Massachusetts" for telling midwestern farmers to "grow Belgium endive," a crop that might appeal to Dukakis and his "Harvard buddies" but not to the American farmer. Quayle claimed that Dukakis had "run up more debt than all the governors" in Massachusetts history. In his closing statement, Quayle said that "the road of Michael Dukakis" meant "bigger government, higher taxes . . . cuts in national defense. Back to the old economics of high interest rates, high inflation, and the old politics of high unemployment."[54]

Quayle devoted the 1992 debate to attacking Clinton as untrustworthy, unprepared for an international crisis, and a tax-and-spend liberal. His opening statement said Clinton would cause higher taxes and fewer jobs and "does not have the strength nor the character to be president of the US,"[55] points he relentlessly made. More than once, he accused Gore of "pulling a Clinton" by saying "one thing one day and another thing the next day." The "fundamental problem with Bill Clinton . . . is trust and character," Quayle said. "Bill Clinton has trouble telling the truth." Accordingly, Clinton could not deal with allies because "truth and integrity are prerequisites to being president of the US." Quayle closed:[56]

> Not one time during this evening, during 90 minutes, did Al Gore tell us why Bill Clinton is qualified to be president. He never answered my charges that Bill Clinton has trouble telling the truth.
>
> The choice is yours. The American people should demand that their president tell the truth. Do you really believe—do you really believe Bill Clinton will tell the truth? And do you, do you trust Bill Clinton to be your president?

Whereas Quayle effectively attacked the opposing standard-bearer, the 1996 and 2000 debates were quite different. When host Jim Lehrer asked Kemp about Dole's unwillingness "to draw personal and ethical differences" with Clinton during the first debate, Kemp responded that he and Dole saw Clinton and Gore as opponents, not enemies, and promised to discuss issues "with dignity and respect."[57] Kemp never attacked Clinton for ethical lapses and repeatedly called Gore "my friend." Gore praised Kemp for speaking against incivility and proclaimed his "enormous respect" for Kemp and Dole, who were "good men."[58] The positive tone elevated discourse but cost Dole, who was trailing, an important opportunity to raise questions about Clinton; Kemp's assertions that it was "beneath [Dole] to go after anyone personally" made it harder for the campaign to do so. Four years later, in their opening statements, Lieberman and Cheney promised to avoid personal attacks, and did,[59] to the consternation of Gore's campaign. The tone changed in 2004. After Cheney's opening discussion of the war in Iraq, Edwards charged, "Mr. Vice President, you are still not being straight with the

American people." Later Edwards accused Cheney of "a complete distortion."[60] Cheney attacked Kerry as having been wrong on all national security issues for three decades.

Candidates who are unknown and relatively inexperienced may be more reluctant to embrace the "hit man" role. Ferraro, for instance, sought to counter her image as "feisty," which called for some restraint. Newcomers Dole and Quayle vigorously attacked their rivals, but Kemp and Lieberman were uncomfortable in that role. Sometimes candidates respond to the opposition. Gore attacked in 1992 but preached civility four years later; Cheney followed the opposite trajectory. Biden was relatively restrained against Palin to avoid appearing a bully, but four years later, after Obama's uninspired debate performance, he ridiculed Republican claims in order to rally the Democratic base and change the narrative. Ryan's discussion was "a bunch of malarkey"; Romney had politicized the attack on America's embassy in Benghazi and denigrated 47 percent of the American people while paying a lower tax rate than someone making $50,000 per year.[61]

Vice-presidential candidates also celebrate the leadership of their ticket mate. In 1984, Bush turned the opening question, on whether he would follow Reagan's policies, into a testimonial to the president, who had "really turned this country around." He had inherited 21 percent interest rates, declining productivity, and "despair." "And this president turned it around and I've been with him every step of the way." Two questions later, Bush ended his criticism of the Carter-Mondale administration by asserting that "Ronald Reagan is delivering leadership." His closing statement listed the accomplishments of Reagan's first term and asserted that "Ronald Reagan is clearly the strong leader of the free world. And I'll be honest with you. It's a joy to serve with a president who does not apologize for the United States of America."[62]

Having missed chances to defend Clinton four years earlier, Gore repeatedly praised Clinton's policies and leadership during the 1996 debate. He opened by discussing "Bill Clinton's positive plan for America's future." Clinton had protected programs on which seniors depended and prevented lobbyists for polluters from gutting the Clean Water Act. When the moderator raised Dole's charge that Clinton had not kept his promises, Gore listed programs where Clinton had met, exceeded, or was in the process of meeting promises. Gore said, "President Clinton showed tremendous courage, vision, wisdom, and leadership" in resolving the war in Bosnia. Gore "was so proud of our President" for his handling of the crisis in Haiti and for his "bold and dynamic leadership" to rescue the Mexican peso.[63]

Kemp was not to be outdone. When Dole's position regarding programs for senior citizens was challenged, Kemp replied, "Does anybody think that Bob Dole, who almost gave his life for his country, who has served in the Senate, who helped save Social Security, crawled out of a fox hole on Riva Ridge in Northern Italy in 1945 to save a wounded radioman? Does anybody think in this country that he could possibly want to move our country ahead and leave anybody behind?" Kemp reprised this image of Dole as wartime hero in his closing sentences:[64]

> Bob Dole, as I said earlier, is a man of courage, a man of principles, a man who crawled out of a fox hole on Riva Ridge in 1945 to save a wounded brethren. The bible says no greater love hath a man than he gave his life. Well, Bob Dole did, just about, he'd been through the valley of the shadow and he as Commander-in-Chief can take this country with the courage of Churchill. The principles of Lincoln and the indefatigable optimism and spirit that this nation expects from its Commander-in-Chief and the next President of the United States, Bob Dole.

Vice-presidential candidates with modest experience are called upon to defend their qualifications. After summarizing Bush's résumé, the first question to Ferraro was "How does your three terms in the House of Representatives stack up against experience like that?" Ferraro was also asked about her qualifications to be commander-in-chief.[65] After PBS's Judy Woodruff asked Quayle in 1988 what qualified him to be vice president, Bentsen suggested that the real question was, "if . . . tragedy should occur," could Bentsen or Quayle be able "without any margin for error, without time for preparation, to take over the responsibility for the biggest job in the world, that of running this great country of ours; to take over the awesome responsibility for commanding the nuclear weaponry that this country has." After Quayle fumbled a question regarding what he would do as acting president, Bentsen reinforced his argument that the question was whether he or Quayle had the "maturity of judgment" and "breadth of experience" to be president.[66]

Brit Hume later referred to Woodruff's question about the "apprehensions" some felt about Quayle "being a heart beat away" and asked Quayle, "What would be the first steps you'd take, and why" if Bush were incapacitated? Quayle said he would "say a prayer" and then "assemble his people and talk" before again defending his qualifications. Hume returned to the topic in the next round. He reminded Quayle of the question and his answer. "What would you do next?" Hume asked. Quayle responded that it was improper to discuss a hypothetical situation and again recited his qualifications. Quayle's continued focus on his qualifications in response to questions about prospective actions caused NBC's Tom Brokaw to say to Quayle, "Surely you must have some plan in mind about what you would do if it fell to you to become President of the United States."

Quayle again characterized the question as one about his qualifications before belatedly appreciating the "what would you do" focus and saying he would gather Bush's advisers. He then discussed his future responsibilities and past experience before making the biggest gaffe in vice-presidential debate history near the end of a long answer: "It is not just age; it's accomplishments, it's experience. I have far more experience than many others that sought the office of vice president of this country. I have as much experience in the Congress as Jack Kennedy did when he sought the presidency. I will be prepared to deal with the people in the Bush administration, if that unfortunate event would ever occur."[67]

Quayle had been warned against using the JFK comparison. As Baker later put it, "Comparing yourself to one of the other team's icons is inherently risky."[68]

Bentsen was ready. He had reacted with disbelief during preparation when advised that Quayle sometimes compared his age or experience with Kennedy's in 1960. "You're no more like Jack Kennedy than George Bush is like Ronald Reagan," Bentsen had responded in rehearsal.[69]

Bentsen unleashed the most famous sequence in debate history. "Senator, I served with Jack Kennedy, I knew Jack Kennedy, Jack Kennedy was a friend of mine. Senator, you are no Jack Kennedy." When Quayle complained that "that was really uncalled for, Senator," Bentsen responded, "You are the one that was making the comparison, Senator — and I'm one who knew him well. And frankly I think you are so far apart in the objectives you choose for your country that I did not think the comparison was well-taken."[70]

Polls judged Bentsen the debate winner, sometimes by a two-to-one margin, and indicated that the debate may have shifted 0 to 3 percent in Dukakis's direction.[71] Yet Quayle also helped his standing. Those who thought Quayle was qualified to be president rose from 37 percent to 47 percent, whereas those who would be worried if Quayle were president dropped from 52 percent to 48 percent.[72]

Although vice-presidential debates often have little impact, some debates may shift a few points. Thomas M. Holbrook found that perceptions of vice-presidential debate performance had some effect on post-debate voter intention and evaluation of vice-presidential candidates in 1984 and 1988.[73] The Cheney-Lieberman debate was followed by a 5 percent shift to the Republicans and Biden-Palin by a small shift to the Democrats.[74] A CBS News poll of uncommitted voters after the 2008 debate concluded that whereas Biden won the debate by more than a two-to-one margin, perceptions of both candidates improved. Still, the results were ominous for the McCain campaign. Although 55 percent of uncommitted voters thought Palin could be vice president, only 44 percent thought she could be an effective president. Some 97 percent of uncommitted voters thought Biden was prepared to be vice president, and 91 percent thought he could be an effective president. And 18 percent of previously uncommitted voters would now vote for Obama, whereas 10 percent favored McCain.[75] A CNN poll found that Biden won the debate, 51 percent to 36 percent; whereas 87 percent thought Biden qualified to be president, only 42 percent thought Palin was.[76]

The Campaign

The rollout, acceptance speech, and debate are the standard high-exposure events of a vice-presidential campaign, but they account for a small fraction of the vice-presidential candidate's time, perhaps 20 percent if debate preparation time is included in the numerator. Candidates spend much of the rest of the campaign traveling the country or, increasingly, the competitive states where the election is contested.

Although vice-presidential candidates generally play a supporting role, how they provide that support varies depending on campaign needs and the resources the running mate brings. Some vice-presidential candidates play very visible campaign roles, either because paired with an incumbent president who adopts a Rose Garden strategy, because chosen as a game-changer, or based on performance.

Incumbent presidents often minimize travel, which puts greater pressure on the vice-presidential candidate. While Ford spent much of the 1976 campaign at the White House, Dole visited forty-four states and traveled more than 60,000 miles in ten and one-half weeks with few days off.[77] To unite Republicans after the Ford-Reagan battle, Dole assumed the responsibility to attack Carter. Dole relentlessly criticized Carter for not knowing or understanding government, for waffling on issues, and for being too liberal.[78] He praised Ford as a great leader who was brave, decent, and honest[79] and whose compassion extended to all Americans.[80]

Dole concentrated on midwestern farm states but visited other venues, too. He focused on secondary markets, often speaking to fewer than 1,000 people. Whereas Ford campaigned in Columbus, Cleveland, and Cincinnati during the closing days, Toledo and Dayton were among Dole's more glamorous stops. Ford went to Houston; Dole to Corpus Christi and Lubbock. Whereas Ford visited Indianapolis, Dole covered Fort Wayne, Evansville, and Terre Haute. In Pennsylvania, Ford went to Philadelphia and Pittsburgh, Dole to Scranton, Erie, and Clark Summit.[81] Dole raised doubts about Carter, engaged the Republican base, and helped Ford carry the farm states,[82] yet many thought his style hurt Ford.[83]

Eight years later, Reagan generally remained at the White House while Bush campaigned energetically for the national ticket and congressional candidates. Bush began attacking Mondale even before the Democratic convention as a liberal Democrat without an economic program, for ignoring human rights abuses in Nicaragua, and for the high inflation and interest rates of the Carter years.[84]

Candidates such as Ferraro and Palin were selected to remake the political landscape and accordingly given high visibility. Ferraro campaigned in large markets, making five trips to Los Angeles, eleven to New York City, three each to Cleveland, Pittsburgh, San Diego, and San Francisco–Oakland, and two each to Chicago, Seattle, San Jose, Sacramento, Hartford, Nashville, and Philadelphia. She appeared with Mondale in New York and Texas in August; at Labor Day parades in New York and Wausau, Wisconsin; at a Columbus Day parade in New York; and in Madison, Wisconsin, the day after the vice-presidential debate.[85] Ferraro attracted large and enthusiastic crowds and much national media. Her utility was compromised, however, by attacks on her husband's business activities. After first agreeing to release his tax returns, Ferraro reversed course, prompting Republicans to suggest that she and her spouse had something to hide.[86] The controversy continued for more than a week, diverting attention from Mondale's campaign themes. Ferraro ultimately addressed these issues in a lengthy press conference on August 21, 1984, where she took questions until reporters had no more.[87] Although nothing disclosed affected Ferraro's qualifications, the controversy damaged her;[88] by mid-September, more viewed her unfavorably than favorably, her negative assessments having doubled in a month.[89]

Palin's selection was conceived as a game-changing pick. Initially, she exceeded expectations. She attracted huge crowds, and the Republican base rallied to McCain.[90] By the end of September, however, after her disastrous Katie Couric interviews,[91] twice as many independents and registered voters said their view of Palin was declining as said it was improving.[92] Whereas after the convention, 52 percent thought Palin qualified to be president (39 percent did not), by late September, those numbers had essentially reversed.[93] By mid-October, 49 percent of registered voters viewed her unfavorably (44 percent favorably), a 27 percent overall drop in four weeks. Although Republicans remained enthusiastic, independents were more negative than positive, a 40 percent negative swing in five weeks. McCain had hoped Palin would attract women voters, but they were much more critical of her than men.[94]

Sometimes vice-presidential campaigns achieve more prominence because the candidate performs well and either attracts favorable comment, is given a larger role, or both. Early on, Bentsen spent much time in the South, especially in Texas, trying "to credentialize" Dukakis with

Reagan Democrats. His campaign initially received so little coverage that he was persuaded to pose before a Buddy Holly statue in Lubbock, Texas, to create a photo opportunity to appeal to the "Bubba" vote and appease frustrated journalists who found their reports receiving little attention.[95]

The vice-presidential debate made Bentsen a star as his "You're no Jack Kennedy" sound bite was rebroadcast. Dukakis spent much of the following day arguing that the Bentsen and Quayle choices revealed that he was the better decision-maker.[96] Dukakis thereafter cast the choice as between two tickets, not two presidential candidates.[97] Bentsen's schedule was revised to include California, New Jersey, Pennsylvania, Missouri, and Arkansas the following week.[98] Bentsen made numerous major televised network appearances during the campaign.[99] After the debate, Dukakis's campaign ran commercials attacking Bush for choosing Quayle.[100] A Dukakis commercial showed Bentsen's "You're no JFK" line, followed by the words "President Quayle?" on the screen.[101] In the closing days, Bentsen campaigned in Chicago, Los Angeles, and throughout Texas;[102] appeared on *Meet the Press* and *Face the Nation*;[103] and was prominently featured in Dukakis's broadcast.[104] By contrast, Quayle was sent to low-visibility venues and uncontested states and did not do national interview shows, appear with Bush, give major speeches, or appear in Republican ads.[105]

Gore left the convention with Clinton on a highly successful bus tour. In all, Clinton and Gore made seven bus trips together, excluding two that lasted less than a day.[106] Clinton's pollster Stan Greenberg found that Gore attracted voters who had doubts about Clinton and recommended using Gore more aggressively in media and scheduling to reassure such voters and reinforce positive images of Clinton.[107]

The vice-presidential candidate's schedule is determined by his or her strengths, campaign needs, and the electoral map. Dole hit the farm states. Lieberman spent time in Florida before Jewish audiences. Biden targeted blue-collar workers, Roman Catholics, and senior citizens in states such as Ohio, Pennsylvania, and Florida.[108] During October 1996, Kemp visited eighteen states, including three trips to Florida covering more than four days and three trips to California covering more than six days. He also campaigned in Arizona, New Mexico, Connecticut, New

Jersey, Ohio, Kentucky, Oregon, Nevada, Tennessee, New York, Massachusetts, New Hampshire, Michigan, Texas, Illinois, and Louisiana, often in population centers.[109] Cheney went on three Sunday-morning talk shows to address some complicated issues.[110]

Many vice-presidential candidates cultivate local media. Dole held several press conferences each day, generally one at each media market. His schedulers included time for individual interviews with local television, radio, and print media. The Bentsen campaign regularly allocated time to local media interviews.[111] Biden did hundreds of local media interviews in 2008, primarily in small towns in competitive states.[112]

CAMPAIGN INTEGRATION

Vice-presidential campaigns are now more closely integrated into the overall effort than used to be the case. Whereas vice-presidential candidates used to hire their own staffs, now presidential campaigns provide the running mate with personnel, a necessity for someone who is a late addition to an enterprise already under way and moving fast. In 1988, the Bush campaign assembled a vice-presidential team that included experienced Republican professionals Stuart Spencer, a former Ford and Reagan adviser; Joseph Canzeri, a former Rockefeller aide; and Ken Khachigian, a former Reagan speechwriter. Quayle's Senate staff was largely excluded. Quayle clashed with Spencer and Canzeri. After the vice-presidential debate, Quayle announced that he would run his own campaign. Spencer left the airplane, and Quayle friends such as Mitch Daniels and Al Hubbard and some Senate colleagues arrived. Lieberman's provided aides arrived at his doorstep moments after Gore invited him to join the ticket. Palin met her team the day before the rollout. The Obama campaign constructed Biden's 2012 staff.

A preassembled staff helps the vice-presidential candidate hit the ground running, promotes campaign coordination, and provides needed expertise. Yet the Quayle experience suggests the advantage of including some of the running mate's associates for their knowledge of, and rapport with, the candidate. Typically, now the provided team is supplemented by some of the running mate's own people. Biden's plane never left unless his longtime associate Ted Kaufman or Mike Donilon was on board.

Campaign staff integration is critical and is facilitated if the vice-presidential candidate has a headquarters presence as well as a traveling staff. Gore surprised the Clinton campaign when he sent close aide Neel to headquarters and had Mark Gearan, the Clinton-provided liaison, generally with him on the road. The "cross-pollination" allowed Neel to know top Clinton people and advocate for Gore at headquarters and put Gearan in close contact with Gore and some of his staff.[113] Gore benefited from the fact that Neel and Gearan were both skillful and well-liked professionals, thereby facilitating the integration of the Clinton and Gore operations with carryover benefits when they took office.

The candidate's attitude and performance also make a big difference. Bush solicited help from Reagan's team so he could stay on message; Quayle willingly attacked his opponents; and Biden accepted instruction from Obama's aides, not an easy adjustment for one used to directing Senate aides. By contrast, Edwards resisted playing second fiddle, insisting on his refrain "Hope is on the way" instead of Kerry's ("Help is on the way"). Palin proved a continual challenge for the McCain campaign staff. Their inability to adapt to their campaign role suggests that Edwards and Palin would not have been successful vice presidents.

VICE-PRESIDENTIAL IMPACT

Presidential campaigns generally do not emphasize the vice-presidential candidate. When they do, it generally means their vice-presidential candidate is perceived more favorably than the rival and that they lack other promising themes. Campaigns that highlight the vice-presidential choice often are in trouble, as was true of the Mondale, Dukakis, and McCain campaigns. On the other hand, the campaigns of Carter in 1976 and Clinton in 1992 emphasized Mondale and Gore, respectively, as part of their successful strategies.

It is overly simplistic to conclude that no one votes for the vice president or that the vice-presidential choice doesn't matter. It is impossible to measure the impact of a running mate. How the presidential candidate would have done alone or with an option not taken cannot be tested in a way that simulates an actual campaign. Although most voters weigh the presidential choice more heavily, that does not render the vice-presidential candidate unimportant. It seems likely that Mondale made a difference in 1976 by shifting a few percentage points to Carter in competitive states such as Ohio and Pennsylvania and that Gore helped change attitudes toward Clinton. Humphrey Taylor of the Harris Poll thought Gore's selection of Lieberman made Gore appear more attractive.[114] Others argued that Cheney reassured voters about Bush.[115] By contrast, Obama focus groups found voters citing the Palin selection as reflecting negatively on McCain.[116] Vice-presidential candidates, like vice presidents, contribute as part of a team even when they are not the featured performer.

Those who minimize the impact of the running mate often note that Bush won even though voters preferred Bentsen to Quayle. This non sequitur simply shows that vice-presidential preference was not decisive, not that it was irrelevant. The Bentsen-Quayle choice probably shifted some voters Dukakis's way but not enough to alter the outcome. Voters preferred Bush to Dukakis for other reasons, and Bentsen's presence did not overcome misgivings that potential swing voters had about Dukakis.

The vice-presidential choice is likely to shift voters only when there is a disparity in perceptions of the vice-presidential candidates among persuadable voters and those who strongly prefer one running mate are indifferent between the presidential candidates. These two conditions rarely coincide, either because both presidential candidates choose well or because few voters are really undecided between the standard-bearers. When both pick well-regarded running mates, there is little reason to weigh the vice-presidential choice. It is not surprising that a choice between Mondale and Bush, Gore and Kemp, Cheney and Lieberman would not affect many voters. It is easy to minimize a shift of a few points, but in a close election, it can be decisive. Stacy Ulbig reports that a typical running mate affects about 1.75 percent of the votes but notes that such an impact could sway enough electoral votes to alter the outcome of a close election such as those in 1976 and 2000.[117]

Campaigns now give vice-presidential candidates greater exposure in competitive states. Moreover, the campaign begins the process of integrating the running mate into the presidential team. When both candidates choose well, the running mate may matter only at the margins. Yet that is where close races are decided.

13

The Vice President
as Successor

Especially as the presidency grew after the New Deal and World War II, the vice president's status as first presidential successor became the common justification of the office. The possibility of presidential death or inability in a nuclear age made a qualified and prepared successor imperative to help ensure continuous presidential leadership. The absence of an intraterm succession for more than forty years after 1974, the second-longest interval in American history without such an event, has somewhat diverted attention from the vice president's successor role. Yet the relative demise of that justification also traces to the development of the White House vice presidency. As the vice presidency has become a robust White House "something," the possibility of becoming "everything" no longer defines its existence.

The development of the White House vice presidency since 1977 has bolstered America's system for handling presidential vacancies and inabilities. In providing a significant ongoing role, the White House vice presidency better positions its occupant to act as successor in response to a presidential vacancy or inability than did the office when the duties were modest and episodic. An engaged vice president is more likely to be knowledgeable about contemporary issues than one remote from decision-making. An active vice president is more likely to be skillful at exercising power than one whose talents have atrophied from idleness. A vice president who has worked regularly with other administration officials is more likely to understand their strengths and weaknesses, their biases and dispositions, than one denied interaction. And succession is likely to operate more smoothly when a member of the president's team, not an outsider, is elevated. Of course, the White House vice presidency does not solve all problems of presidential continuity, but it helps. Presidential inability still presents challenges, as does succession beyond the vice presidency, a subject beyond the scope of this book.

Moreover, even without an intraterm succession, events since 1977 have left their mark. The Reagan assassination attempt on March 30, 1981, exposed problems regarding presidential continuity. The disability provisions of the Twenty-Fifth Amendment received their first applications during this period. New challenges in presidential continuity have tested vice-presidential behavior. New precedents have developed, demonstrating how repeated practice can shape institutional norms.

Background

Between 1841 and 1974, nine vice presidents succeeded to the presidency following the death or, in 1974, resignation of their predecessors. Although the Constitution originally intended that a vice president would simply exercise presidential power and duties, not assume the office, in case of removal, death, resignation, or inability, the Tyler Precedent, discussed in chapter 2, established the alternative view. The precedent was followed seven times from 1850 to 1963 as vice presidents were treated as president, not simply acting president, following the incumbent's death. Not every presidential illness constitutes presidential inability, but power clearly should have been transferred during the eighty days between the shooting of James Garfield and his death in 1881, during at least some of the time between Woodrow Wilson's stroke on October 2, 1919, and the end of his term on March 4, 1921, and when Dwight Eisenhower suffered a heart attack in 1955 and a stroke two years later. Before the ratification of the Twenty-Fifth Amendment in 1967, the Constitution was unclear regarding (1) who could determine whether the president was disabled, (2) based on what standard, and (3) whether such a decision removed the president permanently from office or simply transferred presidential powers and duties during his disability.[1]

In addition to the constitutional gaps, succession and inability presented political problems. Succession events invariably challenged vice presidents, who often came from rival wings of the party, especially in the nineteenth century, when party leaders completed the ticket. Even when presidents largely chose their own running mates, the trauma of presidential death required vice presidents to find the right balance between asserting leadership and deferring to their predecessor's memory. Presidential inability presented unique challenges due to constitutional ambiguities, the lack of precedents, and factual uncertainties not likely to arise following presidential death, resignation, or removal.

Section One of the Twenty-Fifth Amendment adopted the Tyler Precedent for presidential death, resignation, and removal but not for presidential inability. As such, the vice president became president following an event permanently displacing the president but simply discharged presidential powers and duties in case of presidential inability. Section Three allowed the president to transfer presidential powers and duties voluntarily to the vice president, upon transmitting to the Speaker of the House of Representatives and President pro tempore of the Senate a written declaration that he was "unable to discharge the powers and duties" of the presidency, and to resume them upon sending a written notice that the disability had ended. Section Four allowed the vice president and a majority of the heads of the executive departments (that is, members of the Cabinet) or such other body as Congress could create in the future to declare presidential inability and transfer presidential powers and duties to the vice president and provided for the president's later resumption of powers. Section Two of the Twenty-Fifth Amendment, providing a means to fill a vice-presidential vacancy, was used to install Ford as vice president in 1973 after Agnew resigned and Rockefeller in 1974 after Ford succeeded to the presidency following Nixon's resignation.[2]

The Reagan Assassination Attempt

On March 30, 1981, only ten weeks into his term, President Reagan was shot as he left a Washington hotel about 2:30 p.m. after delivering a speech. Reagan and his Secret Service detail did not realize he had been wounded, and his limousine headed for the White House, but upon seeing Reagan coughing blood, his agent diverted the motorcade to a hospital.[3] Reagan's aides soon learned that the president had been shot,[4] and some Cabinet officials and White House aides gathered in the White House situation room while Reagan's three top aides—Baker, Meese, and Deaver—went to the hospital. En route to Austin, Texas, Bush was advised that Reagan was "in serious condition" and encouraged to return.[5] Bush canceled his Austin schedule and embarked on the two-and-one-half-hour flight to Washington, D.C.[6]

At 3:37 p.m., White House aide David Gergen confirmed that Reagan had been shot and that doctors were deciding whether to remove the bullet. He reported that Reagan's condition was stable, that Bush was returning to Washington, and that various Cabinet members and presidential assistants were at the White House.[7] Haig cabled American embassies essentially this information.[8]

After watching a televised briefing during which Deputy Press Secretary Larry Speakes could not state who was running the American government, Haig rushed upstairs to the briefing room, commandeered the podium, and, breathless, announced that "we are in close touch with the Vice President, who is returning to Washington," that ranking Cabinet officials had gathered in the situation room, that Reagan's condition was "stable, now undergoing surgery," and that "no alert measures" were presently necessary or contemplated. Haig proclaimed, "As of now, I am in control here in the White House" and erroneously stated that he followed Bush in the line of succession.[9] Haig's statement was curious because he had known that line well as Nixon's and Ford's chief of staff when the vice presidency was twice vacant and Democratic Speaker of the House Carl Albert was next in line.[10] When Haig returned to the situation room, Weinberger said Haig had misstated America's military status because Weinberger had directed a small change.[11] Weinberger (and others) thought Haig's briefing had overstated Haig's authority and had "unnerved the world."[12]

Leading officials were unaware of the Twenty-Fifth Amendment. Theodore Olson, assistant attorney general for the Office of Legal Counsel, first studied it that day.[13] White House counsel Fred Fielding had not completed preparing a manual to address such situations but had drafted documents to transfer authority from Reagan to Bush.[14] Fielding explained the disability provisions of the Twenty-Fifth Amendment to those in the situation room, but Fielding recalled that "their eyes glazed over" upon hearing of it.[15] Haig later wrote that he and other senior Cabinet members thought discussing the subject was "premature and inappropriate" and that preparing paperwork was "ill-advised."[16] When Richard Darman, then a Reagan assistant, saw papers to invoke the Twenty-Fifth Amendment, he had them removed for safe-keeping, with Baker's approval.[17] Baker, Meese, and Deaver decided against invoking the Twenty-Fifth Amendment. Regardless of the legal formalities, a Cabinet member would be unlikely to trigger the amendment in opposition to Reagan's closest aides.

Upon arriving in Washington, Bush rejected advice that he helicopter to the White House, flew instead to the Naval Observatory, and traveled by car to the White House. Upon entering the situation room, Bush took control and encouraged others to operate as normally as possible.[18] About thirty minutes after Bush arrived, Reagan's surgeon pronounced the president "clear of head,"[19] although he remained on a respirator and on morphine for hours.[20] Bush said favorable reports of Reagan's condition obviated any need to consider the Twenty-Fifth Amendment.[21] He deflected the suggestion that he sign the Dairy Price Support Bill the next day if Reagan was unable to do so but agreed to accept Reagan's national security briefing and to hold various meetings in Reagan's absence. Bush emphasized the importance of giving accurate information to the public. The group agreed to issue a reassuring statement before markets opened the next day and were told the assassination attempt was not part of a larger conspiracy.[22] At 8:20 p.m., Bush announced that Reagan had "emerged from this experience with flying colors and with the most optimistic prospects for a complete recovery" and that "the American Government is functioning fully and effectively" and "with skill and with care."[23]

The Office of Legal Counsel in the Justice Department issued interpretations to help implement the Twenty-Fifth Amendment on April 3, 1981. It concluded that transfer occurred under Section Three or Four when the declaration was sent, not received, and that all parties need not sign a declaration under Section Four if they had reliably assented to it. And it opined that if the president were incapable of making a conscious decision "for a substantial period of time," the Twenty-Fifth Amendment should be invoked.[24]

Bush remained visible after the shooting. The next morning, he chaired a Cabinet meeting and met with the bipartisan congressional leadership. He visited Reagan at the hospital and announced that the president was doing very well. He volunteered that there was "no need for any emergency procedures, the power of the Vice President to do anything," and said he "absolutely" would not be assuming any special powers but would simply cover some of Reagan's meetings that he normally attended. Things would be "business as usual to the best we can do it."[25] Bush met with the Netherlands prime minister and in the postmeeting announcement referred again to Reagan's positive prognosis and said the government was functioning normally.[26] Two days later, Bush met separately with the deputy prime minister of Poland and the foreign minister of Turkey, reported on advances in those relationships, and again referred to Reagan's progress.[27] Bush performed ceremonial duties and issued statements for Reagan, such as congratulating the Senate on passing budget legislation.[28] Bush saw Reagan in the hospital on March 31 and on April 2, 3, 5, 7, 8, and 10, more often than any officials other than the Baker-Meese-Deaver triumvirate.[29]

Reagan came close to dying following the shooting. He later suffered a high fever; his condition remained critical for several days and shocked officials even after his return to the White House.[30] Reagan's White House physician, Dr. Daniel Ruge, later said that the Twenty-Fifth Amendment should have been invoked before Reagan went under anesthesia and remained in place for at least one or two days. Ruge regretted not having raised the subject.[31]

The Reagan assassination attempt produced two significant takeaways regarding the vice president as successor: one relating to Bush's conduct, the other addressing presidential inability more generally. Bush's behavior was a model of competent, circumspect leadership, which impressed Reagan's team and greatly enhanced his standing. Secretary of the Interior James Watt, no Bush admirer, noted Bush's loyalty to Reagan and self-confidence.[32] Speakes observed that Bush "instantly took command."[33] Haig referred to Bush's "stout good sense."[34] Deaver termed Bush "superb."[35]

The Reagan assassination attempt also revealed challenges in making Sections Three and Four operational. The administration was new, relationships were forming, and decision-makers were ignorant of the Twenty-Fifth Amendment and the law of succession. Administration insiders were unprepared for the trauma of a presidential shooting. They understood that presidential succession could make "a fundamental difference" in policy and personnel,[36] and Baker did not want to arouse suspicions among Reagan associates regarding Bush and him, especially since Bush had been Reagan's chief opponent for the 1980 nomination and Baker his campaign manager.[37] If they were "seen grabbing power at the first instance," their behavior might create "some difficulties and some problem."[38] Baker, Meese, and Deaver anticipated that Reagan would shortly regain decision-making ability and that the amendment could be invoked later if necessary.[39] They wanted to present the government as functioning normally, not raise questions about Reagan's health and age.[40] The lack of precedent also impeded invoking the Twenty-Fifth Amendment. Darman thought Reagan's associates in the situation room "capable of chaotic, emotional, half-informed discussion," confused regarding Reagan's condition, and capable of precipitous action.[41]

Had Reagan been disposed to transfer power under Section Three before surgery, Bush would have been hard-pressed to exercise it on *Air Force Two*. The lack of secure voice communications presented one difficulty.[42] Even if the Cabinet had sought to invoke Section Four, Bush possibly could not have transmitted a written statement under Section Four while airborne in a world prior to faxes and e-mails.[43] although perhaps the vice president's assent to a written declaration sent by the Cabinet would have sufficed, as the Justice Department concluded.[44] Baker argued that the correct decision was made but thought that the second-guessing had properly produced refined procedures.[45]

Planned Transfers of Power

The years since 1977 have produced precedents regarding transfer of presidential power to the vice president when the president undergoes an anticipated procedure under anesthesia.

CARTER'S HEMORRHOID ATTACK

The Carter administration had one occasion to consider invoking Section Three when Carter suffered a hemorrhoid attack on December 21, 1978. Carter called Mondale at 6:12 a.m. and during a three-minute conversation told him to stand by in case Carter underwent surgery. The administration apparently planned to transfer power, but that became unnecessary, as Carter's problems resolved without surgery.[46]

REAGAN'S CANCER SURGERY

The first temporary transfer of power came on July 13, 1985, when Reagan had surgery under general anesthesia to remove a large, cancerous polyp from his intestines. By then, Fielding had finished the presidential continuity manual and Bush had served more than a term as Reagan's loyal and engaged vice president. Yet again, the administration mishandled the situation.

Reagan had anticipated less-significant surgery under minor sedation and had decided not to transfer power absent complications. After tests on July 12 revealed the need for major surgery under anesthesia, Reagan decided to transfer power.[47] Bush was in Kennebunkport, Maine, when advised of Reagan's decision and returned to Washington after weighing whether doing so would appear presumptuous and whether remaining in Maine would seem unduly casual.[48]

Regan and Fielding provided Reagan with alternative letters transferring power.[49] Reagan signed one acknowledging Section Three but expressing doubt that its drafters "intended its application to situations such as the instant one." Nonetheless, "consistent with my longstanding arrangement with Vice President George Bush, and not intending to set a precedent binding" future presidents, Reagan transferred presidential powers and duties to Bush beginning with the administration of anesthesia.[50] Reagan signed the letter at 10:32 a.m. and was anesthetized at 11:28 a.m. Bush was not advised that he was acting president until 11:50 a.m.[51] While Reagan was unconscious, Bush hit his head on a concrete surface while playing tennis. For at least two minutes, Bush also was unconscious.[52]

In fact, the framers of the Twenty-Fifth Amendment clearly contemplated surgery under general anesthesia as an appropriate occasion to invoke Section Three.[53] Indeed, a month earlier, the Reagan Justice Department had concluded that "a written declaration pursuant to §3 could be prepared by the President in anticipation of an expected temporary disability, for example, if a President were scheduled to undergo surgery that would require general anesthetic and would result in the President's being unconscious for a significant length of time."[54] Reagan and close associates later conceded that he had used Section Three.[55]

Reagan reclaimed power at 7:22 p.m.[56] via a second, much shorter letter advising the designated legislative leaders that he was "able to resume the discharge of the Constitutional powers and duties of the Office of the President of the United States."[57] Reagan's aides had decided that the president's ability to read and understand that letter reclaiming power was evidence that the inability was over.[58] Reagan's resumption of power so soon after emerging from general anesthesia was premature. Indeed, the White House physician, Dr. John Hutton, advised Bush to be ready in case he needed to act as president during the next eight to ten hours.[59]

Following Reagan's surgery, Bush covered some events for Reagan. Reporters noted that Bush did not visit Reagan during the first few days after surgery, although some others did; Bush said he did not want to impose on Reagan's convalescence.[60] Bush met with Reagan on July 17, four days after the surgery.[61]

Reagan's aversion to setting a precedent was curious. Virtually any sort of presidential action regarding potentially recurring events might be a precedent. The danger is not with precedents but with bad precedents. Good precedents minimize the need for a full decision-making process each time a recurring event arises and make once-novel situations normal and acceptable. And precedents can be distinguished and ignored, where appropriate, or discarded if unworkable.

The situation facing Reagan was appropriate for precedent formation. He clearly could not exercise presidential powers and duties while under general anesthesia. Bush, his loyal and trusted vice president, could do so, and the amendment contemplated transfer in such circumstances. The costs of transfer were negligible, the benefits substantial. Anesthesia, major surgery, hospitalization, and a cancer diagnosis were disorienting, and Reagan should have deferred reclaiming authority for a short time.[62]

Again, advance preparation would have helped. Reagan confronted the situations at inopportune moments. He decided which letter to sign shortly after learning that he probably had cancer and with limited time to reflect. He was given the letter reclaiming power without much thought regarding whether he was able to act as president. Reagan would have benefited from precedents regarding transfer and resumption of power, some contingency planning, or both.

George H. W. Bush: Contingency Planning

During the 1988 campaign, Bush said it had not occurred to him to make arrangements for Quayle to act as president if Bush became disabled and doubted that advance arrangements could be made since circumstances dictated the propriety of a transfer.[63] A Miller Center study in 1988 had recommended that the president, vice president, chief of staff, and White House physician "consider what to do in medical contingencies" during the transition.[64] Bush began developing a contingency plan during the transition and approved it in mid-April 1989.[65] During the process, the Bushes, Quayles, White House physician Dr. Burton Lee, and White House counsel C. Boyden Gray met to discuss circumstances under which a transfer would occur.[66] Bush wrote that the White House was trying to develop procedures to transfer power in case Bush was involved in an accident. The challenging situation, he recognized, was if "I go gaga, or get some horrible degenerating disease." Bush said, "One has to prepare for even the worse contingencies, even though nobody likes talking about those things."[67] According to one of Bush's doctors, the plan "removed any questions or ambiguities" regarding when power should be transferred and "provided an advance directive by the president for certain specific actions to be taken by designated individuals if a medical condition or injury impaired his functional capacity to the extent that he could no longer perform the constitutional responsibilities of his office."[68] Bush "made sure people know what to do in case the amendment has to be invoked," Quayle said.[69] Bush apparently did not resolve the situation in which the Cabinet and president disagreed regarding whether he was disabled, and his physicians declared that in case of doubt, the White House medical office would "be most hesitant" to find a disability.[70] The Clinton administration subsequently adopted the Bush procedures.[71]

Section Three: Further Applications (and Near Applications)

GEORGE H. W. BUSH: ATRIAL FIBRILLATION

Two years later, Bush came close to invoking Section Three of the Twenty-Fifth Amendment. He collapsed while jogging on May 4, 1991, due to atrial fibrillation. After medicine failed to restore his usual heartbeat, doctors planned for Bush to undergo a procedure under general anesthesia to return his heart to its normal rhythm on the morning of May 6, 1991. When Marlin Fitzwater learned of the plans, he thought, "Anesthesia means unconscious, and that means the Twenty-fifth Amendment."[72] Sununu was reluctant to announce that Bush might transfer power to Quayle for fear that such news would be unsettling.[73] Fitzwater argued that Americans should not first learn of a transfer over their morning coffee. Ultimately, with Bush's approval, Fitzwater issued a statement on May 5, 1991, disclosing that if medication did not restore Bush's normal heartbeat, doctors might perform an electrical cardioversion under general anesthesia, which would briefly incapacitate Bush and make the vice president acting president "under the 25th amendment."[74] The following morning, Fitzwater announced that Bush's heart had regained its normal rhythm for six hours and that, although the arrhythmia had returned, Bush's physicians had decided to forgo the electrical cardioversion because he was responding to medication. Fitzwater announced that Bush would be discharged, would meet with former Soviet Foreign Minister Eduard Shevardnadze at 1:30 p.m., and would handle other business.[75]

The episode revived discussion of Quayle's fitness to be president; upon Bush's return to the White House, one of the few media questions addressed that subject. "Hey, he has my full support, always has, and he's doing a first-class job,"[76] Bush replied.

When Bush became ill during a visit to Japan and vomited at a state dinner, Chief of Staff Sam Skinner was sufficiently concerned that he called Quayle to advise him that he might have to act as president. A skeptical Quayle reached First Lady Barbara Bush in Japan, who confirmed that Bush simply had the flu.[77]

CLINTON'S KNEE SURGERY

The possibility of transferring power to Gore arose on March 14, 1997, when Clinton had surgery under local anesthetic to repair torn tendons adjacent to his knee. Clinton did not transfer power, but Press Secretary Mike McCurry implied that if a general anesthesia was used, the Twenty-Fifth Amendment would be invoked under existing arrangements.[78] Clinton's White House physician, Dr. E. Connie Mariano, had given similar advice.[79] Clinton's doctors intentionally avoided using anesthetics that would alter his mental status so that he remained alert and could take any needed action.

GEORGE W. BUSH: TWO SECTION THREE TRANSFERS

George W. Bush twice briefly transferred power to Cheney when he underwent colonoscopies under general anesthesia. The first instance occurred on June 29, 2002, the second July 21, 2007. Cheney was acting president for a little over two hours each time[80] and took no official action.

SUMMATION

Contrary to his stated intentions, Reagan did provide a precedent, and a useful one. Bush and Clinton were prepared to transfer power to Quayle and Gore, respectively, if their medical procedures involved general anesthesia, and George W. Bush twice transferred power to Cheney. These actions created a practice that the president will transfer power to the vice president before planned surgery under anesthesia. In a nuclear and post-9/11 age, it makes sense for the president to transfer presidential powers and duties before receiving general anesthesia.

Section Four: Involuntary Transfers

The logic behind a Section Three transfer when the president has planned surgery under general anesthesia also recommends transfer to the vice president under Section Four when the president is unconscious due to an unplanned event. An unconscious president cannot discharge presidential powers and duties regardless of whether the cause was anticipated or not. The unplanned scenario will be much more difficult to navigate, however, because the president cannot initiate transfer and the need arises unexpectedly. It will likely require response as interested parties process emotions and thoughts in a crisis.

When the president has had no real opportunity to transfer power voluntarily before losing consciousness, a vice president and Cabinet might feel less inhibited about exercising Section Four.[81] Such action would not be perceived as contrary to the president, who had no real opportunity to act. The Reagan assassination attempt presented essentially this situation because the administration was unprepared to address the situation before surgery began. There may be concern that Section Four action will be perceived as ominous and suggest a pessimistic prognosis. That implication will diminish as transfer becomes routine and, in any event, must be balanced against the risks that an unconscious president will signal vulnerability and invite adverse action.

When the president could, but does not, transfer power to the vice president, action under Section Four will be more difficult. The fact that the president implicitly elected not to transfer power would suggest unwillingness to act and put the vice president and Cabinet in an awkward position. Some circumstances might justify using Section Four even when the president has elected not to invoke Section Three. Deterioration of the president's condition and/or the national security context would present the most likely justification for using Section Four under this scenario. But when a president is unconscious yet retains power, the vice president and Cabinet will likely act only under clear and compelling circumstances.

The most difficult situation occurs when, in George H. W. Bush's formulation, the president is "gaga" or suffers a "horrible degenerating disease." In at least some such instances, it is conceivable that a president may resist transferring power. If so, the vice president and Cabinet will find themselves in the awkward position of having to declare a president disabled involuntarily. The likelihood that Section Four will be invoked in such circumstances will depend on a variety of factors, including the severity of the president's condition, the extent to which it has been publicly manifested, and the circumstances facing the administration.

Reagan's performance late in his presidency led some to question his fitness to serve. When Howard Baker replaced Regan as chief of staff on February 27, 1987, he dispatched two aides to debrief the White House staff. They heard that Reagan was disoriented and raised the possibility of invoking the Twenty-Fifth Amendment. Reagan later attributed the comments to "Don Regan's men" and called them "a complete lie."[82] Baker concluded that Reagan was "fully functional" after meeting with him and ended any such consideration.[83] Some others found the president somewhat disengaged at times during his second term, but there was no other known discussion of Section Four.[84]

The White House vice presidency, of course, increases the likelihood of action because the vice president will have worked closely with the president, the Cabinet, and senior White House staff and will probably have developed some rapport with them. Nonetheless, the dynamics will vary based on the circumstances. Bush's relationship with Reagan and his associates on March 30, 1981, was different from the closeness that developed. A vice president will have different relationships with different presidential chiefs of staff, counsels, and physicians, and their dispositions will vary, as will those of different individuals who serve in key Cabinet positions.

The vice president remains in a particularly delicate position, especially when any ambiguity exists regarding presidential inability. Absent factual clarity and consensus among administration insiders that the president's condition warrants invoking Section Four, a vice president is unlikely to act in order to avoid appearing opportunistic. The support of the first spouse, chief of staff, presidential physician, and Cabinet is likely to be important. The Miller Center commission rightly pointed out that the vice president's situation will be enhanced by the Cabinet's willingness "to play an active and visible role" in any Section Four determination.[85]

Although the White House vice presidency and the Twenty-Fifth Amendment substantially improve America's ability to ensure presidential continuity, limitations remain. Formally, a vice president acting under Sections Three and Four has the same powers and duties as the president, but in reality, his or her role will often be more limited. Short of an emergency, it seems highly unlikely that a vice president will take presidential action when power is transferred during a presidential surgery. He or she is unlikely to fire the secretary of state, nominate federal judges, veto legislation, issue pardons, deliver a State of the Union address, or deploy troops unless the president is disabled for a lengthy period and circumstances require action.[86] Except when the president's disability is clearly permanent or long-lasting or an emergency exists, the vice president is likely simply to be available to act if needed. That is a valuable safeguard, especially in a nuclear age, but it is not the same as having presidential leadership.

Continuity of Government after 9/11

Cheney had participated in continuity-of-government exercises during the Reagan administration, but his long-standing concern regarding presidential continuity came to the fore after 9/11. He absented himself from a ceremony at the Washington National Cathedral a few days later and again when Bush addressed a Joint Session of Congress on September 20, 2001. Cheney recognized the illogic of the traditional practice of excusing a low-level Cabinet official in case a calamity wiped out the line of succession, circumstances that would call for the vice president, not someone far down the line. For a short time during Bush's first term, Cheney sometimes worked from undisclosed locations to minimize the chance that a terrorist attack could eliminate Bush and him.[87] In late October 2001, the intelligence community feared Al-Qaeda would launch another attack using some radiological device targeting the White House. Although Bush refused to leave the White House, Cheney admonished him that the question was continuity of government, not individual courage, and announced he was moving to a secure, undisclosed place.[88] Cheney's undisclosed locations included Camp David, the Naval Observatory, and his Wyoming home.[89] The practice generated considerable comment.

Even after 9/11, Cheney and Bush were together on occasion; they simply tried not to be predictable or obvious about it. As time passed, they spent less time physically separated and resumed normal operations. And Biden has not routinely absented himself from the White House as a security precaution.

Vice-Presidential Inability

Although the constitution provides mechanisms to transfer power from a disabled president, no provision exists for determining vice-presidential inability. This gap becomes significant because Section Three and especially Section Four assign specific roles to the vice president when a president is disabled. Although a president might transfer power to the next in line absent a vice president, Section Four specifies the vice president's participation, and if a vice president were de facto disabled, the provision would appear inoperable. Accordingly, there might be no way to declare a president disabled while the vice president was indisposed, and, if the president died while the vice president was disabled, the ability of the "officer" next in line to act as president might be questioned.

In view of the gap, Cheney's precarious health raised special grounds for concern. He had suffered three heart attacks before the November 2000 election and a fourth between the election and inauguration. Shortly after taking office, Cheney executed a letter of resignation to be effective upon delivery to the secretary of state. He entrusted it to Addington and instructed that it be given to Bush "if the need ever arises." He apparently did not specify what would trigger Addington's duty to deliver the letter beyond Cheney's incapacitation. Cheney told Bush of the letter.[90] Cheney's subsequent health history confirmed the prudence of this measure. He had a defibrillator placed in his chest to regulate his heartbeat in 2001 and a new one in July 2007. He had surgery for aneurysms behind his knees in September 2005, shortness of breath from medication in 2006, and a blood clot in his leg after foreign travel in 2007. On November 26, 2007, he had a procedure to correct atrial fibrillation. In October 2008, Cheney had to cancel his campaign schedule due to atrial fibrillation that required an outpatient procedure to restore his heart's normal rhythm. Several years after leaving office, he had a heart transplant.

Clinton: Resignation

In January 1998, the allegation that Clinton had had an affair with White House intern Monica Lewinsky prompted questions regarding whether Clinton might resign. Although then and later McCurry dismissed the speculation as not serious,[91] some thought Clinton might be headed toward resignation. Clinton, of course, did not resign and was acquitted after being tried for impeachment.

Conclusion

Several developments have combined to better ensure presidential continuity. The Twenty-Fifth Amendment provided clarity and procedures to handle some issues of presidential inability and to increase the likelihood of a vice president at virtually all times. The development of the White House vice presidency was consistent with the amendment's implicit vision. It has increased the likelihood of relatively harmonious presidential transitions following death, resignation, or removal and ensured that presidential inability will be addressed.

The amendment and the White House vice presidency alone cannot handle all continuity problems that involve the vice presidency, but during recent decades, administrations have created precedents to address some gaps. Procedures have developed to handle various contingencies such as using Section Three when the president receives general anesthesia and Cheney's action in furnishing a contingent resignation to address vice-presidential disability.

Contingency planning presents another beneficial development. Presidents should make clear to government officials their wishes that Sections Three and Four be used whenever they are disabled. These episodes, though infrequent, will provide useful precedents in making transfer routine when such exceptional events occur. The White House vice presidency will help in making this course palatable and in managing disruption.

14

The Political Future of Vice Presidents

The vice presidency emerged as the best presidential springboard during Nixon's vice presidency and has retained that status ever since. Service as vice president does not guarantee later election as president, but it generally increases the incumbent's chances more than other positions. In some respects, the development of the White House vice presidency has even further enhanced the vice president's chances. Vice-presidential roles are now more likely to present the second officer as a presidential figure. The closer relationship between president and vice president increases the likelihood that vice presidents will receive administration support. Vice presidents have scheduling flexibility and can claim assignments to strengthen their standing.

Yet some recent developments, including some by-products of the White House vice presidency, diminish the office's springboard advantage compared with the Nixon-to-Rockefeller period. A vice president's closer involvement with the administration complicates efforts to separate from an unpopular president or his policies. The demands of the White House vice presidency may limit time to mount a presidential campaign. Moreover, some future vice presidents may, like Cheney, disclaim presidential ambitions because the White House vice presidency is an attractive career destination, and some presidential candidates may prefer a running mate who they think will focus entirely on the administration's success, not on a future presidential run.

Independently, the change to a presidential nominating system of primaries and caucuses eliminates an advantage of earlier vice presidents and poses new challenges. Vice Presidents Nixon and Humphrey secured the presidential nomination based on relationships they formed with state and local leaders through their partisan activities. The vice president's political work still confers benefits, but the modern nomination process cushions the advantage. Vice presidents are now more subject to challenge for presidential nominations, and the heightened expectations from their stature make a poor showing even more costly.

Historical Background

Although the successes of Adams and Jefferson initially made the vice presidency the most promising presidential springboard, that advantage dissipated as parties formed and ticket-balloting emerged. Thomas Jefferson preferred Secretary of State James Madison to Aaron Burr and acted to undermine Burr's position. Madison's two vice presidents died in office, which helped another Virginian, James Monroe, advance. After 1801, only one incumbent nineteenth-century vice president, Martin Van Buren, was elected president, and only one other, John Breckenridge, received significant electoral college support for president.[1]

In deriding the vice presidency as a presidential springboard, some observe that few sitting vice presidents—only Adams, Jefferson, Van Buren, and Bush—have been elected president.[2] Vice presidents do face formidable challenges, but the fact that only four of forty-seven incumbent vice presidents won presidential election is misleading.[3] Since nine vice presidents succeeded to the presidency; nine others died in, or resigned from, the second office; and eleven served with presidents who sought reelection in circumstances where the vice president never really had a chance to run as an incumbent, the relevant denominator for sitting vice presidents who might have sought the presidency is closer to eighteen (47 − [9 + 9 + 11]). Of the eighteen, eight (44 percent) won a presidential nomination, and the four mentioned (22 percent) were elected. Three sitting vice presidents who were defeated—Nixon, Humphrey, and Gore—barely lost, and Nixon was later elected.

Accordingly, the odds of a vice president being elected or nominated are much better than commonly suggested. Most office holders will find that being vice president improves their prospects. Humphrey, Mondale, Bush, and Gore each failed to secure the presidential nomination before being vice president but won it after serving as vice president. Since 1900, only 3 sitting senators, 4 sitting governors, and 2 Cabinet officers were elected president, even though at any time there were 90 to 100 senators, 45 to 50 governors, and 8 to 15 Cabinet secretaries.

Vice-presidential service boosted presidential aspirations during the 1953–1977 period[4] and continues to do so. Of the six vice presidents since Carter's presidency, three (Mondale, Bush, and Gore) won their party's nomination, Bush was elected president, and Gore won the popular vote. Quayle was twice an unsuccessful presidential candidate, and Cheney disclaimed presidential aspirations. Biden's presidential prospects were complicated by the presence of Hillary Clinton, the 2008 Democratic runner-up; by the death of his son in May 2015; and by uncertainty whether he retained presidential aspirations at age seventy-two after two unsuccessful attempts. Nonetheless, polls in summer and fall 2015 suggested considerable support for a Biden candidacy, far more than in 2008, before he decided against a run.

Samuel Popkin has argued that a successor seeking to retain the White House after his party has held the White House for two terms faces formidable challenges.[5] Most vice presidents fall into this group because their opportunity comes after their president's second term. This inherent obstacle does not alone make the vice presidency a worse presidential springboard than other positions because any successor candidate faces this challenge, as Adlai Stevenson and John McCain learned. Yet the vice presidency enhances almost any public figure's chance of being nominated.

Vice-Presidential Advantages

The vice presidency offers advantages in pursuing a presidential run, including stature, recognition, and distinctiveness. The office holder ranks behind only the president; becomes widely known;[6] and, unlike, for example, senators or governors, need not distinguish himself from others with the same title. Vice presidents often operate in settings with a presidential aura.[7] This advantage has increased since 1977 as vice presidents have undertaken more substantive roles. They can extract political advantage from diplomatic work, as Bush did when he used footage from trips to Poland and the Middle East in campaign commercials[8] and escorted Gorbachev in the United States.[9] Two days after Dukakis named Bentsen as his running mate, Bush addressed the United Nations Security Council during a debate regarding an Iranian resolution denouncing the United States for shooting down an Iranian airplane. Bush sought the assignment to achieve visibility in a presidential setting when Dukakis was otherwise dominating the news.[10] Such advantages arise in domestic contexts, too. In June 1988, Bush toured drought-stricken farm states with Secretary of Agriculture Richard Lyng.[11]

Gore also increased his stature through foreign travel. When the Kyoto climate-change talks seemed destined for failure, Gore flew to Japan, used his influence with Clinton to strengthen America's commitment, and gave a speech that helped salvage the process.[12] High-profile trips to Russia and China offered opportunities to position himself as a statesman; a trip to the Middle East to coincide with Israel's fiftieth anniversary allowed him to curry favor with American Jews.[13]

The vice president also is positioned to develop rewarding political relationships[14] by speaking at party meetings, fund-raising for fellow politicians, and campaigning for their election. The second office makes its occupant a draw. A two-term vice president such as Bush, Gore, or Biden will have performed those functions for six years and three election cycles before seeking the presidency. Bush campaigned for Republican candidates in 1982, 1984, and 1986 and raised millions for candidates and the national and state party organizations.[15] His perpetual travel generated friendships and political IOUs from Republican officials. In addition to endorsements, this work may bring organizational help and preferred speaking slots. Sununu, a Bush supporter, invited Bush to give the keynote speech at a luncheon for party activists in March 1987, whereas other candidates got two to five minutes.[16]

Similarly, Gore was active on the campaign trail in 1994 and especially 1996 and 1998. During the latter, he traveled widely as Clinton's problems with the Lewinsky affair limited his campaign activity.[17] Gore visited key primary states; before September 30, 1998, he had visited New Hampshire three times that year.[18] He was the keynote speaker at the New York State Democratic Convention in 1998.[19] During the first six years of his vice presidency, he traveled to California, the largest source of delegates and electoral votes and a fund-raising haven, more than fifty times.[20]

In addition to political appearances, the vice president has resources to exploit for political advantage, and these have grown with vice-presidential influence. They include access to the president and other decision-makers, visits to the West Wing or Naval Observatory, and participation on vice-presidential missions. Bush invited citizens from Iowa and New Hampshire to breakfast with Gorbachev. Whereas other candidates fly in ordinary planes, the vice president travels in *Air Force Two* and vice-presidential limousines with Secret Service protection, all of which signal power and importance.[21]

Finally, the vice president can arrange domestic travel to states with important caucuses and primaries. Bush frequently traveled to critical states, such as California, Florida, and Texas, and to Iowa and New Hampshire, the first caucus and primary states, respectively. Craig Fuller and campaign director Lee Atwater came from Reagan's staff, thereby expanding Bush's reach to Reaganites. Bush raised nearly $4 million in 1985, more than three times the amount raised by his nearest competitor, Kemp. His political action committee had nine paid consultants and a staff of twenty-four by the end of 1985 and directors in states such as Iowa, New Hampshire, and Michigan.[22] By July 1987, he had raised nearly as much as his five Republican rivals who filed Federal Election Commission disclosures and had by far the most-developed fund-raising operation.[23]

The vice presidency helps a public figure achieve greater fame. Only 56 percent could identify Gore when Clinton chose him in 1992. By then, Gore had served in Congress for sixteen years, sought the presidential nomination, and twice been considered for the vice presidency. By the first Clinton-Gore inauguration, 85 percent had an opinion about Gore, and 94 percent did on the eve of the 2000 Democratic convention.[24]

An incumbent vice president seeking the presidential nomination might be expected to limit the field. The few examples do not reveal a pattern. Bush was the front-runner in 1988, but his opponents were Dole, Kemp, Governor Pierre du Pont, evangelist Pat Robertson, Laxalt, Haig, and others.[25] Bush was not automatically seen as Reagan's political heir. Some associated him with the more moderate, eastern wing of the party. Laxalt was Reagan's close friend, Kemp was an economic conservative hero, and Robertson appealed to social conservatives. Although many senators supported their leader, Dole, and conservative congressmen backed Kemp, Bush's extensive party work paid dividends. By contrast, Gore was clearly Clinton's heir apparent. Gore dominated the 1996 convention, and the third night featured him. Clinton routinely praised him lavishly.[26] Other than Bill Bradley, other plausible Democratic candidates opted not to run. In 2016, Hillary Clinton's unique stature eclipsed Biden. She had run almost a dead-even campaign for the 2008 Democratic nomination, had high visibility for more than two decades, and would be the first woman nominated for president. Biden's planning was complicated by the death of his son in May 2015. Still, Biden attracted considerable support before deciding not to run on October 21, 2015.

Vice-Presidential Disadvantages

Vice presidents also face problems running for president, some of which are unique to their position or complicated by it. The main challenges are emerging from the presidential shadow and avoiding responsibility for the administration's unpopular policies. The two problems are similar, in that both involve separating from the president, but different in that all vice presidents encounter the first but not necessarily the second.

EMERGING FROM THE PRESIDENT'S SHADOW

Vice presidents running for president must emerge from the president's shadow to establish an identity as a leader. For four, or more likely eight, years they loyally promote the president's agenda and ambitions. That behavior casts them as a subordinate, not the principal. Service as vice president can cost a political figure a separate identity. Most vice presidents have few opportunities to receive public credit for ideas or actions. When the vice president receives recognition, it is generally as the junior member of the team, as a follower, not leader, in an unequal partnership. "You look number two to them," Mondale said.[27] The problem is more difficult for a sitting, than past, vice president because the incumbent's role requires continued deference, whereas the former vice president has opportunity to reestablish a separate identity. This difficulty is probably greatest for those who serve presidents such as Reagan and Clinton, who dominated the scene, but it is not confined merely to them.

The office may be diminishing. George H. W. Bush, a war hero at twenty, former CIA director, and diplomat, was derided as a lapdog by conservative columnist George Will and as someone who had placed his virility in a blind trust by Garry Trudeau in the *Doonesbury* cartoon strip. Gore, a man who took brave positions in administration councils, was caricatured for standing stiffly by Clinton's side.

That perception may be costly. In July 1987, a *New York Times*/CBS News poll asked voters what they thought Vice President George Bush did when he and Reagan disagreed. Only 15 percent of registered Republicans and 13 percent of all registered voters thought Bush publicly spoke his mind. Some 39 percent of Republicans thought Bush articulated Reagan's views, whereas about one-third thought he said nothing. Yet 55 percent of Republicans thought Bush should publicly speak his mind. Although 47 percent of likely Republican primary voters viewed Bush favorably (23 percent did not), less than one-quarter thought of him as strong, and only 52 percent felt confident in his ability to handle a crisis.[28] Two leading scholars cited polls in 2000 that showed voters who emphasized strong leadership preferred Governor George Bush to Vice President Al Gore almost two to one, a finding they attributed to the vice presidency more than the candidates.[29]

It is not just public perceptions that must be altered. The vice president also has to adjust. He needs to replace the public deference that has defined his vice-presidential service with a more assertive approach. As Mondale put it, a vice president running for president needs to focus "within himself to feel like the President, talk like the President, lead like the President."[30]

Yet an incumbent vice president is in a delicate position. Positive changes must be suggested without trashing the status quo of which the vice president is a part. Some suggestions might be perceived as criticisms of the administration. Why did not the vice president raise these ideas sooner, and if he or she did, why were they not adopted? Some presidential loyalists may resent perceived criticism.

Bush's extreme reluctance to disagree publicly with Reagan compounded his problem. He resisted advice to distance himself from Reagan and refused to break with Reagan on any significant issue until May 1988, when he announced that he would not negotiate with drug dealers. At the time, the administration was considering doing just that with Noriega, who was under indictment on drug charges. Even then, Bush was uncomfortable breaking with Reagan and agreed not to argue strongly against the deal once made.[31]

Instead, Bush emphasized the future and suggested subtle differences with administration policies. For instance, he supported bilingual education and more spending on education.[32] In his announcement speech, he urged more racial harmony and "greater tolerance" and more spending on education and efforts to protect the environment.[33] Although Reagan had said he would consider a tax increase to reach a budget compromise, Bush opposed any tax increase.[34] Bush also sought to distinguish himself stylistically, saying he would adopt a hands-on managerial approach and would bring new people into government to provide a fresh outlook.[35]

Gore faced a similar problem. Although Gore tried to claim credit for the budget surpluses and job creation of the Clinton presidency, he went to great lengths to separate from Clinton's ethical lapses. In his announcement, he pledged to marshal the "moral leadership" of the presidency to fight for America's families. On the day he announced his candidacy, Gore criticized Clinton's conduct in the Lewinsky affair.[36] He moved his campaign headquarters to Nashville in September 1999.[37] He avoided the White House from May 22, 2000, until returning for meetings on the Middle East crisis in mid-October.[38] He selected as his running mate the first Democratic senator to condemn Clinton regarding the Lewinsky scandal. Gore rarely referred to Clinton during the campaign, although Lieberman more freely spoke of the accomplishments of the Clinton-Gore administration.[39] During the campaign, Gore occasionally took positions at odds with the administration. In September, he called on Clinton to release at least five million barrels of oil from government reserves to help control oil prices.[40] Yet even following the Lieberman selection, a *Time*/CNN poll found that 45 percent thought Gore was more a creation of Clinton choosing him as vice president, whereas only 42 percent saw him as primarily a candidate in his own right.[41]

Several standard events help facilitate the transition from follower to leader. First, the vice-presidential selection allows the vice president/presidential candidate to move from junior to senior partner. Reagan-Bush gave way to Bush-Quayle, Clinton-Gore to Gore-Lieberman. Second, the convention signals the transition. Usually the outgoing president speaks on its first day, during which he celebrates his vice president/successor. Reagan highlighted the record of his two terms and connected Bush to those accomplishments. Bush was "someone who is not afraid to speak his mind and who can cut to the core of an issue, someone who never runs away from a fight, never backs way from his beliefs, and never makes excuses."[42] Twelve years later, Clinton performed the same service for Gore. After outlining the administration's accomplishments, he praised Gore, who was "always there" speaking his mind on "the most difficult issues." Gore, Clinton said, "is one strong leader" who "understands the future" more than anyone else.[43] The president and vice president then meet after the president leaves the convention site and before the vice president arrives, symbolizing the passing of leadership. The vice president's acceptance speech then allows him to articulate his vision as the party's new leader.

GUILT BY ASSOCIATION

Vice presidents are more likely to share blame for an administration's mistakes than to receive credit for successes. Although Bush characterized himself as "co-pilot" for seven years and claimed he knew how to "land that plane in the storm,"[44] Haig suggested Bush was not in the "cockpit" but along for "an economy ride in the back of the plane."[45] Unhappy voters tend to seek a candidate outside the administration. One poll found that Iowa Republicans who approved of Reagan's performance divided about evenly between Bush and Dole, whereas those who disapproved of the president favored Dole by more than a two-to-one margin.[46]

Revelations regarding the Iran-contra affair crystallized this problem for Bush. Dole could criticize the administration's conduct, but the affair presented a "lose-lose" situation for Bush. Bush had trumpeted his involvement in decision-making, especially in foreign policy. If he was part of the decision-making, he could not escape responsibility for the choices made. If he was not involved in the crucial meetings, was he really a central player?[47] When the stock market lost more than 22 percent of its value on October 19, 1987, Bush was seen as likely to be most hurt, yet unlike his rivals, he had to support the administration's course.[48]

Vice presidents face constraints in separating from administration policy. They do not want to alienate their colleagues by seeking to escape responsibility. If their efforts to dissociate themselves are not well grounded, they may face push-back from administration personnel. When Bush distanced himself from the sale of arms to Iranians, Secretary of State Shultz contradicted him.[49] When Gore condemned Clinton's behavior with Lewinsky in a televised interview the evening he announced, Clinton aides reported that the president was upset,[50] even though Clinton said he took "no offense" and praised Gore for articulating a vision for the future.[51] Finally, the vice president may suffer if voters think him disloyal or willing to abandon associates when expedient.

Dukakis's standard speech criticized Bush for his silence when Reagan made controversial decisions or attacked him for positions he took as vice president.[52] Of course, Bush won, which shows that these obstacles are not necessarily insurmountable. Bush benefited from an improving national mood. A *New York Times*/CBS poll found in mid-September 1988 that 55 percent approved of Reagan's handling of his job and 57 percent were optimistic about the economy.[53]

Like Reagan, Clinton retained high approval ratings, yet Clinton fatigue hurt Gore. In late March 1999, Pew found that 74 percent were tired of problems associated with Clinton and 60 percent of those favored Bush. Independents preferred Gore to Clinton, 56 percent to 34 percent.[54] About five months later, a *Washington Post*/ABC poll found that more than half of the electorate were tired of Clinton and preferred a different direction. Although 83 percent did not blame Gore for Clinton's ethical lapses, Gore also did not benefit from Clinton's high job approval.[55] In early 2000, an ABC News/*Washington Post* poll found voters equally divided as to whether or not Gore was "too close" to Clinton for the country to turn the page.[56] Bush attempted to tie Gore to Clinton's ethical lapses. He frequently vowed to restore honor and integrity, and sometimes decency, to the White House and challenged Gore to state clearly his views regarding Clinton's sexual conduct.[57]

FORMER VICE PRESIDENTS

Former vice presidents are in a somewhat different position. They have had time to establish an independent identity as a leader but still may find the administration's record a burden. In 1984, Mondale was not perceived as simply vice presidential, but the Carter administration was unpopular, and he remained associated with it. The public record showed his loyalty to Carter but not the policies he had opposed. Although Mondale did not reveal his disagreements with Carter, memoirs of associates and journalistic accounts reported some episodes. It became known that Mondale had opposed the malaise speech, grain embargo, and sale of some weapons to Saudi Arabia.[58]

Mondale argued that as vice president, his job was to give Carter his best judgment but then to help implement the president's decisions. The public should judge him on his policies for the future, not those of the Carter administration. In his acceptance speech, he dealt with his service as Carter's vice president in a single sentence ("Then, an honest, caring man—Jimmy Carter—picked me as his running mate and in 1976 I was elected vice president") and their defeat in the next ("And in 1980, Ronald Reagan beat the pants off us"). Mondale said he had listened to Americans and learned from that experience, which had equipped him with a "new realism." "If Mr. Reagan wants to re-run the 1980 campaign: Fine. Let them fight over the past. We're fighting for the American future."[59] Reagan's campaign tied Mondale to Carter. It ran advertisements containing pictures of Mondale with Carter, and associated Mondale with unpopular policies and outcomes of the Carter years.[60]

Quayle made abbreviated runs for president in 1996 and 2000. After experiencing some health issues, Quayle withdrew from the 1996 race less than three weeks after his informal entry. He cited family disruption, not health, as the motivation, although some speculated that the health episodes may have impacted his appeal to major donors.[61] Four years later, Quayle withdrew in September 1999 after concluding that he could not raise sufficient funds to compete with then governor George Bush in nineteen contests over a month. Quayle had raised $3.5 million, less than one-tenth of what Bush had attracted,[62] and received only 5 percent of Republican poll support, whereas Bush exceeded 60 percent.[63]

Helping the Vice President: The Reagan Example

No president so effectively helped his vice president succeed him as Reagan did in 1988. Although some viewed Reagan's neutrality during the primaries as indicating reservations about Bush, Reagan insisted his status as the Republican leader dictated that position but continued:[64]

> The Vice President, I think, has been the finest Vice President in my memory in this country. He has participated in all the major operations. . . . He's an executive Vice President. He's a major part. He's one of only two of us that are chosen by all the people in this country for the jobs that we hold. And so, he understands that— but I have to remain neutral until the decision is made by the party as to who their nominee will be.

Reagan clearly preferred Bush. They met to discuss the campaign,[65] and Reagan discreetly communicated his support to others.[66]

Although Bush declared in February 1987 that his presidential campaign might create some "friction" between his views and some administration policies,[67] he did not really split with Reagan on any substantive issue until after securing the nomination. Bush's loyalty may have dictated this attitude, but Reagan was also very popular with Republican primary voters and caucus participants, so Bush's position had strategic merit, too.[68] After supporting Reagan for seven years, separating required some finesse to avoid appearing insincere, disloyal, opportunistic, or all of the foregoing.

Bush began poorly. His dismal third-place finish, behind Dole and Robertson, in the Iowa caucus jeopardized his campaign.[69] The New Hampshire primary presented a "do or die" situation. Bush conducted essentially a retail campaign in diners and truck stops, attacked Dole, and brought in Senator Barry M. Goldwater to help him attract Reagan supporters. Bush tied himself closely to Reagan, and the president's popularity in the state helped him. He benefited from the endorsement of Sununu and Representative Judd Gregg. Ultimately, Bush won 38 percent of the Republican vote to Dole's 29 percent.[70] Reagan wrote that Bush's victory in the New Hampshire primary "made my day" even though he needed to maintain public neutrality.[71]

Reagan saw the 1988 election as a referendum on his presidency and made Bush's success an objective of his last year in office. Kenneth Duberstein, Reagan's last chief of staff, worked to assist Bush. Nixon's advice on how a president could help his vice president was solicited, and that former president and vice president met with the Reagans at the White House on July 28, 1988.[72] Reagan thought Nixon's ideas made "great good sense."[73] Duberstein also coordinated administration behavior with the Bush campaign, something the close ties between Bush's advisers and Reagan's team facilitated.

Reagan was fully engaged in the effort to elect Bush. He and Bush discussed the campaign for an hour on June 8, 1988, in the White House residence. A month later, Duberstein arranged a lunch with Reagan; some Bush campaign principals; and Duberstein, Laxalt, Stuart Spencer, and a few others, followed by another meeting a few days later. Reagan held a Cabinet meeting on July 12, 1988, to energize its members regarding Bush's campaign.[74]

Reagan endorsed Bush once the vice president secured the nomination, promising attendees at a Republican fund-raiser that he would "work as hard as I can" for Bush.[75] When some portrayed Reagan's initial statement as "terse" and unenthusiastic,[76] the White House released a statement proclaiming Reagan as "enthusiastic" and "fully committed." Bush had Reagan's "full confidence" and "total support." Bush was a "partner in all we have accomplished."[77] Reagan frequently cited Bush's work in reducing federal regulations and combating the drug trade. His weekly radio address after the Republican convention spotlighted Bush. He said that now "all Americans could see what I've seen for 8 years: dedication, integrity, and commitment to principle; a strong man and a strong leader. I've said many times that George has the experience, the credentials, the savvy, and the—well—the just plain grit to be President of the United States." He credited Bush with "playing a vital role" in the arms-reduction agreement between the United States and the Soviet Union and in creating new jobs by reducing federal regulations. Bush had "always given me straight-from-the-shoulder advice and counsel on how we could advance our vision for the future, and he's always been candid with me when we disagreed."[78] Four days later, he said that "no one has been closer to my side and has contributed more to our success than George Bush." He continued: [79]

I've worked more closely with George Bush these two terms than with any other member of the administration. I've seen him keep a cool head in hot crises. I've seen his leadership and vision. I've given him some of the most sensitive and difficult tasks that we've had, and he has never let me or the country down.

I once said that he is a great Vice President, but I know and I've seen that it didn't come easily. George Bush is a man of action, a man accustomed to command. The Vice Presidency doesn't fit easily on such a man. But George Bush is also a patriot. And so, he made it fit, and he served with a distinction no one has ever matched. Day in, day out, I've sought George Bush's counsel from the very first day of our administration. Believe me, no one is better prepared to lead America into the next decade and to the threshold of the next century, to continue the work that we've begun, to finish the task that is before us, than President George Bush.

Reagan made personnel moves to help Bush. Bush was consulted on, and approved of, Reagan's choice of former Pennsylvania governor Richard Thornburgh as Meese's replacement.[80] Although Reagan initially resisted letting Baker resign as treasury secretary to run Bush's campaign, arguing that Baker could help Bush most at treasury, he acceded when Bush personally appealed to him[81] and appointed another close Bush friend, Nicholas Brady, to the treasury post. Thornburgh and Brady continued in Bush's administration.

In response to Bush's arguments, Reagan agreed not to veto legislation requiring sixty days' notice of plant closings or layoffs[82] and to veto the Defense Authorization Bill on the grounds that the Democratic Congress had threatened national security. When the Palestine Liberation Organization appeared likely to meet America's stated formulation for beginning a dialogue in September 1988, Duberstein became "deeply concerned" that such a development would hurt Bush.[83] Reagan frequently attacked Dukakis as a liberal[84] and questioned Dukakis's mental stability, calling him an "invalid" in a press conference.[85] Reagan also praised Bush's choice of Quayle as "outstanding" and "excellent,"[86] cited Quayle's "energy and enthusiasm,"[87] and compared his national security experience favorably with Dukakis's.[88]

Reagan campaigned energetically for Bush, who welcomed his help. In the closing two and one-half weeks, Reagan visited thirteen states— North Carolina, Kentucky, Maryland, Missouri, Arkansas, California, Nevada, Wisconsin, Ohio, Illinois, New Jersey, Michigan, Texas, and California again.[89] Reagan's popularity helped Bush. On election day, 53 percent approved of Reagan's performance, whereas only 40 percent disapproved. More than 80 percent who approved of Reagan voted for Bush.[90]

In his victory speech, Bush acknowledged his huge debt to Reagan immediately after saluting the American people. He thanked Reagan for "turning our country around and for being my friend, and for going the extra mile on the hustings." Reagan was "simply one of the most decent men" Bush had ever met.[91]

Clinton and Gore

Clinton's early support helped position Gore as the preferred successor. Gore was given prominence at the 1996 convention, with the third night devoted to his speech. Clinton frequently praised Gore effusively. In announcing Christopher's resignation as secretary of state, Clinton praised Christopher for chairing the vice-presidential search, which had produced "the most unique partnership" and "the most influential and constructive" vice president.[92] Clinton indicated his support for Gore before the second term began. The White House allowed Gore to make presidential-level announcements and gave Gore associates important positions in the White House and Democratic National Committee.[93] Clinton also sponsored fund-raisers for Gore months before the first caucuses and primaries.[94]

Clinton wanted to help Gore, but their relationship deteriorated during the last years of their terms, and Clinton's role became limited as Gore distanced himself. Gore repeatedly criticized Clinton's behavior in connection with Lewinsky, absented himself from the White House, moved his campaign to Nashville, and rarely spoke with Clinton.[95] Clinton aides spoke openly of the president's anger over Gore's behavior and his dissatisfaction with the course of the Gore campaign[96] and leaked that Clinton favored George Mitchell or Bob Graham as Gore's running mate.[97]

Clinton was prepared to campaign energetically for Gore. In fact, Clinton spent part of more than half of the sixty-eight days between September 1, 2000, and the election making campaign speeches in New York, California, New Mexico, Michigan, Colorado, Washington, Connecticut, Indiana, Pennsylvania, Massachusetts, Texas, Kentucky, and Arkansas, mostly for candidates for the Senate, such as First Lady Hillary Clinton, or the House or state Democratic parties, though Clinton also made the case for Gore. During the last three weeks of the campaign, he spent part of only one day (November 5) in a competitive state (Arkansas) and did not campaign the day before the election. Journalists commented on Clinton's absence from the Gore campaign.[98] Gore never asked him to do more.

Vice-Presidential Candidates on Defeated Tickets

Defeated vice-presidential candidates not named Franklin D. Roosevelt have not fared particularly well in presidential politics. Some twelve years separated FDR's 1920 vice-presidential defeat and his first of four elections as president, and his subsequent success seems tenuously linked to the earlier experience. Before 1976, no defeated vice-presidential candidate later received his party's nomination. Edmund S. Muskie was the Democratic front-runner in 1972, but his campaign imploded for various reasons. Others, including Earl Warren, Henry Cabot Lodge, and Sargent Shriver, received some subsequent presidential consideration, but none came close to nomination. Some later served in significant positions—Warren as chief justice; Muskie as secretary of state; Frank Knox as secretary of the navy; Lodge as ambassador to South Vietnam, Germany, and the Paris peace talks; Joseph Robinson as Senate majority leader; Charles L. McNary as Senate minority leader; and John Sparkman as chair of Senate committees on foreign relations and banking.

Since 1976, two defeated vice-presidential candidates, Mondale and Dole, later received their party's presidential nomination, although Mondale, having served as vice president prior to his loss, belongs in a different category. Of the eight candidates defeated in their first vice-presidential race, Dole later received his party's nomination, twenty years later and after unsuccessful attempts in 1980 and 1988. Lieberman ran for the Democratic nomination in 2004 but won no delegates and only once received as much as 11 percent of the primary vote. Edwards ran in 2008 but finished well behind Obama and Clinton. None of the other first-time losers ran for president, although Ryan might be a strong candidate in the future. Yet Bentsen served as secretary of the treasury, Dole as Senate majority leader, Mondale as ambassador to Japan, and Ryan as speaker of the House of Representatives.

Conclusion

Like any public office, the vice presidency presents obstacles as a presidential springboard. Emerging from the presidential shadow and separating from unpopular positions present challenges. As the office has become more robust, the vice president has more presidential opportunities, yet the office may also attract some lacking in presidential ambition. Nonetheless, the office remains the best presidential springboard. Without exception, the presidentially ambitious White House vice presidents emerged as more formidable presidential candidates after their terms than they had been before that service.

15

The Problems with the Vice Presidency

The White House vice presidency has become influential and has strengthened American government. Nonetheless, the office remains difficult and controversial. The difficulty relates to a perception that the office frustrates and diminishes its occupants. The controversy stems from the belief that the institution conflicts with basic tenets of our constitutional system.

In one sense, these problems are quite different. Frustration and diminution may reduce vice-presidential job satisfaction but do not present governance problems unless they deter able people from accepting the vice presidency or interfere with their performance. Neither presently seems a problem. The concern that the vice presidency is constitutionally problematic presents more serious questions regarding the propriety of the office.

Both problems challenge the general account of this book. If the vice presidency is so substantial, why are vice presidents diminished or frustrated? And if the office offends basic principles, does it merit celebration? This chapter addresses, and rejects, these critiques.

Frustration and Diminution

Vice-presidential frustration is nothing new. Adams and Jefferson voiced misgivings, and many of their successors found creative, sometimes pungent, ways to echo their sentiments. Rockefeller said each of his eight immediate predecessors was "frustrated,"[1] ranging from Garner, who famously ranked the nation's second office below "a pitcher" or a "bucket" of some warm liquid (although exactly what he said and when he said it is a mystery),[2] to Lyndon Johnson, who called the office "nothing" and "detested every minute of it,"[3] to Humphrey, who compared it to "being naked in the middle of a blizzard with no one to even offer you a match to keep you warm,"[4] to Gerald R. Ford, who, according to Cheney, "hated" his time as vice president as Watergate overtook the Nixon administration.[5]

These disparagements predated the White House vice presidency, yet that more-robust institution has not eliminated the grievance. Mondale became despondent in early 1979.[6] Bush admitted "frustrations" in 1984[7] and later told Quayle that the vice presidency "was a real character-builder."[8] Quayle acknowledged "frustrations" and "challenges" in the office, which he found "awkward" and "confining."[9]

Those who did not publicly admit frustration still experienced diminution. Gore, according to his biographer, found his first two years "deeply frustrating" due to the constraints of his office. Later he was mocked as wooden and for inflating his résumé. The Department of Justice seriously considered prosecuting him over his fund-raising for the 1996 Clinton-Gore campaign, and his presidential aspirations were impacted as he spent much of his second term defending Clinton after the president lied about an extramarital affair with a White House intern.[10] Cheney was mocked for running the search that culminated in his own selection, for working in "undisclosed locations," and for being the first vice president in 200 years to shoot someone. He saw his closest aide convicted of a felony for misconduct during his service, and Bush refused to grant a pardon despite Cheney's pleas. His final poll ratings were underwater. Biden was lampooned by satirists more than any vice president since Quayle. Even the robust White House vice presidency does not immunize its occupants from indignities long associated with the office.

In part, the problems are not unique to the vice presidency. Recent presidents have also suffered embarrassments. Carter and George H. W. Bush were not reelected. Clinton was humiliated by disclosures about the Lewinsky affair and impeached, a demerit he shares only with Andrew Johnson. Reagan and George W. Bush were derided as lightweights. The latter left office with abysmal poll ratings.

Yet the vice presidency presents challenges. Frustration is almost inevitable because the office relegates a first-rank leader to a supporting role. Although a vice president attends high-level meetings, the president decides. The head of a Cabinet department has decisions to make, yet the vice president makes few and must restrain himself.[11] As Quayle put it, as vice president "it is impressed upon you that you are Number Two, not Number One. And if you forget that, the President's staff will remind you."[12]

It is not simply that the vice president does not set policy. He has limited ability to distance himself from disagreeable decisions. A senator can cast a vote or give a speech to record publicly her view and achieve some catharsis. The vice president is generally limited to stating opinions in administration councils, and even then often cautiously because airing disagreement outside confidential settings risks leaks that may embarrass the president, vice president, or both. Moreover, the vice president is expected publicly to defend, or at least explain, the administration's positions notwithstanding his own disagreement.

Former Republican Party chair Frank Fahrenkopf said that the vice presidency "is a miserable, tough job" because "you must take your views and your own personality and swallow them. Your job is to be there as part of the team, to assist, and to help."[13] In fact, good vice presidents need to express their views, forcefully, to the president, not swallow them, but it is a tough job that requires discipline. It forces someone accustomed to the limelight to operate behind the scenes in a context in which he cannot claim credit but does shoulder some blame. Vice presidents who are politically ambitious are saddled with unpopular administration policies when they seek office yet often are not rewarded for administration success. The vice president often has trouble shaping an identity. After Quayle had been in office for eight months, some 45 percent of poll respondents did not know enough to have an opinion about him.[14]

The solution is not to fill the office with followers. A White House vice president must be a leader. He or she may, after all, become "everything" following a presidential death, inability, resignation, or removal. Less contingently, the vice president must interact effectively with heads of state and domestic officials, including the president of the United

States. And he or she must be strong enough to speak candidly to the president.

Of course, some effort might be made to screen prospective running mates who seem unable to be a subordinate. LBJ and Rockefeller obviously were not good bets for success as number twos. By contrast, their backgrounds suggested that George H. W. Bush and Cheney could function well in subordinate roles. Mondale had deferred to Humphrey and Gore to his father, which might have inspired confidence that they could adjust to the vice presidency. Quayle was much junior to Bush, so an understudy role seemed to fit him better than Dole. Prudent presidential candidates think about whether a running mate can function as a number two. Carter reached that conclusion about Mondale, Clinton about Gore, and Bush about Cheney, and it probably explains partly why Bush chose Quayle instead of Dole.

Yet such a filter is an imperfect remedy. Some might have doubted that Biden could adjust to the vice presidency, yet he did. And will a presidential candidate facing a competitive race (e.g., Kennedy) pass on someone with the political juice to help corral 270 electoral votes (e.g., Johnson) because of doubts over how that running mate will function as vice president? Probably not. Some, like Mondale and Bush, who seemed well equipped for the vice presidency found the experience trying even though they performed well.

Ultimately, frustration is part of the price of the White House vice presidency. Vice presidents are no longer bored or inconsequential, but their office requires hard adjustments. They must accept limitations; in return, they benefit. Vice presidents do not set policy, but they were not elected president. They are expected loyally to provide public support, but in return, they participate in high-level decision-making and troubleshooting. Yes, a member of Congress has independence, but he or she attends few meetings in the Oval Office or Situation Room and rarely, if ever, represents America on the international stage. Mondale, Bush, Quayle, Gore, Cheney, and Biden, not to mention Dole, Bentsen, Kemp, Lieberman, Edwards, and Ryan, thought the price worth paying—at least going in.

There are ways to minimize the frustration. Developing and preserving compatibility with the president helps. Mondale, Bush, Quayle,

Cheney, and Biden sustained affection for the presidents they served; that no doubt helped them handle awkward aspects of their jobs. It is useful for vice presidents to remember they were elected vice president, not president. If they believe the ticket is in the right order, they are probably better able to accept a subordinate position. Even if they think it should be inverted, the people thought otherwise. Policy creation or implementation may not end up exactly as the vice president prefers, but they often can exercise influence and help shape outcomes. Taking some visible roles helps, too, as White House vice presidents have done. Working for an understanding president makes a difference. Carter through Obama seem to have behaved decently to their vice presidents.

Moreover, the positive trajectory of the office offers reason for optimism. The characterizations of the mid-1970s of the office as "hopeless" and a "maiming experience" rested on more than 185 years of American history yet were soon rendered obsolete. Recent experience provides reason to hope that the distant past is not prologue and that future vice presidents may find the office increasingly less frustrating. Indeed, Quayle described the vice presidency as not "fun" but "very rewarding" and "very fulfilling."[15] Cheney said he would "miss" being vice president, which was "an amazing experience." "I've loved being Vice President. It's been a great job."[16]

The Unambitious Vice President

In fact, Cheney valued the vice presidency so much that he committed eight years to it even though he did not regard it as a presidential stepping-stone. That attitude made him anomalous among recent vice presidents, yet Cheney and others cited this disposition as beneficial. Chapter 9 suggested that Cheney and others have exaggerated his lack of ambition as a source of his influence. The discussion that follows considers whether the unambitious vice president provides a better model.

The argument for the unambitious vice president proceeds from the assumption that removing a vice president's presidential ambition will produce better performance. A vice president who is not weighing his own political future, the argument goes, will find his agenda more closely aligned with the president's. This common interest will make the vice president's advice more objective and more credible. Conflict between the president and his staff and the Office of the Vice President will be reduced because all will share a common objective. An unambitious vice president will have more time for governance once freed of the need to position him- or herself for a presidential run. Others will be more willing to work with the vice president whom they will not see as a competitor.

There is something to be said for these arguments but also something to be said against them.[17] Lack of presidential ambitions will not necessarily translate into greater loyalty to the president's agenda. In fact, a vice president who does not need the president's support might feel freer to pursue a distinct agenda. An unambitious vice president may be less inhibited, especially during the second term, in separating from administration policies, even publicly.

To be sure, mounting a presidential campaign adds a burden to the vice president's schedule and distracts from current governance work. Yet that activity also has value to the current administration. Bush may have paid a price for Cheney's relative lack of political orientation. Cheney was not focused on the Iowa caucuses, but he also did not cultivate independent voters to persuade them of the merit of administration policies. Perhaps the administration would have fared better had Cheney been more concerned about maintaining political support. In some instances, greater political sensitivity might have helped; the near mass exodus from the justice department in March 2004, the media inaccessibility following the accidental shooting of Whittington, and the bombastic defense of the enhanced interrogation program come to mind.

An unambitious vice president may not be perceived as a rival, but he also may sacrifice something in present political clout by renouncing future ambitions. The Bush administration may have been less powerful during the second term because domestic and foreign leaders knew there would be no third term. The rise of the vice presidency as a presidential springboard was helped by the Twenty-Second Amendment, which precludes presidents from seeking a third term, but a vice president who appears as the president's political heir and as a formidable candidate helps preserve the power of a second-term president. Whereas others had reason to think Reagan's and Clinton's policies might continue, Cheney's attitude made clear there would be no Bush third term. Moreover, Cheney's posture meant that Bush's policies lacked an advocate in the 2008 campaign. Republican and Democratic presidential candidates could distance themselves from the administration without an energized defender.

Finally, a preference for unambitious vice presidents would eliminate from the pool of potential running mates many of each generation's ablest political leaders. Vice-presidential candidates Mondale, Dole, Bush, Bentsen, Quayle, Gore, Kemp, Lieberman, Cheney, Edwards, and Biden had run, or later ran, for president, and only Cheney renounced further ambitions when he joined the ticket. In addition, many of those recently considered for the vice presidency were also presidential aspirants—Baker, Muskie, Glenn, Church, Dukakis, Gephardt, Graham, Kerrey, Kerry, Hillary Clinton, and Romney, among others. Eliminating such candidates would be part of the cost of preferring an unambitious running mate.

With its advantages, the unambitious vice presidency also presents problems for democratic governance. Sustainable policy requires political support, from the public and from other officials. An ambitious vice president helps preserve the democratic link between administration policy and public opinion, especially during a second term, by engaging in a democratic dialogue in which he or she tries to convince the public of the wisdom of administration policies and receives citizen feedback.

Of course, some of the problems identified here may have related to Cheney's disposition and approach, not his lack of presidential ambition. Perhaps a vice president with different sensibilities might lack presidential ambition yet be more democratically attuned.

Ultimately, there are advantages, but also disadvantages, to a politically unambitious vice president. In the abstract, it is hard to balance the gains from increased focus and perhaps from eliminating the vice president's conflicting interests (real and perceived) against the consequences of a double-lame-duck administration, reduced democratic engagement, and a smaller pool of vice-presidential candidates because of eliminating future presidential aspirants. The balance probably depends somewhat on the identity of the unambitious vice president. Bush and Cheney trumpeted the benefit of a vice president who issued an early Sherman statement without publicly acknowledging the accompanying costs. Prudent presidents, presidential candidates, and voters will consider the complete equation. It seems unwise to state a blanket preference for unambitious vice presidents, especially given the impact that approach would have on the pool of available candidates.

The Imperial Vice Presidency

The Cheney tenure raised another, unprecedented question regarding the vice presidency, namely whether the office holder had too much executive power. Some referred to an "imperial vice presidency,"[18] a novel characterization given the office's history and reputation.

Vice presidents differ from others in the president's inner circle in at least five fundamental ways: (1) they are elected to office; (2) they are the constitutional successor; (3) they have a relationship with both political branches; (4) they carry a background in electoral politics; and (5) the president cannot remove them during the term for which they were elected. The first four characteristics enhance vice-presidential stature and power, but the last feature cuts both ways. Tenure strengthens the vice president. Disagreeing with the president may cost access and influence but not the job. On the other hand, the fact that the president cannot remove the vice president reinforced the past bias against empowering him. Some, including Rumsfeld, suggested that a vice president assume a Cabinet portfolio, an idea Ford and George W. Bush rejected[19] and presidential scholar Stephen Hess called "the silliest idea of all."[20] Some worried about the embarrassment to an administration if a president removed the number two from the Cabinet post even while he completed the vice-presidential term. Mondale explained why departmental commitments would inhibit, not develop, vice-presidential influence.

Vice-presidential tenure was not a problem as long as vice presidents were peripheral. In proposing a more engaged vice presidency, Mondale recognized that the Constitution vests executive power in the president and made certain, for constitutional, political, and personal reasons, that his actions had Carter's authorization. Mondale, Bush, Quayle, and Gore served without credible suggestion that they usurped presidential power, nor has any such claim been made regarding Biden. The problem, to the extent there was one, was unique to the Bush-Cheney pairing.

Cheney, of course, denied that he exceeded his authority, a notion he disparaged as "an urban legend";[21] Bush characterized as "myth" the idea that Cheney ran the White House.[22] Although Cheney was neither president nor copresident, sometimes he acted without appropriate restraint in circumventing normal decision-making processes or in disregarding Bush's political interests.[23] Some members of Cheney's staff also acted imperiously.[24]

The problem related largely to three features: Bush delegated broad operational authority to Cheney; Cheney and some on his staff circumvented normal deliberative decision-making processes to achieve ends that were controversial within the administration; and Cheney, like other vice presidents, had extensive private presidential access during which time he and the president could discuss matters confidentially. The confluence of Bush's leadership style and Cheney's aggressive operational approach occasionally produced outcomes not fully vetted within the administration. Cheney prepared the letter changing position on climate change, but Bush signed it without hearing from Powell, O'Neill, and Whitman. Cheney produced the order on military commissions, but Bush issued it without hearing from stakeholders. Bush recognized the threatened Department of Justice resignations were a big deal and said he had been unaware of the department's refusal to bless the warrantless surveillance program until March 10, when it was about to end, even though the problem had been brewing for some time. "Why didn't I know about this?" Bush asked in the morning and was told Card had first learned of the situation the prior night. Of course, Cheney knew of the problem, which he and his office were handling. Bush later learned that Attorney General Ashcroft was hospitalized, which was "news to me."[25] Readers of the *New York Times* had been informed four days earlier that Ashcroft was in intensive care, that James Comey was in charge, and that Ashcroft would be hospitalized for "days."[26] Ashcroft's surgery had been announced on March 9.[27] Bush, unhappily, acted to preserve the program without the Department of Justice's signature on

March 10, but when he turned in that night, he was "irritated" and felt he did not know but planned to learn the "full story." Two mornings later he learned that Comey was the acting attorney general and that senior Department of Justice leaders were about to resign. Bush was unwilling to re-create Nixon's Saturday Night Massacre experience so accommodated the department's concerns but made clear that he did not want "to be blindsided like that again." He attributed the debacle to poor judgment in deciding what matters to present to the president.[28] If a problem involving the imminent demise of a "vital" national security program and a brewing rupture with the Department of Justice in a presidential election year did not merit the president's earlier attention, one wonders what short of war would. The point is that Bush's leadership style apparently allowed him to contemplate Cheney and others handling critical matters without his input, and Cheney did not feel compelled to keep him advised. As of spring 2004, at least, Bush countenanced—indeed was complicit in—some of Cheney's "imperial" behavior. Cheney would have acted quite differently as vice president to Carter, George H. W. Bush, Clinton, Obama, or even Reagan.

Cheney was not as circumspect as other White House vice presidents. Political ambition did not drive his behavior; ideology or a belief that national security depended on his policies did. Whereas other vice presidents tried to expose the president to various options or viewed their role as implementers and articulators of the president's policy, Cheney had a different orientation. He was interested in ends, not means, in outcomes, not protecting the decision-making process.[29]

That leaves the third feature, the White House vice president's private access to the president, a prerogative that allows him to withhold advice when others are present. That privilege immunized vice-presidential comment from direct rebuttal, yet typically vice presidents were weighing in after, or in the context of, a full airing of views. That did not always occur in the George W. Bush administration.

The answer is not to eliminate the vice president's right of private access. The sensitivity of his position requires it, and he can be most useful to the president sometimes in privately thinking aloud with him. In fact, sometimes a vice president's participation in larger discussions may chill deliberation if others assume his view reflects the president's preference.

The risk comes when the vice president advocates policies or presents programs that have not received a full airing before the president embraces them. The remedy in such instances is for the president or vice president to test such ideas with others to make certain that decision is based on appropriate deliberation. Cheney did just that when Rockefeller proposed new programs to Ford that had not been considered by other involved officials. Bush was predisposed to Cheney's suggestions during the first years and sometimes did not seek such a presentation; Cheney apparently did not insist that his recommendations be exposed to discussion.

Private vice-presidential access facilitates presidential decision-making by encouraging robust discussion in meetings and providing the president with advice from a fellow politician who is positioned to take a holistic view of issues. It only becomes a problem if the basic decision-making process is flawed.

The Constitutional Vice Presidency

Cheney's service raised another issue regarding the vice presidency: whether it belongs to the executive or legislative branch. Early in Bush's first term, Cheney invoked executive privilege to shield deliberations of the energy task force from scrutiny by the General Accounting Office of Congress. Later, Cheney claimed immunity from federal disclosure requirements on the ground that the Office of the Vice President is not an "executive agency." That claim ultimately rested primarily on statutory grounds, but Cheney's office had asserted constitutional grounds that it did not abandon.[30] Cheney later said that the vice president has "a foot in both camps,"[31] an understanding he flexed in February 2008 when, as president of the Senate, he signed an amicus brief in a case before the Supreme Court taking a stronger view of the Second Amendment than had the Bush administration.[32] Although many, including White House chief of staff Josh Bolten,[33] challenged Cheney's minimization of the executive nature of his office, some argued that the vice president is exclusively a legislative officer and that the executive acts of Cheney and others were unconstitutional or at least imprudent.[34]

The constitutional text associates the vice president with each branch, as chapter 2 discussed. The original intent of the Constitution imposed on the vice president the duty to preside over the Senate and identified him primarily as a legislative officer.[35] Vice presidents spent most of their time in the legislative branch until the Nixon vice presidency.

During the first two-thirds of the twentieth century, a series of precedents strengthened the vice president's ties to the executive branch. Presidents primarily initiated these actions; vice presidents agreed to them; and the Congress acquiesced in, and even endorsed, them by making the vice president a member of the National Security Council. That ongoing history linked the vice president more securely to the executive branch, and no one complained that the vice president rarely discharged the constitutional duty to preside over the Senate. The Twenty-Fifth Amendment expressed a constitutional vision of the vice presidency as a functioning part of the executive branch. Although it addressed only presidential succession and inability and filling vice-presidential vacancies, it rested on the premises that the office is an indispensable part of the executive branch and that the vice president should be compatible with the president.[36] The ongoing practice of the last century and the implications of the Twenty-Fifth Amendment make clear that the vice president has the constitutional power to discharge the White House vice presidency.

Formally, the Constitution's text links the vice president to both branches, and even those who view the office as executive do not argue that he cannot preside over the Senate or break tie votes. Reb Brownell has improved on the notion of the vice president as a constitutional hybrid by arguing that the vice president acts in only one branch at a time and by calling him a "constitutional chameleon."[37] The vice president clearly does act as a legislative officer when he presides over the Senate, but no one really sees him as such when he breaks a tie vote. Legally, the vote is his, but it is hard to imagine that a White House vice president will not act, and be seen, as the administration's agent in exercising that function. That premise supported the Clinton-Gore joke that whenever Gore voted in the Senate, the administration won.[38] More importantly, as a practical matter, virtually everything consequential that the vice president does occurs in the executive branch. People of the stature and ability of recent vice presidents take the office for its executive role. Vice presidents from both parties have ignored their duty to preside over the Senate save on ceremonial occasions or when a tie seems likely, as it rarely does.[39] No one claims the vice president is derelict in his duties for not presiding over the Senate even though the text imposes that duty and the original intent of the Constitution required it.[40] The vice president almost always wears executive skin.

Democracy and the Vice Presidency

The candidacies of Quayle and Palin have in part prompted academic criticism of vice-presidential selection and election[41] as undemocratic[42] because (1) presidential nominees choose their running mate, and (2) the electoral system denies citizens the opportunity to vote separately for vice president, thereby giving voters reason to attach relatively little significance to the second spot.[43] The issue prompts concern because the vice president is the first presidential successor, the presidency is the most important job in the world, and more than 20 percent of the presidents succeeded from the vice presidency following their predecessors' death or resignation.[44]

These criticisms overlook democratic aspects of vice-presidential selection and election and ignore the necessary relationship of current arrangements to the growth of the office. The system has become progressively more democratic through the increased visibility of the selection process and of vice-presidential candidates and the greater saliency of the office.[45] These factors encourage presidential candidates to choose able running mates and provide citizens with greater reason and opportunity to consider them. The current system appropriately balances democratic accountability and other constitutional values.

Although sometimes defended,[46] the original system had undemocratic features. Electors would be members of the political elite who would exercise discretion to mediate popular will; a vice president could be elected with minority electoral support (Jefferson, 1796); and once political parties slated tickets with understood candidates for president and vice president, the president could be the intended vice president, as almost occurred in 1800.

Some attack vice-presidential selection for giving the presidential nominee "alone" the right to decide on the vice president.[47] In fact, selection is not so unilateral. The elaborate process involves broad consultation and lengthy and public consideration of various options. The timing of selection, before the convention and campaign, virtually guarantees that presidential nominees will consider the likely reaction of delegates and of the electorate. Conventions have reason not to repudiate the standard-bearer's choice, but they do provide a check, as McCain acknowledged in retreating from his plan to choose Lieberman. Most recent vice-presidential nominees have been popular with the convention.

Others complain that vice presidents lack popular support because voters do not ballot separately for the two positions and weight the presidential candidates more heavily.[48] Yet some do weigh the vice-presidential candidates.[49] Following party conventions from 1984 to 2000, Gallup polls revealed that anywhere from 44 percent (in 1984) to 83 percent (in 1992 and 1996) said a vice-presidential selection made voters more or less likely to support a ticket.[50] Slightly more than 50 percent of voters rated Bush's and Kerry's vice-presidential selections as "extremely" or "very" important factors in their 2004 votes. Although the vice-presidential choice was less important than leadership characteristics and policy regarding terrorism, Iraq, and the economy, it was more important than party identification or debate performance.[51] In August 2008, 30 percent of registered voters (and almost 50 percent of undecided voters) said Obama's and McCain's eventual running-mate choices would have "a great deal of influence" on their vote.[52]

Presidential candidates act as if they expect the vice-presidential choice to impact voters. Most presidential nominees since 1976 have chosen running mates of national stature whom they had reason to believe would gain wide acceptance, which may minimize the perceived impact of vice-presidential candidates. This group surely includes Mondale, Bush, Bentsen, Gore, Kemp, Cheney, Lieberman, Edwards, Biden, and Ryan. Many of the exceptions—such as Dole, Ferraro, Quayle, and Palin—were chosen by candidates who trailed and may have made a riskier selection in hope of a high reward.

Vice-presidential candidates now receive significant exposure. The convention acceptance speech, rollout, and debate spotlight the running mate, and information-age technology guarantees the instant dissemination of newsworthy remarks wherever uttered. Some tickets emphasize their vice-presidential candidate, as did Carter (1976) and Dukakis (1988). Clinton said Gore's selection "had a lot to do with my election" and that the decision turned out to be "bigger than you might have thought."[53]

The current system limits, but does not prevent, citizens from weighing the running mates. Intense feelings may affect votes, especially for those relatively indifferent between the competing presidential candidates.[54] Carter campaign manager Hamilton Jordan reported that internal surveys suggested that Mondale added 3 percent to Carter's 1976 vote. One 1988 survey found that 43 percent of Dukakis voters said Bentsen's presence on the ticket influenced their vote, whereas 41 percent saw Quayle as a negative. And a CBS News exit poll reported that nearly 11 percent said Bentsen' s presence influenced their vote for Dukakis and 4.3 percent said the choice of Quayle as the Republican vice-presidential candidate accounted for their vote for Bush.[55]

It seems likely that voters generally either prefer the successful vice-presidential candidate to his opponent or are indifferent between the running mates. Indeed, except for Quayle, recent vice presidents have scored well on favorability polls following their elections. The vexing case remains of the unpopular vice-presidential candidate who rides the standard-bearer's popularity, as occurred when Quayle became vice president even though voters preferred Bentsen by wide margins (63 percent to 32 percent in one survey).[56] That outcome was anomalous. Voters' preference for Bentsen probably did not cost Bush more heavily because misgivings about Dukakis rivaled concerns about Quayle.

Some, like Richard Friedman, acknowledge that an elected vice president would not necessarily be a better vice president but argue that separate voting would "guarantee that if we choose a poor vice-president it is because we as a populace have made a poor choice, not because we have denied ourselves the democratic opportunity to choose."[57] Yet proposed reforms are either not more democratic or would undermine other important constitutional values, including the White House vice presidency.

Some suggested reforms would nominate vice-presidential candidates through vice-presidential primaries, by allowing the convention to select the vice-presidential nominee, or by separating the popular vote for president and vice president.[58] The reforms of vice-presidential nomination are seriously defective. Vice-presidential primaries would diminish public choice by shrinking the pool of those willing to be considered.[59] Presidential candidates, such as Johnson (1960), Bush (1980), Edwards, and Biden, would be precluded from running if the vice-presidential primaries ran concurrently with the presidential events, as would close supporters of prospective candidates such as Mondale (1976). Many appealing vice-presidential candidates, including Mondale, Bentsen, Gore, Kemp, Cheney, and Ryan, did not seek the presidential nomination. It seems unlikely they would have competed for the second spot.

Scheduling the vice-presidential events after the presidential primaries[60] would reduce the pool. Some would not participate absent a sign that the presidential nominee would welcome their selection. Campaign debts of unsuccessful presidential candidates would make another race unappealing. The victor of a vice-presidential primary involving such a restricted pool would not enjoy the "popular legitimacy" of the winner of the presidential nomination. Vice-presidential primaries would probably draw an unrepresentative electorate, especially if conducted separately.

Nor could conventions independently select a vice-presidential nominee. Only Stevenson (1956) in the last sixty years has allowed the convention to choose, a strategy that confirmed impressions that he was too indecisive to be president. A presidential nominee will not silently allow the convention to choose a running mate who may impair his electoral prospects. Delegates will defer to the presidential nominee to whom they are loyal to avoid embarrassing him and because he may become president. Nor is it realistic to expect improvement if the presidential nominee offered the convention a list of several acceptable running mates from which it would select the nominee. Presidential candidates would either submit a stacked list or communicate their choice. Candidates would resist a convention focused on, and likely to prove divisive over, the vice-presidential nomination.

Separate elections would add other undemocratic aspects to those in the nominating process. Presidential and vice-presidential candidates, running separately, would have less incentive to harmonize their appeals. The electorate would be even more challenged to digest a campaign featuring four distinct messages.

If the reforms worked as their proponents hope, the vice president would achieve nomination and office, or both, independently of the presidential candidate. This independence would reverse the positive developments of the White House vice presidency. The biggest problems would occur if the president and vice president came from different parties. The vice president would lose the access upon which the White House vice presidency depends.[61] Even if the two highest officers shared party allegiance, their relationship would be transformed. The bonds of mutual loyalty and dependency would dissipate if the running mate was not the standard-bearer's choice. A separately elected vice president would have a distinct electoral constituency rather than belonging to the president's team. Their independent political identities would foster suspicion and competition. The vice president would become a less-frequent adviser and presidential troubleshooter. Moreover, he would become an alternative president with his or her own constituency, an independent political figure ready to serve as a public critic of presidential policies.[62]

A vice president who was less engaged in the daily work of the executive branch would be less prepared to serve as successor. Arrangements for handling presidential inability, which envision a close relationship between the vice president and administration, would be compromised. If a president and vice president came from opposing parties, presidential succession would produce an intraterm transfer of partisan power that would infringe on the premise that a party controlling the presidency should have a four-year term.

Whether separate election would enhance vice-presidential quality would depend on vice-presidential nomination. Most recent vice presidents have been among the ablest political figures of their times. Their high caliber is due to the incentives in the current system to select an eminent running mate and the appeal of the office. If the presidential nominee lost the right to choose his running mate, vice-presidential quality would decline significantly due to an inferior candidate pool.

Even if the presidential nominee retained the right to select the vice-presidential candidate who would compete separately, quality might suffer. Different calculations would drive vice-presidential choice. There would be less reason to consider impact on the presidential race. The presidential candidate would draw less strength from the vice-presidential candidate, would have less control over him or her, and might prefer to avoid a strong and independent vice-presidential candidate. It is hard to imagine Dole selecting Kemp to run for vice president if Kemp could be separately elected.

Some have proposed remedying these problems by removing the second office from the election process and allowing the president-elect to nominate a vice president after the election subject to confirmation by the House and Senate under the Twenty-Fifth Amendment. It seems bizarre to regard the confirmation procedure that was created as a surrogate for election as more democratic than an election itself. Proponents suggest this approach would remove political considerations and allow the president-elect to choose someone to help in governing.[63] Yet those political considerations are part and parcel of democratic government.

Aside from its less-democratic pedigree, this reform would introduce disadvantages. It would complicate the task of unifying parties. A president-elect would begin the postelection phase by having to select a vice-presidential nominee and shepherd him or her through the bicameral confirmation process, one that would be more intrusive and contentious than the normal advice-and-consent process because of the political nature of the vice presidency and its value as a presidential springboard. Instead of having the vice president–elect help form an administration, the president-elect and his or her closest associates would have yet another major personnel matter to handle. The new vice president would lose the advantages from having helped produce the election victory and from helping create the new government. The transition period would be spent securing confirmation, a process that might extend into the early months of the administration. Patterns of interaction would be established that did not include the new vice president in the early days.

The more-democratic arrangements that some reformers propose are unlikely in practice to yield the anticipated benefits and are likely to impose substantial costs, including diminution of the pool of vice-presidential candidates.[64] The systems for selecting vice-presidential candidates and electing vice presidents have improved markedly in recent decades, including in their fit with democratic values. Moreover, the proposed changes, by separating the vice presidency from the presidency, will diminish the vice presidency, weaken the presidency, and compromise the overall system of presidential succession and inability.

The challenge remains to enhance the democratic aspects of the vice presidency without prohibitive cost elsewhere in the governmental system. Meaningful reform is more likely to come from developing informal institutions that give presidential candidates incentives to choose highly qualified running mates and that allow voters ample opportunity to examine them in action. Some such changes could come from developing new expectations of national candidates such as that they submit to town-hall events and media interviews from a cross-spectrum of the electorate. Ultimately, democratizing the vice presidency, along with other positive changes in our political system, will depend on citizen demands for more pervasive changes in our political system.

The White House vice presidency rests heavily on the association between the presidency and vice presidency. Its development during the past four decades has been one of the few bright spots in the trajectory of our constitutional institutions. It makes little sense to weaken the foundations of that success.

16

Conclusion

The creation of the White House vice presidency is the most impressive development in American political institutions during the past four decades. It has made robust an office that had generally been insignificant, and, in doing so, has contributed to the functioning of the presidency and American government. The accomplishment is especially striking given the troubled history of the vice presidency and the downward trajectory of other constitutional institutions during this period of vice-presidential growth. The enhanced vice presidency has emerged, and endured, without any new statutory or constitutional mandates. This development shows that governmental institutions can change dramatically in positive directions through practices developed by the creative and skillful work of enlightened political leaders and imitated by their successors.

The White House vice presidency culminated the migration of the vice presidency to the executive branch. That process began in the early twentieth century, accelerated with the Nixon vice presidency, and received constitutional sanction in the Twenty-Fifth Amendment, which envisioned the office as executive. Yet at the end of Ford's presidency, the vice presidency remained peripheral and controversial, the humiliating failure of Rockefeller's vice presidency having left the office with an uncertain future. That changed as Carter and Mondale introduced a new model, one their successors have sustained and embellished: the White House vice presidency.

The institution prior to Carter and Mondale had the following features. The presidential nominee chose a running mate after little deliberation at the convention's end. Vice presidents performed disjointed executive functions as occasional presidential advisers, task force chairs, foreign emissaries, administration spokespersons, and political surrogates. Vice-presidential staffs had grown, yet vice presidents and their assistants operated outside the president's inner circle. Perceived as rivals, they were often excluded. The office's primary rationale was to provide a presidential successor, its primary attraction as a presidential springboard.

The White House vice presidency is quite different. The vice president now is the product of an increasingly elaborate selection process that gives the subject great visibility, encourages presidential candidates to think about the office, and convinces most that their choice matters. Some still choose poorly, but most recognize the political wisdom and governing virtue of selecting a high-quality and compatible running mate. The promise of a vice-presidential debate encourages the choice of an able running mate and increases attention to the vice-presidential candidates, as do other new campaign events, such as the vice-presidential rollout. The vice president–elect now helps select personnel and set priorities during the transition. His or her presence at the administration's creation confers influence and signals importance.

The most significant changes relate to the consequential role vice presidents now play in office. The White House vice presidency rests largely on Mondale's vision of the vice president as a senior, across-the-board adviser and troubleshooter on significant matters. Mondale saw his role as helping Carter solve problems by offering candid judgments, exposing the president to a robust policy process, and then helping him implement his decisions. Mondale thought a vice president could provide a politically astute sounding board who largely shared the president's interests and holistic view of the political and policy landscape and a troubleshooter for matters that needed high-level attention. Carter gave Mondale resources to allow him to function as designed. "Mondale gave the job a definition that it had never had before," Quayle later wrote.[1]

Carter's and Mondale's successors have followed the basic contours of the Mondale model. Each administration embraced the conception of the vice president as a senior adviser and troubleshooter, but most of Mondale's successors also took on some long-term operational assignments. Mondale's successors also retained the essential vice-presidential resources although with variations in the way they were deployed. All six presidents supported their vice presidents by word and deed, although some, such as Carter and Clinton, were particularly generous in the frequency and quality of their praise. All vice presidents spent a lot of time with the president. Some saw the presidents in a scheduled way. Bush, Quayle, and Cheney, for instance, began most days with several Oval Office meetings. Some vice-presidential aides became major players in the White House.

Four decades of experience reveal some basic characteristics of the White House vice presidency. First, its parts are interrelated and interdependent. Selection influences performance in office. A presidential candidate who chooses a running mate who is not presidential and compatible will not have a presidential and compatible vice president. And a vice president who is not able and compatible will be less influential as an adviser and less useful as a troubleshooter, conditions likely to increase vice-presidential frustration. The six presidents beginning with Carter chose pretty well, and their vice presidents contributed as advisers and in operational roles. Some exclude Quayle from this assessment, yet he clearly was politically and personally compatible with Bush, understood his role and operated within it, and effectively contributed needed talents.

Vice-presidential duties are also interrelated. Being a senior adviser makes the vice president a more effective troubleshooter because he is perceived to speak for, and have access to, the president. That insider status makes the vice president valuable to foreign leaders and domestic officials. Troubleshooting expands the information and insights vice presidents have to contribute as advisers. Delivering enhances their standing. Political work provides information and capital and is a prerequisite for survival. The vice president's internal clout and external credibility reinforce each other. White House vice presidents perform interrelated functions, not discrete tasks.

This discussion suggests a second feature of a White House vice presidency: a vice president must balance roles that sometimes impose inconsistent, even conflicting demands. He must advise yet also operate and do both across a broad range of issues: foreign, domestic, economic, political, personnel. In order to advise, the vice president must be informed and available, yet troubleshooting takes him out of the White House, and sometimes out of Washington, D.C., or the country, and consumes time and energy. The vice president cannot be in the Situation Room and speaking in China or Los Angeles simultaneously. Yet these (and other) roles are important parts of the job, so a vice president must figure out how to accommodate the various demands of the White House vice presidency. Conflicts are inherent in the job; if the vice president is going to commit his time to its highest and best use, he must guard that resource by not crowding his day with things others could do.

Third, the White House vice presidency is flexible. The six White House vice presidents have each done it differently. Mondale avoided ongoing line assignments, but they constituted much of Gore's operational role. Bush, Quayle, and Biden did something between those two models. Mondale, Bush, Quayle, Cheney, and Biden spent much time dealing with legislators, but Gore spent less time on the Hill. Cheney was not particularly useful in dealing with the opposite party, but Biden excelled across the aisle. Bush was a frequent foreign emissary all over the globe and advised Reagan extensively on foreign policy. Quayle's travel was more targeted, and his most significant advising role drew on his legislative and political insights. Cheney traveled less, especially during the first term, but took some significant trips to war zones and other tense regions. Biden focused on a range of international trouble spots and opportunities during his two terms. Bush and Gore spent much of their second terms running for president. Cheney did not. Mondale and Quayle had to begin reelection campaigning early because Carter and Bush faced primary challenges. Vice presidents operate differently from each other because of the diverse leadership styles of their presidents; the needs of the administration; the problems they face; and the particular talents, expertise, and orientations each contributes. The White House vice presidency can accommodate variation.

Even so, the White House vice presidency adds the most value when its occupant functions not as a subject-matter specialist but as a political generalist. An irate George H. W. Bush instructed the media in December 1988 that a reason the office had "emerged" was that "the Vice President is a generalist."[2] That does not mean that a vice president cannot have special areas of substantive interest or expertise, as, for instance, Bush had in intelligence, Quayle in "Star Wars," or Gore in the environment. Yet a White House vice president's role is not to provide expertise in one or two specific areas; others can do that. Rather, the essential and unique role is to see the entire field as does the president, to provide candid advice that integrates policy and politics to produce sustainable programs, and to expand the president's capacity by executing assignments that require attention at the highest level. Anticipating a Gore vice presidency in October 1992, Richard Neustadt, Gore's former professor, observed that Gore had something to offer Clinton "of enormous and unique utility," a shared "special vantage point" that encompassed the diversity of issues a president faced. "What a prospective asset to the President!" Neustadt wrote. "Somebody with whom he genuinely can kick around choices in the same terms as are relevant for him himself: a very special sounding-board." And Neustadt appreciated that the vice president's job security was an asset that guaranteed "a certain independence of judgment."[3] Neustadt, who, of course, knew something about political institutions and behavior, was really celebrating Mondale's vision of vice-presidential advising.

Fourth, each White House vice presidency is dynamic. They change with the rhythms of the political calendar, personnel moves, problems presented, performance, and fluctuations in relations, including between the president and vice president. Midterm and presidential election years force vice presidents to be on the road more, which affects advising, foreign travel, and other troubleshooting. Baker's departure as Reagan's White House chief of staff deprived Bush of a close ally next door but also meant that Reagan needed him more for political advice. As Clinton's second chief of staff, Panetta introduced more discipline in the White House, which helped Gore. Josh Bolten's assumption of that position was not so fortuitous for Cheney.

Performance matters, too. Bush's conduct following the Reagan assassination attempt showcased his good judgment and loyalty. Gore's role expanded with his success in the NAFTA debate and with REGO and his growing bond with Clinton as they tried to rescue their political careers after the 1994 midterm debacle. Biden's ability to close deals with Republicans helped Obama achieve some of his goals. He clearly developed and sustained a close relationship with Obama that seemed enduring as he approached the final year of his term. By contrast, Cheney's mistakes cost him.

Vice presidencies differ in a second term. A reelected president is more confident and more knowledgeable than at his first inauguration and is liberated from electoral concerns, all of which may lessen his dependency on his vice president. Yet four years of joint service may have strengthened the personal and political bond and allowed the vice president to demonstrate talent and loyalty. Other close presidential associates may return to private life or move to the Cabinet, but the vice president remains, just down the hall. Bush, Gore, and Biden began their second terms in stronger positions. But a second-term vice president may spend less time just down the hall, especially if running for president, an activity that may introduce some perspectives that differ from the president's. Yet Bush's standing grew as Reagan made Bush's election a priority. Clinton anointed Gore as his successor very early, but their relationship disintegrated due to the Lewinsky affair and differences over Gore's campaign. Cheney had abandoned presidential ambitions, and his influence declined in the second term. The president and vice president may become closer or more distant.

Finally, the White House vice presidency is characterized by dependency. Vice presidents rely on presidents for assignments; each president largely determines what and how much the vice president will do. That has been true since the Nixon vice presidency brought the office into the executive branch and remains so now that recent vice presidents have made the enormous leap into the inner circle. The assignments come more frequently, are more substantive and important, and are part of an integrated workload. Instances of public independence remain—Bush and Noriega, Gore and Lewinsky, Cheney and same-sex marriage and the Second Amendment amicus brief.[4] Yet such occasions are exceptional. Generally, vice presidents are publicly loyal, not only when they agree with presidential decisions but also when policy decisions or their implementation run counter to their advice.

In one sense, involvement makes White House vice presidents more dependent than their predecessors. Their president-focused activities are far more significant, but that fact gives them more to lose. Yet in two other respects, White House vice presidents are less dependent than their recent predecessors. First, the institutionalization of the White House vice presidency makes vice-presidential involvement expected, not discretionary. Since the last six vice presidents have been advisers and troubleshooters with a standard set of resources, the next vice president will be less dependent on the next president for that role and those resources. That is not to say that reversion to earlier models is impossible, if, for instance, the president and vice president came from opposing parties under the contingent electoral system or split politically. The former is historically improbable, and powerful incentives mitigate against the latter. The far greater likelihood is that the White House vice presidency will be a continuing part of America's institutional arrangements going forward. Absent some such anomalous event, deviation will require some explanation. Until further notice, the roles and resources of the White House vice presidency accompany the job.

Second, White House vice presidents benefit from the changed nature of their relationship with the president. Dependence runs both ways. Presidents now rely on vice presidents in new ways. Presidents recognize that they need help in dealing with an increasingly challenging set of problems and a larger, more complicated bureaucracy and that the White House vice presidency can provide some of it. Presidents now see that the White House vice presidency strengthens their administrations and makes them better presidents by providing them with counsel from an experienced politician who largely shares their interests and with assistance from a high-level troubleshooter. A presidential candidate who chooses poorly sacrifices a substantial governing asset.

The president depends on the vice president politically, too. The presidential nominating system with its emphasis on primaries and caucuses now makes the president vulnerable to a renomination challenge. A vice president could even challenge a president, although that seems unlikely. More likely, a president will look to the vice president to help him withstand a renomination contest, as Carter did to Mondale and Bush did to Quayle. And the president looks to the vice president to help with reelection.

The White House vice presidency has existed for nearly ten presidential terms across six presidencies: three Democratic, three Republican.

The institution has served presidents who were relatively new to Washington when first elected, as five of the six were. It also served when George H. W. Bush, the consummate insider, was president and during the second terms of Reagan, Clinton, George W. Bush, and Obama when they no longer were strangers to national government or international affairs. It has continued under presidents who were micromanagers, such as Carter, and under those who focused on broad themes, such as Reagan and George W. Bush; under those who were politically sensitive, such as Reagan and Clinton, and less politically attuned, such as Carter and George H. W. Bush; under those popular with their party's base, such as Reagan and George W. Bush, and those who were not, such as Carter and George H. W. Bush; under those with effective, and ineffective, chiefs of staff and with no chief of staff, such as the early Carter. It has worked for vice presidents oriented to domestic or legislative politics and to those who preferred diplomacy. It has worked in the first and second terms, for those hoping to run for president, and for those without that ambition. It has worked even when the principals' past rivalries or personalities raised questions about their ability to coexist. Of course, it has experienced occasional difficulties, and a vice president such as Edwards or Palin who was not presidential or vice-presidential would tax the institution. Yet the success and resilience of the White House vice presidency during the past four decades encourages optimism. Vice-presidential success is not inevitable, but it certainly is possible for those who understand their role and discharge it with skill.

The endurance of the White House vice presidency suggests another theme of this book: that lasting institutional reform can occur through informal means. Repeated practice is a powerful engine of constitutional change that can allow governmental bodies to evolve to forms quite different from, even inconsistent with, their original design or history to accommodate new conditions. The Constitution's text and original intent seem to envision the vice president as the Senate's presiding officer, a commitment that would impede the contemporary role.[5] Fortunately, practice has taken institutional reality in an entirely different direction with widespread support.

The White House vice presidency essentially rests on a series of practices that have developed and been refined over time in a phenomenon resembling a nonjudicial version of the common-law process.[6] That is true of those features which associated the vice presidency with the executive branch before Carter and Mondale took office. It is also true of the defining characteristics of the White House vice presidency—the general adviser and troubleshooter roles and the associated resources—and the supportive system of vice-presidential selection and campaigns (the lengthy vetting, rollout, and debate) and the transition role.

In most instances, Carter, sometimes in response to Mondale's suggestions, adopted a feature to serve the needs of his campaign or administration. The new practice did not bind Carter's and Mondale's successors, yet in most instances, subsequent candidates or administrations adopted the innovation, sometimes with modifications. Carter's successors stopped publicly announced candidate interviews, vetting expanded, and most of Mondale's successors accepted some ongoing line assignments. New institutions developed, such as the preconvention rollout. Yet most of Carter's innovations survived. And as each new campaign or administration adopted a precedent, it became more conventional, the presumptive arrangement. Such entitlements or expectations could be reclaimed only at a cost. In 1992, Quayle emphasized to Gore the value of the West Wing office and urged him to retain it regardless of who else wanted it.[7] He later characterized as "a fool" any future vice president who loses that precious asset.[8] Clinton could hardly deny Gore resources Mondale, Bush, and Quayle had enjoyed over the prior sixteen years, even if he had wanted to do so. A media frenzy would ensue if a president decided to banish the vice president from the White House or refused to break bread with him once a week. As Neustadt challenged, "Try drafting the press release."[9]

As subsequent presidencies established new vice-presidential practices, the protected list expanded. Carter had included Mondale in the transition meetings; Reagan involved Bush, Bush Quayle, and Clinton Gore. Mondale got the president's daily intelligence brief; so have his successors. Reagan included Bush in daily meetings regarding national security and with the chief of staff; Bush did the same with Quayle and Clinton with Gore. Cheney began with everything Gore had, and although Cheney's tenure evoked suggestions that his office had become imperial, Biden essentially inherited those resources. Yes, there were adjustments. Biden did not run the presidential transition, but he was included in a significant way, as were two close associates. The role and resources of the White House vice presidency continued and expanded.

The White House vice presidency took shape from the repetition of accumulated precedents. The logic, workability, and flexibility of the model made it appealing. Repetition entrenched practices by converting novelty to routine, making them institutional, not personal. Expectations developed and established the White House vice presidency as the new norm. Deviation required explanation and became less likely because the status quo has its own pull, especially when working well, as the White House vice presidency has.

The experience of the White House vice presidency raises the question of whether the process that produced such significant and beneficial institutional reform there can work similar magic elsewhere in American government, at least in other areas that lend themselves to informal change.

Replication might depend on understanding what Carter, Mondale, and company did and how they did it. They began by conceiving innovations regarding the vice presidency that would enhance government and were workable. The new vice-presidential selection system, the vice-presidential debate, the transition role, and the adviser-troubleshooter vice president all were sensible and plausible. After identifying each idea, they needed to achieve buy-in among the other necessary participants. In most cases, that was easily done. Carter could dictate the new selection system, although he needed the acquiescence of attractive prospective running mates. The two campaigns agreed to the vice-presidential debate. Carter included Mondale in the transition. Carter accepted Mondale's vice-presidential vision and resource requests and added some others, such as the West Wing office, that he saw were important. The reforms had to be properly resourced. They needed to be implemented successfully to demonstrate their efficacy, no small challenge given the lack of precedents and the stresses that accompany the problems that come to the Oval Office. This process required communicating their vision to their associates and others and acting to protect it.

These steps created practices that worked for Carter and Mondale. Perpetuating them required other actions. The merits of each new institution needed to be communicated to successors. Sometimes visibility or participation simplified that task. Mondale had participated in Carter's vice-presidential selection process, so he understood its structure and was predisposed to its form. But later search leaders communicated with their copartisan predecessors to learn the structure and mechanics. Many participants—Johnson, Cheney, Culvahouse, Christopher—reappeared in different roles.

Transmitting the White House vice presidency required a more difficult, and more interesting, educational effort. The perpetuation of its basic elements required the active role that Mondale, and later his successors, played in recommending it. After the 1980 election, Mondale and his staff educated Bush and his team on the Mondale model and the resources needed to sustain it. The Mondale team was proud of its model yet concerned that advances would be lost because Reagan and Bush had been rivals. Bush (or allies) had to pitch it to Reagan and demonstrate again that it added value. Vice presidents transmitted lessons about the office on a bipartisan basis. Mondale later spoke with Quayle, Gore, and Biden and shared the December 9, 1976, memo with them. Bush spoke with Quayle, as did Nixon, and Quayle spoke to Cheney, although Cheney had already developed an understanding with Bush.[10] Staff communications occurred, too, and many presidential and vice-presidential aides took with them to new jobs the knowledge of the vice presidency from prior service.

Yet the model would not have traveled if it had lacked merit. Incoming administrations adopted the White House vice presidency because it worked for presidents and vice presidents. The model made sense for presidents because it made the vice president an instrument of presidential success, an extra asset to deploy, help for the president now, not simply a standby for a postpresident future. The model made sense to vice presidents, too, by offering a more engaging four (or eight) years than earlier arrangements and giving them the chance to make a difference about things that matter.

The returns from the enhanced vice-presidential role furnished its best recommendation. Its flexibility was an asset because it could be adapted to different administrations, personalities, contexts, styles, and preferences without losing definition. Presidencies succeeded or not, but presidents, vice presidents, and their associates concluded that the White House vice presidency added value.

In some respects, the White House vice presidency better lent itself to creation through informal change than many other projects. Transmission of it benefited from the absence of resistance. Historically, presidents and their inner circles had resisted significant vice-presidential roles. Eisenhower could not imagine a role for Nixon that his chief advisers would accept. Kennedy viewed as ludicrous Johnson's efforts to obtain a West Wing office and meaningful assignments. Johnson was not called for advice because he did not read the cables, a problem Kennedy could have remedied, but that solution apparently exceeded the presidential imagination or desire. Johnson abused Humphrey, Nixon disparaged Agnew. Ford did not resist a role for Rockefeller, but Rumsfeld and Cheney did, and Ford did not insist. He had other things to do.

The pattern of resistance ended with Carter. He was predisposed to strengthening the vice presidency, and his commitment grew as he came to know, like, and value Mondale. Mondale's vice-presidential vision, Carter's commitment of resources, and Mondale's performance made the enterprise even more appealing. The president's support and insistence that his staff cooperate eliminated possible resistance to the White House vice presidency. Reagan accepted the White House vice presidency, as did Bush, Clinton, Bush, and Obama. Resistance disappeared because presidents and their aides saw the White House vice presidency as beneficial. The Senate was happy to have the vice president occupied elsewhere, and the public generally thought it better to use than to ignore the vice president. The White House vice presidency became the new orthodoxy

In theory, at least, change that requires agreement between just two people, where one chooses the other and they share some political interests, comes more easily than that which requires bipartisan cooperation or interbranch agreement. In many other situations, some significant players will resist change, based on either partisanship or concerns regarding separation of powers or federalism.

In other respects, though, the development of the White House vice presidency had to overcome extraordinary obstacles that will not normally exist. First, the past. The premise of precedent-driven reform is that the status quo tends to sustain itself, especially as it becomes more deeply entrenched. If so, 188 years of mostly adverse history posed a formidable barrier. Second, a unique constitutional feature presented a significant obstacle, namely the fact that the vice president is the one major player in the executive branch whom the president cannot replace before the second term. That immunity to removal inhibited presidents from giving their vice presidents meaningful assignments. Vice-presidential assignment had generally been justified either to give the vice president something to do or to make him a better presidential successor; neither gave the president much benefit. Mondale's ability to offer a different vision, and to demonstrate its efficacy, overcame these impediments.

There was also an element of serendipity involved. The right people were in place at the right time. Presidents Johnson or Nixon would not have been receptive as Carter and later Reagan and Bush were. Johnson, Agnew, or Rockefeller would not have handled the vice presidency as well as did Mondale or Bush or Biden. Carter and Mondale were there when it counted, and their successors generally followed their example to support the new institution.

In essence, the vice presidency was in some ways an easier case for informal reform than may be encountered elsewhere, but in other respects it faced challenges. Ultimately, what turned history, overcame constitutional impediment, and redirected incentive was leadership, Mondale's in conceiving a workable, new vision of the office and Carter's in accepting and improving it, and both of their conduct in implementing it. Their examples showed how the vice presidency could enhance an administration and encouraged imitation.

Justice Louis D. Brandeis once wrote, "Knowledge is essential to understanding, and understanding should precede judging."[11] Mondale began by collecting as much knowledge about the vice presidency as he could in order to understand its past problems and its possibilities. His approach was distinctive from prior efforts of presidents, vice presidents, and academics in trying to understand the institution comprehensively before prescribing a set of assignments. The vision of the vice president as an adviser and troubleshooter reflected that understanding. Mondale also understood how to create and present the new vision. Rather than emphasizing the successor role, he made the vice presidency useful on a noncontingent basis. Rather than pursuing his interests, his December 9 memorandum focused on contributing to Carter's success. Rather than equating influence with turf, he embraced access as the ticket to consequence and saw turf as a source of problems. And although he invented something without precedent, he did so by taking roles vice presidents had episodically performed and recasting them in a new and coherent way that gave them substance.

Carter demonstrated bold leadership in his commitment to the undertaking. It was, after all, Carter who pioneered a new selection process, Carter who invited Mondale to run a coordinated campaign, Carter who made space for Mondale in the campaign, Carter who included Mondale in transition activity, Carter who agreed to Mondale's proposal but added important resources to it such as the West Wing office, and Carter who recognized the need to convey repeatedly his support for Mondale to create a new paradigm even if just for his administration and who repeatedly did so.

Carter and Mondale and their associates implemented the new arrangement during four stressful years. Although given no good precedents to follow, they left many behind. Finally, Mondale and his associates selflessly educated Bush and his team regarding the merits of the new model. Their commitment to their creation, and a sense of propriety, overcame partisan reasons not to help their past and future opponent.

Many of Carter's and Mondale's successors also demonstrated impressive political behavior in implementing the White House vice presidency. It took a lot for Reagan to overcome his misgivings about Bush and for Bush to conduct himself in such a way as to override that earlier impression. It took a lot for Bush to overlook Quayle's troubled campaign and poll numbers and for Quayle to add value to Bush's administration in different ways notwithstanding the continuing abuse he took. It took a lot for Clinton to make space for Gore and for Gore to assume a heavy burden of advising, operational, and political duties. It took a lot for Bush to include Cheney as he did and for Cheney to accumulate the degree of influence he had during the first term. It took a lot for Obama to overlook Biden's occasional gaffes—although he did so in part because he recognized that the benefits Biden brought far exceeded those costs—and for Biden to adjust to working for someone else and to do so with such loyalty, skill, and restraint.

White House vice presidents have acted as leaders as well as followers. That was certainly the case when Mondale criticized Carter's approach to the presidency or saved Indochinese boat people, when Bush coaxed Reagan to a less bellicose position regarding the Soviet Union, when Quayle forcefully urged Bush not to abandon his "no new taxes" pledge or chastised Latin American leaders over human rights abuses, when Gore debated Perot or negotiated with Chernomyrdin, when Cheney directed operations on 9/11 or set some useful precedents regarding continuity of government, and when Biden challenged Obama's other advisers over Afghanistan policy or implemented the recovery program or found compromises with McConnell.

White House vice presidents, like others, have made mistakes, sometimes serious ones. Yet the institution Carter and Mondale created and their successors developed has enhanced American government. Its creation and endurance should inspire hope in the possibility of institutional evolution and regeneration and of constructive political leadership, and its example provides lessons for others to apply.

NOTES

Chapter 1: Introduction

1. *The Diary of William Maclay and Other Notes on Senate Debates,* ed. Kenneth R. Bowling and Helen E. Veit (Baltimore, MD: Johns Hopkins University Press, 1988), 9:6.

2. 2 Annals of Cong. 281 (1791).

3. Quoted in Michael Nelson, "Background Paper," in *A Heartbeat Away* (New York: Priority Press Publications, 1988), 19, 30.

4. Thomas R. Marshall, *A Hoosier Salad: Recollections of Thomas R. Marshall, Vice President and Hoosier Philosopher* (Indianapolis, IN: Bobbs-Merrill, 1925), 368.

5. Quoted in Henry Kissinger, *Years of Upheaval* (Boston: Little, Brown, 1982), 90–91.

6. Shirley Anne Warshaw, *The Co-Presidency of Bush and Cheney* (Stanford, CA: Stanford University Press, 2009).

7. Paul C. Light, *Vice-Presidential Power: Advice and Influence in the White House* (Baltimore, MD: Johns Hopkins University Press, 1984).

8. Irving G. Williams, *The Rise of the Vice Presidency* (Washington, DC: Public Affairs Press, 1956).

9. Joel K. Goldstein, *The Modern American Vice Presidency: The Transformation of a Political Institution* (Princeton, NJ: Princeton University Press, 1982).

10. John Adams served two terms under Washington; Daniel Tompkins under James Monroe; Thomas Marshall under Woodrow Wilson; John Nance Garner under Franklin D. Roosevelt; Nixon under Eisenhower; and Agnew under Nixon, although neither completed the second term.

Chapter 2: The Vice Presidency through History

1. U.S. Const., art. I, sec. 3, cl. 4 ("The Vice President of the United States shall be President of the Senate, but shall have no Vote, unless they be equally divided").

2. U.S. Const., art. II, sec. 1, cl. 6 ("In Case of the Removal of the President from Office, or of his Death, Resignation, or Inability to discharge the Powers and Duties of the said Office, the Same shall devolve on the Vice President, and the Congress may by Law provide for the Case of Removal, Death, Resignation or Inability, both of the President and Vice President, declaring what Officer shall then act as President, and such Officer shall act accordingly, until the Disability be removed, or a President shall be elected").

3. The points in the next few paragraphs are developed in greater detail in Joel K. Goldstein, "The New Constitutional Vice Presidency," *Wake Forest Law Review* 30, no. 3 (1995): 505, 510–515.

4. Max Farrand, ed., *The Records of the Federal Convention of 1787* (New Haven, CT: Yale University Press, 1911), 2:537; Cecilia M. Kenyon, ed., *The Antifederalists* (Boston: Northeastern University Press, 1985), 193, 305.

5. Farrand, *The Records of the Federal Convention of 1787*, 2:537.

6. 8 Annals of Cong. 21 (1803) (remarks of Sen. Jonathan Dayton).

7. *The Federalist* No. 68 (Alexander Hamilton).

8. Farrand, *The Records of the Federal Convention of 1787*, 2:537; *The Federalist* No. 68 (Hamilton); Kenyon, *The Antifederalists*, 220, 305.

9. Goldstein, "The New Constitutional Vice Presidency," 513.

10. The ideas in the following paragraphs are developed more fully in Joel K. Goldstein, "Constitutional Change, Originalism, and the Vice Presidency," *University of Pennsylvania Journal of Constitutional Law* 16, no. 2 (2013): 369, 386–392.

11. *The Federalist* No. 68 (Hamilton).

12. *The Diary of William Maclay and Other Notes on Senate Debates*, ed. Kenneth R. Bowling and Helen E. Veit (Baltimore, MD: Johns Hopkins University Press, 1988), 9:6.

13. U.S. Const., art. I, sec. 3, cl. 5 ("The Senate shall choose their other Officers, and also a President pro tempore, in the Absence of the Vice President, or when he shall exercise the Office of President of the United States").

14. *Diary of William Maclay*, 9:6.

15. Farrand, *The Records of the Federal Convention of 1787*, 2:536–537.

16. U.S. Const. art. II, sec. 1, cl. 6.

17. Farrand, *The Records of the Federal Convention of 1787*, 2:495.

18. John D. Feerick, *From Failing Hands* (New York: Fordham University Press, 1965), 48, 50–51.

19. C. F. Adams, ed., *The Works of John Adams*, 10 vols. (Boston: Little, Brown, 1856), 1:460.

20. Thomas Jefferson to James Madison, January 1, 1797, in *The Writings of Thomas Jefferson*, Paul Leicester Ford, ed. (New York: G. P. Putnam's Sons, 1896), 7:98–99.

21. Thomas Jefferson to Dr. Benjamin Rush, January 22, 1797, in ibid., 7:113, 114.

22. Harold C. Relyea, "The Executive Office of the Vice President: Constitutional and Legal Considerations," *Presidential Studies Quarterly* 40, no. 2 (June 2010): 327, 328.

23. Quoted in Mark O. Hatfield with the Senate Historical Office, *Vice Presidents of the United States, 1789–1993* (Washington, DC: Government Printing Office, 1997), 7.

24. Dumas Malone, *Jefferson and the Ordeal of Liberty* (Boston: Little, Brown, 1962), 300, 319.

25. Jefferson to Madison, January 22, 1797, in *The Writings of Thomas Jefferson*, 7:107, 108.

26. Abigail Adams to Mary Smith Cranch, July 4, 1790, in *Adams Family Correspondence*, Margaret A. Hogan et al., eds. (Cambridge, MA: Belknap Press of Harvard University Press, 2009), 9:73, 74.

27. 6 Annals of Cong. 1580, 1581 (1797).

28. Noble Cunningham, Jr., *In Pursuit of Reason: The Life of Thomas Jefferson* (Baton Rouge: Louisiana State University Press, 1987), 221.

29. Akhil Reed Amar, *America's Constitution: A Biography* (New York: Random House, 2005), 168, 336–341.

30. 13 Annals of Cong. 21, 22 (Sen. Dayton), 22–23 (Sen. Jackson), 23 (Sen. Hillhouse).

31. David P. Currie, *The Constitution in Congress: The Jeffersonians, 1801–1829* (Chicago: University of Chicago Press, 2001), 44–45.

32. U.S. Const. amend XII.

33. Senate Historical Office, "President Pro Tempore," United States Senate, accessed July 25, 2015, http://www.senate.gov/artandhistory/history/common/briefing/President_Pro_Tempore.htm#2.

34. 13 Annals of Cong. 143–145 (Sen. White), 155 (Sen. William Plumer), 733–734 (Rep. Taggart), 750–751 (Rep. Roger Griswold).

35. Milton Lomask, *Aaron Burr: The Years from Princeton to Vice President, 1756–1805* (New York: Farrar, Straus and Giroux, 1979), 301–304.

36. Hatfield with the Senate Historical Office, *Vice Presidents of the United States*, 53–57, 74–76, 83–115, 138–141, 152–153.

37. Ibid., 181–187, 251–253, 264, 289–290.

38. Roy E. Brownell II, "The Independence of the Vice Presidency," *New York University Journal of Legislation and Public Policy* 17, no. 2 (2014): 297, 325–334.

39. John P. Kaminski, *George Clinton: Yeoman Politician of the New Republic* (Madison, WI: Madison House, 1993), 278–279, 289–290.

40. John Niven, *John C. Calhoun and the Price of Union* (Baton Rouge: Louisiana State University Press, 1988), 169–177, 185–186.

41. Hatfield with the Senate Historical Office, *Vice Presidents of the United States*, 254, 264–265, 273.

42. Michael J. Gerhardt, *The Forgotten Presidents: Their Untold Constitutional Legacy* (Oxford: Oxford University Press, 2013), 39–40.

43. Calhoun served as vice president to John Quincy Adams and Jackson but was not elected to serve during Jackson's second term.

44. Woodrow Wilson, *Congressional Government* (Boston: Houghton Mifflin, 1885), 162.

45. Theodore Roosevelt to H. C. Lodge, July 1, 1899; Roosevelt to Lodge, December 11, 1899, in *Selections from the Correspondence of Theodore Roosevelt and Henry Cabot Lodge, 1884–1918* (New York: Charles Scribner's Sons, 1925), 1:404, 426.

46. Roosevelt to Lodge, January 30, 1900, in ibid., 1:441, 442.

47. Woodrow Wilson, *Constitutional Government in the United States* (New York: Columbia University Press, 1908), 130.

48. Diary of Colonel House, May 24, 1916, in *The Papers of Woodrow Wilson*, Arthur S. Link, ed. (Princeton, NJ: Princeton University Press, 1981), 37:103, 105.

49. James Bryce, *The American Commonwealth* (New York: Macmillan, 1928), 1:300, 402.

50. "Coolidge Agrees to Sit in Cabinet at Harding's Wish," *New York Times*, December 17, 1920, 1.

51. *The Autobiography of Calvin Coolidge* (New York: Cosmopolitan Books, 1929), 164.

52. "Dawes Is Unwilling to Sit in Cabinet," *New York Times*, February 5, 1925, 2; "Coolidge to Drop Harding Precedent," *New York Times*, November 27, 1924,

18; "Dawes Won't Sit in Cabinet, Refusing Coolidge Offer," *New York Times*, November 26, 1924, 1.

53. "Curtis to Join in Cabinet Meetings: Will Participate in First One Today," *New York Times*, March 8, 1929, 1.

54. "Prizes Vice Presidency: 'Best Job I've Ever Had,' Says Marshall; 'No Responsibilities,'" *New York Times*, November 28, 1918, 2.

55. Quoted in Louis Ludlow, *From Cornfield to Press Gallery: Adventures and Reminiscences of a Veteran Washington Correspondent* (Washington, DC: W. F. Roberts, 1924), 312.

56. "Vice President Has No Work to Bother Him, Dawes Asserts," *New York Times*, August 16, 1927, 1.

57. Mildred Adams, "Busy Mr. Garner Is Ready for Congress," *New York Times*, December 30, 1934, SM5.

58. Hatfield with the Senate Historical Office, *Vice Presidents of the United States*, 388–390, 401–404; Irving G. Williams, "The American Vice-Presidency and Foreign Affairs," *World Affairs* 120, no. 2 (Summer 1957): 39–40.

59. 50 U.S.C. 402.

60. Joel K. Goldstein, "Vice-Presidential Behavior in a Disability Crisis: The Case of Thomas R. Marshall," *Politics and Life Sciences* 33, no. 2 (2014): 44–45.

61. Hatfield with the Senate Historical Office, *Vice Presidents of the United States*, 390–393, 401–403.

62. Harry S. Truman, *Memoirs: 1945, Year of Decisions* (New York: Doubleday, 1955), 19–20; David McCullough, *Truman* (New York: Simon & Schuster, 1992), 333, 337, 376–379.

63. "Marshall Opposed to Seat in Cabinet," *New York Times*, December 5, 1920, 4.

64. *Autobiography of Calvin Coolidge*, 161.

65. "Dawes and Curtis Disagree on Rules," *New York Times*, March 5, 1929, 4.

66. William R. Tansill, "Memorandum: Number of Dates Certain Vice Presidents Actually Presided over the Senate," Library of Congress Legislative Reference Service, June 27, 1955, 2.

67. 95 Cong. Rec. 480 (1949).

68. Floyd M. Riddick, interview by Donald K. Ritchie, Senate Oral History Project, June 26, July 12, 1978, II: 45; III: 66, http://www.senate.gov/artandhistory/history/oral_history/Floyd_M_Riddick.htm; Estimated Presiding Time of the Vice Presidents from 1949–1958, Senate Historical Office Files.

69. Joel K. Goldstein, "Veepwatch, Part 1: The Swing State Selection Myth," Sabato's Crystal Ball, April 5, 2012, http://www.centerforpolitics.org/crystalball/articles/veepwatch-part-1-the-swing-state-selection-myth.

70. Gerald Pomper, *Nominating the President: The Politics of Convention Choice* (Evanston, IL: Northwestern University Press, 1963), 150.

71. Since George Clinton died April 20, 1812, and James S. Sherman died October 30, 1912, the seven deaths occurred over 100 years, 6 months, and 10 days.

72. Clinton L. Rossiter, "The Reform of the Vice-Presidency," *Political Science Quarterly* 63, no. 3 (September 1948): 383.

73. Lucius Wilmerding, Jr., "The Vice Presidency," *Political Science Quarterly* 68, no. 1 (March 1953): 17–41, 19.

74. Joel K. Goldstein, *The Modern American Vice Presidency: The Transformation of a Political Institution* (Princeton: Princeton University Press, 1982), 15–45.

75. Richard Moe, *Roosevelt's Second Act: The Election of 1940 and the Politics of War* (Oxford: Oxford University Press, 2013), 228–240.

76. Herbert Brownell with John P. Burke, *Advising Ike: The Memoirs of Attorney General Herbert Brownell* (Lawrence: University Press of Kansas, 1993), 51, 78–79, 120; Dwight D. Eisenhower, *Waging Peace, 1956–1961* (Garden City, NY: Doubleday, 1965), 6; Richard M. Nixon, *RN: The Memoirs of Richard Nixon* (New York: Grosset and Dunlap, 1978), 167.

77. Goldstein, *The Modern American Vice Presidency*, 302–303.

78. Jeffrey Frank, *Ike and Dick: Portrait of a Strange Political Marriage* (New York: Simon & Schuster, 2013), 80–85.

79. Eisenhower, *Waging Peace*, 6.

80. Frank, *Ike and Dick*, 109–119, 165–181.

81. Robert A. Caro, *The Years of Lyndon Johnson: The Passage of Power* (New York: Alfred A. Knopf, 2012), 173–174.

82. Robert Dallek, *Flawed Giant: Lyndon Johnson and His Times, 1961–1973* (New York: Oxford University Press, 1998), 12.

83. Goldstein, *The Modern American Vice Presidency*, 161, 162–163; Dallek, *Flawed Giant*, 17–20.

84. "Johnson to Get Offices in Sight of White House," *New York Times*, March 1, 1961, 18.

85. The President's News Conference, March 1, 1961, *Public Papers of the Presidents of the United States: John F. Kennedy, 1961* (Washington, DC: Government Printing Office, 1962), 135, 138.

86. Memorandum, Nicholas Katzenbach to Lyndon B. Johnson, "Participation of the Vice President in the Affairs of the Executive Branch," March 9, 1961, http://www.justice.gov/sites/default/files/olc/opinions/1961/03/31/op-olc-supp-v001-p0214_0.pdf, 219–220.

87. Memorandum, Nicholas Katzenbach to Attorney General Robert F. Kennedy, "Delegation of Presidential Powers to the Vice President," June 22, 1961, http://fas.org/irp/agency/doj/olc/062261.pdf, 2.

88. See Minutes of the Democratic Conference, Tuesday, January 3, 1961, in *Minutes of the Senate Democratic Conference, 1903–1964*, ed. Donald Ritchie (Washington, DC: Government Printing Office, 1998), 577–579.

89. William Proxmire, interview by Michael L. Gillette, February 4, 1986, Lyndon Baines Johnson Presidential Library, Austin, TX, http://web2.millercenter.org/lbj/oralhistory/proxmire_william_1986_0204.pdf, 31–32; Caro, *The Years of Lyndon Johnson*, 168; Dallek, *Flawed Giant*, 8.

90. See John D. Feerick, *The Twenty-Fifth Amendment: Its Complete History and Applications*, 3rd ed. (New York: Fordham University Press, 2014).

91. Goldstein, "The New Constitutional Vice Presidency," 526–534.

92. Goldstein, *The Modern American Vice Presidency*, 233–237.

93. Paul T. David, "The Vice Presidency: Its Institutional Evolution and Contemporary Status," *Journal of Politics* 29, no. 4 (November 1967): 721.

94. Joel K. Goldstein, "More Agony Than Ecstasy: Hubert H. Humphrey as Vice President," in *At the President's Side: The Vice Presidency in the Twentieth*

Century, ed. Timothy Walch (Columbia: University of Missouri Press, 1997), 107, 116; Goldstein, *The Modern American Vice Presidency*, 154–155.

95. See Michael Nelson, *Resilient America: Electing Nixon in 1968, Channeling Dissent, and Dividing Government* (Lawrence: University Press of Kansas, 2014).

96. William H. Rehnquist, "Memorandum for the Honorable Edmund L. Morgan, Deputy Counsel to the President, re Advisory Commission on Intergovernmental Relations," February 7, 1969, http://fas.org/irp/agency/doj/olc/020769.pdf, 2.

97. Paul C. Light, *Vice-Presidential Power: Advice and Influence in the White House* (Baltimore, MD: Johns Hopkins University Press, 1984), 69–72.

98. Jules Witcover, *Very Strange Bedfellows: The Short and Unhappy Marriage of Richard Nixon and Spiro Agnew* (New York: PublicAffairs, 2007), 35, 111–130.

99. "Rockefeller Is Praised for Stint of Four Days," *New York Times*, January 18, 1975, 15.

100. James P. Pfiffner, *The Modern Presidency* (New York: St. Martin's, 1994), 4–5, 51–108.

101. Goldstein, *The Modern American Vice Presidency*, 249–270.

102. See ibid., 46–89, for a discussion of the selection process during much of this period.

103. Donald Rumsfeld, *Known and Unknown: A Memoir* (New York: Sentinel, 2011), 111–114.

104. Hubert H. Humphrey, *The Education of a Public Man: My Life and Politics* (Garden City, NY: Doubleday, 1976), 298–299; Carl Solberg, *Hubert Humphrey: A Biography* (New York: W. W. Norton, 1984), 244–246.

105. Max Kampelman, *Entering New Worlds: The Memoirs of a Private Man in Public Life* (New York: HarperCollins, 1991), 165–166.

106. Joshua M. Glasser, *The Eighteen-Day Running Mate: McGovern, Eagleton, and a Campaign in Crisis* (New Haven, CT: Yale University Press, 2012), 100–101, 108, 110, 113–116, 132, 270.

107. Goldstein, "The New Constitutional Vice Presidency," 543–544; Arthur M. Schlesinger, Jr., "On the Presidential Succession," *Political Science Quarterly* 89, no. 3 (Fall 1974): 475.

108. Stephen E. Ambrose, *Nixon: The Education of a Politician, 1913–1962* (New York: Simon & Schuster, 1987), 384.

109. Ibid., 439–442; Frank, *Ike and Dick*, 154–155.

110. The President's News Conference, August 24, 1960, *Public Papers of the Presidents: Dwight D. Eisenhower, 1960–1961* (Washington, DC: Government Printing Office, 1961), 647, 657–658.

111. Nigel Bowles, *The White House and Capitol Hill: The Politics of Presidential Persuasion* (New York: Clarendon, 1987), 38, 39.

112. Caro, *The Years of Lyndon Johnson*, 169–172; Dallek, *Flawed Giant*, 8–9.

113. Harry McPherson, *A Political Education: A Washington Memoir* (Boston: Houghton Mifflin, 1988), 184.

114. Eric F. Goldman, *The Tragedy of Lyndon Johnson* (New York: Dell, 1969), 243.

115. The President's News Conference, February 4, 1965, *Public Papers of the Presidents of the United States: Lyndon B. Johnson, 1965* (Washington, DC: Government Printing Office, 1966), 1:131.

116. Solberg, *Hubert Humphrey*, 270–274; Goldstein, "More Agony Than Ecstasy," 103, 108–110.

117. Witcover, *Very Strange Bedfellows*, 60.

118. Ibid., 56–57, 61–63, 65–68; Tom Korologos, interview by Richard Norton Smith, May 21, 2009, Gerald R. Ford Presidential Foundation, http://geraldr fordfoundation.org/centennial/oralhistory/wp-content/uploads/2013/05/Tom -Korologos-1-and-2.pdf, 7–8.

119. Witcover, *Very Strange Bedfellows*, 150–154, 187–195.

120. Quoted in Goldstein, *The Modern American Vice Presidency*, 171.

121. James Cannon, *Gerald R. Ford: An Honorable Life* (Ann Arbor: University of Michigan Press, 2013), 125–130.

122. Feerick, *The Twenty-Fifth Amendment*, 135–157.

123. John O. Marsh, interview by Richard Norton Smith, October 7, 2008, Gerald R. Ford Oral History Project, http://geraldrfordfoundation.org/centennial/oral history/wp-content/uploads/2013/05/Jack-Marsh.pdf, 11.

124. Feerick, *The Twenty-Fifth Amendment*, 159–164; James Cannon, "Gerald R. Ford and Nelson A. Rockefeller: A Vice Presidential Memoir," in Walch, ed., *At the President's Side*, 136.

125. Light, *Vice-Presidential Power*, 9–10, 69–72; Relyea, "The Executive Office of the Vice President," 31.

126. Feerick, *The Twenty-Fifth Amendment*, 167–189; Richard Norton Smith, *On His Own Terms: A Life of Nelson Rockefeller* (New York: Random House, 2014), 643–644.

127. R. W. Apple, Jr., "Outlook for Rockefeller; Long Experience in Running Things Is Expected to Reinforce President," *New York Times*, December 20, 1974, 1; "The New Vice President," *New York Times*, December 20, 1974, 36.

128. Smith, *On His Own Terms*, 344–345, 539–540.

129. Cannon, "Gerald R. Ford and Nelson A. Rockefeller," 141–142; Rumsfeld, *Known and Unknown*, 184.

130. Rumsfeld, *Known and Unknown*, 184.

131. Jack Marsh to Gerald Ford, "Role of the Vice President," December 20, 1974, Cheney 10 Rockefeller-Nelson-Role as V.P. 12/20/74, Gerald R. Ford Presidential Library, Ann Arbor, MI.

132. Linda Charlton, "Rockefeller Gets Key Job Guiding Domestic Council," *New York Times*, December 22, 1974, 1, 27.

133. Seymour M. Hersh, "Ford Names Rockefeller to Head Inquiry into CIA; Wants Report in 90 Days," *New York Times*, January 6, 1975, 1.

134. Peter Wallison, interview by Richard Norton Smith, November 18, 2009, Gerald R. Ford Oral History Project, http://geraldrfordfoundation.org/centennial /oralhistory/wp-content/uploads/2013/05/Peter-Wallison.pdf, 15–16, 21–22.

135. Jim Cannon, interview by Richard Norton Smith, June 10, 2009, Gerald R. Ford Oral History Project, http://geraldrfordfoundation.org/centennial/oral history/wp-content/uploads/2013/05/Jim-Cannon.pdf, 6–7.

136. Stephen Hess to Jimmy Carter, Memorandum, December 13, 1976, in Stephen Hess, *Organizing the Presidency*, rev. ed. (Washington, DC: Brookings Institution, 1988), 257.

137. Rumsfeld, *Known and Unknown*, 185–186; Dick Cheney with Liz Cheney, *In My Time: A Personal and Political Memoir* (New York: Simon & Schuster, 2011), 80; Cannon interview, 9–10.

138. Rumsfeld, *Known and Unknown*, 185–187; David Burnham, "Rockefeller Plan Splits Ford Aides," *New York Times*, September 5, 1975, 27.

139. Joseph Lelyveld, "Rockefeller Making an Impact on Policy," *New York Times*, September 27, 1975, 1; Joseph Lelyveld, "Vice President with Clout: Rockefeller Has Made Something of His New Job," *New York Times*, September 28, 1975, 188.

140. Smith, *On His Own Terms*, 661–663.

141. Rumsfeld, *Known and Unknown*, 195.

142. Smith, *On His Own Terms*, 676–677; Rumsfeld, *Known and Unknown*, 201–202.

143. Wallison interview, 35–36.

144. Donald Rumsfeld, interview with Richard Norton Smith, March 31, 2009, Gerald R. Ford Oral History Project, http://geraldrfordfoundation.org/centennial /oralhistory/wp-content/uploads/2013/05/Donald-Rumsfeld.pdf, 19.

145. Arthur M. Schlesinger, "On the Presidential Succession," *Political Science Quarterly* 89, no. 3 (Autumn 1974): 475–505; Arthur M. Schlesinger, Jr., "Is the Vice Presidency Necessary?" *Atlantic Monthly*, May 1974, 37–44.

146. Henry Kissinger, *Years of Upheaval* (Boston: Little, Brown, 1982), 90–92.

147. Eugene J. McCarthy, "Memories of Hubert: A Politician Too Good to Be Vice President," *New Republic*, February 18, 1978, 21, 23.

148. Humphrey, *Education of a Public Man*, 367.

CHAPTER 3: LAYING THE FOUNDATION

1. George S. McGovern, *Grassroots: The Autobiography of George McGovern* (New York: Random House, 1977), 193–198.

2. John D. Feerick, *The Twenty-Fifth Amendment: Its Complete History and Applications*, 3rd ed. (New York: Fordham University Press, 2014), 141–145, 167–185.

3. Jules Witcover, *Marathon: The Pursuit of the Presidency, 1972–1976* (New York: Viking, 1977), 361.

4. Walter F. Mondale, Lecture, February 17, 1981, 5 (on file with author).

5. Witcover, *Marathon*, 360.

6. Jimmy Carter, *Keeping Faith: Memoirs of a President* (Toronto, Ontario: Bantam Books, 1982), 35–36.

7. Jimmy Carter, Hamilton Jordan, Charles Kirbo, and Pat Caddell, Press Conference, July 15, 1976, in *The Presidential Campaign of 1976: Jimmy Carter* (Washington, DC: Government Printing Office, 1978), 1:329–330.

8. Carter, *Keeping Faith*, 35.

9. Ibid., 36.

10. Carter et al., Press Conference, July 15, 1976, 1:330–331; Martin Schram, *Running for President: A Journal of the Carter Campaign* (New York: Pocket Books, 1977), 224.

11. Charles Kirbo, interview by Charles O. Jones et al., Jimmy Carter Oral History Project, University of Virginia, January 5, 1983, http://web1.millercenter.org /poh/transcripts/ohp_1983_0105_kirbo.pdf, 13–14.

12. Richard Moe, Memorandum to Mondale, "V-P Nomination," undated, Vice Presidential Selection 1976 folder, Box 7, Richard Moe Papers, Special Collections, University of Maryland Library, College Park, MD.

13. Walter F. Mondale, in discussion with author, November 16, 2006; Walter F. Mondale with David Hage, *The Good Fight: A Life in Liberal Politics* (New York: Scribner, 2010), 157–158.

14. Mondale with Hage, *The Good Fight*, 158.

15. Ibid., 158–159.

16. Mondale, discussion.

17. Carter, *Keeping Faith*, 36–37.

18. Richard Moe, in discussion with author, October 23, 2006.

19. Linda Charlton, "Mondale, on Questionnaire from Carter, Told of Two 'Minor Questions' Raised about His Campaign Funds," *New York Times*, August 3, 1976, 17.

20. Kirbo interview, 14.

21. Muskie met with Carter on July 5, 1976, and Mondale and Glenn on the morning and afternoon, respectively, of July 8.

22. Comments of Hamilton Jordan and Jody Powell in *Campaign for President: The Managers Look at '76*, ed. Jonathan Moore and Janet Fraser (Cambridge, MA: Ballinger Publishing, 1977), 112.

23. Richard Moe, "The Making of the Modern Vice Presidency: A Personal Remembrance," *Minnesota History* (Fall 2006): 88, 91; Mondale with Hage, *The Good Fight*, 161.

24. Richard Moe, Memorandum to Mondale, "Re: The Conversation," June 21, 1976, Vice Presidential Selection 1976 folder, Box 7, Richard Moe papers, Special Collections, University of Maryland Library, College Park, MD.

25. Carter, *Keeping Faith*, 37.

26. Jimmy Carter, *White House Diary* (New York: Farrar, Straus and Giroux, 2010), 89.

27. Carter et al., Press Conference, 1:345.

28. Mondale with Hage, *The Good Fight*, 163.

29. Mondale, discussion.

30. Carter, *Keeping Faith*, 36.

31. Bethine Church, *A Lifelong Affair: My Passion for People and Politics* (Washington, DC: Francis Press, 2003), 245; LeRoy Ashby and Rod Gramer, *Fighting the Odds: The Life of Senator Frank Church* (Pullman: Washington State University Press, 1994), 524–525.

32. Ashby and Gramer, *Fighting the Odds*, 525; Schram, *Running for President*, 225.

33. Ashby and Gramer, *Fighting the Odds*, 523–524; Carroll Hubbard to Jimmy Carter, June 29, 1976, Series 10.6, Box 1, folder 18, Frank Church Collection, Boise State University Library, Boise, ID; Schram, *Running for President*, 230–231.

34. Rosalynn Carter, *First Lady from Plains* (Boston: Houghton Mifflin, 1984), 135–136; Carter et al., Press Conference, 1:343.

35. Carter, *Keeping Faith*, 36–37.

36. R. W. Apple, Jr., "Carter Promises No. 2 Spot Will Go to 1 of 7 Queried," *New York Times*, July 12, 1976, A1, C20; Schram, *Running for President*, 231, 233.

37. Charles Mohr, "Carter to Begin Talks on Ticket," *New York Times*, July 5, 1976, 1, 16.

38. Schram, *Running for President*, 225.

39. Carter et al., Press Conference, 1:331–332.

40. Schram, *Running for President*, 225, 226; Bert Lance with Bill Gilbert, *The Truth of the Matter: My Life in and out of Politics* (New York: Summit Books, 1991), 64; Charles Mohr, "Carter Ends Interviews on Running Mate," *New York Times*, July 13, 1976, 1, 25; R. W. Apple, Jr., "Humphrey Hailed," *New York Times*, July 14, 1976, 1, 16.

41. R. W. Apple, Jr., "A Jubilant Party," *New York Times*, July 16, 1976, A1, A11.

42. James Reston, "Gov. Carter's Strategy," *New York Times*, July 16, 1976, 17.

43. Jimmy Carter, interview from *U.S. News and World Report*, September 13, 1976, reprinted in *The Presidential Campaign of 1976: Jimmy Carter*, 1:734, 736–737.

44. Linda Charlton, "Mondale's Staff Preparing for Campaign," *New York Times*, July 19, 1976, 13.

45. Moe, discussion.

46. Richard Moe, Memorandum to Mondale, "Meeting with Governor Carter," July 21, 1976, Mondale Papers, Minnesota Historical Society, St. Paul, MN.

47. Richard Moe and Michael Berman, interview by James Ceaser et al., Jimmy Carter Oral History Project, University of Virginia, January 15–16, 1982, http://web1.millercenter.org/poh/transcripts/ohp_1982_0115_moe.pdf, 5, 7–8; Michael Berman, "The Vice President in Retrospective," February 21, 1981, 8, 1984 Campaign Files, Speech Files, Mondale Papers, Minnesota Historical Society, St. Paul, MN.

48. Eliot Cutler (Mondale campaign aide and deputy director of Office of Management and Budget), in discussion with author, November 2, 2006.

49. Jimmy Carter and Walter Mondale, Press Conferences, July 27, 28, and 29, 1976, in *The Presidential Campaign of 1976: Jimmy Carter*, 1:353–377.

50. Carter and Mondale, Press Conference, July 27, 1976, 353, 360–361.

51. Jimmy Carter, Press Conference, August 18, 1976, in *The Presidential Campaign of 1976: Jimmy Carter*, 1:393, 399–400.

52. Jimmy Carter and Walter Mondale, Press Conference, September 3, 1976, in *The Presidential Campaign of 1976: Jimmy Carter*, 1:573, 575.

53. John M. Crewdson, "Rizzo Tells Mondale He Will Get Out Vote," *New York Times*, November 2, 1976, 19.

54. Kennedy and Nixon had considered adding such an encounter or including their running mates in a fifth debate. Herbert A. Seltz and Richard D. Yoakam, "Production Diary of the Debates," in *The Great Debates: Background, Perspective, Effects*, ed. Sidney Kraus (Bloomingdale: Indiana University Press, 1962), 118–120. Similarly, in 1968, the Democrats had proposed a vice-presidential debate as part of a series.

55. Louis Harris, "It's Mondale over Dole," The Harris Survey, October 7, 1976.

56. "1976 Debates," accessed April 17, 2015, http://www.debates.org/index.php?page=1976-debates#oct-15-1976.

57. John P. Robinson, "The Polls," in *The Great Debates: Carter v. Ford, 1976*, ed. Sidney Kraus (Bloomington: Indiana University Press, 1979), 263.

58. R. W. Apple, Jr., "Economy Is Stressed by Dole and Mondale during Sharp Debate," *New York Times*, October 16, 1976, 1; David M. Alpern, "Now, the Veep-stakes," *Newsweek*, October 25, 1976, 30.

59. Finlay Lewis, *Mondale: Portrait of an American Politician* (New York: Perennial Library, 1984), 193.

60. "Vice-Presidential Debate in Houston," October 15, 1976, American Presidency Project, University of California, Santa Barbara, http://www.presidency.ucsb.edu/ws/?pid=62249.

61. Mondale, discussion.

62. Mondale with Hage, *The Good Fight*, 169.

63. Quoted in Alan Schroeder, *Presidential Debates: Fifty Years of High-Risk TV*, 2nd ed. (New York: Columbia University Press, 2008), 254–255.

64. Quoted in Schram, *Running for President*, 372, 366.

65. "No. 2 Made His Points," *Time*, November 15, 1976, 35.

66. Bob Dole, interview with Jim Lehrer, November 10, 1999, http://www.pbs.org/newshour/spc/debatingourdestiny/interviews/dole.html.

67. Harris, "It's Mondale over Dole."

68. Jimmy Carter, speech to National Women's Agenda Conference, October 2, 1976; Jimmy Carter, statement in Los Angeles, October 7, 1976, in *The Presidential Campaign of 1976: Jimmy Carter*, 1: 876, 879, 881, 918, 921.

69. R. W. Apple, Jr., "Carter Emphasizing Mondale as an Asset," *New York Times*, October 29, 1976, 18.

70. Elizabeth Drew, *American Journal: The Events of 1976* (New York: Random House, 1977), 491, 513; Mondale with Hage, *The Good Fight*, 170.

71. Jimmy Carter, Speech in Columbus, Ohio, October 16, 1976; Jimmy Carter, Speech at Kennedy-Lawrence Dinner in Pittsburgh, PA, October 27, 1976, in *The Presidential Campaign of 1976: Jimmy Carter*, 1:1037, 1044, 1087, 1089.

72. The Third Carter-Ford Presidential Debate, October 22, 1976, Commission on Presidential Debates, http://www.debates.org/index.php?page=october-22-1976-debate-transcript.

73. "No. 2 Made His Points," 35.

74. Alpern, "Now, the Veepstakes," 30; Apple, "Carter Emphasizing Mondale as an Asset," 18.

75. Jon Nordheimer, "Reagan Hints at Active Role in Shaping G.O.P. Future," *New York Times*, November 5, 1976, 16.

76. Frank Lynn, "Carter's Victory in New York State Offsets Loss of Connecticut, Jersey," *New York Times*, November 3, 1976, 19.

77. Mondale, discussion.

78. Moe, discussion.

79. Jack Watson, Memorandum to Jimmy Carter, "Transition Overview," November 3, 1976, Transition Files, Mondale Papers, Minnesota Historical Society, St. Paul, MN, 6.

80. "Transcript of News Conference Held by President-Elect Carter in Plains, Georgia," *New York Times*, November 5, 1976, 14.

81. "Transcript of News Conference Held by President-Elect Carter in Georgia," *New York Times*, November 16, 1976, 32.

82. David E. Rosenbaum, "Carter Views Jobs as the Top Priority," *New York Times*, December 11, 1976, 12; James T. Wooten, "Carter Spends Much of the Day on Military Affairs," *New York Times*, January 14, 1977, 46.

83. Charles Mohr, "Carter Is Pessimistic after Seeing Economic Advisers," *New York Times*, December 2, 1976, 1.

84. James T. Wooten, "Jackson, Following 3-Hour Meeting with Carter in Plains, Ga., Says They Talked Only about Energy Policy," *New York Times*, December 16, 1976, 23.

85. Lance with Gilbert, *The Truth of the Matter*, 119–120.

86. Charles Mohr, "Carter Now Terms Economy Improved; Leaves Plan in Doubt," *New York Times*, December 28, 1976, 1; Charles Mohr, "Carter to Continue Talks on Economy," *New York Times*, December 29, 1976, 9.

87. "Carter Backs Move for Europe Parley," *New York Times*, January 6, 1977, 6.

88. Eileen Shanahan, "Carter and Party Leaders Reach Accord on Tax Cuts and Spending; All Taxpayers to Get '77 Rebate," *New York Times*, January 8, 1977, 1.

89. Hamilton Jordan, interview by Charles O. Jones et al., Jimmy Carter Oral History Project, University of Virginia, November 6, 1981, http://web1.millercenter.org/poh/transcripts/ohp_1981_1106_jordan.pdf, 19.

90. Moe, discussion; Charles Mohr, "Carter Meets with Woman and 4 Men on Major Administration Posts," *New York Times*, December 8, 1976, 20.

91. Moe and Berman interview, 34.

92. "Carter Names 4 Transition Aides on Foreign Policy," *New York Times*, November 12, 1976, 10.

93. Moe and Berman interview, 10.

94. "Mondale Says He Will Speak Out When He Disagrees with Carter," *New York Times*, December 31, 1976, 7.

95. Moe and Berman interview, 26–27.

96. "Carter Says He Believes Brezhnev Will Keep Word on No Early Test," *New York Times*, December 23, 1976, 13.

97. Quoted in James T. Wooten, "Califano, Sorensen, Schlesinger Named to Key Carter Posts," *New York Times*, December 24, 1976, 1, A11.

98. Charles Mohr, "Carter Bids Cabinet Fulfill His Pledges," *New York Times*, December 29, 1976, 1, 12.

99. "I Look Forward to the Job," interview with Jimmy Carter, *Time*, January 3, 1977, reprinted in Don Richardson, ed., *Conversations with Carter* (Boulder, CO: Lynne Rienner, 1998), 63, 64.

100. Leslie H. Gelb, "Mondale Is Expected to Have Real Power," *New York Times*, December 26, 1976, 1.

101. Mondale, discussion.

CHAPTER 4: THE MONDALE MODEL

1. Richard Moe, Memorandum to Mondale, "Re: The Conversation," June 21, 1976, National Politics—Carter/Mondale Campaign—vice presidential selection 1976, Box 7, Richard Moe papers, University of Maryland Library, College Park, MD.

2. Jules Witcover, *Marathon: The Pursuit of the Presidency, 1972–1976* (New York: Viking, 1977), 361; see also chapter 3 of this book.

3. Charles Mohr, "Carter Describes Muskie as Qualified for Ticket," *New York Times*, July 6, 1976, 1.

4. Walter F. Mondale, in discussion with the author, November 16, 2006.

5. Ibid.

6. Moe, "The Conversation," 1, 2.

7. Richard Moe and Michael Berman, interview by James Ceaser et al., Jimmy Carter Oral History Project, University of Virginia, January 15–16, 1982, http://web1.millercenter.org/poh/transcripts/ohp_1982_0115_moe.pdf, 4.

8. Mondale, discussion.

9. Jimmy Carter Press Conference, July 15, 1976, in *The Presidential Campaign of 1976: Jimmy Carter* (Washington, DC: Government Printing Office, 1978), 324, 325.

10. Robert B. Barnett, "The Vice Presidency: A Preliminary Report Prepared for Senator Walter F. Mondale, Democratic Vice Presidential Nominee," undated, Office of Staff Secretary, 1976 Transition File, Vice President's Role 12/76 folder, Container 3, Carter Presidential Library, Atlanta, GA.

11. Ibid., 21–23, 25.

12. Ibid., 26–27.

13. Ibid.

14. Ibid., 29–31. Mondale's markings do not appear on the Carter Library version but are present on a copy that is on file with the author.

15. Ibid., 31–32.

16. Ibid., 33–34.

17. Nelson Rockefeller to Walter Mondale, November 3, 1976, Transition Files, Mondale Papers, Minnesota Historical Society.

18. Nelson Rockefeller, "Observations on the Relationship between the President and Vice President," November 5, 1976, Transition Files, Vice-Presidential Papers, Mondale Papers, Minnesota Historical Society.

19. "No. 2 Made His Points," *Time*, November 15, 1976, 35.

20. Ted Van Dyk to Walter Mondale, Memorandum, the Vice President's Office, November 29, 1976, Transition Files, Mondale Papers, Minnesota Historical Society. See also Ted Van Dyk, *Heroes, Hacks and Fools: Memoirs from the Political Inside* (Seattle: University of Washington Press, 2007), 167–168.

21. Richard Moe to Walter Mondale, "Your Next Conversation with Governor Carter Regarding Your Assignments as Vice President," November 30, 1976, Mondale Papers, Minnesota Historical Society.

22. Moe and Berman interview, 5.

23. Richard Moe, "The Making of the Modern Vice Presidency: A Personal Reflection," *Minnesota History* (Fall 2006): 88, 92–93.

24. Walter F. Mondale with David Hage, *The Good Fight: A Life in Liberal Politics* (New York: Scribner 2010), 171.

25. Mondale to Carter, "The Role of the Vice President in the Carter Administration," December 9, 1976, 1-2, Mondale Papers, Minnesota Historical Society, http://www2.mnhs.org/library/findaids/00697/pdf/Mondale-CarterMemo.pdf.

26. Ibid., 2.
27. Ibid., 2–9.
28. Ibid., 11.
29. Ibid., 6.
30. Mondale, discussion.
31. Moe and Berman interview, 5.
32. Mondale, discussion.
33. Moe and Berman interview, 5.
34. Mondale, discussion.
35. Ibid.
36. Mondale with Hage, *The Good Fight*, 171–172.
37. Mondale's memo had briefly referred to vice-presidential office arrangements in a footnote, concluding that "I prefer to think of access in the terms expressed here and would prefer to maintain the space with adequate staff offices in the Executive Office Building." Mondale to Carter, "The Role of the Vice President," 5n.
38. Moe and Berman interview, 21–22.
39. Stephen Hess to Jimmy Carter, Memorandum, December 13, 1976, in Stephen Hess, *Organizing the Presidency*, rev. ed. (Washington, DC: Brookings Institution, 1988), 256–258.
40. Mondale with Hage, *The Good Fight*, 181; Paul C. Light, *Vice-Presidential Power: Advice and Influence in the White House* (Baltimore, MD: Johns Hopkins University Press, 1984), 76–77, 162–165.
41. Moe and Berman interview, 6; Michael Berman, "The Vice President in Retrospective," February 21, 1981, 10, 1984 Campaign Files, Speech Files, Mondale Papers, Minnesota Historical Society, St. Paul, MN.
42. Bertram Carp and David M. Rubenstein, interview by David Clinton et al., Jimmy Carter Oral History Project, University of Virginia, March 6, 1982, http://web1.millercenter.org/poh/transcripts/ohp_1982_0306_carp.pdf, 10–11.

CHAPTER 5: IMPLEMENTING THE MONDALE MODEL

1. "Vice President Mondale's Trip to Europe and Japan," statement by the White House press secretary, January 22, 1977, *Public Papers of the Presidents of the United States: Jimmy Carter, 1977* (Washington, DC: Government Printing Office, 1977), 1:8.
2. "Vice President Mondale's Trip to Europe and Japan: Remarks of the President and the Vice President on the Vice President's Departure," January 23, 1977, *Public Papers of the Presidents of the United States: Jimmy Carter 1977* (Washington, DC: Government Printing Office, 1977), 1:11, 12.
3. Steven M. Gillon, *The Democrats' Dilemma: Walter F. Mondale and the Liberal Legacy* (New York: Columbia University Press, 1992), 215–216.
4. "Vice President Mondale's Trip to Europe and Japan," February 1, 1977, *Public Papers of the Presidents of the United States: Jimmy Carter, 1977* (Washington, DC: Government Printing Office, 1977), 1:57.
5. "Vice President Mondale's Trip to Europe and Japan," news conference of the Vice President, February 2, 1977, 1:58.
6. This information is based on a review of Carter's Daily Diary, Jimmy Car-

ter Presidential Library, http://www.jimmycarterlibrary.gov/documents/diary, and Mondale's schedules, Special Assistant for Scheduling Files, Vice Presidential Papers, Mondale Papers, Minnesota Historical Society, St. Paul, MN.

7. "Summary Analysis of the Vice President's Time through July 31, 1977," Office of the Chief of Staff Files, Hamilton Jordan's Confidential Files, Vice President, Box 37, Jimmy Carter Presidential Library, Atlanta, GA; Michael Berman to A. Denis Clift et al., "Six Months Evaluation," July 25, 1977, Administrative Assistant to President of the Senate Files, Vice Presidential Papers, Mondale Papers, Minnesota Historical Society.

8. Michael Berman, "The Vice President in Retrospective," February 21, 1981, 12, 1984 Campaign Files, Speech Files, Mondale Papers, Minnesota Historical Society.

9. Berman to Clift et al., "Six Months Evaluation."

10. Swearing-in Ceremony for Members of the Cabinet, Remarks at the Ceremony, January 23, 1977, *Public Papers of the Presidents of the United States: Jimmy Carter, 1977* (Washington, DC: Government Printing Office, 1977), 1:12.

11. "Report to the American People, Remarks from the White House Library," February 2, 1977, *Public Papers of the Presidents of the United States: Jimmy Carter, 1977* (Washington, DC: Government Printing Office, 1977), 1:69, 76.

12. Radio-Television News Directors Association, "Interview with Members of the Board of Directors of the Association," April 29, 1977, *Public Papers of the Presidents of the United States: Jimmy Carter, 1977* (Washington, DC: Government Printing Office, 1977), 1:747, 748–749.

13. "The President's Trip to London, Newcastle, and Geneva: Remarks on Departure from the White House," May 5, 1977, *Public Papers of the Presidents of the United States: Jimmy Carter, 1977* (Washington, DC: Government Printing Office, 1977), 1:809.

14. Charles Mohr, "Mondale Seen Settling into Role of 'Senior Adviser' to President," *New York Times,* April 29, 1977, 1.

15. Hedrick Smith, "Lance Departure: A Mondale Gain as Carter Confidant," *New York Times,* September 29, 1977, 39; Jimmy Carter, *White House Diary* (New York: Farrar, Straus and Giroux, 2010), 109.

16. Jack Nelson, "Carter Calls Mondale Role in Administration 'Critical,'" *Los Angeles Times,* September 29, 1977, B1.

17. The President's News Conference of September 29, 1977, *Public Papers of the Presidents of the United States: Jimmy Carter, 1977* (Washington, DC: Government Printing Office, 1978), 2:1684, 1689.

18. Michael Berman to Richard Moe, "Evaluation of 1977 and Suggestions for 1978," February 18, 1978, Chief of Staff Richard Moe Files, Vice Presidential Papers, Mondale Papers, Minnesota Historical Society.

19. Walter Mondale to Jimmy Carter, "Review of My Vice Presidency," September 6, 1977, Office of the Chief of Staff Files, Hamilton Jordan's Confidential Files, Vice President, Box 37, Jimmy Carter Presidential Library.

20. Richard Moe to Walter Mondale, "First Year Review," February 24, 1978, 1, Review of Vice Presidency, Chief of Staff Richard Moe Files, Vice Presidential Papers, Mondale Papers, Minnesota Historical Society.

21. Berman to Moe, "Evaluation of 1977 and Suggestions for 1978."

22. Moe to Mondale, "First Year Review."

23. Paul C. Light, *Vice-Presidential Power: Advice and Influence in the White House* (Baltimore, MD: Johns Hopkins University Press, 1984), 177.

24. Curtis Wilkie, "No Regrets," *Mpls. St. Paul* magazine, March 1979, 53.

25. Bertram Carp (Carter deputy director of domestic policy), discussion with the author, December 4, 2006; Mohr, "Mondale Seen Settling into Role of 'Senior Adviser' to President."

26. Richard Moe and Michael Berman, interview by James Ceaser et al., Jimmy Carter Oral History Project, University of Virginia, January 15–16, 1982, http://web 1.millercenter.org/poh/transcripts/ohp_1982_0115_moe.pdf, 107.

27. Carter, *White House Diary*, 87.

28. Walter Mondale, in discussion with author, January 10, 2007; Walter F. Mondale with David Hage, *The Good Fight: A Life in Liberal Politics* (New York: Scribner, 2010), 187.

29. Richard Moe, in discussion with author, October 23, 2006.

30. Mondale, discussion; Moe and Berman interview, 32.

31. Moe to Mondale, "Talking Points Monday Lunch Agenda" (undated but apparently for April 11, 1977), Material from the Jimmy Carter Presidential Library, Vice Presidential Papers, Mondale Papers, Minnesota Historical Society; Daily Diary of President Jimmy Carter, April 11, 1977, 2.

32. Moe to Mondale, "Monday Lunch Talking Points," August 19, 1977, Material from the Jimmy Carter Presidential Library, Vice Presidential Papers, Mondale Papers, Minnesota Historical Society. Carter phoned Baker and Goldwater during his lunch with Mondale; Daily Diary of President Jimmy Carter, August 22, 1977, 2.

33. Carter, *White House Diary*, 87.

34. Mondale with Hage, *The Good Fight*, 253.

35. A. Denis Clift to Walter Mondale, "Lunch with President, Wednesday, February 27, 1980," 12:30 p.m., February 26, 1980, Material from the Jimmy Carter Presidential Library, Vice Presidential Papers, Mondale Papers, Minnesota Historical Society.

36. Moe to Mondale, "Talking Points for Luncheon with the President—Monday, March 10, 1980," March 7, 1980, Material from the Jimmy Carter Presidential Library, Vice Presidential Papers, Mondale Papers, Minnesota Historical Society.

37. Moe to Mondale, "Talking Points for Luncheon with the President—Tuesday, March 25, 1980," March 24, 1980, Material from the Jimmy Carter Presidential Library, Vice Presidential Papers, Mondale Papers, Minnesota Historical Society.

38. Moe to Mondale, "Talking Points for Luncheon with the President—Monday, April 7, 1980," April 7, 1980, Material from the Jimmy Carter Presidential Library, Vice Presidential Papers, Mondale Papers, Minnesota Historical Society.

39. Walter Mondale, in discussion with author, November 16, 2006.

40. Ibid.; Mondale with Hage, *The Good Fight*, 179.

41. 438 U.S. 265 (1978).

42. Mondale with Hage, *The Good Fight*, 177–180; Gillon, *The Democrats' Dilemma*, 193–194.

43. Griffin B. Bell with Ronald J. Ostrow, *Taking Care of the Law* (New York: William Morrow, 1982), 28–29.

44. Finlay Lewis, *Mondale: Portrait of an American Politician* (New York: Perennial Library, 1984), 207–208; Martin Schram, "When Mondale Speaks, Carter

Listens," *Newsday*, December 3, 1978, 1; Daily Diary of Jimmy Carter, September 28, 1978, 6.

45. Jimmy Carter, *Keeping Faith: Memoirs of a President* (Toronto, Ontario: Bantam Books, 1982), 492–493; Carter, *White House Diary*, 406.

46. Daily Diary of President Jimmy Carter, March 3, 1980, 3–4; Mondale Calendar, March 3, 1980, Mondale Papers, Minnesota Historical Society.

47. "Jimmy Carter: Israeli Settlements and the Status of Jerusalem Statement on the U.S. Vote in the Security Council of the United Nations," March 3, 1980, *Public Papers of the Presidents of the United States: Jimmy Carter, 1980* (Washington, DC: Government Printing Office, 1981), 1:427.

48. Mondale, discussion, November 16, 2006.

49. Ibid.; Moe and Berman interview, 104.

50. Zbigniew Brzezinski, *Power and Principle: Memoirs of the National Security Adviser, 1977–1981* (New York: Farrar, Straus and Giroux, 1983), 34, 35.

51. Mondale, discussion, November 16, 2006.

52. Moe and Berman interview, 71.

53. Hamilton Jordan, *Crisis: The Last Year of the Carter Presidency* (New York: G. P. Putnam's Sons, 1982), 43; Mondale with Hage, *The Good Fight*, 179, 182.

54. Quoted in Lewis, *Mondale*, 206.

55. Brzezinski, *Power and Principle*, 33; Jordan, *Crisis*, 43; Mondale with Hage, *The Good Fight*, 181.

56. Light, *Vice-Presidential Power*, 144–148.

57. Berman, "The Vice President in Retrospective," 8; Moe and Berman interview, 5.

58. Moe and Berman interview, 10.

59. Lynne Olson, "Mondale Aides Feel They Are Full Partners," *Baltimore Sun*, August 28, 1977, 1, 3.

60. Light, *Vice-Presidential Power*, 98–99.

61. Mondale, discussion, November 16, 2006; Carter, *White House Diary*, 89–90.

62. Lewis, *Mondale*, 201–203, 209–210; Mondale with Hage, *The Good Fight*, 183, 186–189, 195, 235–237.

63. Carter, *Keeping Faith*, 476.

64. Jordan, *Crisis*, 100.

65. Carter, *Keeping Faith*, 482–483.

66. Walter Mondale to Hamilton Jordan, "Reorganization," April 3, 1978, 1978FE, Vice President's Central Subject Files, Vice Presidential Papers, Mondale Papers, Minnesota Historical Society.

67. Walter Mondale to Jimmy Carter, "Observations on Your Presidency," April 19, 1978, Material from the Jimmy Carter Presidential Library, Vice Presidential Papers, Mondale Papers, Minnesota Historical Society.

68. Carter, *Keeping Faith*, 115–116; Gillon, *The Democrats' Dilemma*, 260–264; Mondale with Hage, *The Good Fight*, 235–238; Elizabeth Drew, "A Reporter at Large: Phase: In Search of a Definition," *New Yorker*, August 27, 1979, 45, 50, 59.

69. Mondale, discussion, January 10, 2007.

70. Terrence Smith, "Carter Cancels Cuts of $2 Billion Proposed in Social Welfare Budget," *New York Times*, December 23, 1978, 1.

71. Lewis, *Mondale*, 216–217.

72. Mondale with Hage, *The Good Fight*, 237–238; Lewis, *Mondale*, 214–215.

73. Bell with Ostrow, *Taking Care of the Law*, 23.

74. Moe and Berman interview, 26, 46.

75. Gillon, *The Democrats' Dilemma*, 191–193; Moe and Berman interview, 46–49.

76. Frank Moore, interview with Dr. Martin Elzy, Jimmy Carter Library & Museum Oral History, July 30–31, 2002, http://www.jimmycarterlibrary.gov/library /oralhistory/clohproject/moore.pdf, 24.

77. Ibid., 56.

78. Mondale with Hage, *The Good Fight*, 186–187.

79. Moe to Mondale, "Monday Lunch Talking Points—July 22, 1977," July 22, 1977; Moe to Mondale, "Talking Points for Luncheon with the President—Monday, November 14, 1977," November 11, 1977, 3, Material from the Jimmy Carter Presidential Library, Vice Presidential Papers, Mondale Papers, Minnesota Historical Society.

80. Walter Mondale to Jimmy Carter, "Warnke Nomination," February 10, 1977, Vice Presidential Papers, Mondale Papers, Minnesota Historical Society.

81. Mondale with Hage, *The Good Fight*, 187–188; Gillon, *The Democrats' Dilemma*, 192–193.

82. Walter Mondale to Jimmy Carter, "Voter Registration Bill," July 14, 1977, Vice Presidential Papers, Mondale Papers, Minnesota Historical Society.

83. Schram, "When Mondale Speaks, Carter Listens," 1, 10.

84. Gillon, *The Democrats' Dilemma*, 223–226.

85. Moe to Mondale, "Monday Lunch Talking Points [for lunch August 29, 1977]—August 26, 1977," Material from the Jimmy Carter Presidential Library, Vice Presidential Papers, Mondale Papers, Minnesota Historical Society.

86. Gillon, *The Democrats' Dilemma*, 224–225.

87. Thomas F. Eagleton (U.S. senator), in discussion with author.

88. Moe to Mondale, "Monday Lunch Talking Points [for lunch August 1, 1977]—August 1, 1977," Material from the Jimmy Carter Presidential Library, Vice Presidential Papers, Mondale Papers, Minnesota Historical Society.

89. William Smith to Mondale, "Breakfast with Robert Byrd and 1980 Democrats," June 4, 1980, Chronological Files, Assistant to the President of the Senate Files, Vice Presidential Papers, Mondale Papers, Minnesota Historical Society.

90. William Smith to Mondale, "Follow-Up on Breakfast with Senate Democrats Running for Re-Election," August 22, 1980, Chronological Files, Assistant to the President of the Senate Files, Vice Presidential Papers, Mondale Papers, Minnesota Historical Society.

91. Berman, "The Vice President in Retrospective," 14.

92. "Vice President Mondale's Trip to Europe," Statement on the Vice President's Trip, May 3, 1977, *Public Papers of the Presidents: Jimmy Carter, 1977* (Washington, DC: Government Printing Office, 1977), 1:785; Mondale with Hage, *The Good Fight*, 199–204; Gillon, *The Democrats' Dilemma*, 218–220.

93. Carter, *White House Diary*, 36.

94. Walter Mondale to Jimmy Carter, "My Meeting with Vorster," April 8, 1977, Material from the Jimmy Carter Presidential Library, Mondale Papers, Minnesota Historical Society. http://www2.mnhs.org/library/findaids/00697/pdfa/00697–001 05.pdf, Mondale Papers, Minnesota Historical Society.

95. Cyrus Vance, *Hard Choices: Critical Years in America's Foreign Policy* (New York: Simon & Schuster, 1983), 265, 278–279; Mondale with Hage, *The Good Fight*, 200–203.

96. Mondale, discussion, November 16, 2006; Walter F. Mondale, interview by David E. Reuther, Foreign Affairs Oral History Project, Association for Diplomatic Studies and Training, April 27, 2004, http://adst.org/wp-content/uploads/2012/09 /Mondale-Walter-F.toc_.pdf, 12–13.

97. Walter Mondale to Jimmy Carter, "Recommended Actions Resulting from My European Trip," May 24, 1977, Material from the Jimmy Carter Presidential Library, Vice Presidential Papers, Mondale Papers, Minnesota Historical Society.

98. "Vice President Mondale's Trip to Europe," 785–786.

99. Mondale to Carter, "Recommended Actions Resulting from My European Trip," 6–8.

100. Mondale to Bob Bergland, February 24, 1978; Mondale to W. Michael Blumenthal, February 24, 1978; Mondale to Juanita Kreps, February 24, 1978; Mondale to Robert Strauss, February 24, 1978; Mondale to John Gilligan, February, 24, 1978; Mondale to James Schlesinger, February 24, 1978, VP Subject Files, 1978 TR2-64, Vice Presidential Papers, Mondale Papers, Minnesota Historical Society.

101. Terence Smith, "Mondale Trip: Reassurance for Asian Allies," *New York Times*, May 8, 1978, A3.

102. Terence Smith, "Mondale Is a Nonexpert Who Matters," *New York Times*, May 14, 1978, E1; David Aaron, interview with Marie Allen, Jimmy Carter Library, December 15, 1980, http://www.jimmycarterlibrary.gov/library/exitInt/Aaron .pdf, 8.

103. Walter Mondale to Jimmy Carter, "Report on Visit to the Pacific," May 11, 1978; Department of State to Dr. Zbigniew Brzezinski, The White House, "Status of Actions from the Vice President's Asian Trip," Material from the Jimmy Carter Presidential Library, Vice Presidential Papers, Mondale Papers, Minnesota Historical Society.

104. Brzezinski, *Power and Principle*, 116–120, 238–246, 249–251, 276, 279–281.

105. William B. Quandt, *Camp David: Peacemaking and Politics* (Washington, DC: Brookings Institution, 1986), 218; Vance, *Hard Choices*, 199.

106. Jimmy Carter, interview by editors and news directors, June 30, 1978, *Public Papers of the Presidents of the United States: Jimmy Carter, 1978* (Washington, DC: Government Printing Office, 1979), 2:1225, 1227.

107. "Vice President Mondale's Visit to Israel," Statement by the President Announcing the Visit, June 14, 1978, *Public Papers of the Presidents of the United States: Jimmy Carter, 1978* (Washington, DC: Government Printing Office, 1979), 1:1090; "Insert for Vice President's Luncheon with President," Monday, June 19, 1978, Material from the Jimmy Carter Presidential Library, Vice Presidential Papers, Mondale Papers, Minnesota Historical Society.

108. "Vice President's Lunch with President, Monday, June 26, 1978," June 25, 1978, Material from the Jimmy Carter Presidential Library, Vice Presidential Papers, Mondale Papers, Minnesota Historical Society; Jimmy Carter interview, June 30, 1978, *Public Papers of the Presidents of the United States: Jimmy Carter, 1978* (Washington, DC: Government Printing Office, 1979), 2:1225, 1227; Quandt, *Camp David*, 196–197.

109. Mondale with Hage, *The Good Fight*, 207; Gillon, *The Democrats' Dilemma*, 235.
110. Terence Smith, "Mondale Says Begin Agrees to a Parley with Egypt and U.S.," *New York Times*, July 3, 1978, A1, 3.
111. Quandt, *Camp David*, 197; Gillon, *The Democrats' Dilemma*, 234–235; Aaron interview, 10.
112. Mondale with Hage, *The Good Fight*, 209; Quandt, *Camp David*, 197; Gillon, *The Democrats' Dilemma*, 235.
113. Mondale with Hage, *The Good Fight*, 209.
114. Daily Diary of President Jimmy Carter, September 5, 6, 7, 8, 10, and 14, 1978.
115. Carter, *Keeping Faith*, 390; Mondale with Hage, *The Good Fight*, 209.
116. Daily Diary of President Jimmy Carter, September 15, 16, and 17, 1978; Mondale with Hage, *The Good Fight*, 209–211; Carter, *White House Diary*, 236–245; A. Denis Clift, *With Presidents to the Summit* (Fairfax, VA: George Mason University Press, 1993), 164–167.
117. Quandt, *Camp David*, 229.
118. Carter, *White House Diary*, 244.
119. Mondale, discussion, November 16, 2006.
120. Mondale with Hage, *The Good Fight*, 211–213.
121. Ibid., 212–214.
122. Mondale with Hage, *The Good Fight*, 214–215; Marty Kaplan, "The Best Speech I Ever Wrote," *Huffington Post*, July 30, 2009, http://www.huffingtonpost.com/marty-kaplan/the-best-speech-i-ever-wr_b_247918.html.
123. Henry Kamm, "Vietnam, at Geneva Parley, Urges U.S. to Accept More of Its Refugees," *New York Times*, July 21, 1979, 1.
124. Press Release, Office of the Vice President's Press Secretary, July 21, 1979, Vice Presidential Papers, Mondale Papers, Minnesota Historical Society, http://www2.mnhs.org/library/findaids/00697/pdf/UNSpeech19790721.pdf.
125. Henry Kamm, "Hanoi Said to Agree to Attempt to Halt Exodus of Refugees," *New York Times*, July 22, 1979, A1, 10; Henry Kamm, "Vietnam Goes on Trial in Geneva over Its Refugees," *New York Times*, July 22, 1979, E5.
126. Mondale with Hage, *The Good Fight*, 215.
127. Vance, *Hard Choices*, 126.
128. Ibid., 115.
129. Brzezinski, *Power and Principle*, 34; Vance, *Hard Choices*, 116.
130. Mondale with Hage, *The Good Fight*, 217–218.
131. Clift, *With Presidents to the Summit*, 183; Mondale with Hage, *The Good Fight*, 217–220.
132. A. Denis Clift to Walter Mondale, "Lunch with President—China Visit," September 4, 1979, Material from the Jimmy Carter Presidential Library, Vice Presidential Papers, Mondale Papers, Minnesota Historical Society.
133. Vice President's Press Secretary, "Text of Address for Delivery by Vice President Mondale at Beijing University," August 27, 1979, Vice Presidential Papers, Mondale Papers, Minnesota Historical Society.
134. Edward Cowan, "Revised Pay Curb Demanded," *New York Times*, December 24, 1979, D1, D3; Edward Cowan, "Ambiguous New Guidelines," *New York Times*, October 5, 1979, D1, D4.

135. Steven Rattner, "Miller Captures Key Policy Role," *New York Times*, November 20, 1979, D1, D12; Steven R. Weisman, "Financial and Political Urgency Called Impetus to Change Aid," *New York Times*, November 2, 1979, D4; Reginald Stuart, "Chrysler Pay Pact to Save $203 Million," *New York Times*, October 26, 1979, A1, D6; Reginald Stuart, "U.S. Said to Abandon Ceiling on Chrysler Aid," *New York Times*, October 25, 1979, D6.

136. A. Denis Clift to Walter Mondale, "Talking Points on Trip to West Africa for Luncheon with President, Wednesday, June 11, 1980," June 11, 1980, Vice Presidential Papers, Mondale Papers, Minnesota Historical Society.

137. Richard Moe to Walter Mondale, "Wednesday Luncheon Points [for October 12, 1977, lunch]," October 11, 1977; Moe to Mondale, "Monday Luncheon Talking Points [for September 19, 1977, lunch]," September 16, 1977, Vice Presidential Papers, Mondale Papers, Minnesota Historical Society.

138. Speech Texts, Vice Presidential Papers, Mondale Papers, Minnesota Historical Society, https://www.hhh.umn.edu/centers/cspg/research/mondale_papers/pdf/Speeches_1977_81_001.pdf.

139. "Opposing Stands Taken by Mondale and Kennedy," *New York Times*, December 11, 1978, D11.

140. Seth S. King, "Reporter's Notebook: Some Fence-Mending Where Few Fences Remain," *New York Times*, January 15, 1978, 16.

141. Terence Smith, "Mondale Previews Carter Energy Plan before Governors," *New York Times*, July 9, 1979, A1; Terence Smith, "Mondale, at Dinner, Defends Carter," *New York Times*, July 8, 1979, 29.

142. "Mondale Seeks Pact Support," *New York Times*, July 17, 1979, A3; Bernard Weinraub, "Mondale Stumps for Arms Pact, but Finds Concern over Energy," *New York Times*, July 19, 1979, A3.

143. Gillon, *The Democrats' Dilemma*, 242–243.

144. Hedrick Smith, "Dismissals Taken as Pre-Campaign Move by Carter," *New York Times*, July 20, 1979, A1; Hedrick Smith, "Mondale Suggested as Possible Nominee," *New York Times*, September 6, 1979, A1.

145. "Vice President Dismisses Report on Potential for Heading Ticket," *New York Times*, September 7, 1979, D13.

146. Gillon, *The Democrats' Dilemma*, 276.

147. Carter, *White House Diary*, 392; Mondale with Hage, *The Good Fight*, 269–271.

148. Staff to Mondale, "Formation of White House Executive Committee," August 31, 1977, Vice Presidential Papers, Mondale Papers, Minnesota Historical Society.

149. Private Sector Initiative Program, "Remarks at a White House Meeting on the Employment Program," May 23, 1978, *Public Papers of the Presidents of the United States: Jimmy Carter, 1978* (Washington, DC: Government Printing Office, 1979), 1:959, 961.

150. Roger Wilkins, "U.S. Begins a Review on Jobs for Youths," *New York Times*, March 19, 1979, A1, D7; Philip Shabecoff, "Carter Asks Outlay of $2 Billion More for Youth Training," *New York Times*, January 11, 1980, A1, D14.

151. Richard Moe to Walter Mondale, "Monday Lunch Agenda" [undated but apparently for April 14, 1977, lunch], Mondale Papers, Minnesota Historical Soci-

ety; Richard Moe to Walter Mondale, "Talking Points for Lunch with President," April 15, 1977, Material from the Jimmy Carter Presidential Library, Vice Presidential Papers, Mondale Papers, Minnesota Historical Society.

152. Moe and Berman interview, 16–17.

153. Richard Moe to Walter Mondale, "Thoughts on the Next Year," January 29, 1979, 6–7, Review of Vice Presidency, Chief of Staff Files, Vice Presidential Papers, Mondale Papers, Minnesota Historical Society.

154. Al Eisele to Dick Moe et al., "Thoughts on 1979 Staff Memo," February 6, 1979, Vice Presidential Papers, Mondale Papers, Minnesota Historical Society.

155. Gillon, *The Democrats' Dilemma*, 251–266.

156. Mondale, discussion, November 16, 2006; Mondale with Hage, *The Good Fight*, 236.

157. Mondale with Hage, *The Good Fight*, 235–237.

158. Gillon, *The Democrats' Dilemma*, 266; "Staff Spats," *Time*, September 17, 1979.

159. "Carter Campaign Unit to Use Mondale Name," *New York Times*, March 16, 1979, A17.

160. The President's News Conference of October 9, 1979, *Public Papers of the Presidents: Jimmy Carter, 1979* (Washington, DC: Government Printing Office, 1980), 2:1836, 1844.

161. Friends of Carter-Mondale, "Remarks at a Fundraising Dinner," October 24, 1979, *Public Papers of the Presidents of the United States: Jimmy Carter, 1979* (Washington, DC: Government Printing Office, 1980), 2:2015.

162. Democratic Presidential Nomination, 1980, "Remarks Announcing Candidacy," December 4, 1979, *Public Papers of the Presidents of the United States: Jimmy Carter, 1979* (Washington, DC: Government Printing Office, 1980), 2:2192.

163. Jimmy Carter, interviewed by Dan Rather, *60 Minutes*, August 10, 1980, reprinted in Don Richardson, ed., *Conversations with Carter* (Boulder, CO: Lynne Riemer, 1998), 191–195.

164. "Remarks at a Meeting of the Democratic National Committee," August 15, 1980, *Public Papers of the Presidents of the United States: Jimmy Carter, 1980* (Washington, DC: Government Printing Office, 1982), 2:1541.

165. "The Presidential Transition and Domestic and Foreign Policy Issues Remarks in a Question-and-Answer Session with Reporters," November 12, 1980, *Public Papers of the Presidents of the United States: Jimmy Carter, 1980* (Washington, DC: Government Printing Office, 1982), 3:2702.

166. Carter, *Keeping Faith*, 39–40.

167. Quoted in Lewis, *Mondale*, 203–204.

168. Richard Moe to Jimmy Carter, November 21, 1980, 1, Richard Moe Memoranda, Chief of Staff Files, Vice Presidential Papers, Mondale Papers, Minnesota Historical Society.

CHAPTER 6: WHY IT WORKED

1. Some ideas in this chapter were suggested in Joel K. Goldstein, "The Rising Power of the Vice Presidency," *Presidential Studies Quarterly* 38, no. 3 (September 2008): 374, 377–378.

2. See generally Joel K. Goldstein, *The Modern American Vice Presidency: The Transformation of a Political Institution* (Princeton, NJ: Princeton University Press, 1982).

3. Paul C. Light, *Vice-Presidential Power: Advice and Influence in the White House* (Baltimore, MD: Johns Hopkins University Press, 1984), 70–73.

4. William G. Mayer, "A Brief History of Vice Presidential Selection," in *In Pursuit of the White House, 2000: How We Choose Our Presidential Nominees*, ed. William G. Mayer (Chatham, NJ: Chatham House, 1999), 355.

5. Walter F. Mondale, in discussion with author, November 16, 2006, and January 10, 2007; Richard Moe and Michael Berman, interview by James Ceaser et al., Jimmy Carter Oral History Project, University of Virginia, January 15–16, 1982, http://web1.millercenter.org/poh/transcripts/ohp_1982_0115_moe.pdf, 6.

6. Mondale, discussion, November 16, 2006.

7. Moe and Berman interview, 96. Bertram Carp and David Rubenstein, interview by David Clinton et al., Jimmy Carter Presidency Project, University of Virginia, March 6, 1982, http://web1.millercenter.org/poh/transcripts/ohp_1982_0306_carp.pdf, 11.

8. Moe and Berman interview, 7; Walter F. Mondale with David Hage, *The Good Fight: A Life in Liberal Politics* (New York: Scribner, 2010), 162–163.

9. Jimmy Carter, interview by Charles O. Jones et al., Jimmy Carter Presidency Project, University of Virginia, November 29, 1982, http://web1.millercenter.org/poh/transcripts/ohp_1982_1129_carter.pdf, 12.

10. Quoted in Finlay Lewis, *Mondale: Portrait of an American Politician* (New York: Perennial Library, 1984), 211.

11. Mondale, discussion, January 10, 2007.

12. Light, *Vice-Presidential Power*, 145–148.

13. Mondale, discussion, November 16, 2006.

14. Michael Berman, "The Vice President in Retrospective," February 21, 1981, 16, 1986 Campaign Files, Speech Files, Mondale Papers, Minnesota Historical Society, St. Paul, MN.

15. Lewis, *Mondale*, 208.

16. Carp and Rubenstein interview, 12.

17. Ibid.

18. Zbigniew Brzezinski, *Power and Principle: Memoirs of the National Security Adviser, 1977–1981* (New York: Farrar, Straus and Giroux, 1983), 35.

19. Carp and Rubenstein interview, 12; Carter interview, 9–10.

20. Carp and Rubenstein interview, 13.

21. Lewis, *Mondale*, 191.

22. Light, *Vice-Presidential Power*, 255–256.

23. "Carter's Plan—Turning Point for Nation? Exclusive Interview with Vice President Walter Mondale," *U.S. News and World Report*, July 23, 1979, 21.

24. Mondale, discussion, January 10, 2007.

25. Stuart Eizenstat, interview by Donald Kettl et al., Jimmy Carter Oral History Project, University of Virginia, January 29–30, 1982, http://web1.millercenter.org/poh/transcripts/ohp_1982_0129_eizenstat.pdf, 50–51; Moe and Berman interview, 9–10, 19–20.

26. Hamilton Jordan, *Crisis: The Last Year of the Carter Presidency* (New York: G. P. Putnam's Sons, 1982), 77.

27. Moe and Berman interview, 7.

28. Frank Moore, interview with Dr. Martin I. Elzy, July 30–31, 2002, Jimmy Carter Library & Museum Oral History, http://www.jimmycarterlibrary.gov/library /oralhistory/clohproject/moore.pdf, 56.

29. Vice President Staff to Walter Mondale, "Formation of White House Executive Committee," Vice Presidential Papers, Mondale Papers, Minnesota Historical Society.

30. Mondale, discussion, January 10, 2007.

31. Carp and Rubenstein interview, 12.

CHAPTER 7: THE WHITE HOUSE VICE PRESIDENCY

1. "Election Night Victory Speech in Los Angeles," November 4, 1980, American Presidency Project, University of California, Santa Barbara, http://www.presidency .ucsb.edu/ws/index.php?pid=76115&st=&st1=.

2. "Reagan-Bush News Conference and the Bush Acceptance Speech," *New York Times*, July 18, 1980, A12.

3. James A. Baker III with Steve Fiffer, *"Work Hard, Study . . . and Keep Out of Politics!" Adventures and Lessons from an Unexpected Public Life* (New York: G. P. Putnam's Sons, 2006), 139.

4. Pendleton James, interview with Stephen F. Knott, Karen M. Hult, and Charles E. Walcott, Ronald Reagan Oral History Project, University of Virginia, Charlottesville, November 3, 2003, http://web1.millercenter.org/poh/transcripts/ohp_2003 _1103_james.pdf, 31–32, 58.

5. George H. W. Bush to President-Elect Ronald Reagan, memorandum, November 10, 1980, in George H. W. Bush, *All the Best: My Life in Letters and Other Writings* (New York: Scribner, 2013), 305–306.

6. James interview, 59; Chase Untermeyer, "Looking Forward: George Bush as Vice President," in *At the President's Side: The Vice Presidency in the Twentieth Century*, ed. Timothy Walch (Columbia: University of Missouri Press, 1997), 160.

7. "Defining a Public Role for Vice Presidents: A Symposium," in *At the President's Side: The Vice Presidency in the Twentieth Century*, ed. Timothy Walch (Columbia: University of Missouri Press, 1997), 205–206.

8. Ibid., 205.

9. David E. Rosenbaum, "Bush Plans to Emulate Mondale Role," *New York Times*, January 21, 1981, B3.

10. George H. W. Bush to Ralph P. Davidson, April 18, 1981, in Bush, *All the Best*, 311–312.

11. Baker with Fiffer, *"Work Hard, Study . . . and Keep Out of Politics!,"* 153; Untermeyer, "Looking Forward," 159.

12. George Bush with Victor Gold, *Looking Forward* (New York: Doubleday, 1987), 231–232.

13. Ronald Reagan, *The Reagan Diaries*, ed. Douglas Brinkley (New York: Harper Perennial, 2007), 432, 442, 490, 590.

14. Ibid., 106, 187, 205, 206, 219, 262, 296, 337, 371, 450, 457, 476, 501, 577.

15. Bush with Gold, *Looking Forward*, 232.

16. George H. W. Bush, "Diary Entry, April 13, 1983," in Bush, *All the Best*, 327; Craig Fuller, interview with Stephen F. Knott and Jeff Chidester, George H. W. Bush Oral History Project, University of Virginia, Charlottesville, May 12, 2004, http://web1.millercenter.org/poh/transcripts/ohp_2004_0512_fuller.pdf, 48–49.

17. Doro Bush Koch, *My Father, My President: A Personal Account of the Life of George H. W. Bush* (New York: Warner Books, 2006), 171.

18. Reagan, *The Reagan Diaries*, 205, 206, 219, 296, 337, 450, 501.

19. Bush, *All the Best*, 321–323, 329–331, 334–336, 342–344, 350–351.

20. George P. Shultz, *Turmoil and Triumph: My Years as Secretary of State* (New York: Charles Scribner's Sons, 1993), 850n2; Caspar W. Weinberger, *Fighting for Peace: Seven Critical Years in the Pentagon* (New York: Warner Books, 1990), 368n; James A. Baker III, interview with Russell Riley, James Sterling Young, and Robert Strong, George H. W. Bush Oral History Project, University of Virginia, Charlottesville, March 17, 2011, http://web1.millercenter.org/poh/transcripts/ohp_2011_0317_baker.pdf, 6.

21. Larry Speakes with Robert Pack, *Speaking Out: The Reagan Presidency from inside the White House* (New York: Charles Scribner's Sons, 1988), 85–86; Ed Rollins with Tom DeFrank, *Bare Knuckles and Back Rooms: My Life in American Politics* (New York: Broadway Books, 1996), 170.

22. Craig Fuller (chief of staff to Vice President Bush), in discussion with author, March 13, 2007.

23. Steven R. Weisman, "Bush Prizes His Behind-the-Scenes Influence," *New York Times*, February 28, 1982, 1, 28.

24. Robert C. McFarlane with Zofia Smardz, *Special Trust* (New York: Cadell and Davies, 1994), 340, 295.

25. Shultz, *Turmoil and Triumph*, 312; Reagan, *The Reagan Diaries*, 169.

26. Michael Deaver, interview with James Sterling Young et al., Ronald Reagan Oral History Project, University of Virginia, Charlottesville, September 12, 2002, http://web1.millercenter.org/poh/transcripts/ohp_2002_0912_deaver.pdf, 15.

27. Kenneth Duberstein (chief of staff to President Reagan), in discussion with author, March 16, 2007.

28. Fuller, discussion.

29. McFarlane, *Special Trust*, 28.

30. Shultz, *Turmoil and Triumph*, 808.

31. Craig Fuller, "The Vice President's Meeting with Mr. Nir, 7/29/86," in *The Tower Commission Report* (New York: Bantam Books, 1987), 385–389.

32. *Final Report of the Independent Counsel for Iran/Contra Matters*, August 4, 1993, http://fas.org/irp/offdocs/walsh/chap_28.htm, vol. 1, ch. 28.

33. Donald Regan, *For the Record: From Wall Street to Washington* (San Diego: Harcourt Brace Jovanovich, 1988), 371–372.

34. Reagan, *The Reagan Diaries*, 477.

35. Herbert Parmet, *George Bush: The Life of a Lone Star Yankee* (New York: Scribner, 1997), 316–317.

36. Shultz, *Triumph and Turmoil*, 1066, 1075.

37. Frank Carlucci, interview with Stephen Knott, Philip Zelikow, and Don Oberdorfer, Ronald Reagan Oral History Project, University of Virginia, Charlottesville, August 28, 2001, http://web1.millercenter.org/poh/transcripts/ohp_2001_0828_carlucci.pdf, 45.

38. Parmet, *George Bush*, 330–332; Shultz, *Triumph and Turmoil*, 1066.

39. Untermeyer, "Looking Forward," 163.

40. Fuller interview, 55.

41. Duberstein, discussion.

42. Fred McClure, interview by James S. Young et al., George H. W. Bush Oral History Project, University of Virginia, Charlottesville, September 20, 2001, http://millercenter.org/president/bush/oralhistory/frederick-mcclure, 12, 64.

43. Joseph A. Pika, "The New Vice Presidency: Dick Cheney, Joe Biden, and the New Presidency," in *The Presidency and the Political System*, 9th ed., ed. Michael Nelson (Washington, DC: CQ Press, 2010), 519.

44. Fuller interview, 49.

45. Fuller, discussion.

46. Alexander Haig, *Caveat: Realism, Reagan and Foreign Policy* (London: Weidenfeld and Nicolson, 1984), 212–214.

47. Reagan, *The Reagan Diaries*, 83–84.

48. Jack Lechelt, *The Vice Presidency in Foreign Policy: From Mondale to Cheney* (El Paso, TX: LFB Scholarly Publishing, 2009), 115.

49. "Bush, Back from China, Says Rift on Taiwan Can Be Healed," *New York Times*, May 19, 1982, A2.

50. George H. W. Bush to Barry Goldwater, May 28, 1982, in Bush, *All the Best*, 318.

51. John F. Burns, "Peking Gives Bush a Bill of Particulars," *New York Times*, October 20, 1985, E2.

52. Lechelt, *The Vice Presidency in Foreign Policy*, 112–117.

53. John Vinocur, "Bush Hopes Arms Talks Continue Even if the Allies Deploy Missiles," *New York Times*, February 6, 1983, 14; John Vinocur, "In Europe, Bush Seeks to Keep Allies in Line," *New York Times*, February 6, 1983, E4.

54. John Vinocur, "Bush Says the U.S. Is 'Deadly Serious' on Weapons Curbs," *New York Times*, February 5, 1983, A1.

55. George H. W. Bush and Brent Scowcroft, *A World Transformed* (New York: Alfred A. Knopf, 1998), 4.

56. George H. W. Bush to Ronald Reagan, memorandum, February 15, 1984, in Bush, *All the Best*, 331–332.

57. Reagan, *The Reagan Diaries*, 219–223.

58. George H. W. Bush to Ronald Reagan, memorandum, March 13, 1985, in Bush, *All the Best*, 342–344.

59. Elaine Sciolino, "Poland and U.S. to Exchange Envoys," *New York Times*, September 23, 1987, A3; "Bush Nudges and Poses as His Cameras Roll," *New York Times*, October 4, 1987, E2; Gerald M. Boyd, "U.S. Agrees to Aid Poland with Debt as Bush Pays Visit," *New York Times*, September 28, 1987, A1, A9; Jackson Diehl, "Poland Seeks U.S. Capital in Wake of Improved Ties; Bush Arriving on Highest Visit since '79," *Washington Post*, September 25, 1987, A1.

60. "The President-Elect's News Conference Announcing the Nomination of Clayton Yeutter as Secretary of Agriculture," December 14, 1988, American Presidency Project, University of California, Santa Barbara, http://www.presidency.ucsb.edu/ws/?pid=85212.

61. Chase Untermeyer, interview by James Sterling Young et al., George H. W. Bush Oral History Project, University of Virginia, Charlottesville, July 27–28, 2000, http://web1.millercenter.org/poh/transcripts/ohp_2000_0727_untermeyer.pdf, 27–28.

62. Hedrick Smith, "Bush Says He Sought to Avoid Acting Like Surrogate President," New York Times, April 12, 1981, 1, 28.

63. George H. W. Bush to Ralph P. Davidson, April 18, 1981, in Bush, All the Best, 311–312.

64. Ronald Reagan, interview with foreign television journalists, May 19, 1988, Public Papers of the Presidents of the United States: Ronald Reagan, 1988 (Washington, DC: Government Printing Office, 1990), 1:610, 615.

65. C. Boyden Gray, "The Coordinating Role of the Vice Presidency," in The Presidency in Transition, ed. James P. Pfiffner and R. Gordon Hoxie et al. (New York: Center for the Study of the Presidency, 1989), 425–429.

66. "Remarks Announcing the Establishment of the Presidential Task Force on Regulatory Relief," January 22, 1981, Public Papers of the Presidents of the United States: Ronald Reagan, 1981 (Washington, DC: Government Printing Office, 1982), 30.

67. "Address before a Joint Session of the Congress on the State of the Union," January 25, 1984, Public Papers of the Presidents of the United States: Ronald Reagan, 1984 (Washington, DC: Government Printing Office, 1986), 1:87, 88.

68. Kenneth B. Noble, "U.S. Expects Deregulation to Save over $150 Billion," New York Times, August 12, 1983, A8.

69. "Memorandum on the Review of Federal Regulatory Programs," December 15, 1986, Public Papers of the Presidents of the United States: Ronald Reagan, 1986 (Washington, DC: Government Printing Office, 1989), 2:1630.

70. "Statement by the Press Secretary on Foreign and Domestic Crisis Management," March 24, 1981, Public Papers of the Presidents of the United States: Ronald Reagan, 1981 (Washington, DC: Government Printing Office, 1982), 285.

71. Baker with Fiffer, "Work Hard, Study . . . and Keep Out of Politics!," 140, 148.

72. Haig, Caveat, 144–150.

73. "Statement Announcing the Establishment of a Federal Anticrime Task Force for Southern Florida," January 28, 1982, Public Papers of the Presidents of the United States: Ronald Reagan, 1982 (Washington, DC: Government Printing Office, 1983), 1:86.

74. "Statement Announcing Actions against Terrorism," June 20, 1985, Public Papers of the Presidents of the United States: Ronald Reagan, 1985 (Washington, DC: Government Printing Office, 1988), 1:800.

75. "Press Briefing by Vice President George Bush," March 6, 1986, VP Task Force, George H. W. Bush Vice Presidential Records, George H. W. Bush Presidential Library, College Station, TX.

76. "Address to the Nation on the Iran Arms and Contra Aid Controversy,"

March 4, 1987, *Public Papers of the Presidents of the United States: Ronald Reagan, 1987* (Washington, DC: Government Printing Office, 1989), 1:208, 210.

77. "Office of Vice President Press Release," June 2, 1987, Terrorism, Press Office, George H. W. Bush Vice-Presidential Records, George H. W. Bush Presidential Library, College Station, TX.

78. Untermeyer interview, 25.

79. "Excerpts from Remarks by Vice President George Bush, American Enterprise Institute's Public Policy Luncheon," December 3, 1986, 5, Press Office, George H. W. Bush Vice-Presidential Records, George H. W. Bush Presidential Library, College Station, TX.

80. "Remarks by Vice President George Bush, International Conference on Terrorism, Washington, D.C.," January 20, 1987, Press Office, George H. W. Bush Vice-Presidential Records, George H. W. Bush Presidential Library, College Station, TX.

81. Chase Untermeyer to Vice President George H. W. Bush, December 21, 1981, Vice President's Trips 1981, Chase Untermeyer Memos, George H. W. Bush Vice-Presidential Records, George Bush Presidential Library, College Station, TX.

82. Adam Clymer, "Bush Urges G.O.P. to Cite the Economy in Courting Voters," *New York Times*, January 13, 1982, A16.

83. Reagan, *The Reagan Diaries*, 106

84. Andrew Rosenthal, "Conservatives Looking to Quayle as Their Top Ally in White House," *New York Times*, November 17, 1988, A1, B12.

85. Dan Quayle, in discussion with author, November 17, 2014; Dan Quayle, *Standing Firm: A Vice-Presidential Memoir* (New York: HarperCollins, 1994), 74–75, 100, 109, 113; Gerald M. Boyd, "Circle of Senior Aides Helps Bush Fill Top Posts," *New York Times*, December 8, 1988, B22.

86. Quayle, *Standing Firm*, 104.

87. Dan Quayle, "Standing Firm," in *At the President's Side: The Vice Presidency in the Twentieth Century*, ed. Timothy Walch (Columbia: University of Missouri Press, 1997), 172.

88. William P. Barr, interview by James S. Young et al., George H. W. Bush Oral History Project, University of Virginia, Charlottesville, April 5, 2001, http://web1 .millercenter.org/poh/transcripts/ohp_2001_0405_barr.pdf, 18.

89. Lechelt, *The Vice Presidency in Foreign Policy*, 162–164.

90. Koch, *My Father, My President*, 267.

91. Quayle, *Standing Firm*, 103.

92. Dan Quayle, interview with James S. Young et al., George H. W. Bush Oral History Project, University of Virginia, Charlottesville, March 12, 2002, http:// web1.millercenter.org/poh/transcripts/ohp_2002_0312_quayle.pdf, 47–48.

93. Bush and Scowcroft, *A World Transformed*, 24.

94. Quayle interview, 56–58.

95. Bernard Weinraub, "Cheney Remarks on Soviet Future Ruffle the White House's Feathers," *New York Times*, May 2, 1989, A1, A18.

96. Quayle, discussion.

97. Quayle interview, 57.

98. John H. Sununu, interview by James S. Young et al., George H. W. Bush Oral History Project, University of Virginia, Charlottesville, June 8–9, 2000, http://web1.millercenter.org/poh/transcripts/ohp_2000_0608_sununu.pdf, 21.

99. Untermeyer interview, 92.

100. Quayle, *Standing Firm*, 217.

101. Ibid., 104–105.

102. Ibid., 192–199.

103. Quayle interview, 41–42.

104. Peter Goldman, Thomas M. DeFrank, Mark Miller, Andrew Murr, and Tom Mathews, *Quest for the Presidency, 1992* (College Station: Texas A & M University Press, 1994), 346–347, 358–359, 365–366.

105. Quayle interview, 30; David Broder and Bob Woodward, *Dan Quayle: The Man Who Would Be President* (New York: Simon & Schuster, 1992), 99-100.

106. George H. W. Bush to David Broder, October 3, 1991, in Bush, *All the Best*, 537.

107. Broder and Woodward, *Dan Quayle*, 99–102.

108. Correspondence between Kennedy and Quayle, June 12, 1991, and July 10, 1991, Hubbard Files, Education [1], Dan Quayle Vice-Presidential Records, George H. W. Bush Presidential Library, College Station, TX.

109. Quayle, *Standing Firm*, 111–113, 187, 196–199, 267–272; Broder and Woodward, *Dan Quayle*, 100–101.

110. Robert Pear, "Senate Favors Sending Arms to Aid Cambodia's Sihanouk," *New York Times*, July 22, 1989, 2.

111. Andrew Rosenthal, "Panel Defeats Attempt to Increase Support for War Planes in Budget," *New York Times*, July 25, 1989, A18.

112. Quayle interview, 67–68.

113. Ibid., 31.

114. Sununu interview, 60.

115. Quayle interview, 60.

116. "Remarks by Vice President Quayle to Military Officers, San Salvador," Friday, February 3, 1989; "Vice President Quayle's Remarks to ESAF, San Salvador," Friday, February 3, 1989, Office of the Chief of Staff, Quayle Speech Files, Dan Quayle Vice-Presidential Records, George H. W. Bush Presidential Library, College Station, TX; Lindsey Gruson, "Quayle's Warning to Salvador Aimed at Congress," *New York Times*, February 5, 1989, 16; Robert Pear, "Quayle Pressed Salvador for Inquiry on Massacre," *New York Times*, February 15, 1989, A6.

117. Quayle, *Standing Firm*, 153–154.

118. Ibid., 136–139.

119. McClure interview, 63.

120. Bush and Scowcroft, *A World Transformed*, 160–161; Colin L. Powell with Joseph E. Persico, *My American Journey* (New York: Random House, 1995), 440–444.

121. Dan Quayle, "Address to the Commonwealth Club of California," May 19, 1992, in Quayle, Standing Firm, 381–387.

122. Dan Quayle, "Address to Faculty and Students at Seton Hall University," November 29, 1990, in Quayle, *Standing Firm*, 369–374.

123. Quayle, "Standing Firm," 174.

124. Quayle interview, 62–63.

125. Quayle, *Standing Firm*, 278.

126. "Press Briefing by Marlin Fitzwater on the Vice President's Role with the Council on Competitiveness," April 4, 1989, Articles [1], Domestic Policy Office and the Council on Competitiveness, Dan Quayle Vice-Presidential Records, George H. W. Bush Presidential Library, College Station, TX.

127. "Minutes, Council on Competitiveness, First Meeting—6/20/89, First Meeting [1, 2], Domestic Policy Office and the Council on Competitiveness," Dan Quayle Vice-Presidential Records, George H. W. Bush Presidential Library, College Station, TX.

128. "Agenda, Council on Competitiveness Meeting of March 20, 1990," March 19, 1990; "Minutes of Council on Competitiveness Meeting with the Vice President on Biotechnology," March 20, 1990, Domestic Policy Office and the Council on Competitiveness, Dan Quayle Vice-Presidential Records, George H. W. Bush Presidential Library, College Station, TX.

129. "Statement by Press Secretary Fitzwater on the Review of Regulatory Issues by the Council on Competitiveness," June 15, 1990, American Presidency Project, University of California, Santa Barbara, http://www.presidency.ucsb.edu/ws/index.php?pid=18606&st=&st1=.

130. Ede Holiday, assistant to the president and secretary of the Cabinet, to Cabinet and agency heads, "Federal Regulations," June 13, 1990, Ede Holiday Memo, Domestic Policy Office and the Council on Competitiveness, Dan Quayle Vice-Presidential Records, George H. W. Bush Presidential Library, College Station, TX.

131. Dan Quayle to heads of executive departments and agencies, "Regulatory Review Process," March 22, 1991, Takings, Allan B. Hubbard, Domestic Policy Office and the Council on Competitiveness, Dan Quayle Vice-Presidential Records, George H. W. Bush Presidential Library, College Station, TX.

132. Broder and Woodward, *Dan Quayle*, 126–127.

133. Quayle interview, 49–50.

134. Barbara Rosewicz, "Panel Led by Quayle Helped Kill Plan to Require Certain Waste Recycling," *Wall Street Journal*, December 20, 1990.

135. "Statement of FDA Drug Review by Vice President Quayle," press release, OVP, Prepared Remarks by the Vice President, Food and Drug Law Institute Conference, December 11, 1991, FDA [1], Allan B. Hubbard Files, Domestic Policy Office and the Council on Competitiveness, Dan Quayle Vice-Presidential Records, George H. W. Bush Presidential Library, College Station, TX.

136. Dan Quayle, "Address to the Annual Meeting of the American Bar Association," August 13, 1991, in Quayle, *Standing Firm*, 375–380.

137. Executive Order 12778, October 23, 1991, 56 Federal Register (No. 207), October 25, 1991; "Remarks on Signing the Executive Order on Civil Justice Reform," October 23, 1991, *Public Papers of the Presidents of the United States: George Bush, 1991* (Washington, DC: Government Printing Office, 1992), 2:1315.

138. Philip J. Hilts, "At Heart of Debate on Quayle Council: Who Controls Federal Regulations?" *New York Times*, December 16, 1991, B11.

139. Broder and Woodward, *Dan Quayle*, 125.

140. John Glenn et al. to Hon. Dennis DeConcini, July 27, 1992, Domestic Policy Office and the Council on Competitiveness, Dan Quayle Vice-Presidential Records, George H. W. Bush Presidential Library, College Station, TX.

141. 138 Cong. Rec. 23123, 24468, 24470 (comments of Rep. Skaggs, Sen. Pryor, Sen. Sasser).

142. 137 Cong. Rec. 14501, 14502 (1991); 138 Cong. Rec. 24471, 24472, 24474, 24475 (1992).

143. "Remarks on Signing the Executive Order Establishing the National Space Council," April 20, 1989, *Public Papers of the Presidents of the United States: George Bush, 1989* (Washington, DC: Government Printing Office, 1990), 1:456.

144. "Remarks on the 20th Anniversary of the Apollo 11 Moon Landing," July 20, 1989, *Public Papers of the Presidents of the United States: George Bush, 1989* (Washington, DC: Government Printing Office, 1990), 2:990, 992.

145. Broder and Woodward, *Dan Quayle*, 147–152; Quayle, *Standing Firm*, 185–187.

146. Quayle, *Standing Firm*, 183–184.

147. Warren Christopher, interview by James S. Young et al., William J. Clinton Presidential History Project, University of Virginia, Charlottesville, April 15–16, 2002, http://web1.millercenter.org/poh/transcripts/ohp_2002_0415_christopher talbott.pdf, 11; Roy M. Neel, interview by Russell L. Riley and Stephen Knott, William J. Clinton Presidential History Project, University of Virginia, Charlottesville, November 14, 2002, http://web1.millercenter.org/poh/transcripts/ohp_2002_1114 _neel.pdf, 54.

148. Warren Christopher, *Chances of a Lifetime* (New York: Scribner, 2001), 160; Al Kamen and Ann Devroy, "In Cabinet Choices, Gore Has Seat at the Head Table; Influence of Vice President-Elect Far Exceeds That of Predecessors," *Washington Post*, December 13, 1992, A23.

149. Thomas "Mack" McLarty III, interview by James Sterling Young et al., William J. Clinton Presidential History Project, University of Virginia, Charlottesville, July 12, 2002, http://web1.millercenter.org/poh/transcripts/ohp_2002_0712_mc larty.pd, 13.

150. Todd S. Purdum, "Two Top Nominees Were Most Likely Candidates All Along," *New York Times*, December 6, 1996, B7.

151. Taylor Branch, *The Clinton Tapes: Wrestling History with the President* (New York: Simon & Schuster, 2009), 401, 403, 408; Press briefing by Mike McCurry, December 4, 1996, American Presidency Project, University of California, Santa Barbara, http://www.presidency.ucsb.edu/ws/?pid=48847.

152. George Stephanopoulos, *All Too Human: A Political Education* (Boston: Little, Brown, 1999), 402; Bob Woodward, *The Choice* (New York: Simon & Schuster, 1996), 13–15, 48.

153. Bill Clinton, *My Life* (New York: Alfred A. Knopf, 2004), 516.

154. Ron Klain (Gore and Biden vice-presidential chief of staff), in discussion with author, September 30, 2010.

155. Stephanopoulos, *All Too Human*, 205.

156. Bill Clinton, "How to Evaluate a President," in *The Clinton Presidency and*

the Constitutional System, ed. Rosanna Perotti (College Station: Texas A & M University Press, 2012), 28.

157. Stephanopoulos, *All Too Human*, 402.

158. Quoted in Joel K. Goldstein, "Reshaping the Model: Clinton, Gore and the New Vice Presidency," in *The Clinton Presidency and the Constitutional System*, ed. Rosanna Perotti (College Station: Texas A & M University Press, 2012), 96.

159. Quoted in Elaine Sciolino and Todd S. Purdum, "Al Gore, One Vice President Who Is Eluding the Shadows," *New York Times*, February 19, 1995, 1, 32.

160. Madeleine Albright with Bill Woodward, *Madam Secretary* (New York: Miramax, 2003), 180.

161. Madeleine K. Albright, interview with Russell Riley, Stephen F. Knott, and Robert Strong, William J. Clinton Presidential History Project, University of Virginia, Charlottesville, August 30, 2006, http://web1.millercenter.org/poh /transcripts/ohp_2006_0830_albright.pdf, 28.

162. Mike McCurry, in discussion with author, October 18, 2005.

163. Elizabeth Drew, *On the Edge: The Clinton Presidency* (New York: Simon & Schuster, 1994), 69–70, 216, 228.

164. Bob Woodward, *The Agenda: Inside the Clinton White House* (New York: Simon & Schuster, 1994), 281.

165. Joseph Lockhart, interview with Russell L. Riley et al., William J. Clinton Presidential History Project, University of Virginia, Charlottesville, September 19–20, 2005, http://web1.millercenter.org/poh/transcripts/ohp_2005_0919_lockhart .pdf, 52.

166. Clinton, *My Life*, 516; Drew, *On the Edge*, 68, 228.

167. Leon Panetta with Jim Newton, *Worthy Fights: A Memoir of Leadership in War and Peace* (New York: Penguin Press, 2014), 104–105, 109.

168. Albright with Woodward, *Madam Secretary*, 180; Bill Turque, *Inventing Al Gore: A Biography* (Boston: Houghton Mifflin, 2000), 301.

169. Drew, *On the Edge*, 215–216.

170. Stephanopoulos, *All Too Human*, 401–403; Elizabeth Drew, *Showdown: The Struggle between the Gingrich Congress and the Clinton White House* (New York: Simon & Schuster, 1996), 217–221, 356–357.

171. Turque, *Inventing Al Gore*, 306–308.

172. Richard Riley, interview by Russell L. Riley, Patrick McGuinn, and Joseph A. Pika, William J. Clinton Presidential History Project, University of Virginia, August 30–31, 2004, http://web1.millercenter.org/poh/transcripts/ohp_2004_0830_riley .pdf, 52–53; Turque, *Inventing Al Gore*, 294–296.

173. Ashton Carter and William Perry, *Preventive Defense: A New Security Strategy for America* (Washington, DC: Brookings Institution Press, 1999), 32, 76.

174. Goldstein, "Reshaping the Model," 90; Turque, *Inventing Al Gore*, 274; Drew, *On the Edge*, 205–209, 358, 360–363, 368, 371, 373.

175. Albright interview, 28.

176. Samuel R. Berger, interview by Russell L. Riley, Timothy Naftali, and Robert Strong, William J. Clinton Presidential History Project, University of Virginia, March 24–25, 2005, http://web1.millercenter.org/poh/transcripts/ohp_2005_0324 _berger.pdf, 36.

177. David J. Rothkopf, *Running the World: The Inside Story of the National Security Council and the Architects of American Power* (New York: Public Affairs, 2005), 311–312.

178. "Remarks Announcing the National Performance Review," March 3, 1993, *Public Papers of the Presidents of the United States: William J. Clinton, 1993* (Washington, DC: Government Printing Office, 1994), 1:233–235.

179. "Teleconference Remarks to the National Association of County Officials," July 19, 1993, *Public Papers of the Presidents of the United States: William J. Clinton, 1993* (Washington, DC: Government Printing Office, 1994), 1:1104, 1106.

180. "Remarks Announcing the Report of the National Performance Review and an Exchange with Reporters," September 7, 1993, *Public Papers of the Presidents of the United States: William J. Clinton, 1993* (Washington, DC: Government Printing Office, 1994), 2:1444.

181. Margaret Carlson, "Where's Al Gore?," *Time*, September 13, 1993.

182. "Hunt on for Government Waste," *New York Times*, March 4, 1993, A23.

183. "Remarks Announcing the National Performance Review," 234.

184. Gwen Ifill, "Gore Jumps into the Job of Cutting U.S. Waste," *New York Times*, August 20, 1993, A20; George S. Church, "Gorezilla Zaps the System," *Time*, September 13, 1993.

185. Al Gore, "From Red Tape to Results: Creating a Government That Works Better and Costs Less," *Report of the National Performance Review*, September 7, 1993, iii.

186. "Remarks to General Services Administration Employees in Franconia, Virginia," September 8, 1993; "Remarks to the Community in Cleveland," September 9, 1993; "Remarks to the North Valley Job Training Partnership in Sunnyvale, California," September 10, 1993; "Remarks and a Question-and-Answer Session on the National Performance Review in Houston, Texas," September 11, 1993, *Public Papers of the Presidents of the United States: William J. Clinton, 1993* (Washington, DC: Government Printing Office, 1994), 2:1452–1454, 1458–1460, 1466–1468, 1469–1474.

187. Seth Faison, "Shove Over Jay, Chevy, Dave. Here's Al," *New York Times*, September 9, 1993, D20; Elizabeth Kolbert, "My Next Guest's Policy Opens Today!" *New York Times*, September 10, 1993, A18; Drew, *On the Edge*, 295–296.

188. "Address before a Joint Session of the Congress on the State of the Union," January 24, 1995, *Public Papers of the Presidents of the United States: William J. Clinton, 1995* (Washington, DC: Government Printing Office, 1996), 1:75, 78.

189. "Remarks on Regulatory Reform," February 21, 1995, *Public Papers of the Presidents of the United States: William J. Clinton, 1995* (Washington, DC: Government Printing Office, 1996), 1:235, 236.

190. "Remarks on the National Performance Review," September 7, 1995, *Public Papers of the Presidents of the United States: William J. Clinton, 1995* (Washington, DC: Government Printing Office, 1996), 2:1317, 1319.

191. Al Gore, *The Best Kept Secrets in Government* (Washington, DC: Government Printing Office, 1996), 1.

192. Clinton, *My Life*, 648. See Goldstein, "Reshaping the Model," 92.

193. Albright interview, 33.

194. Strobe Talbott, *The Russia Hand: A Memoir of Presidential Diplomacy* (New York: Random House, 2002), 59–61, 64–65.

195. Carter and Perry, *Preventive Defense*, 25–26, 49.

196. "Background Briefing by Senior Administration Official," June 21, 1994, American Presidency Project, University of California, Santa Barbara, http://www.presidency.ucsb.edu/ws/?pid=59731.

197. "Press Briefing by National Security Adviser Tony Lake," October 22, 1995, American Presidency Project, University of California, Santa Barbara, http://www.presidency.ucsb.edu/ws/?pid=59506.

198. Warren Christopher, *In the Stream of History: Shaping Foreign Policy for a New Era* (Stanford, CA: Stanford University Press, 1998), 96n6.

199. Talbott, *The Russia Hand*, 9, 85–86.

200. Ibid., 265.

201. "Remarks Prior to Discussions with Prime Minister Viktor Chernomyrdin of Russia and an Exchange with Reporters," January 30, 1996, *Public Papers of the Presidents of the United States: William J. Clinton, 1996* (Washington, DC: Government Printing Office, 1997), 1:114.

202. "Remarks at a Democratic National Committee Dinner on Amelia Island," November 1, 1997, *Public Papers of the Presidents of the United States: William J. Clinton, 1997* (Washington, DC: Government Printing Office, 1999), 2:1480, 1481.

203. "The President's News Conference with President Mandela of South Africa," October 5, 1994, *Public Papers of the Presidents of the United States: William J. Clinton, 1994* (Washington, DC: Government Printing Office, 1995), 2:1699.

204. "The President's News Conference with President Nelson Mandela of South Africa in Cape Town," March 27, 1998, *Public Papers of the Presidents of the United States: William J. Clinton, 1998* (Washington, DC: Government Printing Office, 1999), 1:448, 449, 450.

205. "Remarks Announcing the Creation of the White House Office on Environmental Policy," February 8, 1993, *Public Papers of the Presidents of the United States: William J. Clinton, 1993* (Washington, DC: Government Printing Office, 1994), 1:62, 63.

206. Philip Elmer-Dewitt, "Not Just Hot Air," *Time*, May 3, 1993.

207. "Remarks Announcing the Creation of the White House Office on Environmental Policy." See Goldstein, "Reshaping the Model," 93, 102–103nn52–56.

208. William Stevens, "Gore, in Japan, Signals That U.S. May Make Some Compromises on Climate," *New York Times*, December 8, 1997, A8.

209. "Gore Exhorts Latins on Saving Environment," *New York Times*, December 8, 1996, 22.

210. Edmund L. Andrews, "New Effort to Settle Data Issues," *New York Times*, January 9, 1995, D1; Edmund L. Andrews, "G.O.P. to Delay a Vote on Communications Bill," *New York Times*, April 5, 1995, D1, D5.

211. "Remarks on Signing the Telecommunications Act of 1996," February 8, 1996, *Public Papers of the Presidents of the United States: William J. Clinton, 1996* (Washington, DC: Government Printing Office, 1997), 1:185, 186–188.

212. "Statement on the New Television Rating System," July 10, 1997, *Public Papers of the Presidents of the United States: William J. Clinton, 1997* (Washington, DC: Government Printing Office, 1999), 2:938.

213. Bill Clinton, interview with Joe Klein of the *New Yorker* in New York City, July 5, 2000, American Presidency Project, University of California, Santa Barbara, http://www.presidency.ucsb.edu/ws/?pid=1257; Riley interview, 53–54.

214. "Memorandum Establishing the President's Community Enterprise Board," September 9, 1993, *Public Papers of the Presidents of the United States: William J. Clinton, 1993* (Washington, DC: Government Printing Office, 1994), 2:1460–1462.

215. "Remarks on Affirmative Action at the National Archives and Records Administration," July 19, 1995, *Public Papers of the Presidents of the United States: William J. Clinton, 1995* (Washington, DC: Government Printing Office, 1996), 2:1106, 1113.

216. David E. Rosenbaum, "Perot Debate Seen as Way to Try to Save Trade Pact," *New York Times*, November 6, 1993, 1.

217. Drew, *On the Edge*, 344–345.

218. "Media Roundtable Interview on NAFTA," November 12, 1993; "Remarks in a Telephone Conversation with Representative Ed Pastor on NAFTA," November 12, 1993, *Public Papers of the Presidents of the United States: William J. Clinton, 1993* (Washington, DC: Government Printing Office, 1994), 2:1959, 1960, 1966, 1967–1968.

219. "The President's News Conference," November 10, 1993, *Public Papers of the Presidents of the United States: William J. Clinton, 1993* (Washington, DC: Government Printing Office, 1994), 2:1942, 1943.

220. B. Drummond Ayres, Jr., "Long a Defender of the Boss, Gore Praises Clinton Courage," *New York Times*, August 18, 1998, A13.

221. Michael Janofsky, "Gore Makes a Strong Statement of His Support for the President," *New York Times*, September 13, 1998, 37.

222. Talbott, *The Russia Hand*, 143–146, 151, 444 n11.

223. Ibid., 310–314.

224. "Remarks on the Military Technical Agreement on Kosovo and an Exchange with Reporters," June 10, 1999, *Public Papers of the Presidents of the United States: William J. Clinton, 1999* (Washington, DC: Government Printing Office, 2000), 1:909, 910.

225. "Gore in Ukraine, Expresses Support for Economic Change," *New York Times*, August 3, 1994, A10.

226. "Memorandum on the Ounce of Prevention Council," September 13, 1994, *Public Papers of the Presidents of the United States: William J. Clinton, 1994* (Washington, DC: Government Printing Office, 1995), 2:1542–1543.

227. "Remarks Announcing the Donation of Cellular Telephones to Neighborhood Watch Groups," July 17, 1996, *Public Papers of the Presidents of the United States: William J. Clinton, 1996* (Washington, DC: Government Printing Office, 1998), 2:1138, 1139.

228. Turque, *Inventing Al Gore*, 298.

229. John F. Harris, "Gore Stings GOP on Campaign Stump," *Washington Post*, November 2, 1998, A1; Michael Janofsky, "Gore Takes Role of No. 1 Campaigner," *New York Times*, October 21, 1998, A20.

230. John Hilley and Lawrence Stein, interview by Russell L. Riley et al., William J. Clinton Presidential History Project, University of Virginia, May 20–21, 2004, http://web1.millercenter.org/poh/transcripts/ohp_2004_0520_stein.pdf, 75–76.

CHAPTER 8: THE TRIUMPH OF THE VICE PRESIDENCY

1. James Mann, *Rise of the Vulcans: The History of Bush's War Cabinet* (New York: Viking, 2004), 261.

2. Stephen F. Hayes, *Cheney: The Untold Story of America's Most Powerful and Controversial Vice President* (New York: HarperCollins, 2007), 299.

3. Barton Gellman, *Angler: The Cheney Vice Presidency* (New York: Penguin Press, 2008), 35–50; Peter Baker, *Days of Fire: Bush and Cheney in the White House* (New York: Doubleday, 2013), 75, 80–81.

4. Gellman, *Angler*, 38–40.

5. Joel K. Goldstein, "Cheney, Vice Presidential Power and the War on Terror," *Presidential Studies Quarterly* 40, no. 1 (2010): 102, 109–110.

6. Baker, *Days of Fire*, 361, 362, 373–374; Dick Cheney with Liz Cheney, *In My Time: A Personal and Political Memoir* (New York: Threshold Editions, 2011), 425.

7. Joshua Bolten (Bush OMB director and chief of staff), in discussion with author, November 23, 2010.

8. Baker, *Days of Fire*, 6.

9. Gellman, *Angler*, 50–51.

10. Bolten, discussion.

11. Richard Cheney, interview by Sam Donaldson and Cokie Roberts, *This Week*, ABC, January 27, 2002, http://georgewbush-whitehouse.archives.gov/vicepresident/news-speeches/speeches/vp20020127.html; Richard Cheney, interview by Campbell Brown, NBC News, January 28, 2002, http://georgewbush-whitehouse.archives.gov/vicepresident/news-speeches/speeches/vp20020128.html.

12. Hayes, *Cheney*, 2.

13. Gellman, *Angler*, 244; Cheney with Cheney, *In My Time*, 314.

14. Richard Cheney and Lynne Cheney, interview by Don Imus, *Imus in the Morning*, MSNBC, January 20, 2005, http://www.nbcnews.com/id/6847999/ns/msnbc-imus_on_msnbc/t/vice-president-cheney-inauguration-day/#.VUUHJ_lVhBc.

15. George W. Bush, *Decision Points* (New York: Broadway Paperbacks, 2010), 86.

16. Baker, *Days of Fire*, 109–110.

17. Ibid., 88.

18. Bush, *Decision Points*, 450–451.

19. Baker, *Days of Fire*, 6.

20. Hayes, *Cheney*, 307.

21. Robert M. Gates, *Duty: A Memoir of a Secretary of War* (New York: Alfred A. Knopf, 2014), 282.

22. Donald Rumsfeld, *Known and Unknown: A Memoir* (New York: Sentinel, 2011), 320.

23. Bush, *Decision Points*, 189, 190, 237–239; Baker, *Days of Fire*, 184–185; Hayes, *Cheney*, 352.

24. Donald Rumsfeld, interview by Bob Woodward, July 6 and 7, 2006, http://www.defense.gov/Transcripts/Transcript.aspx?TranscriptID=3744.

25. Gellman, *Angler*, 56.

26. Baker, *Days of Fire*, 92.

27. Hayes, *Cheney*, 3, 335–345.

28. Baker, *Days of Fire*, 216.

29. Cheney with Cheney, *In My Time*, 399; Hayes, *Cheney*, 391–392; Bob Woodward, *Plan of Attack* (New York: Simon & Schuster, 2004), 391–392.

30. Baker, *Days of Fire*, 95–97; Gellman, *Angler*, 82–91.

31. Condoleezza Rice, *No Higher Honor: A Memoir of My Years in Washington* (New York: Crown, 2011), 42; Baker, *Days of Fire*, 96–97.

32. Cheney with Cheney, *In My Time*, 317–318; Baker, *Days of Fire*, 101–102.

33. Baker, *Days of Fire*, 103.

34. Ibid., 233–234, 273–274; Gellman, *Angler*, 255–275.

35. For a fuller account, see Goldstein, "Cheney, Vice Presidential Power and the War on Terror," 118–120.

36. Baker, *Days of Fire*, 173–175.

37. Gellman, *Angler*, 162–168.

38. Baker, *Days of Fire*, 313–314.

39. Ibid., 193–195.

40. Cheney with Cheney, *In My Time*, 369–371, 383, 386, 399.

41. Paul Kengor, "Cheney and Vice Presidential Power," in *Considering the Bush Presidency*, ed. Gary L. Gregg II and Mark J. Rozell (New York: Oxford University Press, 2004), 160, 166.

42. John P. Burke, *Becoming President: The Bush Transition, 2000–2003* (Boulder, CO: Lynne Rienner, 2004), 97.

43. Jack Goldsmith, *The Terror Presidency: Law and Judgment inside the Bush Administration* (New York: W. W. Norton, 2007), 76, 128.

44. Glenn Kessler and Peter Slevin, "Cheney Is Fulcrum of Foreign Policy," *Washington Post*, October 13, 2002, http://www.washingtonpost.com/wp-dyn /content/article/2002/10/13/AR2006051500660.html.

45. Baker, *Days of Fire*, 87; Glenn Kessler, "With Vice President, He Shaped Iraq Policy," *Washington Post*, October 29, 2005, http://www.washingtonpost.com /wp-dyn/content/article/2005/10/28/AR2005102802139.html.

46. Lawrence Wilkerson, interview, *Frontline*, PBS, December 13, 2005, http:// www.pbs.org/wgbh/pages/frontline/darkside/interviews/wilkerson.html.

47. Goldstein, "Cheney, Vice Presidential Power and the War on Terror," 110; Goldsmith, *Terror Presidency*, 77–78.

48. Rice, *No Higher Honor*, 17.

49. Gellman, *Angler*, 54.

50. Baker, *Days of Fire*, 99–100.

51. Ibid., 7, 247–248.

52. Bush, *Decision Points*, 244; Baker, *Days of Fire*, 209–210, 215–216.

53. Baker, *Days of Fire*, 278–279.

54. Rice, *No Higher Honor*, 231.

55. Richard Cheney, interview by Michael Nelson, The Election of 2004—Collective Memory Project, SMU Center for Presidential History, November 18, 2014, http://cphcmp.smu.edu/2004election/richard-cheney, 12.

56. Hayes, *Cheney*, 350–351.

57. Baker, *Days of Fire*, 373–374.

58. Ibid., 416–419, 426.

59. Cheney with Cheney, *In My Time*, 442–443.

60. Ibid., 409–410.

61. Baker, *Days of Fire*, 7, 10, 385–386, 418–419, 454, 461, 529, 535–537, 556–557, 566–568.

62. Cheney with Cheney, *In My Time*, 471–472; Gates, *Duty*, 172–176.

63. Gates, *Duty*, 176.

64. Baker, *Days of Fire*, 476–478.

65. Gellman, *Angler*, 355.

66. Cheney with Cheney, *In My Time*, 429–430.

67. Rice, *No Higher Honor*, 502.

68. Baker, *Days of Fire*, 578–580.

69. Gates, *Duty*, 98, 584.

70. Baker, *Days of Fire*, 401.

71. Ibid., 401–402, 427.

72. Gates, *Duty*, 98.

73. "Remarks Prior to a Meeting with the National Energy Policy Development Group and an Exchange with Reporters," January 29, 2001, *Public Papers of the Presidents of the United States: George W. Bush, 2001* (Washington, DC: Government Printing Office, 2003), 1:30.

74. Hayes, *Cheney*, 314.

75. "Remarks Announcing the Energy Plan in St. Paul, Minnesota," May 17, 2001, *Public Papers of the Presidents of the United States: George W. Bush, 2001* (Washington, DC: Government Printing Office, 2003), 1:534–538.

76. "Statement on Domestic Preparedness against Weapons of Mass Destruction," May 8, 2001, *Public Papers of the Presidents of the United States: George W. Bush, 2001* (Washington, DC: Government Printing Office, 2003), 1:498–499.

77. Cheney with Cheney, *In My Time*, 318–319.

78. Hayes, *Cheney*, 308–309.

79. Gellman, *Angler*, 57.

80. Hayes, *Cheney*, 309; Gellman, *Angler*, 62–67.

81. Gellman, *Angler*, 77–80.

82. Cheney with Cheney, *In My Time*, 308–313; Hayes, *Cheney*, 399–405.

83. Hayes, *Cheney*, 403–405; Cheney with Cheney, *In My Time*, 310–313.

84. Baker, *Days of Fire*, 220–221; Hayes, *Cheney*, 383–384.

85. Cheney with Cheney, *In My Time*, 350–351; Gellman, *Angler,* 153; Goldstein, "Cheney, Vice Presidential Power and the War on Terror," 116–117.

86. Cheney with Cheney, *In My Time*, 359; Baker, *Days of Fire*, 428.

87. Cheney with Cheney, *In My Time*, 507–509; Baker, *Days of Fire*, 611, 621–622.

88. Hayes, *Cheney*, 332–333; Gellman, *Angler*, 114–118.

89. "Remarks in Sarasota, Florida on the Terrorist Attack on New York City's World Trade Center," September 11, 2001, *Public Papers of the Presidents of the United States: George W. Bush, 2001* (Washington, DC: Government Printing Office, 2003), 2:1098.

90. Hayes, *Cheney*, 335–343.

91. "Remarks at Barksdale Air Force Base, Louisiana, on the Terrorist Attacks,"

September 11, 2001, *Public Papers of the Presidents of the United States: George W. Bush, 2001* (Washington, DC: Government Printing Office, 2003), 2:1098, 1099.

92. See Goldstein, "Cheney, Vice Presidential Power and the War on Terror," 106–107; Gellman, *Angler*, 118–125.

93. Hayes, *Cheney*, 3, 345.

94. Cheney with Cheney, *In My Time*, 348–349; Gellman, *Angler*, 139–143, 162–173.

95. Goldstein, "Cheney, Vice Presidential Power and the War on Terror," 115–121.

96. Cheney with Cheney, *In My Time*, 348–349; Baker, *Days of Fire*, 163–165; Gellman, *Angler*, 140–143.

97. Gellman, *Angler*, 289–296.

98. Bush, *Decision Points*, 172–174; Goldstein, "Cheney, Vice Presidential Power and the War on Terror," 116–118.

99. Gellman, *Angler*, 311–313, 316–320.

100. Bush, *Decision Points*, 173, 174.

101. Goldstein, "Cheney, Vice Presidential Power and the War on Terror," 120–121; Hayes, *Cheney*, 479–482.

102. Cheney with Cheney, *In My Time*, 369.

103. Hayes, *Cheney*, 368–369.

104. Rice, *No Higher Honor*, 170–171; Jack Lechelt, *The Vice Presidency in Foreign Policy: From Mondale to Cheney* (El Paso, TX: LFB Scholarly Publishing, 2009), 262–267.

105. Baker, *Days of Fire*, 221–222.

106. Cheney with Cheney, *In My Time*, 387–388; Rumsfeld, *Known and Unknown*, 491.

107. Rice, *No Higher Honor*, 180.

108. George Tenet with Bill Harlow, *At the Storm Center: My Years at the CIA* (New York: HarperCollins, 2007), 315–317.

109. Rumsfeld, *Known and Unknown*, 449–450; Cheney with Cheney, *In My Time*, 396–397.

110. Baker, *Days of Fire*, 514, 519–520, 528–529.

111. Joseph A. Pika, "The Vice Presidency: Dick Cheney, Joe Biden, and the New Vice Presidency," in *The Presidency and the Political System*, 9th ed., ed. Michael Nelson (Washington, DC: CQ Press, 2010), 509, 519.

112. Cheney with Cheney, *In My Time*, 371–380; Hayes, *Cheney*, 369–373.

113. Richard Cheney, interview by Bob Schieffer, *Face the Nation*, CBS, March 24, 2002, http://georgewbush-whitehouse.archives.gov/vicepresident/news-speeches/speeches/vp20020324-1.html; Richard Cheney, interview by Wolf Blitzer, *Late Edition*, CNN, March 24, 2002, http://georgewbush-whitehouse.archives.gov/vicepresident/news-speeches/speeches/vp20020324-2.html; Richard Cheney, interview by Tim Russert, *Meet the Press*, NBC, March 24, 2002, http://georgewbush-whitehouse.archives.gov/vicepresident/news-speeches/speeches/vp20020324.html.

114. Cheney with Cheney, *In My Time*, 426–427; Hayes, *Cheney*, 466–471.

115. Cheney with Cheney, *In My Time*, 497–500.

116. David E. Sanger, "Cheney Warns Pakistan to Act against Terrorists," *New York Times*, February 27, 2007, A9.

117. "Press Briefing by a Senior Administration Official on the Vice President's Trip to the Middle East," March 15, 2008. http://georgewbush-whitehouse.archives .gov/news/releases/2008/03/text/20080315–2.html.

118. "Remarks by Vice President Cheney and Prime Minister Maliki of Iraq in Photo Opportunity," March 17, 2008, http://georgewbush-whitehouse.archives.gov /news/releases/2008/03/20080317.html; "Remarks by Vice President Cheney, General David Petraeus and Ambassador Ryan Crocker in Press Availability," March 17, 2008, http://georgewbush-whitehouse.archives.gov/news/releases/2008/03/200803 17-6.html.

119. Hayes, *Cheney*, 430–433.

120. Cheney with Cheney, *In My Time*, 426–428; Jad Mouawad, "Such Good Friends Again," *New York Times,* August 6, 2005, C1.

121. Hayes, *Cheney*, 305–307.

122. "Remarks by the Vice President at the Annual Meeting of the Associated Press in Toronto," April 30, 2001, http://georgewbush-whitehouse.archives.gov/vice president/news-speeches/speeches/vp20010430.html; "Remarks by the Vice President at the U.S. Chamber of Commerce Rally Supporting the Bush Administration's Energy Plan," May 25, 2001, http://georgewbush-whitehouse.archives.gov/vice president/news-speeches/speeches/vp20010525.html; "Remarks by the Vice President to U.S. Energy Association Efficiency Forum," June 13, 2001, http://georgew bush-whitehouse.archives.gov/vicepresident/news-speeches/speeches/vp20010613 .html; "Remarks by the Vice President at Town Hall Energy Meeting, Community College of Allegheny County in Pittsburgh, Pennsylvania," July 16, 2001, http:// georgewbush-whitehouse.archives.gov/vicepresident/news-speeches/speeches/vp 20010716–2.html.

123. Richard Cheney, interview by Tim Russert, *Meet the Press*, NBC, September 16, 2001, http://georgewbush-whitehouse.archives.gov/vicepresident/news -speeches/speeches/vp20010916.html.

124. James P. Pfiffner, *Power Play: The Bush Presidency and the Constitution* (Washington, DC: Brookings Institution, 2008), 163.

125. Bob Kemper and Jeff Zeleny, "Cheney, Once an Asset, Sees Star Dim," *Chicago Tribune*, August 1, 2002, http://articles.chicagotribune.com/2002-08-01/news /0208010279_1_jennifer-millerwise-vice-president-dick-cheney-white-house.

126. Mike Allen, "Cheney's Turn in the Public Eye; Vice President Emerges from Isolation as He Drums Up Small Town Support," *Washington Post*, August 29, 2004, A32.

127. Baker, *Days of Fire*, 387–389; Cheney with Cheney, *In My Time*, 322–324.

128. Bush, *Decision Points*, 97–99; Baker, *Days of Fire*, 396–401.

129. Hayes, *Cheney*, 407–408; Gellman, *Angler*, 259–261.

130. Richard Cheney, interview by Mark Knoller, CBS Radio, January 7, 2009, http://georgewbush-whitehouse.archives.gov/news/releases/2009/01/20090107-7 .html.

131. Edward Kaufman (U.S. senator and former Biden chief of staff), in discussion with author, May 6, 2014.

132. Ibid.

133. Some sense of the time Obama and Biden spent together is apparent from the parts of their schedules made publicly available each day at the White House web site, https://www.whitehouse.gov/schedule/complete. It provides a limited listing of certain standard events and thus understates their interactions.

134. Gates, *Duty*, 283, 288.

135. Ron Klain (former Biden chief of staff), in discussion with author, September 30, 2010.

136. Bob Woodward, *Obama's Wars* (New York: Simon & Schuster, 2010), 160.

137. Klain, discussion.

138. Quoted in Mark Leibovich, "Speaking Freely, Biden Finds Influential Role," *New York Times*, March 29, 2009, 1, 16.

139. Bruce Reed (former Biden chief of staff), in discussion with author, August 29, 2014.

140. Woodward, *Obama's Wars*, 64–73.

141. Ibid., 80–81.

142. Gates, *Duty*, 342.

143. Hillary Rodham Clinton, *Hard Choices* (New York: Simon & Schuster, 2014), 130, 138; Leon Panetta with Jim Newton, *Worthy Fights: A Memoir of Leadership in War and Peace* (New York: Penguin Press, 2014), 254.

144. Woodward, *Obama's Wars*, 160.

145. Jules Witcover, *Joe Biden: A Life of Trial and Redemption* (New York: HarperCollins, 2010), 456–468.

146. Gates, *Duty*, 563–565; Mark Landler, "Obama's Growing Trust in Biden Is Reflected in His Call on Troops," *New York Times*, June 25, 2011, A4, 9.

147. Reed, discussion.

148. Barack Obama, interview by Chris Matthews, *Hardball*, MSNBC, December 5, 2013, http://www.nbcnews.com/id/53755285/ns/msnbc-hardball_with_chris _matthews/t/hardball-chris-matthews-thursday-december-th/#.VTvGFSFViko.

149. Reed, discussion; Klain, discussion.

150. Office of the Vice President press release, "Vice President Biden in Iraq to Meet with Iraqi Leaders and Visit U.S. Troops," September 15, 2009, https:// www.whitehouse.gov/the-press-office/vice-president-biden-iraq-meet-with-iraqi -leaders-and-visit-us-troops-91509.

151. Klain, discussion.

152. Kaufman, discussion.

153. "Address before a Joint Session of Congress, February 24, 2009," *Public Papers of the Presidents of the United States: Barack Obama, 2009* (Washington, DC: Government Printing Office, 2010), 1:145, 147.

154. White House press release, "Vice President Biden to Oversee the Administration's Implementation of the Recovery Act's Provisions," February 23, 2009, https://www.whitehouse.gov/the-press-office/vice-president-biden-oversee -administrations-implementation-recovery-acts-provision.

155. Michael Grunwald, *The New New Deal: The Hidden Story of Change in the Obama Era* (New York: Simon & Schuster, 2012), 256–259; Office of the Vice President press release, "Remarks by the Vice President on the 200 Days of the

American Recovery and Reinvestment Act," September 3, 2009, https://www.white house.gov/the-press-office/remarks-vice-president-200-days-american-recovery -amd-reinvestment-act.

156. Michael Grunwald, "It's Official: The Stimulus Isn't a Waste of Money," *Time*, October 1, 2010.

157. "Memoranda for the Heads of Executive Departments and Agencies re: White House Task Force on Middle Class Working Families," January 30, 2009, https://www.whitehouse.gov/the_press_office/memorandum_for_the_heads_of _executive_departments_and_agencies.

158. Grunwald, *The New New Deal*, 208–209.

159. Klain, discussion.

160. Peter Baker, "Gamble by Obama Pays Off with Final Approval of Arms Control Pact," *New York Times*, December 23, 2010, A6, A8.

161. Bob Woodward, *The Price of Politics* (New York: Simon & Schuster, 2012), 69–78; Carl Hulse and Jackie Calmes, "Biden and G.O.P. Leader Helped Hammer Out Bipartisan Tax Accord," *New York Times*, December 7, 2010, A24.

162. Woodward, *The Price of Politics*, 340–341, 347–352.

163. David A. Farenthold, Paul Kane, and Lori Montgomery, "How McConnell and Biden Pulled Congress away from the Fiscal Cliff," *Washington Post*, January 2, 2013, http://www.washingtonpost.com/politics/how-mcconnell-and-biden-pulled -congress-away-from-the-fiscal-cliff/2013/01/02/992fe6de-5501-11e2-8e84-e933f 677fe68_story.html.

164. Office of the Vice President press release, "Remarks by Vice President Biden at 45th Munich Conference on Security Policy," February 7, 2009, https:// www.whitehouse.gov/the-press-office/remarks-vice-president-biden-45th-munich -conference-security-policy.

165. Office of the Vice President press release, "Remarks by Vice President Joe Biden on Asia-Pacific Policy," July 19, 2013, https://www.whitehouse.gov/the-press -office/2013/07/19/remarks-vice-president-joe-biden-asia-pacific-policy.

166. Office of the Vice President press release, "Background Conference Call with Senior Administration Official on Vice President Biden and Dr. Jill Biden's Trip to India and Singapore," July 19, 2013, https://www.whitehouse.gov/the-press-office /2013/07/19/background-conference-call-senior-administration-officials-vice -president.

167. Office of the Vice President press release, "Readout of Vice President Biden's Meeting with Prime Minister Shinzo Abe of Japan," July 26, 2013, https://www .whitehouse.gov/the-press-office/2013/07/26/readout-vice-president-bidens -meeting-prime-minister-shinzo-abe-japan.

168. White House press release, "Remarks by the President in a Press Confer- ence," December 19, 2012, https://www.whitehouse.gov/the-press-office/2012/12 /19/remarks-president-press-conference.

169. Philip Rucker and Peter Wallsten, "Biden's Gun Task Force Met with All Sides but Kept Its Eye on the Target," *Washington Post*, January 19, 2013, http:// www.washingtonpost.com/politics/bidens-gun-task-force-met-with-all-sides-but -kept-its-eye-on-the-target/2013/01/19/520d77a6-60c5-11e2-b05a-605528f6b712 _story.html.

170. White House press release, "Remarks by the President and Vice President on Gun Violence," January 16, 2013, https://www.whitehouse.gov/the-press -office/2013/01/16/remarks-president-and-vice-president-gun-violence.

CHAPTER 9: DETERMINANTS OF VICE-PRESIDENTIAL ROLE
1. See James A. Baker III with Steve Fiffer, "*Work Hard, Study . . . and Keep Out of Politics!*" *Adventures and Lessons from an Unexpected Public Life* (New York: G. P. Putnam, 2006), 157; Herbert Parmet, *George Bush: The Life of a Lone Star Yankee* (New York: Scribner, 1997), 245–246.
2. Chase Untermeyer, "Looking Forward: George Bush as Vice President" in *At the President's Side: The Vice Presidency in the Twentieth Century,* ed. Timothy Walch (Columbia: University of Missouri Press, 1997), 159–160.
3. Hedrick Smith, "Again, President Is Drawing Conservatives' Ire," *New York Times,* January 13, 1982, A14.
4. Ronald Reagan, interview with foreign television journalists, May 19, 1988, *Public Papers of the Presidents of the United States: Ronald Reagan, 1988* (Washington, DC: Government Printing Office, 1990), 1:610, 615.
5. George Bush with Victor Gold, *Looking Forward* (New York: Doubleday, 1987), 222.
6. Steven R. Weisman, "Bush Prizes His Behind-the-Scenes Influence," *New York Times,* February 28, 1982, 1, 26
7. Baker with Fiffer, "*Work Hard, Study . . . and Keep Out of Politics!,*" 138–139, 157; Doro Bush Koch, *My Father, My President: A Personal Account of the Life of George H. W. Bush* (New York: Warner Books, 2006), 175.
8. Craig Fuller (chief of staff to Vice President Bush), in discussion with author, March 13, 2007.
9. Prior to becoming vice president, Bush had served two terms in the House of Representatives, as ambassador to the United Nations, as chair of the Republican National Committee, as chief of the U.S. Liaison Office to China, and as director of the CIA. He had been runner-up to Nelson Rockefeller for vice president in 1974 and to Reagan in the 1976 primaries.
10. Bush with Gold, *Looking Forward,* 227–230.
11. George H. W. Bush to President-Elect and Mrs. Ronald Reagan, November 10, 1980, in George H. W. Bush, *All the Best: My Life in Letters and Other Writings* (New York: Scribner, 2013), 303.
12. Bush with Gold, *Looking Forward,* 231; Baker, with Fiffer, "*Work Hard, Study . . . and Keep Out of Politics!,*" 157.
13. Bush to Reagan, July 5, 1983, in Bush, *All the Best,* 329, 330.
14. Bush to Reagan, March 13, 1985, in Bush, *All the Best,* 342, 343.
15. Ronald Reagan, *The Reagan Diaries,* ed. Douglas Brinkley (New York: Harper Perennial, 2007), 317.
16. James F. Kuhn, interview by Stephen F. Knott and Darby Morrisroe, Ronald Reagan Oral History Project, University of Virginia, Charlottesville, March 7, 2003, http://web1.millercenter.org/poh/transcripts/ohp_2003_0307_kuhn.pdf, 54.
17. "The President's News Conference," February 11, 1986, *Public Papers of the*

Presidents of the United States: Ronald Reagan, 1986 (Washington, DC: Government Printing Office, 1988), 1:200, 206–207.

18. Paul Laxalt, interview by Stephen F. Knott, James Sterling Young, and Erwin Hargrove, Ronald Reagan Oral History Project, University of Virginia, Charlottesville, October 9, 2001, http://web1.millercenter.org/poh/transcripts/ohp_2001_10 09_laxalt.pdf, 52; James Baker III, interview by Russell L. Riley, James Sterling Young, and Robert Strong, George H. W. Bush Oral History Project, University of Virginia, Charlottesville, March 17, 2011, http://web1.millercenter.org/poh /transcripts/ohp_2011_0317_baker.pdf, 20; Edwin Meese, "The Reagan Presidency," in *Leadership in the Reagan Presidency*, ed. Kenneth W. Thompson (Lanham, MD: University Press of America, 1993), 2:223, 232–233.

19. Michael Deaver, interview by James Sterling Young et al., Ronald Reagan Oral History Project, University of Virginia, Charlottesville, September 12, 2002, http://web1.millercenter.org/poh/transcripts/ohp_2002_0912_deaver.pdf, 60.

20. Reagan, *The Reagan Diaries*, 281.

21. John H. Sununu, interview by James S. Young et al., George H. W. Bush Oral History Project, University of Virginia, Charlottesville, June 8–9, 2000, http://web1 .millercenter.org/poh/transcripts/ohp_2000_0608_sununu.pdf, 11.

22. Reagan, *The Reagan Diaries*, 492.

23. Parmet, *George Bush*, 273.

24. Deaver interview, 15.

25. Untermeyer, "Looking Forward," 160–162; Deaver interview, 60.

26. E. Pendleton James, interview by Stephen F. Knott, Karen M. Hult, and Charles E. Walcott, Ronald Reagan Oral History Project, University of Virginia, Charlottesville, November 3, 2003, http://web1.millercenter.org/poh/transcripts /ohp_2003_1103_james.pdf, 46.

27. Francis X. Clines, "The Vice President: No Comment on the Future," *New York Times*, February 25, 1983, A18; Untermeyer, "Looking Forward," 165.

28. Reagan, *The Reagan Diaries*, 498, 528–529.

29. George P. Shultz, *Turmoil and Triumph: My Years as Secretary of State* (New York: Charles Scribner's Sons, 1993), 11, 275, 317, 423.

30. Max Kampelman, *Entering New Worlds: The Memoirs of a Private Man in Public Life* (New York: HarperCollins, 1991), 264.

31. Colin L. Powell with Joseph E. Persico, *My American Journey* (New York: Random House, 1995), 332.

32. Frank Carlucci, interview with Stephen Knott, Philip Zelikow, and Don Oberdorfer, Ronald Reagan Oral History Project, University of Virginia, Charlottesville, August 28, 2001, http://web1.millercenter.org/poh/transcripts/ohp_2001_0828_car lucci.pdf, 24.

33. Jack Lechelt, *The Vice Presidency in Foreign Policy: From Mondale to Cheney* (El Paso, TX: LFB Scholarly Publishing, 2009), 103–104.

34. George J. Church, "The Education of a Standby," *Time*, January 30, 1989, 27; Robin Toner, "Optimistic Mood Greets 41st President," *New York Times*, January 20, 1989, A1, A12.

35. David Broder and Bob Woodward, *Dan Quayle: The Man Who Would Be President* (New York: Simon & Schuster, 1992), 89–90.

36. Dan Quayle, interview with James S. Young et al., George H. W. Bush Oral

History Project, University of Virginia, Charlottesville, March 12, 2002, http://web1
.millercenter.org/poh/transcripts/ohp_2002_0312_quayle.pdf, 53.

37. "The President-Elect's News Conference Announcing the Nomination of
Clayton Yeutter as Secretary of Agriculture," December 14, 1988, American Presidency Project, University of California, Santa Barbara, http://www.presidency.ucsb
.edu/ws/?pid=85212.

38. R. W. Apple, Jr., "Possibility of a Reunited Germany Is No Cause for Alarm,
Bush Says," *New York Times*, October 25, 1989, A1, A12.

39. George H. W. Bush interview by Linda Douglas, Jim Lampley, and Paul
Moyer, June 15, 1991, *Public Papers of the Presidents of the United States: George
Bush, 1991* (Washington, DC: Government Printing Office, 1992), 1:663, 666–668.

40. Dan Quayle, in discussion with author, November 17, 2014.

41. Dan Quayle, "Standing Firm," in *At the President's Side: The Vice Presidency
in the Twentieth Century*, ed. Timothy Walch (Columbia: University of Missouri
Press, 1997), 174.

42. R. W. Apple, Jr., "Is Quayle Out of Tune on U.S. Soviet Policy?" *New York
Times*, October 20, 1989, A14.

43. Thomas L. Friedman, "Handling Gorbachev: A Debate among Skeptics,"
New York Times, November 21, 1989, A10.

44. Quoted in Parmet, *George Bush*, 486.

45. Quayle interview, 80.

46. Quayle, discussion.

47. William Schneider, "Suddenly, the Quayle Factor Revives," *National Journal*,
May 11, 1991, 1146; Michael Barone and Kenneth T. Walsh, "His Place at the Table,"
U.S. News and World Report, May 20, 1991, 20; David Broder, "The Quayle Question," *Washington Post*, May 7, 1991, http://www.washingtonpost.com/archive
/opinions/1991/05/07/the-quayle-question/2c1d5416-56d9-4a58-99eb-7aa9eb
502556.

48. Jack W. Germond and Jules Witcover, *Mad as Hell: Revolt at the Ballot Box,
1992* (New York: Warner Books, 1993), 398–399.

49. Roy M. Neel, interview by Richard Riley and Stephen Knott, William J. Clinton Presidential History Project, University of Virginia, Charlottesville, November
14, 2002, http://web1.millercenter.org/poh/transcripts/ohp_2002_1114_neel.pdf, 57.

50. Elizabeth Drew, *On the Edge: The Clinton Presidency* (New York: Simon &
Schuster, 1994), 228.

51. Taylor Branch, *The Clinton Tapes: Wrestling History with the President*
(New York: Simon & Schuster, 2009), 202.

52. Neel interview, 68.

53. Ibid., 68–69; Drew, *On the Edge*, 226.

54. Richard Moe, in discussion with author, July 14, 2014.

55. Neel interview, 70.

56. Branch, *The Clinton Tapes*, 599.

57. Ibid., 599–600.

58. George Stephanopoulos, *All Too Human: A Political Education* (Boston: Little, Brown, 1999), 402.

59. Robert B. Reich, *Locked in the Cabinet* (New York: Alfred A. Knopf, 1997),
241.

60. Drew, *On the Edge*, 67–68.

61. Branch, *The Clinton Tapes*, 74; Bill Turque, *Inventing Al Gore: A Biography* (Boston: Houghton Mifflin, 2000), 283–286.

62. Joel K. Goldstein, "Reshaping the Model: Clinton, Gore, and the New Vice Presidency," in *The Clinton Presidency and the Constitutional System*, ed. Rosanna Perotti (College Station, TX: Texas A & M University Press, 2012), 91–95.

63. Bob Woodward, *The Choice* (New York: Simon & Schuster, 1996), 13–15, 48–49.

64. "Remarks at a Democratic National Committee Dinner on Amelia Island," November 1, 1997, *Public Papers of Presidents of the United States: William J. Clinton, 1997* (Washington, DC: Government Printing Office, 1999), 2:1480, 1481.

65. "Remarks at a National Conference of Democratic Mayors Dinner," August 12, 1997, *Public Papers of the Presidents of the United States: William J. Clinton, 1997* (Washington, DC: Government Printing Office, 1999), 2:1092.

66. John Hilley and Lawrence Stein, interview by Russell L. Riley et al., William J. Clinton Presidential History Project, University of Virginia, May 20–21, 2004, http://web1.millercenter.org/poh/transcripts/ohp_2004_0520_stein.pdf, 76.

67. Richard L. Berke, "Gore's Stumble Entices Rivals for 2000 Race," *New York Times*, March 11, 1997, A1, A20.

68. Joseph Lockhart, interview with Russell L. Riley et al., William J. Clinton Presidential History Project, University of Virginia, Charlottesville, September 19–20, 2005, http://web1.millercenter.org/poh/transcripts/ohp_2005_0919_lockhart .pdf, 52.

69. Dick Cheney with Liz Cheney, *In My Time: A Personal and Political Memoir* (New York: Threshold Editions, 2011), 305.

70. Donald Rumsfeld, *Known and Unknown: A Memoir* (New York: Sentinel, 2011), 320; Bob Woodward, *Plan of Attack* (New York: Simon & Schuster, 2004), 429–430.

71. Joseph A. Pika, "The Vice Presidency: Dick Cheney, Joe Biden, and the New Vice Presidency," in *The Presidency and the Political System*, 9th ed., ed. Michael Nelson (Washington, DC: CQ Press, 2010), 522

72. Richard Cheney, interview by Sean Hannity, *Sean Hannity Radio Show*, January 12, 2009, http://georgewbush-whitehouse.archives.gov/news/releases/2009/01 /20090112–6.html; Richard Cheney, interview by Jim Lehrer, *News Hour with Jim Lehrer*, PBS, January 14, 2009, 9.

73. Richard Cheney, interview by *Time* magazine, October 18, 2006, http:// georgewbush-whitehouse.archives.gov/news/releases/2006/10/20061021–1.html.

74. Cheney with Cheney, *In My Time*, 305.

75. James Pfiffner, "Organizing the 21st Century White House," in *Rivals for Power: Presidential-Congressional Relations*, 5th ed., ed. James A. Thurber (Lanham, MD: Rowman & Littlefield, 2013), 63–86.

76. Joel K. Goldstein, "Cheney, Vice Presidential Power and the War on Terror," *Presidential Studies Quarterly* 40, no. 1 (2010): 108.

77. Peter Baker, *Days of Fire: Bush and Cheney in the White House* (New York: Doubleday, 2013), 100.

78. Cheney with Cheney, *In My Time*, 300.

79. Paul Kengor, "Cheney and Vice Presidential Power," in *Considering the Bush Presidency,* ed. Gary L. Gregg II and Mark J. Rozell (New York: Oxford University Press, 2004), 160, 161.

80. See Goldstein, "Cheney, Vice Presidential Power and the War on Terror," 107–111, for further discussion of some of these factors.

81. Baker, *Days of Fire,* 6–7.

82. Barton Gellman, *Angler: The Cheney Vice Presidency* (New York: Penguin Press, 2008), 325.

83. Joseph Carroll, "Americans' Ratings of Dick Cheney Reach New Lows," *Gallup,* July 18, 2007, http://www.gallup.com/poll/28159/americans-ratings-dick-cheney -reach-new-lows.aspx; "Political Ratings of U.S. Leaders Rise Moderately since Last Month," *Harris Poll #71,* September 15, 2006, Table 6, http://www.harrisinteractive .com/vault/Harris-Interactive-Poll-Research-for-Immediate-Release-2006-09.pdf.

84. Baker, *Days of Fire,* 441–446; Cheney with Cheney, *In My Time,* 250–252.

85. George W. Bush, *Decision Points* (New York: Broadway Paperbacks, 2010), 87.

86. Ibid., 86.

87. Robert M. Gates, *Duty: A Memoir of a Secretary of War* (New York: Alfred A. Knopf, 2014), 7.

88. Baker, *Days of Fire,* 426; Gellman, *Angler,* 364.

89. Baker, *Days of Fire,* 452.

90. Gellman, *Angler,* 364.

91. Richard Cheney, interview by Martha Raddatz, ABC News, March 19, 2008, http://georgewbush-whitehouse.archives.gov/news/releases/2008/03/text/2008 0319-5.html.

92. Roger Simon, "McCain Bashes Cheney over Iraq Policy," *Politico,* January 22, 2007, http://www.politico.com/news/stories/0107/2390.html.

93. Gellman, *Angler,* 387–388.

94. Mark Halperin and John Heilemann, *Double Down: Game Change, 2012* (New York: Penguin, 2014), 71.

95. Edward Kaufman (U.S. senator and former Biden chief of staff), in discussion with author, May 6, 2014.

96. Halperin and Heilemann, *Double Down,* 71–72.

97. Hillary Rodham Clinton, *Hard Choices* (New York: Simon & Schuster, 2014), 234.

98. Gates, *Duty,* 288.

99. Bob Woodward, *Obama's Wars* (New York: Simon & Schuster, 2010), 159– 160, 217, 221, 240, 262–263, 270–272.

100. Mark Leibovich, "For a Blunt Biden, an Uneasy Supporting Role," *New York Times,* May 8, 2012, A1.

101. Mary Bruce, "Joe Biden Advised against the Osama Bin Laden Raid," *ABC News,* January 30, 2012, http://abcnews.go.com/blogs/politics/2012/01/joe-biden -advised-against-the-osama-bin-laden-raid.

102. Clinton, *Hard Choices,* 22–23.

103. Ron Klain (former Biden chief of staff), in discussion with author, September 30, 2010.

104. Kaufman, discussion.

105. Halperin and Heilemann, *Double Down*, 299-300.

106. Rahm Emanuel, "Joe Biden: Vice President," *Time*, April 21, 2011, http://content.time.com/time/specials/packages/article/0,28804,2066367_2066369_2066099,00.html.

107. White House press release, "Remarks by the President in Eulogy in Honor of Beau Biden," June 6, 2015, https://www.whitehouse.gov/the-press-office/2015/06/06/remarks-president-eulogy-honor-beau-biden.

CHAPTER 10: THE VICE-PRESIDENTIAL SELECTION PROCESS

1. Joel K. Goldstein, *The Modern American Vice Presidency: The Transformation of a Political Institution* (Princeton: Princeton University Press, 1982), 46–89.

2. William G. Mayer, "A Brief History of Vice Presidential Selection," in *In Pursuit of the White House, 2000: How We Choose Our Presidential Nominees*, ed. William G. Mayer (New York: Chatham House, 2000), 345.

3. See, e.g., "Report of the Study Group on Vice-Presidential Selection," Institute of Politics, John F. Kennedy School of Government, Harvard University, June 14, 1976, 10–11.

4. Mark Hiller and Douglas Kriner, "Institutional Change and the Dynamics of Vice Presidential Selection," *Presidential Studies Quarterly* 38, no. 3 (2008): 401, 403–406; Mayer, "A Brief History," 355–356; Donald S. Collat, Stanley Kelley, Jr., and Ronald Rogowski, "The End Game in Presidential Nominations," *American Political Science Review* 75, no. 2 (June 1981): 426–435.

5. The most recent prior instance was 1964, when Lyndon Johnson chose Hubert H. Humphrey.

6. Gerald Ford, *A Time to Heal: The Autobiography of Gerald R. Ford* (New York: Berkley Books, 1979), 388.

7. Phil Buchen to Dick Cheney, August 2, 1976, Vice Presidential Selection 1976 Forms Sent to Potential Candidates, Philip Buchen Files, Box 64, Gerald R. Ford Presidential Library, Ann Arbor, MI.

8. "Letter to 1976 Republican National Convention Delegates Requesting Suggestions for the Vice-Presidential Nominee," July 31, 1976, *Public Papers of the Presidents of the United States: Gerald R. Ford, 1976–77* (Washington, DC: Government Printing Office, 1979), 3:2113–2114.

9. Donna [surname unknown] to Jack Marsh, August 18, 1976, Political Affairs, Ford (8), Presidential Handwriting Files, Box 37, Gerald R. Ford Presidential Library, Ann Arbor, MI.

10. Robert Hartmann to Ford, untitled, undated memo, Memos President (2), Box 131, Hartmann Papers, Gerald R. Ford Presidential Library, Ann Arbor, MI.

11. "Rockefeller Backed as No. 2," *New York Times*, August 15, 1976, 24.

12. William J. Casey to Gerald R. Ford, July 29, 1976, Political Affairs (7), Presidential Handwriting Files, Box 37, Gerald R. Ford Presidential Library, Ann Arbor, MI.

13. Robert O. Anderson to Gerald R. Ford, July 27, 1976, Correspondence—Vice President (2), President Ford Committee, Box 83, Gerald R. Ford Presidential Library, Ann Arbor, MI.

14. Charles Percy to Gerald R. Ford, August 6, 1976, Political Affairs, Ford (8), Presidential Handwriting Files, Box 37, Gerald R. Ford Presidential Library, Ann Arbor, MI.

15. Jonathan Moore and Janet Fraser, eds., *Campaign for President: The Managers Look at '76* (Cambridge: Ballinger Publishing, 1977), 47–48.

16. "Text of Reagan Statement," *New York Times*, July 27, 1976, 15.

17. Moore and Fraser, *Campaign for President*, 47–51; James M. Naughton, "Connally Favors Ford's Candidacy as 'Better Choice,'" *New York Times*, July 28, 1976, 1, 10; James M. Naughton, "Ford Is Endorsed by Top Delegate from Mississippi," *New York Times*, July 29, 1976, 1, 15; James M. Naughton, "Ford Backed by Two Key Mississippians," *New York Times*, July 31, 1976, 1, 9.

18. Warren Weaver, Jr., "Sears Seeks to Force Ford to Name Running Mate," *New York Times*, August 10, 1976, 14; R. W. Apple, Jr., "Ford to Be Pushed by Reagan Forces on Running Mate," *New York Times*, August 15, 1976, 1, 24.

19. Ford, *A Time to Heal*, 387.

20. Ibid., 386–387.

21. James A. Baker III with Steve Fiffer, *"Work Hard, Study . . . and Keep Out of Politics!" Adventures and Lessons from an Unexpected Public Life* (New York: G. P. Putnam's Sons, 2006), 2–3.

22. Moore and Fraser, *Campaign for President*, 64–65.

23. Ford, *A Time to Heal*, 388–391; Martin Schram, *Running for President: A Journal of the Carter Campaign* (New York: Pocket Books, 1977), 260–264.

24. Carter (Kirbo), Mondale (John Reilly), Dukakis (Paul Brountas), and Romney (Beth Myers) are examples.

25. Clinton and Gore (Warren Christopher), George W. Bush (Cheney), Kerry (James Johnson), and McCain (Arthur B. Culvahouse, Jr.) chose prominent party insiders.

26. Clinton (Christopher, civil rights leader Vernon Jordan, and Governor Madeleine Kunin), Dole (Robert Ellsworth, Ann McLaughlin, and Rod DeArment), and Obama (Johnson, Eric Holder, and Caroline Kennedy) involved committees that sometimes included intimates and/or insiders.

27. David Barstow and Katharine Q. Seelye, "In Selecting a No. 2, No Detail Too Small," *New York Times*, August 9, 2000, A1, A17.

28. Jim VandeHei and Dan Balz, "Now, the Kerry Team Looks for a No. 2," *Washington Post*, March 4, 2004, http://www.washingtonpost.com/archive/politics/2004/03/04/now-the-kerry-team-looks-for-a-no-2/6b5c05e0-cb2f-45f3-849b-b899c38d0fdf.

29. Warren Christopher, *Chances of a Lifetime* (New York: Scribner, 2001), 145.

30. Richard Stengel, "The Democrats: An Indelicate Balance," *Time*, July 25, 1988, 20, 21.

31. Robin Toner, "In Key Role for Dukakis, a Friend Who Plays Close to the Vest," *New York Times*, June 14, 1988, B6.

32. Karen Tumulty, "The Gleam Team," *Time*, July 19, 2004.

33. Christopher, *Chances of a Lifetime*, 147.

34. Robert F. Ellsworth to Bob Dole, June 25, 1996, Robert J. Dole Presidential

Campaign Papers, Box 309, Folder 11, Robert J. Dole Archive and Special Collections, University of Kansas, Lawrence.

35. Gerald M. Boyd, "Bush Is Lining Up Prospects for No. 2 Spot on the Ticket," *New York Times*, July 28, 1988, A1, 18.

36. Christopher, *Chances of a Lifetime*, 147.

37. Peter Goldman, Thomas M. DeFrank, Mark Miller, Andrew Murr, and Tom Mathews, *Quest for the Presidency, 1992* (College Station: Texas A & M University Press, 1994), 278-279.

38. Christopher, *Chances of a Lifetime*, 148–149.

39. Mark Halperin and John Heilemann, *Double Down: Game Change, 2012* (New York: Penguin, 2014), 345.

40. Dan Balz and Milton Coleman, "Mondale to Name Ferraro Running Mate Today," *Washington Post*, July 12, 1984, A1.

41. Elizabeth Drew, *Election Journal: Political Events of 1987–1988* (New York: William Morrow, 1989), 215.

42. Christopher, *Chances of a Lifetime*, 148–149, 151–152.

43. Dick Cheney with Liz Cheney, *In My Time: A Personal and Political Memoir* (New York: Simon & Schuster, 2011), 256–257.

44. Halperin and Heilemann, *Double Down*, 345.

45. James Hamilton (principal or coprincipal Democratic vetter, 2000, 2004, and 2008), in discussion with author, August 22, 2014.

46. Terry M. Neal and Dan Balz, "GOP Hails Cheney's Inclusion on Ticket; Democrats Prepare to Fight 'Big Oil,'" *Washington Post*, July 26, 2000, A1.

47. Joe Lieberman and Hadassah Lieberman with Sarah Crichton, *An Amazing Adventure* (New York: Simon & Schuster, 2003), 9.

48. Barton Gellman, *Angler: The Cheney Vice Presidency* (New York: Penguin Press, 2008), 6.

49. Alison Mitchell, "Cheney as the Finalist; Bush Did the Screening," *New York Times*, July 26, 2000, A18.

50. Christopher, *Chances of a Lifetime*, 151.

51. Barstow and Seelye, "In Selecting a No. 2, No Detail Too Small."

52. Jonathan Moore, ed., *Campaign for President: The Managers Look at '84* (Boston: Auburn House Publishing, 1986), 141, 145.

53. Geraldine A. Ferraro with Linda Bird Francke, *Ferraro: My Story* (Toronto, Ontario: Bantam Books, 1985), 26–29; George J. Church and Ed Magnuson, "A Break with Tradition," *Time*, July 23, 1984, 12, 13.

54. Richard Stengel, "The Democrats: An Indelicate Balance," *Time*, July 25, 1988, 20, 21.

55. Hamilton, discussion.

56. "Exhaustive Search Comes Down to Late-Night Choice; Immediate Effort to Announce Decision Fizzled Because Bentsen Had Shut Off Phone," *Washington Post*, July 13, 1988, A6.

57. Lieberman and Lieberman, *An Amazing Adventure*, 9–10.

58. Hamilton, discussion.

59. Edward Walsh, "Dukakis Interviews Prospective Running Mates; Governor Meets with Gephardt, Gore; Jackson Says 'Interests Have Converged,'" *Washington Post*, July 6, 1988, A5; Paul B. Brountas, interview by Andrea L. Hommedieu,

George J. Mitchell Oral History Project, Bowdoin College, Brunswick, ME, April 12, 2010, http://digitalcommons.bowdoin.edu/cgi/viewcontent.cgi?article=1022& context=mitchelloralhistory, 14.

60. Peter Goldman and Tom Mathews, *The Quest for the Presidency, 1988* (New York: Simon & Schuster, 1989), 320–321.

61. Marisa M. Kashino, "A. B. Culvahouse: The Man Who Vetted Sarah Palin," *Washingtonian*, April 21, 2011, http://www.washingtonian.com/articles/people/ab -culvahouse-the-man-who-vetted-sarah-palin.

62. Hamilton, discussion.

63. Larry J. Sabato, *Feeding Frenzy: How Attack Journalism Has Transformed American Politics* (New York: Free Press, 1991), 84.

64. Gerald M. Boyd, "Bush Prunes Running-Mate List; Doles, Quayle and Three Others Stay," *New York Times*, August 13, 1988, 1; Drew, *Election Journal*, 243.

65. Stuart Spencer, interview with Paul B. Freedman et al., Ronald Reagan Oral History Project, University of Virginia, Charlottesville, November 15–16, 2001, http://web1.millercenter.org/poh/transcripts/ohp_2001_1115_spencer.pdf, 102.

66. Sabato, *Feeding Frenzy*, 82.

67. Richard L. Berke, "Invisible, Subtle Race Is on to Reach the Heights of No. 2," *New York Times*, May 3, 2000, A1.

68. Quoted in David Broder and Bob Woodward, *Dan Quayle: The Man Who Would Be President* (New York: Simon & Schuster, 1992), 16.

69. Ibid., 21–26; Dan Quayle, *Standing Firm: A Vice-Presidential Memoir* (New York: HarperCollins, 1994), 18–20.

70. Boyd, "Bush Is Lining Up Prospects for No. 2 Spot on the Ticket," A1.

71. Broder and Woodward, *Dan Quayle*, 29.

72. "What the Bush Ticket Needs," *New York Times*, August 6, 1988, 7.

73. Lieberman and Lieberman, *An Amazing Adventure*, 10–15.

74. Jim VandeHei and Dan Balz, "Kerry Picks Edwards as Running Mate: Mass. Senator Calls Ex-Rival a Man of Middle-Class Values," *Washington Post*, July 7, 2004, A1.

75. LeRoy Ashby and Rod Gramer, *Fighting the Odds: The Life of Senator Frank Church* (Pullman: Washington State University Press, 1994), 522.

76. "Dodd Criticizes Method of Filling Party Ticket," *New York Times*, June 30, 1984, 6; Bernard Weinraub, "Mondale Feels the Pressure to Choose a Running Mate," *New York Times*, July 7, 1984, 1; George J. Church, "Aiming for a Good Show," *Time*, July 16, 1984.

77. Howell Raines, "Mondale Touches All the Bases but Doesn't Manage to Score," *New York Times*, July 8, 1984, E1.

78. Michael Oreskes, "Dukakis Talks to Gephardt and Gore," *New York Times*, July 6, 1988, A14.

79. Goldman et al., *Quest for the Presidency, 1992*, 280–281; Jack W. Germond and Jules Witcover, *Mad as Hell: Revolt at the Ballot Box, 1992* (New York: Warner Books, 1993), 329–330.

80. John Heilemann and Mark Halperin, *Game Change: Obama and the Clintons, McCain and Palin, and the Race of a Lifetime* (New York: HarperCollins, 2010), 335.

81. Stephen Hayes, *Cheney: The Untold Story of America's Most Powerful and Controversial Vice President* (New York: HarperCollins, 2007), 277–278; Cheney with Cheney, *In My Time*, 254–255.

82. Cheney with Cheney, *In My Time*, 256.

83. Gellman, *Angler*, 1–10.

84. Hayes, *Cheney*, 278–279.

85. George W. Bush, *Decision Points* (New York: Broadway Paperbacks, 2010), 67.

86. Cheney with Cheney, *In My Time*, 257–258.

87. Frank Bruni and Eric Schmitt, "Looking for Just the Right Fit, Bush Finds It in Dad's Cabinet," *New York Times*, July 25, 2000, A1; Adam Nagourney and Frank Bruni, "Gatekeeper to Running Mate; Cheney's Road to Candidacy," *New York Times*, July 28, 2000, A1, A14.

88. Cheney with Cheney, *In My Time*, 258–259.

89. Mary Cheney, *Now It's My Turn: A Daughter's Chronicle of Political Life* (New York: Threshold Editions, 2006), 1–4.

90. Bush, *Decision Points*, 65, 68; Cheney with Cheney, *In My Time*, 259.

91. Cheney with Cheney, *In My Time*, 259; Bush, *Decision Points*, 69.

92. Cheney with Cheney, *In My Time*, 259–260.

93. Gellman, *Angler*, 21–22; Nagourney and Bruni, "Gatekeeper to Running Mate," A1.

94. Cheney with Cheney, *In My Time*, 260.

95. Ibid., 262.

96. Gellman, *Angler*, 23; Nagourney and Bruni, "Gatekeeper to Running Mate," A1.

97. Cheney with Cheney, *In My Time*, 262–264; Karl Rove, *Courage and Consequence: My Life as a Conservative in the Fight* (New York: Simon & Schuster, 2010), 169–171.

98. Cheney with Cheney, *In My Time*, 264.

99. Alison Mitchell and Frank Bruni, "McCain Said to Be Willing to Run as Bush's No. 2," *New York Times*, July 21, 2000, A14.

100. Cheney with Cheney, *In My Time*, 264–265. The Constitution does not, as some have said, prohibit a president and vice president from being from the same state. It simply prohibits an elector from voting for a presidential and vice-presidential candidate from the elector's state.

101. Alison Mitchell, "Top Choice Seen for Bush's No. 2," *New York Times*, July 22, 2000, A1, A11.

102. Bush, *Decision Points*, 66.

103. Gellman, *Angler*, 21–23.

104. Associated Press, "McCain Compiles List of Running Mates," NBC.com, April 2, 2008, http://www.nbcnews.com/id/23916421/ns/politics-decision_08/t/mccain-compiles-list-running-mates/#.VUY6oflViko.

105. Heilemann and Halperin, *Game Change*, 353–358; Dan Balz and Haynes Johnson, *The Battle for America, 2008: The Story of an Extraordinary Election* (New York: Viking, 2009), 328–331.

106. Kashino, "A. B. Culvahouse"; Heilemann and Halperin, *Game Change*, 358–364; Balz and Johnson, *The Battle for America, 2008*, 332–335.

107. Balz and Johnson, *The Battle for America, 2008*, 333.

108. Richard L. Berke, "The Quarterback at the Game's End," *New York Times*, August 10, 1996, A1, 10; William Gibson, "Kemp Surges in VP Race," *Sun Sentinel*, August 9, 1996, http://articles.sun-sentinel.com/1996-08-09/news/9608080670 _1_bob-dole-s-veepstakes-pivotal-midwest-states-kemp.

109. Roderick A. DeArment, interview by Richard Norton Smith, August 17, 2007, Robert J. Dole Oral History Project, University of Kansas, Lawrence, https:// docs.google.com/gview?url=http://dolearchivecollections.ku.edu/collections/oral _history/pdf/dearment_rod_2007-08-17.pdf, 21–22.

110. "I'm Kind of Moderate," *Time*, June 16, 1980, 15; Ronald Reagan to Hon. Samuel L. Devine, June 26, 1980, in Ronald Reagan, *Reagan: A Life in Letters* (New York: Free Press, 2003), 246.

111. Alexander Haig, *Caveat: Realism, Reagan and Foreign Policy* (London: Weidenfeld and Nicolson, 1984), 9.

112. Richard B. Cheney, interview by Philip Zelikow et al., George H. W. Bush Oral History Project, University of Virginia, Charlottesville, March 16–17, 2000, http://web1.millercenter.org/poh/transcripts/ohp_2000_0316_cheney.pdf, 30.

113. Ed Magnuson, "Inside the Jerry Ford Drama," *Time*, July 28, 1980, 16, 18; Howell Raines, "Ford Advisers Reportedly Asked Wide Concessions from Reagan," *New York Times*, July 18, 1980, A1, A11.

114. Cheney with Cheney, *In My Time*, 140.

115. Raines, "Ford Advisers Reportedly Asked Wide Concessions from Reagan"; Ronald Reagan to Hon. John Davis Lodge, August 18, 1980, and Ronald Reagan to William Simon, August 11, 1980, in Reagan, *Reagan*, 248, 251–252.

116. Cheney with Cheney, *In My Time*, 140.

117. Michael Deaver with Mickey Herskowitz, *Behind the Scenes* (New York: William Morrow and Company, 1987), 95–96.

118. Elizabeth Drew, "A Reporter at Large: 1980: The Republican Convention," *New Yorker*, August 11, 1980, 38, 56–57; Tom Shales, "Back to You, CBS," *Washington Post*, July 17, 1980, D1.

119. Lyn Nofziger, interview by Steven F. Knott and Russell Riley, Ronald Reagan Oral History Project, University of Virginia, Charlottesville, March 6, 2003, http://web1.millercenter.org/poh/transcripts/ohp_2003_0306_nofziger.pdf, 32; Alan Greenspan, *The Age of Turbulence: Adventures in a New World* (New York: Penguin Press, 2007), 89–91.

120. Edwin Meese, *With Reagan: The Inside Story* (Washington, DC: Regnery Gateway, 1992), 45; Drew, "A Reporter at Large: 1980: The Republican Convention," 38.

121. Goldman and Mathews, *The Quest for the Presidency, 1988*, 171–172.

122. Goldman et al., *Quest for the Presidency, 1992*, 282.

123. Katharine Q. Seelye, "Critic of Clinton," *New York Times*, August 8, 2000, A1, A21; Katharine Q. Seelye, "Gore and Advisers Gather to Select a Running Mate," *New York Times*, August 7, 2000, A17.

124. Boyd, "Bush Prunes Running Mate List."

125. Baker with Fiffer, "*Work Hard, Study . . . and Keep Out of Politics!*," 246.

126. Goldman and Mathews, *The Quest for the Presidency, 1988*, 318.

127. Ibid., 318–319.

128. Drew, *Election Journal*, 244; James A. Baker III, interview with James S. Young et al., George H. W. Bush Oral History Project, University of Virgina, Charlottesville, January 29, 2003, http://web1.millercenter.org/poh/transcripts/ohp _2000_0129_baker.pdf, 12.

CHAPTER 11: CRITERIA FOR SELECTION

1. George Bush with Victor Gold, *Looking Forward: An Autobiography* (New York: Doubleday, 1987), 7.

2. Brountas to Dukakis, "Memorandum Regarding Vice Presidential Selection," June 8, 1988, 4 (on file with author).

3. Warren Christopher, *Chances of a Lifetime* (New York: Scribner, 2001), 145, 152–153.

4. Karl Rove, *Courage and Consequence: My Life as a Conservative in the Fight* (New York: Simon & Schuster, 2010), 166–167, 171.

5. See generally Michael Nelson, "Choosing the Vice President," *PS: Political Science and Politics* 21, no. 4 (Fall 1988): 858–868.

6. "Letter to 1976 Republican National Convention Delegates Requesting Suggestions for the Vice-Presidential Nominee," July 31, 1976, *Public Papers of the Presidents of the United States: Gerald R. Ford, 1976–1977* (Washington, DC: Government Printing Office, 1979), 3:2113–2114; Gerald Ford, *A Time to Heal: The Autobiography of Gerald R. Ford* (New York: Berkley Books, 1979), 388.

7. "News Conference by Vice President Bush and Senator Dan Quayle," August 17, 1988, American Presidency Project, University of California, Santa Barbara, http://www.presidency.ucsb.edu/ws/?pid=85220.

8. Dick Cheney with Liz Cheney, *In My Time* (New York: Simon & Schuster, 2011), 256.

9. Stephen F. Knott and Jeffrey L. Chidester, *At Reagan's Side: Insiders' Recollections from Sacramento to the White House* (Lanham, MD: Rowman & Littlefield, 2009), 63; Stuart Spencer, interview with Paul B. Freedman et al., Ronald Reagan Oral History Project, University of Virginia, Charlottesville, November 15–16, 2001, http://web1.millercenter.org/poh/transcripts/ohp_2001_1115_spencer.pdf, 52–53.

10. Mark Halperin and John Heilemann, *Double Down: Game Change, 2012* (New York: Penguin, 2014), 351–355.

11. Quoted in Katharine Q. Seelye, "The Vice President; Democrats Say Bush's Choice Gives Gore a Freer Hand," *New York Times*, July 26, 2000, A20.

12. Nelson, "Choosing the Vice President," 859, 864, 865–866.

13. Rove, *Courage and Consequence*, 166–167, 171.

14. Christopher, *Chances of a Lifetime*, 145–146; George W. Bush, *Decision Points* (New York: Broadway Paperbacks, 2010), 66–67.

15. Kennedy had actually served in Congress for nearly fourteen years, whereas Quayle was completing his twelfth year.

16. Joel K. Goldstein, *The Modern American Vice Presidency: The Transformation of a Political Institution* (Princeton, NJ: Princeton University Press, 1982), 83–85.

17. See Mark Hiller and Douglas Kriner, "Institutional Change and the Dynamics of Vice Presidential Selection," *Presidential Studies Quarterly* 38, no. 3 (Sep-

tember 2008): 401, 412–413; Jody C. Baumgartner, *The American Vice Presidency Reconsidered* (Westport, CT: Praeger Publishers, 2006), 42–49.

18. Frank Newport, "Palin Unknown to Most Americans," August 30, 2008, *Gallup*, http://www.gallup.com/poll/109951/palin-unknown-most-americans.aspx.

19. Richard E. Fenno, Jr., *The Making of a Senator: Dan Quayle* (Washington, DC: CQ Press, 1989).

20. James A. Baker III with Steve Fiffer, *"Work Hard, Study . . . and Keep Out of Politics!" Adventures and Lessons from an Unexpected Public Life* (New York: G. P. Putnam's Sons, 2006), 98.

21. Elizabeth Kolbert, "Dole, in Choosing Kemp, Buried a Bitter Past Rooted in Doctrine," *New York Times*, September 29, 1996, 1, 18.

22. Halperin and Heilemann, *Double Down*, 354–355.

23. Jody C. Baumgartner and Peter L. Francia, *Conventional Wisdom and American Elections: Exploding Myths, Exploring Misconceptions*, 2nd ed. (Lanham, MD; Rowman & Littlefield, 2010), 67–68, 73–74, 80–81.

24. Lee Sigelman and Paul J. Wahlbeck, "The 'Veepstakes': Strategic Choice in Presidential Running Mate Selection," *American Political Science Review* 91, no. 4 (December 1997): 855, 856.

25. Knott and Chidester, *At Reagan's Side*, 63.

26. Colin L. Powell with Joseph E. Persico, *My American Journey* (New York: Random House, 1995), 554.

27. David M. Halbfinger, "McCain Is Said to Tell Kerry He Won't Join," *New York Times*, June 12, 2004, A1, A11.

28. Ford, *A Time to Heal*, 389.

29. Goldstein, *The Modern American Vice Presidency*, 75–76.

30. "News Conference by Vice President Bush and Senator Dan Quayle."

31. "Address Accepting the Presidential Nomination at the Republican National Convention in New Orleans," August 18, 1988, American Presidency Project, University of California, Santa Barbara, http://www.presidency.ucsb.edu/ws/?pid=25955.

32. "Remarks at a National Conference of Democratic Mayors Dinner," August 12, 1997, *Public Papers of the Presidents of the United States: William J. Clinton, 1997* (Washington, DC: Government Printing Office, 1999), 2:1092.

33. Taylor Branch, *The Clinton Tapes: Wrestling History with the President* (New York: Simon & Schuster, 2009), 599. For further development of these ideas regarding the Gore selection, see Joel K. Goldstein, "Reshaping the Model: Clinton, Gore, and the New Vice Presidency," in *The Clinton Presidency and the Constitutional System*, ed. Rosanna Perotti (College Station: Texas A & M University Press, 2012), 87–89.

34. Scott Reed, interview by Brien R. Williams, Robert J. Dole Oral History Project, University of Kansas, November 8, 2007, http://dolearchivecollections.ku .edu/collections/oral_history/pdf/reed_scott_2007-11-08.pdf, 18.

35. Jonathan Moore, ed., *Campaign for President: The Managers Look at '84* (Boston: Auburn House Publishing, 1986), 140, 220.

36. Richard L. Burke, "A Bold Move for Identity," *New York Times*, August 8, 2000, A1, A21; Katharine Q. Seelye, "Critic of Clinton," *New York Times*, August 8, 2000, A1.

37. Roderick A. DeArment, interview by Richard Norton Smith, August 17, 2007, Robert J. Dole Oral History Project, University of Kansas, Lawrence, https://

docs.google.com/gview?url=http://dolearchivecollections.ku.edu/collections/oral _history/pdf/dearment_rod_2007-08-17.pdf, 7.

38. Some information here was presented in Joel K. Goldstein, "Veepwatch Part 1: The Swing State Selection Myth," Sabato's Crystal Ball, April 5, 2012, http://www.centerforpolitics.org/crystalball/articles/veepwatch-part-1-the-swing -state-selection-myth.

39. Quoted in Seelye, "Critic of Clinton," A1.

40. George S. Sirgiovanni, "Dumping the Vice President: An Historical Overview and Analysis," *Presidential Studies Quarterly* 24, no. 4 (Fall 1994): 781.

41. Richard Norton Smith, *On His Own Terms: A Life of Nelson Rockefeller* (New York: Random House, 2014), 676–677; Cheney with Cheney, *In My Time*, 90.

42. Max Friedersdorf, interview by Stephen Knott and Russell L. Riley, Ronald Reagan Oral History Project, University of Virginia, October 24–25, 2002, http://web1.millercenter.org/poh/transcripts/ohp_2002_1024_friedersdorf.pdf, 37–38.

43. Cheney with Cheney, *In My Time*, 102–103.

44. Peter Goldman, Thomas M. DeFrank, Mark Miller, Andrew Murr, and Tom Mathews, *Quest for the Presidency, 1992* (College Station: Texas A & M University Press, 1994), 279.

45. Dennis Ross, *The Missing Peace: The Inside Story of the Fight for Middle East Peace* (New York: Farrar, Straus and Giroux, 2004), 86; Goldman et al., *Quest for the Presidency, 1992*, 377–379.

46. Marlin Fitzwater, *Call the Briefing! Bush and Reagan, Sam and Helen: A Decade with Presidents and the Press* (New York: Times Books, 1995), 349; Goldman et al., *Quest for the Presidency, 1992*, 380.

47. Fitzwater, *Call the Briefing!*, 349; Baker with Fiffer, "*Work Hard, Study . . . and Keep Out of Politics!,*" 317–318; Goldman et al., *Quest for the Presidency, 1992*, 373; Jack W. Germond and Jules Witcover, *Mad as Hell: Revolt at the Ballot Box, 1992* (New York: Warner Books, 1993), 399.

48. Richard B. Cheney, interview by Philip Zelikow et al., George H. W. Bush Oral History Project, University of Virginia, March 16–17, 2000, http://web1.miller center.org/poh/transcripts/ohp_2000_0316_cheney.pdf, 163–164. Cheney did not share his view with Bush.

49. Ed Rollins with Tom DeFrank, *Bare Knuckles and Back Rooms: My Life in American Politics* (New York: Broadway Books, 1996), 262–263.

50. Tom Morgenthau, "The Quayle Question," *Newsweek*, August 3, 1992, 24.

51. Powell with Persico, *My American Journey*, 553–554.

52. Goldman et al., *Quest for the Presidency, 1992*, 375–376, 703–704.

53. Frank Newport, "Most Americans Want Dick Cheney to Stay on GOP Ticket," July 16, 2004, *Gallup Poll*, http://www.gallup.com/poll/12370/most -americans-want-dick-cheney-stay-gop-ticket.aspx.

54. Baker with Fiffer, "*Work Hard, Study . . . and Keep Out of Politics!,*" 317–318.

55. Goldman et al., *Quest for the Presidency, 1992*, 381, 382.

56. Baker with Fiffer, "*Work Hard, Study . . . and Keep Out of Politics!,*" 318.

57. Fitzwater, *Call the Briefing*, 351.

58. Goldman et al., *Quest for the Presidency, 1992*, 385.

59. Cheney with Cheney, *In My Time*, 417–418.

60. Bush, *Decision Points*, 86–87.

61. Peter Baker, *Days of Fire: Bush and Cheney in the White House* (New York: Doubleday, 2013), 282–284.

62. Newport, "Most Americans Want Dick Cheney to Stay on GOP Ticket."

63. Halperin and Heilemann, *Double Down*, 78.

64. "Press Briefing by Press Secretary Jay Carney, 11/01/2013," https://www.whitehouse.gov/the-press-office/2013/11/01/press-briefing-press-secretary-jay-carney-11012013.

65. Joel K. Goldstein, "Sorry Folks—Biden Is Here to Stay," *Washington Post*, August 28, 2010, http://www.washingtonpost.com/wp-dyn/content/article/2010/08/27/AR2010082704480.html.

CHAPTER 12: VICE-PRESIDENTIAL CAMPAIGNS

1. Bill Peterson, "Floor Fight Threatened by NOW, Convention Battle Vowed if Nominee Selects a Male," *Washington Post*, July 2, 1984, A1; Sandra Salmans, "Women May Fight for Ticket Spot, NOW's Leader Says," *New York Times*, July 2, 1984, A1.

2. George J. Church and Ed Magnuson, "A Break with Tradition," *Time*, July 23, 1984, 12.

3. Bernard Weinraub, "'Difficult' Decision," *New York Times*, July 13, 1984, A1; David S. Broder and Bill Peterson, "Exciting Choice; Bold Decision Greeted with Enthusiasm, Caution," *Washington Post*, July 13, 1984, A1; William Raspberry, "Walter the Bold," *Washington Post*, July 13, 1984, A17; Tom Wicker, "Mondale and His Party," *New York Times*, July 17, 1984, A21; "Transcript of Mondale Announcement and Representative Ferraro's Reply," *New York Times*, July 13, 1984, A8.

4. David E. Rosenbaum, "Democrats Praise Selection, Many Feminists Are Elated," *New York Times*, July 13, 1984, A8.

5. Adam Clymer, "Range of Pluses and Minuses Found in Poll on Rep. Ferraro," *New York Times*, July 14, 1984, A1, 6; "Survey Gives an Edge to Reagan-Bush Ticket," *Newsweek*, July 15, 1984, 27.

6. Church and Magnuson, "A Break with Tradition," *Time*, July 23, 1984, 12, 15; Jane Perlez, "Rep. Ferraro Asks Bush for Debates in Fall Campaign," *New York Times*, July 14, 1984, A1.

7. Jane Perlez, "Rep. Ferraro Reconsiders Remark about Religion," *New York Times*, July 16, 1984, A1.

8. Bernard Weinraub, "Exuberant Welcome Given Mondale and Rep. Ferraro," *New York Times*, July 17, 1984, A13.

9. Robin Toner, "Dukakis Battles Bruised Feelings in Jackson Camp," *New York Times*, July 14, 1988, A1, 20. Michael Oreskes, "Democrats Strive to Ward Off Clash at the Convention," *New York Times*, July 17, 1988, 1, 17.

10. James A. Baker III with Steve Fiffer, "*Work Hard, Study . . . and Keep Out of Politics!*" *Adventures and Lessons from an Unexpected Public Life* (New York: G. P. Putnam's Sons, 2006), 250.

11. Dan Quayle, *Standing Firm: A Vice-Presidential Memoir* (New York: Harper Collins, 1994), 4–8.

12. Herbert Parmet, *George Bush: The Life of a Lone Star Yankee* (New York: Scribner, 1997), 346; Elizabeth Drew, *Election Journal: Political Events of 1987–1988* (New York: William Morrow, 1989), 248–249.

13. Larry J. Sabato, *Feeding Frenzy: How Attack Journalism Has Transformed American Politics* (New York: Free Press, 1991), 118–119, 156–171.

14. Quayle, *Standing Firm*, 30.

15. "News Conference by Vice President Bush and Senator Dan Quayle," August 17, 1988, American Presidency Project, University of California, Santa Barbara, http://www.presidency.ucsb.edu/ws/?pid=85220; Drew, *Election Journal*, 249–250.

16. Quayle, *Standing Firm*, 33–34. Quayle said the phone calls were made to obtain information, not to use influence to receive special treatment.

17. Jack W. Germond and Jules Witcover, *Whose Broad Stripes and Bright Stars? The Trivial Pursuit of the Presidency, 1988* (New York: Warner Books, 1989), 390.

18. Richard Darman, *Who's in Control? Polar Politics and the Sensible Center* (New York: Simon & Schuster, 1996), 189–190.

19. David R. Runkel, ed., *Campaign for President: The Managers Look at '88* (Dover, MA: Auburn House Publishing, 1989), 209.

20. Germond and Witcover, *Whose Broad Stripes and Bright Stars?*, 394; Gerald M. Boyd, "Quayle Declares He Broke No Rules to Get into Guard," *New York Times*, August 20, 1988, A1, 8.

21. E. J. Dionne, Jr., "Bush Struggling to Shed Questions on Quayle Service," *New York Times*, August 21, 1988, 1, 24.

22. Michael Kramer, "Can Bush Survive Quayle?" *U.S. News and World Report*, August 29, 1988, 24, 25; Ed Rollins with Tom DeFrank, *Bare Knuckles and Back Rooms: My Life in American Politics* (New York: Broadway Books, 1996), 191.

23. Sabato, *Feeding Frenzy*, 53.

24. Roy M. Neel, interview by Russell L. Riley and Stephen F. Knott, William J. Clinton Presidential History Project, University of Virginia, Charlottesville, November 14, 2002, http://web1.millercenter.org/poh/transcripts/ohp_2002_1114_neel.pdf, 38–39.

25. "Days before or after the First Day of Convention Vice-Presidential Nominees Were Selected, 1968–2012," American Presidency Project, University of California, Santa Barbara, http://www.presidency.ucsb.edu/data/vp_selection.php. The information in the chart for the Kemp selection is wrong. He was chosen on August 10, 1996, two days before the convention began.

26. Frank Newport, "Palin Unknown to Most Americans," *Gallup*, August 30, 2008, http://www.gallup.com/poll/109951/palin-unknown-most-americans.aspx, 5; Lydia Saad, "Reaction to Ryan as V.P. Pick among Least Positive Historically," *Gallup*, August 13, 2012, http://www.gallup.com/poll/156545/reaction-ryan-pick-among-least-positive-historically.aspx, 4.

27. Jon Cohen, "Positive Views of Ryan Jump Higher after Pick," *Washington Post*, August 13, 2012, http://www.washingtonpost.com/blogs/the-fix/post/positive-views-of-ryan-jump-higher-after-pick/2012/08/13/32251614-e55b-11e1-9739-eef99c5fb285_blog.html.

28. Saad, "Reaction to Ryan as V.P. Pick among Least Positive Historically."

29. Catalina Carnia, "USAT/Gallup Poll: Paul Ryan Gets Low Marks for VP,"

USA Today, August 13, 2012, http://content.usatoday.com/communities/onpolitics/post/2012/08/paul-ryan-poll-vice-president-mitt-romney-/1#.VbsH2PlViko.

30. Jack W. Germond and Jules Witcover, *Mad as Hell: Revolt at the Ballot Box, 1992* (New York: Warner Books, 1993), 333; Peter Goldman, Thomas M. DeFrank, Mark Miller, Andrew Murr, and Tom Mathews, *Quest for the Presidency, 1992* (College Station: Texas A & M University Press, 1994), 282–283; Bill Turque, *Inventing Al Gore: A Biography* (Boston: Houghton Mifflin, 2000), 249.

31. Warren Christopher, *Chances of a Lifetime* (New York: Scribner, 2001), 155.

32. Turque, *Inventing Al Gore*, 249.

33. Samuel L. Popkin, *The Candidate: What It Takes to Win—and Hold—the White House* (New York: Oxford University Press, 2012), 186.

34. "Remarks Introducing Governor Sarah Palin as the 2008 Republican Vice Presidential Nominee in Dayton, Ohio," August 29, 2008, American Presidency Project, University of California, Santa Barbara, http://www.presidency.ucsb.edu/ws/index.php?pid=78529; "Remarks Accepting Senator McCain's Nomination as the Republican Nominee for Vice-President in Dayton, Ohio," August 29, 2008, American Presidency Project, University of California, Santa Barbara, http://www.presidency.ucsb.edu/ws/index.php?pid=78574.

35. Newport, "Palin Unknown to Most Americans."

36. Mark Halperin and John Heilemann, *Double Down: Game Change, 2012* (New York: Penguin, 2014), 356; Jeff Zeleny and Jim Rutenberg, "Romney Chooses Ryan, Pushing Fiscal Issues to the Forefront," *New York Times*, August 12, 2012, A1.

37. Frank Newport, "Americans Split on Paul Ryan; One in Four Have No Opinion," *Gallup*, August 29, 2012, http://www.gallup.com/poll/156986/americans-split-paul-ryan-one-four-no-opinion.aspx.

38. David W. Moore, "Edwards Pick Compares Favorably with Recent Vice Presidential Candidates," *Gallup*, July 7, 2004, http://www.gallup.com/poll/12298/edwards-pick-compares-favorably-recent-vice-presidential-candidates.aspx.

39. Ibid.; Newport, "Palin Unknown to Most Americans," 4; Saad, "Reaction to Ryan as V.P. Pick among Least Positive Historically," 5.

40. Keating Holland, "The Vice Presidential 'Bounce' Factor," CNN, August 8, 2008, http://www.cnn.com/2008/POLITICS/08/08/veep.bounce/index.html?iref=nextin.

41. Jeffrey M. Jones, "Romney Sees No Immediate Bounce from Ryan V.P. Pick," *Gallup*, August 15, 2012, http://www.gallup.com/poll/156692/romney-sees-no-immediate-bounce-ryan-pick.aspx.

42. "Geraldine Ferraro Acceptance Speech," July 20, 1984, http://www.americanrhetoric.com/speeches/gferraroacceptanceaddress.html.

43. "Palin's Speech at the Republican National Convention," *New York Times*, September 3, 2008, http://elections.nytimes.com/2008/president/conventions/videos/transcripts/20080903_PALIN_SPEECH.html.

44. Frank Newport, "Republicans' Enthusiasm Jumps after Convention," *Gallup*, September 8, 2008, http://www.gallup.com/poll/110107/republicans-enthusiasm-jumps-after-convention.aspx.

45. "Gore Acceptance Speech," July 16, 1992, http://www.speeches-usa.com/Transcripts/al_gore-1992dnc.htm.

46. Edward Walsh, "Cheney Attacks Gore and Clinton; Republicans Nominate Bush as His No. 2 Nod with a Partisan Blast," *Washington Post*, August 3, 2000, A1.

47. "Text of Dick Cheney's Speech," CBS News, August 2, 2000, http://www .cbsnews.com/news/text-of-dick-cheneys-speech/.

48. Walter F. Mondale, "Acceptance Speech," Democratic National Convention, New York, NY, August 14, 1980, Speech Files, Mondale Papers, Minnesota Historical Society, St. Paul, MN.

49. "1992 Acceptance Speech," August 21, 1992, http://articles.latimes.com /1992–08–21/news/mn-5796_1_republican-convention.

50. "Transcript: Vice President Biden's Convention Speech," September 6, 2012, NPR, http://www.npr.org/2012/09/06/160713378/transcript-vice-president-bidens -convention-speech.

51. Information taken from "Debate History," 1976–2012, at Commission on Presidential Debates, http://www.debates.org/index.php?page=debate-history.

52. Thomas B. Edsall, "Bush Presses Attack in Heartland; Dukakis Seen Unleashing IRS 'Army'; Poll Indicates Dead Heat," *Washington Post*, September 29, 1988, A16; *New York Times*/CBS News Poll; "The Vice-Presidential Candidates: Voters' Views before the Debate," *New York Times*, October 5, 1988, A30.

53. Joseph Carroll, "Americans' Ratings of Dick Cheney Reach New Lows," *Gallup*, July 18, 2007, 7, http://www.gallup.com/poll/28159/americans-ratings-dick -cheney-reach-new-lows.aspx.

54. "The Bentsen-Quayle Vice-Presidential Debate," October 5, 1988, Commission on Presidential Debates, http://www.debates.org/index.php?page=october -5-1988-debate-transcripts.

55. "The Gore-Quayle-Stockdale Vice-Presidential Debate," October 13, 1992, Commission on Presidential Debates, http://www.debates.org/index.php?page= october-13-1992-debate-transcript.

56. Ibid.

57. "The Gore-Kemp Vice-Presidential Debate," October 9, 1996, Commission on Presidential Debates, http://www.debates.org/index.php?page=october-9-1996 -debate-transcript.

58. Ibid.

59. "The Lieberman-Cheney Vice-Presidential Debate," October 5, 2000, Commission on Presidential Debates, http://www.debates.org/index.php?page=october -5-2000-debate-transcript.

60. "The Cheney-Edwards Vice-Presidential Debate," October 5, 2004, Commission on Presidential Debates, http://www.debates.org/index.php?page=october-5 -2004-transcript.

61. "October 11, 2012, Debate Transcript," Commission on Presidential Debates, http://www.debates.org/index.php?page=october-11-2012-the-biden-romney-vice -presidential-debate.

62. "The Bush-Ferraro Vice-Presidential Debate," October 11, 1984, Commission on Presidential Debates, http://www.debates.org/index.php?page=october-11-1984 -debate-transcript.

63. "The Gore-Kemp Vice-Presidential Debate."

64. Ibid.

65. "The Bush-Ferraro Vice-Presidential Debate."

66. "The Bentsen-Quayle Vice-Presidential Debate."

67. Ibid.

68. Baker with Fiffer, *"Work Hard, Study . . . and Keep Out of Politics!,"* 273.

69. Quoted in Alan Schroeder, *Presidential Debates: Fifty Years of High-Risk TV*, 2nd ed. (New York: Columbia University Press, 2008), 52.

70. "The Bentsen-Quayle Vice-Presidential Debate."

71. George Skelton, "Voters Indicate Quayle Hurts Bush's Chances," *Los Angeles Times*, October 11, 1988, http://articles.latimes.com/1988-10-11/news/mn-3765_1_times-poll; Mark Blumenthal, "What's a Win? VP Debates Election," Pollster.com, October 3, 2008, http://www.pollster.com/blogs/whats_a_win_vp_debate_edition.html; Gary Langer, "Gallup, Harris Polls Find Slight Bush Edge," Associated Press, October 12, 1988, http://www.apnewsarchive.com/1988/Gallup-Harris-Polls-Find-Slight-Bush-Edge/id-d31cd68be0c38e3dc6c481f53bd2270f. The *Los Angeles Times* poll seemed to suggest the possibility of a larger shift, although its range of uncertainty was high.

72. Blumenthal, "What's a Win?"

73. Thomas Holbrook, "The Behavioral Consequences of Vice-Presidential Debates: Does the Undercard Have Any Punch?" *American Politics Quarterly* 22, no. 4 (1994): 469, 474–477.

74. Andrew Dugan, "Vice Presidential Debates Rarely Influence Voters," *Gallup*, October 10, 2012, http://www.gallup.com/poll/157994/vice-presidential-debates-rarely-influence-voters.aspx.

75. "Uncommitted Voters: The Vice-Presidential Debate," October 2, 2008, CBS News Poll, http://www.cbsnews.com/htdocs/pdf/2008VPDebate_poll.pdf.

76. "Debate Poll Says Biden Won, Palin Beats Expectations," CNN.com, October 3, 2008, http://www.cnn.com/2008/POLITICS/10/03/debate.poll.index.html?eref=onion.

77. Douglas E. Kneeland, "Dole Replies to Criticism That He Hurt Ford's Chances," *New York Times*, November 5, 1976, A1, A15.

78. "Speech to National Conference of State Legislators," September 3, 1976, 2; "Speech to Gala in Newport, Rhode Island," September 4, 1976, 3; "Speech to UPI Editors Conference," October 8, 1976, 5, 7; "Remarks by Senator Bob Dole, G.O.P. Fund Raiser, Birmingham, Alabama," Robert J. Dole Senate Papers—Personal/Political Files, Box 40, Folders 10, 11, 25, 17, Robert J. Dole Archive and Special Collections, University of Kansas, Lawrence.

79. "Speech to Gala in Newport, Rhode Island," 1.

80. "Speech to Association of Builders and Contractors, Boston, Ma.," September 16, 1976, 10, Robert J. Dole Senate Papers—Personal/Political Files, Box 40, Folder 15, Robert J. Dole Archive and Special Collections, University of Kansas, Lawrence.

81. President Ford's schedule was determined from searching campaign documents at the American Presidency Project web site. Senator Dole's schedule was determined from his 1976 campaign schedules at Robert J. Dole Senate Papers—Personal/Political Files, Box 40, Robert J. Dole Archive and Special Collections, University of Kansas, Lawrence.

82. Stuart Spencer, interview with Paul B. Freedman et al., Ronald Reagan Oral History Project, University of Virginia, Charlottesville, November 15–16, 2001, http://web1.millercenter.org/poh/transcripts/ohp_2001_1115_spencer.pdf, 42–43.

83. Kneeland, "Dole Replies to Criticism That He Hurt Ford's Chances."

84. Stephen Engelberg, "Bush Opens Attack on Mondale; Cites Foreign and Domestic Policy," New York Times, July 15, 1984, 1, 28.

85. "Ferraro Trip Summary," Box 64, Campaign 1984, Itinerary Summary, Geraldine A. Ferraro Papers, Marymount Manhattan College, New York, NY.

86. Howell Raines, "G.O.P. Seizes 'Genderless Issue' of Tax Return to Attack Ferraro," New York Times, August 14, 1984, A1, A19.

87. "She Answers Questions in 2-Hour Session and Hopes for 'New Year,'" New York Times, August 22, 1984, A1, B5.

88. Sabato, Feeding Frenzy, 12, 105, 126; Steven M. Gillon, The Democrats' Dilemma: Walter F. Mondale and the Liberal Legacy (New York: Columbia University Press, 1992), 369–370.

89. David E. Rosenbaum, "Poll Shows Many Choose Reagan Even If They Disagree with Him," New York Times, September 19, 1984, 1, B9.

90. "Views of Palin Fluid as Spotlight Remains on GOP Ticket," Pew Research, September 18, 2008, 2, http://www.people-press.org/files/legacy-pdf/451.pdf.

91. John Heilemann and Mark Halperin, Game Change: Obama and the Clintons, McCain and Palin, and the Race of a Lifetime (New York: HarperCollins, 2010), 398–400, 403; Dan Balz and Haynes Johnson, The Battle for America, 2008: The Story of an Extraordinary Election (New York:Viking, 2009), 354–358.

92. "Interest in Economic News Surges," Pew Research, October 1, 2008, 2–3, http://www.people-press.org/files/legacy-pdf/457.pdf.

93. "Obama Boosts Leadership Image and Regains Lead over McCain," Pew Research, October 1, 2008, 1, http://www.people-press.org/files/legacy-pdf/456.pdf.

94. "Growing Doubts about McCain's Judgment, Age and Campaign Conduct," Pew Research, October 21, 2008, 13–14, http://www.people-press.org/files/legacy-pdf/462.pdf.

95. Mike McCurry, in discussion with author, March 16, 2007.

96. Robin Toner, "Quayle Reflects Badly on Bush, Dukakis Asserts," New York Times, October 7, 1988, B6.

97. "I Believe in an America That's in Command of Its Destiny," New York Times, October 25, 1988, A26.

98. Bill Lambrecht, "Bentsen Sharpens His Attacks, Broadens Schedule," St. Louis Post Dispatch, October 10, 1988; Kent Jenkins, Jr., "Bentsen Now Playing 'Higher Visibility Role,'" Washington Post, October 9, 1988, A18; Drew, Election Journal, 303.

99. Tom Sherwood, "Reputation Enhanced, Sen. Bentsen Awaited Double Verdict," Washington Post, November 9, 1988, A31.

100. Michael Oreskes, "Bush and Dukakis Try to Capitalize on Latest Debate," New York Times, October 7, 1988, A1, B6.

101. Andrew Rosenthal, "Invoking Kennedy Triumph, Dukakis Tours Connecticut," New York Times, November 4, 1988, A19.

102. Warren Weaver, Jr., "Bentsen, Stumping in Texas, Calls Race Dead Heat," New York Times, November 7, 1988, B15; Douglas Jehl, "Bentsen Gets Bigger

Campaign Role; Dukakis Aides Alter Strategy and Decide to Feature Him on TV," *Los Angeles Times*, October 27, 1988, http://articles.latimes.com/1988-10-27/news /mn-487_1_bentsen-dukakis-campaign.

103. Richard L. Berke, "Quayle Role as Phantom of Campaign," *New York Times*, November 7, 1988, A1; Warren Weaver, Jr., "Bentsen to Move from Supporting Cast to Role with More T.V. Time," *New York Times*, October 27, 1988, B14.

104. E. J. Dionne, Jr., "Candidates Wage Battle to Dawn of Election Day," *New York Times*, November 8, 1988, A1, 19.

105. Spencer interview, 103–104; Berke, "Quayle Role as Phantom of Campaign."

106. Germond and Witcover, *Mad as Hell*, 381–384, 387–388.

107. Stan Greenberg to Bill Clinton, "Re: Reclaiming the Dialogue," September 22, 1992, in Goldman et al., *Quest for the Presidency, 1992*, 719–722.

108. John M. Broder, "Hitting the Backroads and Having Less to Say," *New York Times*, October 31, 2008, A20.

109. "Long Range Planning Schedule for Jack Kemp," October 1996, Kemp October Travel Schedule 1996, Robert J. Dole Presidential Campaign Papers, Box 331, Folder 16, Robert J. Dole Archive and Special Collections, University of Kansas, Lawrence.

110. Terry M. Neel, "Cheney Defends Attacks on Military Preparedness; Nominee Says Drug Benefit Plan Is Underway," *Washington Post*, August 28, 2000, A8.

111. Warren Weaver, Jr., "Bentsen Seeks Local Angle over Big Picture," *New York Times*, September 25, 1988, 27.

112. Broder, "Hitting the Backroads and Having Less to Say," A20; *Campaign for President: The Managers Look at 2008* (Lanham, MD: Rowman & Littlefield, 2009), 154–155.

113. Neel interview, 41; Robert Boorstin, interview by Diane D. Blair, Diane D. Blair Papers, University of Arkansas, November 19, 1992, http://pryorcenter.uark .edu/projects/Diane%20D.%20Blair/BOORSTIN-Robert-O/transcripts/BOOR STIN-Robert-O-nBob-Blair-19921119-FINAL.pdf, 23–25.

114. Humphrey Taylor, "The Lieberman Effect," *Harris Poll*, no. 54, September 20, 2000.

115. Rhodes Cook, "Vice Presidential Candidates Who Helped the Ticket," October 2, 2008, http://blogs.wsj.com/capitaljournal/2008/10/02/vice-presidential -candidates-who-helped-the-ticket/b.

116. David Plouffe, *The Audacity to Win: The Inside Story and Lessons of Barack Obama's Historic Victory* (New York: Viking, 2009), 334.

117. Stacy G. Ulbig, *Vice Presidents, Presidential Elections, and the Media: Second Fiddles in the Spotlight* (Boulder, CO: FirstForumPress, 2013), 101–102.

CHAPTER 13: THE VICE PRESIDENT AS SUCCESSOR

1. See generally John D. Feerick, *From Failing Hands* (New York: Fordham University Press, 1965).

2. See generally John D. Feerick, *The Twenty-Fifth Amendment: Its Complete History and Applications*, 3rd ed. (New York: Fordham University Press, 2014), 125–189; Joel K. Goldstein, *The Modern American Vice Presidency: The Transformation of a Political Institution* (Princeton, NJ: Princeton University Press, 1982), 239–248.

3. Herbert L. Abrams, *"The President Has Been Shot": Confusion, Disability, and the 25th Amendment in the Aftermath of the Attempted Assassination of Ronald Reagan* (New York: W. W. Norton, 1992), 55–56.

4. Richard Darman, *Who's in Control? Polar Politics and the Sensible Center* (New York: Simon & Schuster, 1996), 47–49; Del Quentin Wilber, *Rawhide Down: The Near Assassination of Ronald Reagan* (New York: Henry Holt, 2011), 112.

5. George Bush with Victor Gold, *Looking Forward: An Autobiography* (New York: Doubleday, 1987), 219–220; Alexander Haig, *Caveat: Realism, Reagan and Foreign Policy* (London: Weidenfeld and Nicolson, 1984), 152; Caspar W. Weinberger, *Fighting for Peace: Seven Critical Years in the Pentagon* (New York: Warner Books, 1990), 85.

6. Herbert Parmet, *George Bush: The Life of a Lone Star Yankee* (New York: Scribner, 1997), 268.

7. "Statement by Assistant to the President David R. Gergen about the Attempted Assassination of the President," March 30, 1981, *Public Papers of the Presidents of the United States: Ronald Reagan, 1981* (Washington, DC: Government Printing Office, 1982), 310.

8. Haig, *Caveat*, 155.

9. "Remarks by Secretary of State Alexander M. Haig, Jr., about the Attempted Assassination of the President, March 30, 1981," *Public Papers of the Presidents of the United States: Ronald Reagan, 1981* (Washington, DC: Government Printing Office, 1982), 311; Feerick, *The Twenty-Fifth Amendment*, 193–196.

10. Haig, *Caveat*, 163–164.

11. Weinberger, *Fighting for Peace*, 87–90.

12. Darman, *Who's in Control?*, 51–53.

13. Wilber, *Rawhide Down*, 165.

14. Fred Fielding, "An Eyewitness Account of Executive 'Inability,'" *Fordham Law Review* 79, no. 3 (2010): 823, 827–829.

15. Ibid., 827.

16. Haig, *Caveat*, 157.

17. James A. Baker III with Steve Fiffer, *"Work Hard, Study . . . and Keep Out of Politics!" Adventures and Lessons from an Unexpected Public Life* (New York: G. P. Putnam's Sons, 2006), 146; Darman, *Who's in Control?*, 54–56.

18. Parmet, *George Bush*, 270–271; Darman, *Who's in Control?*, 57.

19. Darman, *Who's in Control?*, 58.

20. Abrams, *"The President Has Been Shot,"* 64–65.

21. Haig, *Caveat*, 162; Wilber, *Rawhide Down*, 193; Darman, *Who's in Control?*, 57.

22. Weinberger, *Fighting for Peace*, 93–95.

23. "Statement by the Vice President about the Attempted Assassination of the President," March 30, 1981, *Public Papers of the Presidents of the United States: Ronald Reagan, 1981* (Washington, DC: Government Printing Office, 1982), 311.

24. Theodore B. Olson, "Presidential Succession and Delegation in Case of Disability," April 3, 1981, *Opinions of the Office of Legal Counsel of the United States Department of Justice*, 5: 91, 93n4, 98, http://www.justice.gov/sites/default/files/olc/opinions/1981/04/31/op-olc-v005-p0091.pdf.

25. "Exchange between the Vice President and Reporters on the President's Recovery Following the Attempted Assassination," March 31, 1981, *Public Papers of the Presidents of the United States: Ronald Reagan, 1981* (Washington, DC: Government Printing Office, 1982), 312.

26. "Remarks of the Vice President and Prime Minister Andreas A. M. van Agt of The Netherlands Following Their Meetings," March 31, 1981, *Public Papers of the Presidents of the United States: Ronald Reagan, 1981* (Washington, DC: Government Printing Office, 1982), 313–314.

27. "Remarks of the Vice President and Deputy Prime Minister Mieczyslaw Jagielski of Poland Following Their Meeting," April 2, 1981, and "White House Statement on the Vice President's Meeting with Minister of Foreign Affairs Ilter Turkmen of Turkey," April 2, 1981, *Public Papers of the Presidents of the United States: Ronald Reagan, 1981* (Washington, DC: Government Printing Office, 1982), 319–320, 322–323.

28. "Remarks of the Vice President on Senate Passage of Federal Budget Legislation," April 3, 1981, *Public Papers of the Presidents of the United States: Ronald Reagan, 1981* (Washington, DC: Government Printing Office, 1982), 324.

29. Ronald Reagan, President's Daily Diary, March 31–April 10, 1981, http://www.reaganfoundation.org/white-house-diary.aspx.

30. Robert E. Gilbert, *The Mortal Presidency: Illness and Anguish in the White House* (New York: Fordham University Press, 1998), 225–229.

31. Lawrence K. Altman, "Presidential Power: Reagan Doctor Says He Erred," *New York Times*, February 20, 1989, A13.

32. Deborah Hart Strober and Gerald S. Strober, *Reagan: The Man and His Presidency* (Boston: Houghton Mifflin, 1998), 123.

33. Larry Speakes with Robert Pack, *Speaking Out: The Reagan Presidency from Inside the White House* (New York: Charles Scribner's Sons, 1988), 9.

34. Haig, *Caveat*, 162.

35. Michael Deaver with Mickey Herskowitz, *Behind the Scenes* (New York: William Morrow and Company, 1987), 7, 28–29.

36. Darman, *Who's in Control?*, 59.

37. Baker with Fiffer, *"Work Hard, Study . . . and Keep Out of Politics!,"* 145–146.

38. Baker quoted in Stephen F. Knott and Jeffrey L. Chidester, *At Reagan's Side: Insiders' Recollections from Sacramento to the White House* (Lanham, MD: Rowman & Littlefield, 2009), 81.

39. Strober and Strober, *Reagan*, 123.

40. Wilber, *Rawhide Down*, 164.

41. Darman, *Who's in Control?*, 53–56.

42. Wilber, *Rawhide Down*, 164.

43. Darman, *Who's in Control?*, 55.

44. Olson, "Presidential Succession and Delegation in Case of Disability," 93 n4.

45. Baker with Fiffer, *"Work Hard, Study . . . and Keep Out of Politics!,"* 145–146.

46. Walter F. Mondale, in discussion with the author, July 28, 2014; Jimmy Carter, Daily Diary, December 21, 1978, http://www.jimmycarterlibrary.gov/documents/diary/1978/d122178t.pdf; Larry L. Simms, "Prior Presidential Disabilities," in *Opinions of the Office of Legal Counsel of the United States Department of Justice*, 5:103.

47. Stuart Taylor, Jr., "Aides Describe Reagan's Choice in Transfer of Power to Bush," *New York Times*, July 15, 1985, A11; Fielding, "An Eyewitness Account of Executive 'Inability,'" 829–830.

48. Parmet, *George Bush*, 306; Ronald Reagan, interview by Hugh Sidey, *Time*, July 25, 1985, http://www.reagan.utexas.edu/archives/speeches/1985/72585b.htm.

49. Fielding, "An Eyewitness Account of Executive 'Inability,'" 830–831.

50. "Letter to the President Pro Tempore of the Senate and the Speaker of the House on the Discharge of the President's Powers and Duties during His Surgery," July 13, 1985, *Public Papers of the Presidents of the United States: Ronald Reagan, 1985* (Washington, DC: Government Printing Office, 1988) 2:919.

51. Taylor, "Aides Describe Reagan's Choice in Transfer of Power to Bush," A11.

52. Marlin Fitzwater, *Call the Briefing! Bush and Reagan, Sam and Helen: A Decade with Presidents and the Press* (New York: Times Books, 1995), 285.

53. Feerick, *The Twenty-Fifth Amendment*, 113.

54. Ralph W. Tarr, "Operation of the Twenty-Fifth Amendment Respecting Presidential Succession," June 14, 1985, in *Opinions of the Office of Legal Counsel*, 9:65, 68.

55. Feerick, *The Twenty-Fifth Amendment*, 198–199; Ronald Reagan, *An American Life* (New York: Simon & Schuster, 1990), 500.

56. Donald Regan, *For the Record: From Wall Street to Washington* (San Diego: Harcourt Brace Jovanovich, 1988), 10.

57. "Letter to the President Pro Tempore of the Senate and the Speaker of the House on the President's Resumption of His Powers and Duties following Surgery," July 13, 1985, *Public Papers of the Presidents of the United States: Ronald Reagan, 1985* (Washington, DC: Government Printing Office, 1988), 2:919–920.

58. Fielding, "An Eyewitness Account of Executive 'Inability,'" 831–832.

59. Dr. John Hutton, interview by Stephen F. Knott, Russell Swerdlow, M.D., and Jeffrey Chidester, Ronald Reagan Oral History Project, University of Virginia, Charlottesville, April 15–16, 2004, http://web1.millercenter.org/poh/transcripts/ohp_2004_0415_hutton.pdf, 11–12.

60. Phil Gailey, "Bush, after a Moment in the Sun, Slips Back into Reagan's Shadow," *New York Times*, July 17, 1985, A1, A16.; Gerald M. Boyd, "Bush Says Reagan Illness Made Him Reflect on Duty," *New York Times*, July 24, 1985, A1, A17.

61. Ronald Reagan, President's Daily Diary, July 17, 1985, http://www.reagan foundation.org/whdpdf/071785.pdf.

62. Robert E. Gilbert, "The Politics of Presidential Illness: Ronald Reagan and the Iran-Contra Scandal," *Politics and the Life Sciences* 33, no. 2 (2014): 58–76.

63. Lawrence K. Altman, "Bush Is Called Exceptionally Fit; Says He Can Now Handle Stress," *New York Times*, November 1, 1988, A1, 28.

64. *Report of the Commission on Presidential Disability and the Twenty-Fifth Amendment*, University of Virginia, 1988, http://web1.millercenter.org/commissions/comm_1988.pdf, 8.

65. Lawrence C. Mohr, M.D., "Medical Considerations in the Determination of Presidential Disability," in *Managing Crisis: Presidential Disability and the Twenty-Fifth Amendment*, ed. Robert E. Gilbert (New York: Fordham University Press, 2000), 97, 104.

66. "Bush and Quayle Discuss Transfer of Power," *New York Times*, April 28, 1989, A12; Feerick, *The Twenty-Fifth Amendment*, 200–201.

67. Bush Diary, April 18, 1989, in George H. W. Bush, *All the Best: My Life in Letters and Other Writings* (New York: Scribner, 2013), 422–423.

68. Mohr, "Medical Consideration in the Determination of Presidential Disability," 104.

69. "The Vice President's View: 'It's an Awkward Job,'" *U.S. News and World Report*, May 20, 1991, 20.

70. Quoted in Fitzwater, *Call the Briefing!*, 286.

71. Ann Devroy and Ruth Marcus, "Clinton Team Follows Bush 'Road Map' on the Transfer of Presidential Power," *Washington Post*, June 14, 1993, http://www.washingtonpost.com/archive/politics/1993/06/14/clinton-team-follows-bush-road-map-on-the-transfer-of-presidential-power/4f1401a4-5d4e-4088-8e89-717368ceccib.

72. Fitzwater, *Call the Briefing!*, 284.

73. Ibid., 289.

74. "Statement by Press Secretary Fitzwater on the President's Health," May 5, 1991, *Public Papers of the Presidents of the United States: George Bush, 1991* (Washington, DC: Government Printing Office, 1992), 1:474.

75. "Statement by Press Secretary Fitzwater on the President's Health," May 6, 1991, *Public Papers of the Presidents of the United States: George Bush, 1991* (Washington, DC: Government Printing Office, 1992), 1:475.

76. "Exchange with Reporters," May 6, 1991, *Public Papers of the Presidents of the United States: George Bush, 1991* (Washington, DC: Government Printing Office, 1992), 1:476.

77. Dan Quayle, in discussion with author, November 17, 2014.

78. "Press Briefing by Mike McCurry and Dr. David Wade," March 14, 1997, American Presidency Project, University of California, Santa Barbara, http://www.presidency.ucsb.edu/ws/?pid=48584.

79. Connie Mariano, "In Sickness and in Health: Medical Care for the President of the United States," in *Managing Crises: Presidential Disability and the Twenty-Fifth Amendment*, ed. Robert E. Gilbert (New York: Fordham University Press, 2000), 83, 93.

80. "List of Vice-Presidents Who Served as 'Acting' President Under the 25th Amendment, Reagan–G. W. Bush," American Presidency Project, University of California, Santa Barbara, http://www.presidency.ucsb.edu/acting_presidents.php.

81. Joel K. Goldstein, "The Vice Presidency and the Twenty-Fifth Amendment: The Power of Reciprocal Relationships," in *Managing Crisis: Presidential Disability and the Twenty-Fifth Amendment*, ed. Robert E. Gilbert (New York: Fordham University Press, 2000), 165, 196–197.

82. Ronald Reagan, *The Reagan Diaries*, ed. Douglas Brinkley (New York: Harper Perennial, 2007), 647.

83. Howard Baker, interview by Stephen Knott, Jeffrey Chidester, and Kurt Hohenstein, Ronald Reagan Oral History Project, University of Virginia, Charlottesville, August 24, 2004, http://web1.millercenter.org/poh/transcripts/ohp_2004_0824_baker.pdf, 3.

84. Frank Carlucci, interview by Stephen Knott, Philip Zelikow, and Don Oberdorfer, Ronald Reagan Oral History Project, University of Virginia, Charlottesville, August 28, 2001, http://web1.millercenter.org/poh/transcripts/ohp_2001_0828_carlucci.pdf, 28–31.

85. *Report of the Commission on Presidential Disability and the Twenty-Fifth Amendment*, 13.

86. Goldstein, "The Vice Presidency and the Twenty-Fifth Amendment," 198–201.

87. Bob Woodward, *Plan of Attack* (New York: Simon & Schuster, 2004), 429–430.

88. Bob Woodward, *Bush at War* (New York: Simon & Schuster, 2002), 270.

89. Dick Cheney with Liz Cheney, *In My Time: A Personal and Political Memoir* (New York: Simon & Schuster, 2011), 337–338.

90. Ibid., 320–322.

91. "Press Briefing by Mike McCurry," January 23, 1998, American Presidency Project, University of California, Santa Barbara, http://www.presidency.ucsb.edu/ws/?pid=48183; "Press Briefing by Mike McCurry," September 11, 1998, American Presidency Project, University of California, Santa Barbara, http://www.presidency.ucsb.edu/ws/?pid=48268.

CHAPTER 14: THE POLITICAL FUTURE OF VICE PRESIDENTS

1. Breckenridge received seventy-two electoral votes as runner-up to Abraham Lincoln in 1860. Vice President George Clinton received six electoral votes in 1808, President (and former Vice President) Van Buren received sixty electoral votes in losing reelection in 1840, and former president and vice president Millard Fillmore received eight electoral votes as a third-party presidential candidate in 1856. Thomas A. Hendricks received forty-two electoral votes in Ulysses Grant's 1872 election twelve years before he was elected as vice president.

2. Julian Zelizer, "Why Biden Won't Win," CNN.com, March 3, 2014, http://www.cnn.com/2014/03/03/opinion/zelizer-biden-wont-win.

3. Joel K. Goldstein, "The Vice-Presidential Advantage," Sabato's Crystal Ball, March 20, 2014, http://www.centerforpolitics.org/crystalball/articles/the-vice-presidential-advantage.

4. Joel K. Goldstein, *The Modern American Vice Presidency: The Transformation of a Political Institution* (Princeton: Princeton University Press, 1982), 249–270.

5. Samuel L. Popkin, *The Candidate: What It Takes to Win—and Hold—the White House* (New York: Oxford University Press, 2012), 191.

6. See generally Goldstein, *The Modern American Vice Presidency*, 254–259.

7. Ibid., 259–262.

8. Elizabeth Drew, *Election Journal: Political Events of 1987–1988* (New York: William Morrow, 1989), 51; Gerald M. Boyd, "Bush and the Mideast: Of Sights and Substance," *New York Times*, August 5, 1986, B5.

9. Gerald M. Boyd, "Gorbachev Visit Called Boon to Bush," *New York Times*, December 12, 1987, 9.

10. Julie Johnson, "Bush to Speak at U.N. Debate on Iran's Plane," *New York Times*, July 14, 1988, A1, A23.

11. Ronald Reagan, *The Reagan Diaries*, ed. Douglas Brinkley (New York: Harper Perennial, 2007), 621.

12. Bill Turque, *Inventing Al Gore: A Biography* (Boston: Houghton Mifflin, 2000), 332–336.

13. Douglas Jehl, "Gore in Mideast, Prods Sides before Talks," *New York Times*, May 4, 1998, A10.

14. Goldstein, *The Modern American Vice Presidency*, 262–264.

15. Chase Untermeyer, "Looking Forward: George Bush as Vice President," in *At the President's Side: The Vice Presidency in the Twentieth Century*, ed. Timothy Walch (Columbia: University of Missouri Press, 1997), 157, 166.

16. Bernard Weinraub, "Bush's Rivals Resent His Advantages," *New York Times*, June 10, 1987, A24.

17. Turque, *Inventing Al Gore*, 350–351.

18. Michael Janofsky, "In New Hampshire, Gore Looks More Presidential," *New York Times*, September 19, 1998, A7.

19. "Gore to Address State Convention," *New York Times*, April 29, 1998, B4.

20. Michael Janofsky, "Gore Building Network in California," *New York Times*, January 24, 1999, 24.

21. Drew, *Election Journal*, 47, 51; Boyd, "Gorbachev Visit Called Boon to Bush," 9.

22. Jack W. Germond and Jules Witcover, *Whose Broad Stripes and Bright Stars? The Trivial Pursuit of the Presidency, 1988* (New York: Warner Books, 1989), 73–74.

23. Richard L. Berke, "National Fund-Raising Base Eludes All but Bush," *New York Times*, September 1, 1987, A12.

24. Frank Newport, "Most Americans Know Al Gore Well," *Gallup*, August 17, 2000, http://www.gallup.com/poll/2626/most-americans-know-gore-well.aspx.

25. James A. Baker III with Steve Fiffer, *"Work Hard, Study . . . and Keep Out of Politics!" Adventures and Lessons from an Unexpected Public Life* (New York: G. P. Putnam's Sons, 2006), 238.

26. See, e.g., "The President's News Conference," December 16, 1997, *Public Papers of the Presidents of the United States: William J. Clinton, 1997* (Washington, DC: Government Printing Office, 1999), 2:1772, 1782.

27. Walter Mondale, interview by Jim Lehrer, *NewsHour with Jim Lehrer*, PBS, August 15, 2000, http://www.pbs.org/newshour/spc/election2000/demconvention /mondale_8–15.html.

28. E. J. Dionne, Jr., "Bush's Presidency Bid Shaky Despite His Lead, Poll Finds," *New York Times*, July 26, 1987, 1, 22.

29. Sidney M. Milkis and Michael Nelson, *The American Presidency: Origins and Development, 1789–2011*, 6th ed. (Washington, DC: CQ Press, 2012), 501.

30. Mondale interview.

31. George H. W. Bush, *All the Best: My Life in Letters and Other Writings* (New York: Scribner, 2013), 386–388.

32. Gerald M. Boyd, "Bush Turns from History to Vision," *New York Times*, May 19, 1987, A26.

33. Gerald M. Boyd, "Pledging Tolerance, Bush Officially Joins 1988 Race," *New York Times*, October 13, 1987, A1.

34. Gerald M. Boyd, "Bush Splits with Reagan on Taxes," *New York Times*, October 24, 1987, A9.

35. Gerald M. Boyd, "Bush Envisions Hands-on Presidency," *New York Times*, November 23, 1987, B12.

36. John M. Broder, "The Lewinsky Episode: First the Scandal, Then the Strain," *New York Times*, March 4, 2000, A12.

37. Turque, *Inventing Al Gore*, 365.

38. Melinda Henneberger and Don Van Natta, Jr., "Once Close to Clinton, Gore Keeps a Distance," *New York Times*, October 20, 2000, A1, 26; Kevin Sack, "The Vice President: Gore Again Alters Day to Meet on Middle East," *New York Times*, October 14, 2000, A15.

39. Richard Perez-Pena, "The Democratic Running Mate: In Praise of the President, Lieberman Is Unabashed Where Gore Is Reticent," *New York Times*, September 3, 2000, 26.

40. Katharine Q. Seelye and David Sanger, "Gore Asks Release of U.S.-Stored Oil to Stabilize Price," *New York Times*, September 22, 2000, A1, A18.

41. "Gore's Leap of Faith: Gore Needed a Bold Veep Move—and Got It," *Time*, August 21, 2000.

42. Ronald Reagan, "Remarks at the Republican National Convention in New Orleans, Louisiana," August 15, 1988, *Public Papers of Presidents of the United States: Ronald Reagan, 1988* (Washington, DC: Government printing Office, 1991), 2:1080, 1084.

43. "Remarks to the Democratic National Convention in Los Angeles, California," August 14, 2000, *Public Papers of Presidents of the United States: William J. Clinton, 2000* (Washington, DC: Government Printing Office, 2001), 2:1650, 1653.

44. E. J. Dionne, Jr., "Bush Draws Foes' Fire in First Debate," *New York Times*, October 29, 1987, A1.

45. Drew, *Election Journal*, 45.

46. Steven V. Roberts, "In Iowa, Tarnish on Reagan Rubs Off on Bush," *New York Times*, January 18, 1988, A1, A13.

47. Herbert Parmet, *George Bush: The Life of a Lone Star Yankee* (New York: Scribner, 1997), 315–320.

48. E. J. Dionne, Jr., "G.OP. Fears Campaign Damage," *New York Times*, October 21, 1987, A1, D12.

49. George P. Shultz, *Turmoil and Triumph: My Years as Secretary of State* (New York: Charles Scribner's Sons, 1993), 808–809.

50. John M. Broder and Don Van Natta, Jr., "Aides Say Clinton Is Angered as Gore Tries to Break Away," *New York Times*, June 26, 1999, A1, 10.

51. William J. Clinton, interview by Wolf Blitzer, *Late Election*, CNN, June 20, 1999, *Public Papers of the Presidents of the United States: William J. Clinton, 1999* (Washington, DC: Government Printing Office, 2000), 1:967, 971.

52. "I Believe in an America That's in Command of Its Destiny," *New York Times*, October 25, 1988, A26; Robin Toner, "Dukakis and Bush Trade Fire in Heavy Barrages; Democrat Denounces Rival's Stand in the Iran-Contra Affair," *New York Times*, August 31, 1988, A1, A16.

53. E. J. Dionne, Jr., "Poll Shows Bush Sets Agenda for Principal Election Issues," *New York Times*, September 14, 1988, A1, A29.

54. "Clinton Fatigue Undermines Gore Poll Standing," *Pew Research Center*, April 17, 1999, http://www.people-press.org/files/legacy-pdf/65.pdf, 3.

55. Dan Balz and Richard Morin, "Clinton-Weary Public Has Doubts about Gore," *Washington Post*, September 8, 1999, A1.

56. Broder, "The Lewinsky Episode."

57. Frank Bruni, "The Texas Governor: Bush Calls on Gore to Denounce Clinton Affair," *New York Times*, August 12, 2000, A11.

58. Bernard Weinraub, "Mondale's Tightrope Act on the Carter Problem," *New York Times*, October 24, 1983, B8.

59. Walter F. Mondale, "Address Accepting the Presidential Nomination at the Democratic National Convention in San Francisco," July 19, 1984, American Presidency Project, University of California, Santa Barbara, http://www.presidency.ucsb.edu/ws/index.php?pid=25972.

60. Jonathan Moore, ed., *Campaign for President: The Managers Look at '84* (Dover, MA: Auburn House Publishing, 1986), 108.

61. Richard Berke, "Facing Financial Squeeze, Quayle Pulls Out of '96 Race," *New York Times*, February 10, 1995, A1, A14.

62. Todd S. Purdum, "Quayle Bids Farewell to the Presidential Race, and Effectively, an Era of His Career," *New York Times*, September 28, 1999, A22.

63. Frank Newport, "Quayle Never Caught on with Republican Voters," *Gallup*, September 28, 1999, http://www.gallup.com/poll/3574/quayle-never-caught-republican-voters.aspx.

64. Ronald Reagan, interview by Tom Brokaw et al., December 3, 1987, *Public Papers of the Presidents of the United States: Ronald Reagan, 1987* (Washington, DC: Government Printing Office, 1989), 2:1425, 1429–1430.

65. Reagan, *The Reagan Diaries*, 566.

66. John H. Sununu, interview by James S. Young et al., George H. W. Bush Oral History Project, University of Virginia, Charlottesville, June 8–9, 2000, http://web1.millercenter.org/poh/transcripts/ohp_2000_0608_sununu.pdf, 11.

67. Gerald M. Boyd, "Bush, Bullets Hot, Recalls the Alamo," *New York Times*, February 20, 1987, A18.

68. David R. Runkel, ed., *Campaign for President: The Managers Look at '88* (Dover, MA: Auburn House Publishing, 1989), 32.

69. R. W. Apple, Jr., "Stunning Result Carries a Grim Message for Bush," *New York Times*, February 9, 1988, B7.

70. E. J. Dionne, Jr., "Gephardt Is Second," *New York Times*, February 17, 1988, A1, B6; E. J. Dionne, Jr., "Bush in Struggle with Surging Dole in New Hampshire," *New York Times*, February 16, 1988, A1, B7.

71. Reagan, *The Reagan Diaries*, 578.

72. Kenneth Duberstein (chief of staff to President Reagan), in discussion with author, March 16, 2007.

73. Reagan, *The Reagan Diaries*, 634.

74. Ibid., 617, 626–629.

75. "Remarks at the Annual Republican Congressional Fundraising Dinner,"

May 11, 1988, *Public Papers of the Presidents of the United States: Ronald Reagan, 1988* (Washington, DC: Government Printing Office, 1990), 1:587, 590.

76. E. J. Dionne, Jr., "Mixed Blessings: Bush as Heir Underlines a Paradox for Republicans," *New York Times*, May 15, 1988, E1.

77. "Statement Endorsing George Bush's Candidacy for President," May 12, 1988, *Public Papers of the Presidents of the United States: Ronald Reagan, 1988* (Washington, DC: Government Printing Office, 1990), 1:590.

78. "Radio Address to the Nation on the Republican National Convention and George Bush," August 20, 1988, *Public Papers of the Presidents of the United States: Ronald Reagan, 1988–89* (Washington, DC: Government Printing Office, 1991), 2:1091–1092.

79. "Remarks at a Presidential Campaign Rally for George Bush in Los Angeles, California," August 24, 1988, *Public Papers of the Presidents of the United States: Ronald Reagan, 1988–89* (Washington, DC: Government Printing Office, 1991), 2:1101, 1104, 1105.

80. A. B. Culvahouse, interview by Stephen F. Knott, Darby Morrisroe, and Karen M. Hult, Ronald Reagan Oral History Project, University of Virginia, Charlottesville, April 1, 2004, http://web1.millercenter.org/poh/transcripts/ohp_2004_0401_culvahouse.pdf, 43.

81. Baker with Fiffer, *"Work Hard, Study . . . and Keep Out of Politics!,"* 240–241.

82. Steven V. Roberts, "President Decides Not to Veto Bill Requiring Notice of Plant Closings," *New York Times*, August 3, 1988, A1, B5.

83. Shultz, *Turmoil and Triumph*, 1035.

84. Steven V. Roberts, "Reagan Courting Texas Democrats," *New York Times*, September 23, 1988, A22; Steven V. Roberts, "Hard-Hitting Campaign Is Opened by President," *New York Times*, August, 24, 1988, B6.

85. "Remarks on the Veto of the National Defense Authorization Act, Fiscal Year 1989 and a Question-and-Answer Session with Reporters," August 3, 1988, *Public Papers of the Presidents of the United States: Ronald Reagan, 1988–89* (Washington, DC: Government Printing Office, 1991), 2:1013, 1016.

86. "Statement on the Selection of Senator Dan Quayle of Indiana as the Republican Vice Presidential Nominee," August 16, 1988, *Public Papers of the Presidents of the United States: Ronald Reagan, 1988–89* (Washington, DC: Government Printing Office, 1991), 2:1087.

87. "Radio Address to the Nation on the Republican National Convention and George Bush," 2:1092.

88. "Remarks at a Presidential Campaign Rally for George Bush in Los Angeles, California," 2:1104.

89. Maureen Dowd, "President, in Vintage Form, Relishes His Final Campaign," *New York Times*, November 7, 1988, A1, B13; Julie Johnson, "The Reagan Campaign Magic: He Isn't Running but He's Winning," *New York Times*, November 3, 1988, B19. The states visited were determined by reviewing locations of Reagan's speeches available at the American Presidency Project web site for October and November 1988.

90. E. J. Dionne, Jr., "Many Split Tickets," *New York Times*, November 9, 1988, A1, A25; George Skelton, "The Times/CNN Poll; Dukakis Lost Own Is-

sue: Competence," *Los Angeles Times*, November 9, 1988, http://articles.latimes .com/1988-11-09/news/mn-270_1_modern-times.

91. "Bush Victory Talk: 'I Mean to Be a President of All the People,'" *New York Times*, November 9. 1988, A27.

92. "Remarks on the Resignation of Secretary of State Christopher and an Exchange with Reporters," November 7, 1996, *Public Papers of the Presidents of the United States: William Clinton, 1996* (Washington, DC: Government Printing Office, 1998), 2:2089, 2090.

93. Richard L. Berke, "Gore's Bandwagon Gets Big Push as Clinton Shows His Enthusiasm," *New York Times*, July 14, 1997, A1, B8.

94. Katharine Q. Seelye, "Gore Stops By; Clinton Plays the Gracious Host," *New York Times*, August 8, 1999, 1; Katharine Q. Seelye, "Clinton Gathers Fund-Raisers and Urges Them to Help Gore," *New York Times*, August 11, 1999, A14.

95. Joseph Lockhart, interview with Russell L. Riley et al., William J. Clinton Presidential History Project, University of Virginia, Charlottesville, September 19–20, 2005, http://web1.millercenter.org/poh/transcripts/ohp_2005_0919_lockhart .pdf, 128, 129.

96. Broder and Van Natta, "Aides Say Clinton Is Angered as Gore Tries to Break Away"; Henneberger and Van Natta, "Once Close to Clinton, Gore Keeps a Distance."

97. Richard L. Berke, "Clinton Tells of His Choices for Vice President," *New York Times*, July 20, 2000, A22.

98. Bill Clinton, interview by Jose Diaz-Balart of Telemundo in New York City, November 4, 2000, *Public Papers of the Presidents of the United States: William Clinton, 2000–2001* (Washington, DC: Government Printing Office, 2002), 3:2497, 2498; press briefing by Jake Siewart, November 6, 2000, American Presidency Project, University of California, Santa Barbara, http://www.presidency.ucsb.edu /ws/?pid=47943. Clinton's campaign activity was determined from the location of his speeches available at the American Presidency Project web site for September through early November 2000.

CHAPTER 15: THE PROBLEMS WITH THE VICE PRESIDENCY

1. Quoted in Mark Hatfield with Senate Historical Office, *Vice Presidents of the United States, 1789–1993* (Washington, DC: Government Printing Office, 1997), 512.

2. See Patrick Cox, "John Nance Garner on the Vice Presidency: In Search of the Proverbial Bucket," Center for American History, University of Texas at Austin, https://www.cah.utexas.edu/documents/news/garner.pdf.

3. Quoted in Doris Kearns, *Lyndon Johnson and the American Dream* (New York: Harper & Row, 1976), 164.

4. Quoted in "The President Giveth and Taketh Away," *Time*, November 14, 1969, 19.

5. Quoted in Stephen F. Hayes, *Cheney: The Untold Story of America's Most Powerful and Controversial Vice President* (New York: HarperCollins, 2007), 2.

6. Steven M. Gillon, *The Democrats' Dilemma: Walter F. Mondale and the Liberal Legacy* (New York: Columbia University Press, 1992), 255–259.

7. George H. W. Bush, *All the Best: My Life in Letters and Other Writings* (New York: Scribner, 2013), 337.

8. "Remarks at the Bush-Quayle Welcoming Rally at the Republican National Convention in Houston, Texas," August 17, 1992, *Public Papers of the Presidents of the United States: George Bush, 1992* (Washington, DC: Government Printing Office, 1993), 2:1370.

9. Dan Quayle, *Standing Firm: A Vice-Presidential Memoir* (New York: Harper-Collins, 1994), 91, 102; quoted in David Broder and Bob Woodward, *Dan Quayle: The Man Who Would Be President* (New York: Simon & Schuster, 1992), 90.

10. Bill Turque, *Inventing Al Gore: A Biography* (Boston: Houghton Mifflin, 2000), 268–269, 326–327, 348–349, 359.

11. Bush, *All the Best*, 337.

12. "Address by Vice President Dan Quayle," The Leader's Lecture Series, September 19, 2000, https://www.senate.gov/artandhistory/history/common/generic/Leaders_Lecture_Series_Quayle.htm.

13. Frank J. Fahrenkopf, Jr., "Reagan as Political Leader," in *Leadership in the Reagan Presidency*, ed. Kenneth W. Thompson (Lanham, MD: University Press of America, 1993), 2:46.

14. R. W. Apple, Jr., "On Quayle in Search of an Image as a Leader," *New York Times*, September 27, 1989, A14.

15. Dan Quayle, interview with James S. Young et al., George H. W. Bush Oral History Project, University of Virginia, Charlottesville, March 12, 2002, http://web1.millercenter.org/poh/transcripts/ohp_2002_0312_quayle.pdf, 46.

16. Richard B. Cheney, interview by Mark Knoller, CBS Radio, January 7, 2009, http://georgewbush-whitehouse.archives.gov/news/releases/2009/01/20090107-7.html.

17. Some of these arguments were addressed in Joel K. Goldstein, "Cheney, Vice Presidential Power and the War on Terror," *Presidential Studies Quarterly* 40, no. 1 (2010): 127–129.

18. Bruce Montgomery, *Richard B. Cheney and the Rise of the Imperial Vice Presidency* (Westport, CT: Praeger, 2009); Sam Tanenhaus, "The Imperial Vice Presidency," *New Republic*, November 19, 2008, http://www.newrepublic.com/article/books/the-imperial-vice-presidency.

19. Donald Rumsfeld, *Known and Unknown: A Memoir* (New York: Sentinel, 2011), 184, 285.

20. Stephen Hess to Jimmy Carter, Memorandum, December 13, 1976, in Stephen Hess, *Organizing the Presidency*, rev. ed. (Washington, DC: Brookings Institution, 1988), 230.

21. Cheney interview, CBS Radio, 5.

22. George W. Bush, *Decision Points* (New York: Broadway Paperbacks, 2010), 87.

23. Goldstein, "Cheney, Vice Presidential Power and the War on Terror," 125–127.

24. Ibid., 127; Condoleezza Rice, *No Higher Honor: A Memoir of My Years in Washington* (New York: Crown, 2011), 17–18, 104–105; Jack Goldsmith, *The Terror*

Presidency: Law and Judgment inside the Bush Administration (New York: W. W. Norton, 2007).

25. Bush, *Decision Points*, 172.

26. Eric Lightblau and Lawrence K. Altman, "Ashcroft in Hospital with Pancreatic Ailment," *New York Times*, March 6, 2004, A9.

27. Department of Justice News Release, "Attorney General John Ashcroft to Undergo Procedure at G. W. Hospital," March 9, 2004, http://www.justice.gov /archive/opa/pr/2004/March/04_ag_148.htm.

28. Bush, *Decision Points*, 172–174.

29. Joseph A. Pika, "The New Vice Presidency: Dick Cheney, Joe Biden, and the New Presidency," in *The Presidency and the Political System*, 9th ed., ed. Michael Nelson (Washington, DC: CQ Press, 2010), 509, 522.

30. David Addington to Hon. John F. Kerry, June 26, 2007, http://www.pegc.us /archive/White_House/addington_letter_20070626.pdf.

31. Richard B. Cheney, interview by Larry King, CNN, July 31, 2007, http:// georgewbush-whitehouse.archives.gov/news/releases/2007/07/20070731-2.html; Cheney interview, CBS Radio.

32. Robert Barnes, "Cheney Joins Congress in Opposing D.C. Gun Ban," *Washington Post*, February 9, 2008, http://www.washingtonpost.com/wp-dyn/content /article/2008/02/08/AR2008020803802.html.

33. Peter Baker, *Days of Fire: Bush and Cheney in the White House* (New York: Doubleday, 2013), 579.

34. Glenn Harlan Reynolds, "Is Dick Cheney Unconstitutional?" *Northwestern University Law Review Colloquy* 102 (November 12, 2007): 110–116; Gene Healy, "Time to Downsize the Imperial Vice-Presidency," Cato Institute, http://www.cato .org/publications/commentary/time-downsize-imperial-vicepresidency.

35. Joel K. Goldstein, "Constitutional Change, Originalism, and the Vice Presidency," *University of Pennsylvania Journal of Constitutional Law* 16, no. 2 (2013): 383–394.

36. Joel K. Goldstein, "The New Constitutional Vice Presidency," Wake Forest Law Review 30, no. 3 (1995): 505, 526–540.

37. Roy E. Brownell II, "A Constitutional Chameleon: The Vice President's Place within the American System of Separation of Powers" (Parts I and II), *Kansas Journal of Law & Public Policy* 24, nos. 1 and 2 (2014, 2015): 1, 294.

38. Bill Clinton, *My Life* (New York: Alfred A. Knopf, 2004), 536.

39. Of White House vice presidents, Cheney broke only eight ties, Bush seven, Gore four, and Mondale one. "Occasions When Vice Presidents Have Voted to Break Tie Votes in the Senate," http://www.senate.gov/artandhistory/history /resources/pdf/VPTies.pdf.

40. Goldstein, "Constitutional Change, Originalism, and the Vice Presidency," 408.

41. Akhil Reed Amar and Vik Amar, "President Quayle?" *Virginia Law Review* 78, no. 4 (1992): 913–947; Richard Albert, "President Palin?" *Huffington Post*, May 28, 2010, http://www.huffingtonpost.com/richard-albert/president-palin_b _593284.html.

42. Sanford Levinson, *Our Undemocratic Constitution: Where the Constitution*

Goes Wrong (and How We the People Can Correct It) (New York: Oxford University Press, 2006), 122–123; Thomas E. Cronin and Michael A. Genovese, *The Paradoxes of the American Presidency* (New York: Oxford University Press, 1998), 340–341.

43. Douglas L. Kriner, "The Vice Presidency Should Be Abolished: Pro," in *Debating the Presidency: Conflicting Perspectives on the American Executive*, 2nd ed., ed. Richard J. Ellis and Michael Nelson (Washington, DC: CQ Press, 2010), 175–176; Richard Albert, "The Evolving Vice Presidency," *Temple Law Review* 78, no. 4 (2005): 811, 870–872.

44. See Joel K. Goldstein, *The Modern American Vice Presidency: The Transformation of a Political Institution* (Princeton, NJ: Princeton University Press, 1982), 10.

45. Michael Nelson, "Choosing the Vice President," *PS: Political Science and Politics* 21, no. 4 (Fall 1988): 858–868.

46. Richard D. Friedman, "Some Modest Proposals on the Vice-Presidency," *Michigan Law Review* 86, no. 7 (1988): 1703, 1728–1729.

47. Albert, "President Palin?"

48. Arthur M. Schlesinger, Jr., "On the Presidential Succession," *Political Science Quarterly* 89, no. 3 (1974): 483–484; Friedman, "Some Modest Proposals on the Vice-Presidency," 1726.

49. Martin P. Wattenberg, "The Role of Vice Presidential Candidate Ratings in Presidential Voting Behavior," *American Politics Quarterly* 23, no. 4 (1995): 504–514.

50. Lydia Saad, "Gore Gains in Race for President as Result of Democratic Convention," *Gallup News Service*, August 21, 2000, http://www.gallup.com/poll/2620/gore-gains-race-president-result-democratic-convention.aspx.

51. Jeffrey M. Jones, "Different Influences Found for Bush, Kerry Voters," *Gallup News Services*, December 16, 2004, http://www.gallup.com/poll/14374/different-influences-found-bush-kerry-voters.aspx.

52. "Vice Presidential Choices, July 31–August 5, 2008," CBS News Poll, August 6, 2008, http://www.cbsnews.com/htdocs/pdf/Jul08B-VP.pdf.

53. Quoted in Jack W. Germond and Jules Witcover, *Mad as Hell: Revolt at the Ballot Box, 1992* (New York: Warner Books, 1993), 333.

54. Goldstein, "The New Constitutional Vice Presidency," 551.

55. Jules Witcover, *Crapshoot: Rolling the Dice on the Vice Presidency* (New York: Crown, 1992), 418.

56. Warren Weaver, Jr., "Bentsen Back in Capital: New Prospect of Power," *New York Times*, November 11, 1988, A23.

57. Friedman, "Some Modest Proposals on the Vice-Presidency," 1729.

58. Amar and Amar, "President Quayle?" 944–948; Friedman, "Some Modest Proposals on the Vice Presidency," 1726–1729.

59. Goldstein, "The New Constitutional Vice Presidency," 555.

60. Albert, "Evolving Vice Presidency," 885.

61. Joel K. Goldstein, "Akhil Reed Amar and Presidential Continuity," *Houston Law Review* 47, no. 1 (2009): 67, 81.

62. Goldstein, "The New Constitutional Vice Presidency," 552.

63. Witcover, *Crapshoot*, 415, 417; Tom Wicker, "How to Choose a Vice President," *New York Times*, August 23, 1988, A21. In his more recent book on the

vice presidency, Witcover appears to favor selection by the presidential nominee, although he does not discuss the possibility of routinely using the Twenty-Fifth Amendment to choose vice presidents. See Jules Witcover, *The American Vice Presidency: From Irrelevance to Power* (Washington, DC: Smithsonian Books, 2014), 514–515, 519–520.

64. For other critiques of reforms addressed herein, see Michael Nelson, "Background Paper," in *A Heartbeat Away* (New York: Priority Press Publications, 1988), 46–52.

CHAPTER 16: CONCLUSION

1. Dan Quayle, "Standing Firm," in *At the President's Side: The Vice Presidency in the Twentieth Century*, ed. Timothy Walch (Columbia: University of Missouri Press, 1997), 172.

2. "The President-Elect's News Conference Announcing the Nomination of Clayton Yeutter as Secretary of Agriculture," December 14, 1988, American Presidency Project, University of California, Santa Barbara, http://www.presidency.ucsb.edu/ws/index.php?pid=85212.

3. Richard Neustadt to Reed Hundt, "Role of the Vice President," October 6, 1992, in *Preparing to Be President: The Memos of Richard E. Neustadt*, ed. Charles O. Jones (Washington, DC: AEI Press, 2000), 128.

4. Roy E. Brownell II, "The Independence of the Vice Presidency," *New York University Journal of Legislation and Public Policy* 17, no. 2 (2014): 352–358.

5. Joel K. Goldstein, "Constitutional Change, Originalism, and the Vice Presidency," *University of Pennsylvania Journal of Constitutional Law* 16, no. 2 (2013): 369, 389–394, 406–408.

6. Ibid., 404.

7. Dan Quayle, "Address," The Leader's Lecture Series, Washington, DC, September 19, 2000, http://www.senate.gov/artandhistory/history/common/generic/Leaders_Lecture_Series_Quayle.htm.

8. Dan Quayle, interview with James S. Young et al., George H. W. Bush Oral History Project, University of Virginia, Charlottesville, March 12, 2002, http://web1.millercenter.org/poh/transcripts/ohp_2002_0312_quayle.pdf, 27.

9. Richard E. Neustadt, "Vice Presidents as National Leaders: Reflections Past, Present, and Future," in *At the President's Side: The Vice Presidency in the Twentieth Century*, ed. Timothy Walch (Columbia: University of Missouri Press, 1997), 189.

10. Barton Gellman, *Angler: The Cheney Vice Presidency* (New York: Penguin Press, 2008), 57–60.

11. *Jay Burns Baking Co. v. Bryan*, 264 U.S. 504, 517, 520 (1924).

SELECTED BIBLIOGRAPHY

ARCHIVAL SOURCES

Ashby-Gramer Collection. Boise State University Library. Boise, ID.

Bush, George H. W. Vice-Presidential Papers. George Bush Presidential Library and Museum. Texas A & M University, College Station.

Cannon, James M. Papers. Gerald R. Ford Presidential Library. Ann Arbor, MI.

Carter, Jimmy. Presidential Papers. Jimmy Carter Presidential Library and Museum. Atlanta, GA.

Church, Frank. Papers. Boise State University. Boise, ID.

Clinton, William J. Digital Library. William J. Clinton Presidential Library and Museum. Little Rock, AR.

Dole, Robert J. Papers. Robert J. Dole Archive and Special Collection. University of Kansas. Lawrence.

Ferraro, Geraldine. Papers. Marymount Manhattan College. New York, NY.

Ford, Gerald R. Papers. Gerald R. Ford Presidential Library. Ann Arbor, MI.

Harris, Patricia. Papers. Library of Congress. Washington, DC.

Hartmann. Robert. Papers. Gerald R. Ford Presidential Library. Ann Arbor, MI.

Moe, Richard. Papers. University of Maryland. Baltimore.

Mondale, Walter F. Papers. Minnesota Historical Society. St. Paul.

Muskie, Edmund S. Papers. Bates College. Lewiston, ME.

Quayle, Dan. Vice-Presidential Papers. George Bush Presidential Library and Museum. Texas A & M University. College Station.

Regan, Donald. Papers. Library of Congress. Washington, DC.

ORAL HISTORY PROJECTS

Blair, Diane P. Project. Pryor Center for Arkansas Oral and Visual History. University of Arkansas. Fayetteville.

Bush, George H. W. Oral History Project. Miller Center. University of Virginia. Charlottesville.

Carter, Jimmy. Presidential Oral History Project. Miller Center. University of Virginia. Charlottesville.

Carter Exit Interview Project. Jimmy Carter Presidential Library and Museum. Atlanta, GA.

Carter Library Oral History Project. Jimmy Carter Presidential Library and Museum. Atlanta. GA.

Clinton, William J. Presidential History Project. Miller Center. University of Virginia. Charlottesville.

Collective Memory Project of the Election of 2004. Center for Presidential History. Southern Methodist University. Dallas, TX.

Dole, Robert J. Oral History Project. Robert J. Dole Archive and Special Collections. University of Kansas. Lawrence.

Ford, Gerald R. Oral History Project. Gerald R. Ford Presidential Foundation. Grand Rapids, MI.

Johnson, Lyndon Baines. Oral History Project. LBJ Presidential Library. Austin, TX.

Mitchell, George J. Oral History Project. George J. Mitchell Department of Special Collections and Archives. Bowdoin College, Brunswick, ME.

Muskie, Edmund S. Oral History Project. Muskie Archives. Bates College, Lewiston, ME.

Reagan, Ronald. Oral History Project. Miller Center. University of Virginia. Charlottesville.

Reichley, A. James. Research Interviews. Gerald R. Ford Presidential Library. Ann Arbor, MI.

U.S. Senate. Oral History Project. U.S. Senate Historical Office, Washington, DC.

White House Transition Interviews. National Archives.

GOVERNMENT DOCUMENTS, REPORTS, AND WEB SITES

Annals of Congress.

Biden, Joe. Vice President of the United States. White House: Barack Obama. https://www.whitehouse.gov/administration/vice-president-biden.

Cheney, Richard B. Vice President of the United States. White House: George W. Bush. http://georgewbush-whitehouse.archives.gov/vicepresident/vpbio.html.

Congressional Record.

Davis, Christopher M. The President Pro Tempore of the Senate: History and Authority of the Office. Congressional Research Service. December 20, 2012.

Gore, Al. Vice President of the United States. http://clinton4.nara.gov/WH/EOP /OVP/VP.html.

Katzenbach, Nicholas, to Attorney General Robert F. Kennedy. "Delegation of Presidential Powers to the Vice President." June 22, 1961.

—— to Lyndon B. Johnson. "Participation of the Vice President in the Affairs of the Executive Branch." March 9, 1961. In *Supplemental Opinions of the Office of Legal Counsel,* ed. Nathan A. Forrester, vol. 1. Washington, DC: Government Printing Office, 2013, http://www.justice.gov/sites/default /files/olc/legacy/2013/07/26/op-olc-supp.pdf, 214–224.

Middle Class Task Force. White House: Barack Obama. https://www.whitehouse. gov/strongmiddleclass.

Olson, Theodore B. "Presidential Succession and Delegation in Case of Disability." April 3, 1981. In *Opinions of the Office of Legal Counsel of the United States Department of Justice,* ed. Margaret Colgate Love. Washington, DC: Government Printing Office, 1981, http://www.justice.gov/sites/default/files/olc/legacy /2014/01/29/op-olc-05.pdf, 5:91–103.

The Presidential Campaign of 1976: Jimmy Carter. Washington, DC: Government Printing Office, 1978.

The Public Papers of the Presidents of the United States: Dwight D. Eisenhower– Barack Obama, 1953–2015. Washington, DC: Government Printing Office.

Rehnquist, William H., to the Honorable Edmund L. Morgan, Deputy Counsel to the President, "Advisory Commission on Intergovernmental Relations." February 7, 1969. Department of Justice, http://fas.org/irp/agency/doj/olc/020769.pdf.

Tansill, William R. "Number of Dates Certain Vice Presidents Actually Presided over the Senate." Library of Congress Legislative Reference Service. June 27, 1955.

Tarr, Ralph W. "Operation of the Twenty-Fifth Amendment Respecting Presidential Succession." June 14, 1985. In *Opinions of the Office of Legal Counsel.* Washington, DC: Government Printing Office, 1985, http://www.justice.gov/sites/default/files/olc/legacy/2014/01/29/op-olc-09.pdf, 9:65–70.

U.S. Senate, http://www.senate.gov.

NEWSPAPERS AND PERIODICALS

National Journal
Newsweek
New Yorker
New York Times
Politico
Time
U.S. News and World Report
Washington Post

BOOKS AND ARTICLES

Abrams, Herbert L. *"The President Has Been Shot": Confusion, Disability, and the 25th Amendment in the Aftermath of the Attempted Assassination of Ronald Reagan.* New York: W. W. Norton, 1992.

Ackerman, Bruce. *The Failure of the Founding Fathers: Jefferson, Marshall and the Rise of Presidential Democracy.* Cambridge, MA: Harvard University Press, 2005.

Adams, Henry. *The Life of Albert Gallatin.* Philadelphia: J. B. Lippincott & Co., 1879.

Adams, John. *The Works of John Adams, Second President of the United States.* Boston: Little, Brown, 1850–1856.

Albert, Richard. "The Evolving Vice Presidency." *Temple Law Review* 78, no. 4 (Winter 2005): 811–896.

Albright, Madeleine, with Bill Woodward. *Madam Secretary.* New York: Miramax, 2003.

Amar, Akhil Reed. *America's Constitution: A Biography.* New York: Random House, 2005.

Amar, Akhil Reed, and Vik Amar. "President Quayle?" *Virginia Law Review* 78, no. 4 (1992): 913–947.

Ambrose, Stephen E. *Nixon: The Education of a Politician, 1913–1962.* New York: Simon & Schuster, 1987.

Ashby, LeRoy, and Rod Gramer. *Fighting the Odds: The Life of Senator Frank Church.* Pullman: Washington State University Press, 1994.

Baker, James A., III, and Thomas M. DeFrank. *The Politics of Diplomacy: Revolution, War and Peace.* New York: Putnam, 1995.

Baker, James A., III, with Steve Fiffer. *"Work Hard, Study . . . and Keep Out of Politics!" Adventures and Lessons from an Unexpected Public Life*. New York: G. P. Putnam's Sons, 2006.

Baker, Peter. *Days of Fire: Bush and Cheney in the White House*. New York: Doubleday, 2013.

Balz, Dan, and Haynes Johnson. *The Battle for America, 2008: The Story of an Extraordinary Election*. New York: Viking, 2009.

Baumgartner, Jody C. *The American Vice Presidency Reconsidered*. Westport, CT: Praeger Publishers, 2006.

Baumgartner, Jody C., and Peter L. Francia. *Conventional Wisdom and American Elections: Exploding Myths, Exploring Misconceptions*, 2nd ed. Lanham, MD: Rowman & Littlefield, 2010.

Bell, Griffin B., with Ronald J. Ostrow. *Taking Care of the Law*. New York: Morrow, 1982.

Bowles, Nigel. *The White House and Capitol Hill: The Politics of Presidential Persuasion*. New York: Oxford University Press, 1987.

Bowling, Kenneth R., and Helen E. Veit, eds. *The Diary of William Maclay and Other Notes on Senate Debates*. Baltimore, MD: John Hopkins University Press, 1988.

Branch, Taylor. *The Clinton Tapes: Wrestling History with the President*. New York: Simon & Schuster, 2009.

Broder, David, and Bob Woodward. *Dan Quayle: The Man Who Would Be President*. New York: Simon & Schuster, 1992.

Brownell, Herbert, with John P. Burke. *Advising Ike: The Memoirs of Attorney General Herbert Brownell*. Lawrence: University Press of Kansas, 1993.

Brownell, Roy E., II. "A Constitutional Chameleon: The Vice President's Place within the American System of Separation of Powers," part 1. *Kansas Journal of Law and Public Policy* 24, no. 1 (2014): 1–77.

———. "A Constitutional Chameleon: The Vice President's Place within the American System of Separation of Powers," part 2. *Kansas Journal of Law and Public Policy* 24, no. 2 (2015): 294–400.

———. "The Independence of the Vice Presidency." *New York University Journal of Legislation and Public Policy* 17, no. 2 (2014): 297–376.

Bryce, James. *The American Commonwealth*. New York: Macmillan, 1928.

Brzezinski, Zbigniew. *Power and Principle: Memoirs of the National Security Adviser, 1977–1981*. New York: Farrar, Straus and Giroux, 1983.

Burke, John P. *Becoming President: The Bush Transition, 2000–2003*. Boulder, CO: Lynne Rienner, 2004.

———. *The Institutional Presidency*. Baltimore, MD: Johns Hopkins University Press, 1992.

Bush, George H. W. *All the Best: My Life in Letters and Other Writings*. New York: Scribner, 2013.

Bush, George H. W., with Vic Gold. *Looking Forward*. New York: Doubleday, 1987.

Bush, George H. W., and Brent Scowcroft. *A World Transformed*. New York: Alfred A. Knopf, 1998.

Bush, George W. *Decision Points*. New York: Broadway Paperbacks, 2010.

Byrd, Robert C. *The Senate, 1789–1989: Addresses on the History of the United States Senate.* Washington, DC: Government Printing Office, 1993.

Cannon, James. *Gerald R. Ford: An Honorable Life.* Ann Arbor: University of Michigan Press, 2013.

———. "Gerald R. Ford and Nelson A. Rockefeller: A Vice Presidential Memoir." In *At the President's Side: The Vice Presidency in the Twentieth Century,* ed. Timothy Walch. Columbia: University of Missouri Press, 1997, 135–143.

Cannon, Lou. *President Reagan: The Role of a Lifetime.* New York: Public Affairs, 1991.

———. *Reagan.* New York: G. P. Putnam's Sons, 1982.

Caro, Robert A. *The Years of Lyndon Johnson: The Passage of Power.* New York: Alfred A. Knopf, 2012.

Carter, Ashton, and William Perry. *Preventive Defense: A New Security Strategy for America.* Washington, DC: Brookings Institution Press, 1999.

Carter, Jimmy. *Keeping Faith: Memoirs of a President.* Toronto, Ontario: Bantam Books, 1982.

———. *White House Diary.* New York: Farrar, Straus and Giroux, 2010.

Carter, Rosalynn. *First Lady from Plains.* Boston: Houghton Mifflin, 1984.

Cheney, Dick, with Liz Cheney. *In My Time: A Personal and Political Memoir.* New York: Threshold Editions, 2011.

Cheney, Mary. *Now It's My Turn: A Daughter's Chronicle of Political Life.* New York: Threshold Editions, 2006.

Christopher, Warren. *Chances of a Lifetime.* New York: Scribner, 2001.

———. *In the Stream of History: Shaping Foreign Policy for a New Era.* Stanford, CA: Stanford University Press, 1998.

Church, Bethine. *A Lifelong Affair: My Passion for People and Politics.* Washington, DC: Francis Press, 2003.

Clift, Denis A. *With Presidents to the Summit.* Fairfax, VA: George Mason University Press, 1993.

Clinton, Bill. *My Life.* New York: Alfred A. Knopf, 2004.

Clinton, Hillary Rodham. *Hard Choices.* New York: Simon & Schuster, 2014.

Collat, Donald S., Stanley Kelley, Jr., and Rogowski, Ronald. "The End Game in Presidential Nominations." *American Political Science Review* 75 (June 1981): 421–435.

Coolidge, Calvin. *The Autobiography of Calvin Coolidge.* New York: Cosmopolitan Book Corporation, 1929.

Cronin, Thomas, and Michael Genovese. *The Paradoxes of the American Presidency.* New York: Oxford University Press, 1998.

Cunningham, Noble, Jr. *In Pursuit of Reason: The Life of Thomas Jefferson.* Baton Rouge: Louisiana State University Press, 1987.

Currie, David P. *The Constitution in Congress: Democrats and Whigs, 1829–1861.* Chicago: University of Chicago Press, 2005.

———. *The Constitution in Congress: The Jeffersonians, 1801–1829.* Chicago: University of Chicago Press, 2001.

Dallek, Robert. *Flawed Giant: Lyndon Johnson and His Times, 1961–1973.* New York: Oxford University Press, 1998.

Darman, Richard. *Who's in Control? Polar Politics and the Sensible Center.* New York: Simon & Schuster, 1996.

David, Paul T. "The Vice Presidency: Its Institutional Evolution and Contemporary Status." *Journal of Politics* 29, no. 4 (November 1967): 721–748.

Deaver, Michael, with Mickey Herskowitz. *Behind the Scenes.* New York: William Morrow, 1987.

Dole, Bob, and Elizabeth Dole with Richard Norton Smith. *The Doles: Unlimited Partners.* New York: Simon & Schuster, 1988.

Dole, Robert. *Unlimited Partners: Our American Story.* New York: Simon & Schuster, 1996.

Drew, Elizabeth. *American Journal: The Events of 1976.* New York: Random House, 1977.

———. *Election Journal: Political Events of 1987–1988.* New York: William Morrow, 1989.

———. *On the Edge: The Clinton Presidency.* New York: Simon & Schuster, 1994.

Eisenhower, Dwight D. *Waging Peace, 1956–1961.* New York: New American Library, 1965.

Fahrenkopf, Frank J., Jr. "Reagan as Political Leader." In *Leadership in the Reagan Presidency: Eleven Intimate Portraits*, ed. Kenneth W. Thompson. Lanham, MD: University Press of America, 1993.

Farrand, Max. *The Records of the Federal Convention of 1787.* New York: Yale University Press, 1966.

Feerick, John D. *From Failing Hands.* New York: Fordham University Press, 1965.

———. "Presidential Succession and Inability: Before and after the Twenty-Fifth Amendment." *Fordham Law Review* 79, no. 3 (December 2010): 907–949.

———. *The Twenty-Fifth Amendment: Its Complete History and Applications*, 3rd ed. New York: Fordham University Press, 2014.

Fenno, Richard E., Jr. *The Making of a Senator: Dan Quayle.* Washington, DC: CQ Press, 1989.

Ferraro, Geraldine, with Linda Bird Francke. *Ferraro: My Story.* Toronto, Ontario: Bantam Books, 1985.

Fielding, Fred. "An Eyewitness Account of Executive 'Inability.'" *Fordham Law Review* 79, no. 3 (December 2010): 823–834.

Fitzwater, Marlin. *Call the Briefing! Bush and Reagan, Sam and Helen: A Decade with Presidents and the Press.* New York: Times Books, 1995.

Ford, Gerald R. *A Time to Heal: The Autobiography of Gerald R. Ford.* New York: Berkley Books, 1979.

Ford, Paul Leicester, ed. *The Writings of Thomas Jefferson*, vol. 7. New York: G. P. Putnam's Sons, 1896.

Frank, Jeffrey. *Ike and Dick: Portrait of a Strange Political Marriage.* New York: Simon & Schuster, 2013.

Friedman, Richard D. "Some Modest Proposals on the Vice-Presidency." *Michigan Law Review* 86, no. 7 (June 1988): 1703–1734.

Gates, Robert M. *Duty: A Memoir of a Secretary of War.* New York: Alfred A. Knopf, 2014.

Gellman, Barton. *Angler: The Cheney Vice Presidency.* New York: Penguin Press, 2008.

Gergen, David. *Eyewitness to Power: The Essence of Leadership: Nixon to Clinton.* New York: Simon & Schuster, 2001.

Gerhardt, Michael J. *The Forgotten Presidents: Their Untold Constitutional Legacy.* Oxford: Oxford University Press, 2013.

Germond, Jack W., and Jules Witcover. *Mad as Hell: Revolt at the Ballot Box, 1992.* New York: Warner Books, 1993.

———. *Whose Broad Stripes and Bright Stars? The Trivial Pursuit of the Presidency, 1988.* New York: Warner Books, 1989.

Gilbert, Robert E., ed. *Managing Crisis: Presidential Disability and the Twenty-Fifth Amendment.* New York: Fordham University Press, 2000.

———. *The Mortal Presidency: Illness and Anguish in the White House.* New York: Fordham University Press, 1998.

———. "The Politics of Presidential Illness: Ronald Reagan and the Iran-Contra Scandal." *Politics and the Life Sciences* 33, no. 2 (Fall 2014): 58–76.

Gillon, Steven M. *The Democrats' Dilemma: Walter F. Mondale and the Liberal Legacy.* New York: Columbia University Press, 1992.

Glasser, Joshua M. *The Eighteen-Day Running Mate: McGovern, Eagleton, and a Campaign in Crisis.* New Haven, CT: Yale University Press, 2012.

Goldman, Eric F. *The Tragedy of Lyndon Johnson.* New York: Dell, 1968.

Goldman, Peter, Thomas M. DeFrank, Mark Miller, Andrew Murr, and Tom Mathews. *Quest for the Presidency, 1992.* College Station: Texas A & M University Press, 1994.

Goldman, Peter, and Tom Mathews. *The Quest for the Presidency, 1988.* New York: Simon & Schuster, 1989.

Goldsmith, Jack. *The Terror Presidency: Law and Judgment inside the Bush Administration.* New York: W. W. Norton, 2007.

Goldstein, Joel K. "Akhil Reed Amar and Presidential Continuity." *Houston Law Review* 47, no. 1 (2010): 67–104.

———. "Cheney, Vice Presidential Power and the War on Terror." *Presidential Studies Quarterly* 40, no. 1 (March 2010): 102–139.

———. "Constitutional Change, Originalism, and the Vice Presidency." *University of Pennsylvania Journal of Constitutional Law* 16, no. 2 (November 2013): 369–411.

———. *The Modern American Vice Presidency: The Transformation of a Political Institution.* Princeton, NJ: Princeton University Press, 1982.

———. "More Agony Than Ecstasy: Hubert H. Humphrey as Vice President." In *At the President's Side: The Vice Presidency in the Twentieth Century*, ed. Timothy Walch. Columbia: University of Missouri Press, 1997, 103–123.

———. "The New Constitutional Vice Presidency." *Wake Forest Law Review* 30, no. 3 (Fall 1995): 505–561.

———. "An Overview of the Vice-Presidency." *Fordham Law Review* 45 (February 1977): 786–804.

———. "Resolved, the Vice Presidency Should Be Abolished: Con." In *Debating the Presidency: Conflicting Perspectives on the American Executive*, 2nd ed., ed. Richard J. Ellis and Michael Nelson. Washington, DC: CQ Press, 2010, 179–186.

———. "The Rising Power of the Vice Presidency." *Presidential Studies Quarterly* 38, no. 3 (September 2008): 374–389.

———. "Taking from the Twenty-Fifth Amendment: Lessons in Ensuring Presidential Continuity." *Fordham Law Review* 79, no. 3 (December 2010): 959–1042.

———. "The Vice Presidency and the Twenty-Fifth Amendment: The Power of Reciprocal Relationships." In *Managing Crisis: Presidential Disability and the Twenty-Fifth Amendment*, ed. Robert E. Gilbert. New York: Fordham University Press, 2000, 165–213.

———. "Vice-Presidential Behavior in a Disability Crisis: The Case of Thomas R. Marshall." *Politics and Life Sciences* 33, no. 2 (Fall 2014): 37–57.

Gore, Al. *The Best Kept Secrets in Government*. Washington, DC: Government Printing Office, 1996.

Gray, C. Boyden. "The Coordinating Role of the Vice Presidency." In *The Presidency in Transition*, ed. James P. Pfiffner and R. Gordon Hoxie. New York: Center for the Study of the Presidency, 1989, 425–429.

Greenspan, Alan. *The Age of Turbulence: Adventures in a New World*. New York: Penguin Press, 2007.

Grunwald, Michael. *The New New Deal: The Hidden Story of Change in the Obama Era*. New York: Simon & Schuster, 2012.

Haig, Alexander. *Caveat: Realism, Reagan and Foreign Policy*. London: Weidenfeld and Nicolson, 1984.

Halberstam, David. *War in a Time of Peace*. New York: Scribner, 2001.

Halperin, Mark, and John Heilemann. *Double Down: Game Change, 2012*. New York: Penguin, 2014.

Hatfield, Mark, with the Senate Historical Office. *Vice Presidents of the United States, 1789–1993*. Washington, DC: Government Printing Office, 1997.

Hayes, Stephen. *Cheney: The Untold Story of America's Most Powerful and Controversial Vice President*. New York: HarperCollins, 2007.

Heilemann, John, and Mark Halperin. *Game Change: Obama and the Clintons, McCain and Palin, and the Race of a Lifetime*. New York: HarperCollins, 2010.

Hess, Stephen. *Organizing the Presidency*, rev. ed. Washington, DC: Brookings Institution, 1988.

Hiller, Mark, and Douglas Kriner. "Institutional Change and the Dynamics of Vice Presidential Selection." *Presidential Studies Quarterly* 38, no. 3 (September 2008): 401–421.

Hogan, Margaret A., et al., eds. *Adams Family Correspondence*, vol. 9. Cambridge, MA: Belknap Press of Harvard University Press, 2009.

Holbrook, Thomas. "The Behavioral Consequences of Vice-Presidential Debates: Does the Undercard Have Any Punch?" *American Politics Quarterly* 22, no. 4 (1994): 469–482.

Humphrey, Hubert H. *The Education of a Public Man*. New York: Doubleday & Co., 1976.

Hunt, Gaillard. *The Writings of James Madison, 1790–1801*. New York: The Knickerbocker Press, 1906.

Jefferson, Thomas. *A Manual of Parliamentary Practice for the Use of the Senate of the United States*. Washington, DC: Samuel Harris Smith, 1801.

Jones, Charles O., ed. *Preparing to Be President: The Memos of Richard E. Neustadt*. Washington, DC: AEI Press, 2000.

Jordan, Hamilton. *Crisis: The Last Year of the Carter Presidency.* New York: G. P. Putnam's Sons, 1982.

Kaminski, John. *George Clinton: Yeoman Politician of the New Republic.* Madison, WI: Madison House, 1993.

Kampelman, Max. *Entering New Worlds: The Memoirs of a Private Man in Public Life.* New York: HarperCollins, 1991.

Kearns, Doris. *Lyndon Johnson and the American Dream.* New York: Harper & Row, 1976.

Kengor, Paul G. "Cheney and Vice Presidential Power." In *Considering the Bush Presidency*, ed. Gary L. Gregg II and Mark J. Rozell. New York: Oxford University Press, 2004, 160–176.

———. *Wreath Layer or Policy Player? The Vice President's Role in Foreign Policy.* Lanham, MD: Lexington Books, 2000.

Kissinger, Henry. *Years of Upheaval.* Boston: Little, Brown, 1982.

Knott, Stephen F., and Jeffrey L. Chidester. *At Reagan's Side: Insiders' Recollections from Sacramento to the White House.* Lanham, MD: Rowman & Littlefield, 2009.

Koch, Doro Bush. *My Father, My President: A Personal Account of the Life of George H. W. Bush.* New York: Warner Books, 2006.

Kraus, Sidney, ed. *The Great Debates: Background, Perspective, Effects.* Bloomington: Indiana University Press, 1962.

———. *The Great Debates, 1976.* Bloomington: Indiana University Press, 1979.

Kriner, Douglas L. "The Vice Presidency Should Be Abolished: Pro." In *Debating the Presidency: Conflicting Perspectives on the American Executive*, 2nd ed., ed. Richard J. Ellis and Michael Nelson. Washington, DC: CQ Press, 2010, 172–179.

Kuroda, Tadahisa. *The Origins of the Twelfth Amendment: The Electoral College in the Early Republic, 1787–1804.* Westport, CT: Greenwood Press, 1994.

Lance, Bert, with Bill Gilbert. *The Truth of the Matter: My Life in and out of Politics.* New York: Summit Books, 1991.

Lechelt, Jack. *The Vice Presidency in Foreign Policy: From Mondale to Cheney.* El Paso, TX: LFB Scholarly Publishing, 2009.

Levinson, Sanford. *Our Undemocratic Constitution: Where the Constitution Goes Wrong (and How We the People Can Correct It).* Oxford: Oxford University Press, 2006.

Lewis, Finlay. *Mondale: Portrait of an American Politician.* New York: Perennial Library, 1984.

Lieberman, Joe, and Hadassah Lieberman with Sarah Crichton. *An Amazing Adventure: Joe and Hadassah's Personal Notes on the 2000 Campaign.* New York: Simon & Schuster, 2003.

Light, Paul C. *Vice-Presidential Power: Advice and Influence in the White House.* Baltimore, MD: Johns Hopkins University Press, 1984.

Link, Arthur S., ed. *The Papers of Woodrow Wilson*, vol. 37. Princeton, NJ: Princeton University Press, 1981.

Lomask, Milton. *Aaron Burr: The Years from Princeton to Vice President, 1756–1805.* New York: Farrar, Straus and Giroux, 1979.

Ludlow, Louis. *From Cornfield to Press Gallery: Adventures and Reminiscences of a Veteran Washington Correspondent.* Washington, DC: W. F. Roberts, 1924.

Malone, Dumas. *Jefferson and the Ordeal of Liberty.* Boston: Little, Brown, 1962.

Mann, James. *Rise of the Vulcans: The History of Bush's War Cabinet.* New York: Viking, 2004.

Mariano, E. Connie. "In Sickness and in Health: Medical Care for the President of the United States." In *Managing Crisis: Presidential Disability and the Twenty-Fifth Amendment,* ed. Robert E. Gilbert. New York: Fordham University Press, 2000, 83–95.

Mayer, William G. *In Pursuit of the White House, 2000: How We Choose Our Presidential Nominees.* New York: Chatham House, 2000.

McClellan, Scott. *What Happened: Inside the Bush White House and Washington's Culture of Deception.* New York: PublicAffairs, 2008.

McCullough, David. *John Adams.* New York: Simon & Schuster, 2001.

———. *Truman.* New York: Simon & Schuster, 1992.

McFarlane, Robert C., with Zofia Smardz. *Special Trust.* New York: Cadell and Davies, 1994.

McGovern, George S. *Grassroots: The Autobiography of George McGovern.* New York: Random House, 1977.

McPherson, Harry. *A Political Education: A Washington Memoir.* Boston: Houghton Mifflin, 1988.

Meese, Edwin. *With Reagan: The Inside Story.* Washington, DC: Regnery Gateway, 1992.

Milkis, Sidney M., and Michael Nelson. *The American Presidency: Origins and Development.* Washington, DC: CQ Press, 2012.

Miller, Amanda Fuchs, ed. *Campaign for President: The Managers Look at 2008.* Lanham, MD: Rowman & Littlefield, 2009.

Moe, Richard. *Roosevelt's Second Act: The Election of 1940 and the Politics of War.* Oxford: Oxford University Press, 2013.

Mohr, Lawrence C. "Medical Considerations in the Determination of Presidential Disability." In *Managing Crisis: Presidential Disability and the Twenty-Fifth Amendment,* ed. Robert E. Gilbert. New York: Fordham University Press, 2000, 97–109.

Mondale, Walter F., with David Hage. *The Good Fight: A Life in Liberal Politics.* New York: Scribner, 2010.

Montgomery, Bruce. *Richard B. Cheney and the Rise of the Imperial Vice Presidency.* Westport, CT: Praeger, 2009.

Moore, Jonathan, ed. *Campaign for President: The Managers Look at '84.* Dover, MA: Auburn House, 1986.

———. *The Campaign for President: 1980 in Retrospect.* Cambridge, MA: Ballinger, 1981.

Moore, Jonathan, and Janet Fraser, eds. *Campaign for President: The Managers Look at '76.* Cambridge, MA: Ballinger, 1977.

Natoli, Marie D. *American Prince, American Pauper: The Contemporary Vice Presidency in Perspective.* Westport, CT: Greenwood Press, 1985.

Nelson, Michael. "Choosing the Vice President." *PS: Political Science and Politics* 21, no. 4 (Fall 1988): 858–868.

———. *A Heartbeat Away.* New York: Priority Press Publications, 1988.

——. *Resilient America: Electing Nixon in 1968, Channeling Dissent, and Dividing Government*. Lawrence: University Press of Kansas, 2014.

Nelson, Michael, ed. *The Presidency and the Political System*, 9th ed. Washington, DC: CQ Press, 2010.

Neustadt, Richard E. "Vice Presidents as National Leaders: Reflections Past, Present, and Future." In *At the President's Side: The Vice Presidency in the Twentieth Century*, ed. Timothy Walch. Columbia: University of Missouri Press, 1997, 183–196.

Niven, John. *John C. Calhoun and the Price of Union*. Baton Rouge: Louisiana State University Press, 1988.

Nixon, Richard M. *RN: The Memoirs of Richard Nixon*. New York: Grosset and Dunlap, 1978.

O'Brien, Lawrence F. *No Final Victories*. Garden City, NY: Doubleday, 1974.

Panetta, Leon, with Jim Newton. *Worthy Fights: A Memoir of Leadership in War and Peace*. New York: Penguin Press, 2014.

Parmet, Herbert. *George Bush: The Life of a Lone Star Yankee*. New York: Scribner, 1997.

Perotti, Rosanna, ed. *The Clinton Presidency and the Constitutional System*. College Station: Texas A & M University Press, 2012.

Pfiffner, James P. *The Modern Presidency*. New York: St. Martin's, 1994.

——. "Organizing the 21st Century White House." In *Rivals for Power: Presidential-Congressional Relations,* 5th ed, ed. James A. Thurber. Lanham, MD: Rowman & Littlefield, 2013, 63–86.

——. *Power Play: The Bush Presidency and the Constitution*. Washington, DC: Brookings Institution, 2008.

Pfiffner, James P., and R. Gordon Hoxie, eds. *The Presidency in Transition*. New York: Center for the Study of the Presidency, 1989.

Pika, Joseph A. "The New Vice Presidency: Dick Cheney, Joe Biden, and the New Presidency." In *The Presidency and the Political System*, 9th ed., ed. Michael Nelson. Washington, DC: CQ Press, 2010, 509–533.

Plouffe, David. *The Audacity to Win: The Inside Story and Lessons of Barack Obama's Historic Victory*. New York: Viking, 2009.

Pomper, Gerald. *Nominating the President: The Politics of Convention Choice*. Evanston, IL: Northwestern University Press, 1963.

Popkin, Samuel L. *The Candidate: What It Takes to Win—and Hold—the White House*. New York: Oxford University Press, 2012.

Powell, Colin L., with Joseph E. Persico. *My American Journey*. New York: Random House, 1995.

Purcell, L. Edward. *Vice Presidents: A Biographical Dictionary*. New York: Facts on File, 2010.

Quandt, William B. *Camp David: Peacemaking and Politics*. Washington, DC: Brookings Institution, 1986.

Quayle, Dan. *Standing Firm: A Vice-Presidential Memoir*. New York: HarperCollins, 1994.

——. "Standing Firm: Personal Reflections on Being Vice President." In *At the President's Side: The Vice Presidency in the Twentieth Century*, ed. Timothy Walch. Columbia: University of Missouri Press, 1997, 169–179.

Reagan, Nancy, with William Novak. *My Turn: The Memoirs of Nancy Reagan.* New York: Random House, 1989.

Reagan, Ronald. *Reagan: A Life in Letters.* New York: Free Press, 2003.

———. *The Reagan Diaries,* ed. Douglas Brinkley. New York: HarperPerennial, 2007.

Regan, Donald. *For the Record: From Wall Street to Washington.* San Diego, CA: Harcourt Brace Jovanovich, 1988.

Reich, Robert B. *Locked in the Cabinet.* New York: Alfred A. Knopf, 1997.

Reynolds, Glenn Harlan. "Is Dick Cheney Unconstitutional?" *Northwestern University Law Review Colloquy* 102 (2007): 110–116.

Rice, Condoleezza. *No Higher Honor: A Memoir of My Years in Washington.* New York: Crown, 2011.

Richardson, Don, ed. *Conversations with Carter.* Boulder, CO: Lynne Rienner, 1998.

Ritchie, Donald, ed. *Minutes of the Senate Democratic Conference, 1903–1964.* Washington, DC: Government Printing Office, 1998.

Rollins, Ed, with Tom DeFrank. *Bare Knuckles and Back Rooms: My Life in American Politics.* New York: Broadway Books, 1996.

Roosevelt, Theodore. *Selections from the Correspondence of Theodore Roosevelt and Henry Cabot Lodge, 1884–1918.* New York: Charles Scribner's Sons, 1925.

Ross, Dennis. *The Missing Peace: The Inside Story of the Fight for Middle East Peace.* New York: Farrar, Straus and Giroux, 2004.

Rossiter, Clinton L. "The Reform of the Vice Presidency." *Political Science Quarterly* 63, no. 3 (September 1948): 383–403.

Rothkopf, David J. *Running the World: The Inside Story of the National Security Council and the Architects of American Power.* New York: PublicAffairs, 2005.

Rove, Karl. *Courage and Consequence: My Life as a Conservative in the Fight.* New York: Simon & Schuster, 2010.

Rumsfeld, Donald. *Known and Unknown: A Memoir.* New York: Sentinel, 2011.

Runkel, David R., ed. *Campaign for President: The Managers Look at '88.* Dover, MA: Auburn House Publishing, 1989.

Sabato, Larry. *Feeding Frenzy: Attack Journalism and American Politics.* New York: Free Press, 1991.

Savage, Charlie. *Takeover: The Return of the Imperial Presidency and the Subversion of American Democracy.* Boston: Little, Brown, 2007.

Schlesinger, Arthur M., Jr. "On the Presidential Succession." *Political Science Quarterly* 89, no. 3 (Fall 1974): 475–505.

Schram, Martin. *Running for President: A Journal of the Carter Campaign.* New York: Pocket Books, 1977.

Schroeder, Alan. *Presidential Debates: Fifty Years of High-Risk TV,* 2nd ed. New York: Columbia University Press, 2008.

Shultz, George P. *Turmoil and Triumph: My Years as Secretary of State.* New York: Charles Scribner's Sons, 1993.

Sigelman, Lee, and Paul J. Wahlbeck. "The 'Veepstakes': Strategic Choice in Presidential Running Mate Selection." *American Political Science Review* 91, no. 4 (December 1997): 855–864.

Simon, William, with John M. Caher. *A Time for Reflection: An Autobiography.* Washington, DC: Regnery Publishing, 2004.

Sirgiovanni, George S. "Dumping the Vice President: An Historical Overview and Analysis." *Presidential Studies Quarterly* 24, no. 4 (Fall 1994): 765–782.

Smith, Richard Norton. *On His Own Terms: A Life of Nelson Rockefeller.* New York: Random House, 2014.

Solberg, Carl. *Hubert Humphrey: A Biography.* New York: W. W. Norton, 1984.

Speakes, Larry, with Robert Pack. *Speaking Out: The Reagan Presidency from Inside the White House.* New York: Charles Scribner's Sons, 1988.

Stephanopoulos, George. *All Too Human: A Political Education.* Boston: Little, Brown, 1999.

Strober, Deborah Hart, and Gerald S. Strober. *Reagan: The Man and His Presidency.* Boston: Houghton Mifflin, 1998.

Strober, Gerald S., and Deborah H. Strober. *Nixon: An Oral History of His Presidency.* New York: HarperCollins, 1994.

Suskind, Ron. *The One Percent Doctrine: Deep inside America's Pursuit of Its Enemies since 9/11.* New York: Simon & Schuster, 2006.

———. *The Price of Loyalty: George W. Bush, the White House, and the Education of Paul O'Neill.* New York: Simon & Schuster, 2004.

"Symposium on the Vice Presidency." *Fordham Law Review* 45 (February 1977): 703–804.

Talbott, Strobe. *The Russia Hand: A Memoir of Presidential Diplomacy.* New York: Random House, 2002.

Tenet, George, with Bill Harlow. *At the Storm Center: My Years at the CIA.* New York: HarperCollins, 2007.

Thurber, James A., ed. *Rivals for Power: Presidential-Congressional Relations,* 5th ed. Lanham, MD: Rowman & Littlefield, 2013.

Truman, Harry S. *Memoirs: 1945, Year of Decisions.* Garden City, NY: Doubleday, 1955.

Turner, Michael. *The Vice President as Policy Maker: Rockefeller in the Ford White House.* Westport, CT: Greenwood Press, 1982.

Turque, Bill. *Inventing Al Gore: A Biography.* Boston: Houghton Mifflin, 2000.

Ulbig, Stacy G. *Vice Presidents, Presidential Elections, and the Media: Second Fiddles in the Spotlight.* Boulder, CO: FirstForumPress, 2013.

Untermeyer, Chase. "Looking Forward: George Bush as Vice President." In *At the President's Side: The Vice Presidency in the Twentieth Century,* ed. Timothy Walch. Columbia: University of Missouri Press, 1997, 157–168.

Vance, Cyrus. *Hard Choices: Critical Years in America's Foreign Policy.* New York: Simon & Schuster, 1983.

Van Dyk, Ted. *Heroes, Hacks and Fools: Memoirs from the Political Inside.* Seattle: University of Washington Press, 2007.

Walch, Timothy, ed. *At the President's Side: The Vice Presidency in the Twentieth Century.* Columbia: University of Missouri Press, 1997.

Wallison, Peter J. *Ronald Reagan: The Power of Conviction and the Success of His Presidency.* Boulder, CO: Westview Press, 2003.

Warshaw, Shirley Anne. *The Co-Presidency of Bush and Cheney.* Stanford, CA: Stanford University Press, 2009.

———. *Powersharing: White House–Cabinet Relations in the Modern Presidency.* Albany: State University of New York Press, 2006.

Wattenberg, Martin P. "The Role of Vice Presidential Candidate Ratings in Presidential Voting Behavior." *American Political Quarterly* 23, no. 4 (October 1995): 504–514.

Weinberger, Caspar W. *Fighting for Peace: Seven Critical Years in the Pentagon.* New York: Warner Books, 1990.

Weizman, Ezer. *The Battle for Peace.* New York: Bantam Books, 1981.

Wilber, Del Quentin. *Rawhide Down: The Near Assassination of Ronald Reagan.* New York: Henry Holt, 2011.

Williams, Irving. *The Rise of the Vice Presidency.* Washington, DC: Public Affairs Press, 1956.

Wilmerding, Lucius, Jr. "The Vice Presidency." *Political Science Quarterly* 68, no. 1 (March 1953): 17–41.

Wilson, Woodrow. *Congressional Government: A Study in American Politics.* Boston: Houghton Mifflin, 1885.

———. *Constitutional Government in the United States.* New York: Columbia University Press, 1908.

Witcover, Jules. *The American Vice Presidency: From Irrelevance to Power.* Washington, DC: Smithsonian, 2014.

———. *Crapshoot: Rolling the Dice on the Vice Presidency.* New York: Crown, 1992.

———. *Joe Biden: A Life of Trial and Redemption.* New York: HarperCollins, 2010.

———. *Marathon: The Pursuit of the Presidency, 1972–1976.* New York: Viking, 1977.

———. *Very Strange Bedfellows: The Short and Unhappy Marriage of Richard Nixon and Spiro Agnew.* New York: PublicAffairs, 2007.

Wolffe, Richard. *Revival: The Struggle for Survival Inside the Obama White House.* New York: Broadway Paperbacks, 2011.

Woodward, Bob. *The Agenda: Inside the Clinton White House.* New York: Simon & Schuster, 1994.

———. *Bush at War.* New York: Simon & Schuster, 2002.

———. *The Choice.* New York: Simon & Schuster, 1996.

———. *Obama's Wars.* New York: Simon & Schuster, 2011.

———. *Plan of Attack.* New York: Simon & Schuster, 2004.

———. *The Price of Politics.* New York: Simon & Schuster, 2012.

SELECTED ONLINE SOURCES

American Presidency Project, University of California, Santa Barbara. http://www.presidency.ucsb.edu.

Commission on Presidential Debates. http://www.debates.org.

Gallup Poll. http://www.gallup.com/home.aspx.

Harris Poll. http://www.harrisinteractive.com/Insights/HarrisVault.aspx.

Pew Research Center. http://www.pewresearch.org.

PollingReport.com. http://www.pollingreport.com/.

President's Daily Diary, WhiteHouseHistory.org. http://www.whitehousehistory.org/whha_about/research-presidential-recordings.html#b.

Rumsfeld, Donald. Rumsfeld Papers. http://papers.rumsfeld.com.

Sabato's Crystal Ball, University of Virginia. http://www.centerforpolitics.org/crystalball.

INDEX

Aaron, David, 79, 82
  as Mondale associate, 45, 50
  NSC role, 63, 64, 75, 96, 99, 100
Abe, Shinzo, 147
Abraham, Spencer, 130, 155
Adams, Abigail, 15
Adams, John, 2, 14, 15, 16, 266
  on vice presidency, 1, 13, 15, 282
  as vice president, 1, 15, 317n10
Adams, John Quincy, 17, 205,
  319n43
Addington, David, 133, 137, 138, 164,
  165, 263
Adelman, Kenneth, 189
Agnew, Spiro T., 32, 94, 174, 206, 313
  resignation as vice president, 32,
  37–38
  selection as Nixon's running mate,
  29, 203
  as vice president, 4, 27–28, 31–32, 35,
  250, 317n10
Ahtisaari, Martti, 126
Ailes, Roger, 197
Albert, Carl, 251
Albright, Madeleine, 120, 121, 123
Alexander, Lamar, 181, 183, 184
Alito, Samuel, 140
Allen, Richard, 152
Ambrose, Stephen, 30
Anderson, Robert O., 176
Andropov, Yuri, 110
Annunzio, Frank, 81
Aquino, Corazon, 116
Arafat, Yasser, 138–139
Armstrong, Anne, 176, 177, 182–183,
  213, 218
Armstrong, William, 181
Ashcroft, John, 290
Atwater, Lee, 197, 269
Augustine, Norman, 180
Axelrod, David, 169
Ayotte, Kelly, 181

Babbitt, Bruce, 181
Baker, Howard, 176, 182–183, 208, 218,
  220, 288
Baker, James, 108, 197, 209
  dump Quayle effort, 222
  impact on Bush as Reagan chief of
  staff, 151–152, 305
  in Reagan attempted assassination
  aftermath, 251–254
  as secretary of state, 114, 116
  as vice-presidential possibility
  (1996), 180
Baker, Newton, 20
Baker, Peter, 131
Baldridge, Malcolm, 106
Balz, Dan, 194
Barkley, Alben W., 22–23
Barnett, Robert, 45, 59, 75
  memorandum on vice presidency,
  54–56, 61
Bayh, Evan, 183, 208, 215, 217, 218
Beame, Abe, 49
Begin, Menachem, 84
Bell, Griffin, 73, 79
Bennett, William, 113, 182, 196, 217
Bentsen, Lloyd, 125, 181–182, 205, 268,
  281, 285, 288, 297
  campaign impact (1988), 216, 233,
  241, 247, 295, 296
  and Dukakis's vice-presidential
  selection process, 185, 187, 190,
  196, 200, 202, 212, 214, 215–217,
  219
  and Mondale's vice-presidential
  selection process, 189–190, 200, 216
  qualifications of, 205, 206–208, 216–
  217, 221
  rollout of, 227–228
  vice-presidential campaign (1988),
  216, 236, 239–241, 243–244, 245
  vice-presidential debate, 236, 239–
  241, 244

[409]